THE FORMATION OF THE MEDIEVAL WEST

The Formation of the Medieval West

STUDIES IN THE ORAL CULTURE OF THE BARBARIANS

Michael Richter

FOUR COURTS PRESS

Set in 11 on 13 Ehrhardt
by Gilbert Gough Typesetting, Dublin

First published by
FOUR COURTS PRESS
Kill Lane, Blackrock, Co. Dublin, Ireland

This edition is not for sale in North America,
where the book is published by
St. Martin's Press, New York.

© Michael Richter 1994

A catalogue record for this title
is available from the British Library.

ISBN 1-85182-153-8

All rights reserved.
No part of this publication may be
reproduced, stored in or introduced into a
retrieval system, or transmitted, in any
form or by any means (electronic,
mechanical, photocopying, recording
or otherwise), without the prior written
permission of both the copyright owner
and publisher of this book.

Printed in Ireland
by Colour Books Ltd,

CONTENTS

PREFACE   vii
ABBREVIATIONS   xv

PART I
THE TRANSFORMATION OF THE ROMAN WORLD

1 Politics   3
2 Religion   27
3 Literacy   45

PART II
APPROACHES TO ORAL CULTURE

4 Approaches to medieval oral culture   81
5 Performers and music   105

PART III
THE EARLY MEDIEVAL EVIDENCE

6 A Carolingian cluster (c.780-840)   125
7 Before the Carolingians   146
8 After the Carolingians   160
9 The Celtic countries   181
10 Oral culture and early vernacular literature   231
11 Results   255

BIBLIOGRAPHY   265
INDEX   289

PREFACE

One of the fundamental problems for the historian is posed by the very medium through which he works. The language in which he approaches and articulates the past is inevitably that of his own world. It is an axiom of the profession that the past is different from the present and, in the case of the early Middle Ages, one may say very different. This makes it particularly necessary to question the extent to which concepts of today are adequate for the past. Problems of this kind are multiplied, if, as generally happens, more than one language is involved in the process of approaching the past. It will become evident in the following chapters that Latin words or phrases which appear to be unproblematical reveal dimensions hitherto overlooked.[1] Something comparable holds for the sources more generally.

In order to stress this point, in this study certain terms are used which derive from the past yet are here used with connotations which may appear unattractive to the modern ear. This is probably true of 'barbarians', especially when it is linked to the concept of 'culture'. A positive approach to those who are called 'barbarians' in the contemporary sources is the main direction of this study; it is true, of course, that in a scholarly work of this nature the writer is forever wondering whether he is taking too romantic a view of 'the noble savage' or whether concepts such as dignity, truthfulness, responsibility or respect for others really apply to the medieval barbarian just as much as courage (sometimes to the point of recklessness), endurance or loyalty.

> Dolentes referimus, quod non solum quidam minores clerici, verum etiam aliqui ecclesiarum praelati, circa commessationes superfluas et confabulationes illicitas, ut de aliis taceamus, fere medietatem noctis expendunt: et somno residuum relinquentes, vix ad diurnum concentum avium excitantur, transcurrendo undique continua syncapa matutinum.

This lament over the moral state of the clergy was formulated at the Fourth

[1] Richter, M., 'Is Latin a key to the early medieval world?' in *Odysseus—Man in history today*, Moscow 1991 (in Russian; to be published in German shortly: 'Latein—ein Schlüssel zur Welt des Mittelalters?' in *Mittellateinisches Jahrbuch*).

Lateran Council in 1215.[2] Given this context, and the strong terms used, the state of affairs described seems to have been deeply entrenched. If this was the situation among the clergy, what might one expect of the flock in their charge? This study attempts to provide not an answer (for there are bound to be very many answers) but approaches to the values held by clerics and lay people in the early Middle Ages, often referred to as either 'dark' or 'Christian' ages. Lateran IV may be taken to prepare one for what to expect.

It has always been very difficult to deal with developments in the early medieval West due to the relatively meagre source material. Yet it is unquestionably a very important period in history, for what developed then laid the foundation of later structures. The relative paucity of available sources also has its attraction in that frequent re-reading of them can result in new insights into the world of which they form a part without being representative.

The aim and purpose of this book is to set the oral culture in the early medieval West into the central position that belongs to it even though the written sources suggest otherwise. As a corollary, the extant written sources are newly assessed, in a dual manner: individually, they are analysed as to what they do tell about the oral tradition, and collectively they are considered for what they are: of rather marginal importance to much of early medieval life, the output of the expertise of some individuals and groups possessed of no great social prestige.

While there are many studies of the period that make passing reference to the oral nature of much of early medieval society, they leave it at that, presumably in the belief that this oral part of the culture cannot be studied properly. The oral aspect of the societies is then quickly relegated to the background, to be given no further attention, and the written sources are accepted as representative of the period. This is an understandable attitude, but it is not the only possible one, as the present study demonstrates. Many of the passages concerning oral culture discussed below have long been known and have been commented upon individually; however, they assume a new physiognomy when properly decoded and when placed in their contemporary cultural context. When that is done, further pieces of information not widely known or used can be pressed into service to strengthen our grasp of oral culture.

True, it is only through the written sources that the oral culture can be investigated at all, but there is a case for arguing that the written sources of the early medieval West have in the past been overvalued. The so-called darkness of the early medieval centuries deserves a positive approach, an attempt to establish what makes this period of European history qualitatively different from what had gone before and what was to follow. That this is

2 c.XVII. *Conciliorum Oecumenicorum Decreta*, Alberigo, J. et al., ed., Basel 1962, p. 219 (Mansi XXII, 1003).

Preface

certainly a difficult task—but, then, the proper treatment of the written sources is, for any period of history, extremely difficult.

This monograph is the first attempt to deal with the oral culture in the early medieval West directly and positively. The absence of guidelines which this implies exposes the researcher to a freedom which can sometimes feel distinctly uncomfortable. But if it is indeed the case that the oral culture is central to most societies at that period, it deserves all the effort necessary to elucidate it.

It is a central concern of this book to explore ways in which the early Middle Ages can be approached in a more nuanced manner with the help of the written sources. These have to be handled carefully; their messages have to be decoded. The sources have to be set into a broader social and cultural context which they, in turn, illuminate, albeit insufficiently. One of the major challenges writing this book involved was the need to come to terms with the phenomenon of oral cultures; however, this also proved exhilarating. As far as oral culture is concerned, one has to learn about the characteristics of such a culture in order to be able to approach the sources with an adequate list of questions. In this respect modern studies of traditional societies have proved to be of great help. Many of these societies have common basic features, especially the importance attached to the spoken word, the care with which language is handled, the respect shown to it. Since there is no guideline available for the early Middle Ages, analogies had to be sought elsewhere. It is a pleasant obligation to record my debt to some scholars in particular whose works I have ruminated even where I did not agree with all the ramifications of their ideas: Eric Havelock, Albert Lord, Walter Ong, Milman Parry and Paul Zumthor.

The nature of the topic, as well as the state of research, has contributed to the structure of this book. In view of the lack of preliminary historical studies, I have felt it necessary to sketch the structures of the societies in the early medieval West while keeping in mind the largely oral nature of their culture (which is only subsequently elucidated). It has proved necessary to deal in more detail than originally envisaged with general issues like the nature and potential of written sources, the strength and weakness of the Latin language in non-Latin environments, the concepts of literacy and conversion, and, basically, the overall perception of the sub- and post-Roman societies in the West. In the last-mentioned field, I build on new approaches by historians who press into service other disciplines such as anthropology, sociology or linguistics.

In the more theoretical section, I lean rather heavily on anthropology. I have done so in the belief that the historian, like the anthropologist, is engaged essentially cross-cultural studies. Unlike the anthropologist, the historian does not perhaps set out sufficiently convinced that what he is investigating is fundamentally different from the world of his personal experience. When investigating what appears familiar, all too easily what is unfamiliar is not given its adequate place, even more so since the unfamiliar is much less evident in the sources. To what extent my use of anthropological stimulation is valid remains to be seen. I have been encouraged, however, by statements like the following: 'Only if we abandon . . . that sweet sense of accomplishment which comes from the parading of habitual skills and address ourselves to problems sufficiently unclarified as to make discovery possible, can we hope to achieve work which will not just reincarnate that of the great men.'[3]

The available sources from the early medieval West are approached from new angles. Incidental and sporadic references, often with pejorative undertones, allow us to conclude that oral culture continued to be a central feature of those societies; in other words, older institutions survived not on the margins but at the very centre of 'Christian' societies.

One of the major results of my research is a profound conviction that the Latin language is a most inadequate tool for grasping aspects of early medieval cultures outside the sphere of Latin. This is of truly crucial importance to a new evaluation of these cultures; for this reason references in the sources to the oral culture are generally quoted in full without a close translation (that would impose yet another barrier between object and observer). Instead, arguments are presented to show why certain terms have to be understood differently from the traditional manner. No source speaks for itself, and in the following pages some sources familiar to historians will reveal new and hitherto unfamiliar aspects.

Due to the exceptionally rich evidence, features of oral culture in the Celtic countries can be studied in greater depth than is possible for the continental societies. That evidence is contained predominantly in sources written in the vernacular rather than Latin, which is a further reason why the Celtic countries are treated separately. However, ultimately there emerge surprising insights into parallels or at least similarities between the Celtic and the other barbarian societies.

Two areas hardly figure at all in this book: Spain and Scandinavia. Both can be taken to have had a rather similar oral culture in the early medieval centuries. However, the Arab conquest of Spain in the early eighth century gave rise to a culture in which the sources are predominantly in Arabic, with which I am not familiar. Scandinavian societies, on the other hand, received Christianity and thereby alphabetic literacy so late that they fall outside the general frame of this work.[4]

3 Geertz, C., 'Religion as a cultural system', in Banton, M., ed., *Anthropological approaches to the study of religion*, London 1966, 1-46, at 2.
4 See most recently Boyer, Régis, *La poésie scaldique* (= Typologie des sources du moyen âge occidental fasc. 62), Turnhout 1992.

Preface xi

The oral culture was intimately bound to the vernacular language of each society. Those who deal with the history of early vernacular literature have tended to look for antecedents of this literature and have concerned themselves with a number of the accounts which I also adduce. However, where this study differs fundamentally from those accounts is in the approach to the early oral culture.[5] There seem to be differences not only in quantity but also in quality between oral culture and vernacular literature and therefore rethinking traditional positions seems unavoidable. In this field I am exposing myself perhaps to most criticism from experts in early medieval literature, and I can only ask them to keep an open mind.

This book is concerned with those aspects of medieval society which were already in existence when Christianity arrived and somehow gained a foothold. 'Barbarian' is a term with multiple meanings in the Middle Ages as had been the case in antiquity; some of these meanings coincide, others do not. In focusing more intensely than usual on the barbarian aspects of the early medieval West I hope to redress the balance, and this by purposefully elaborating the strength and potential of barbarian culture, its purpose and functions. I hope that this study will stimulate others to constructive considerations of the nature of the oral culture and will encourage them to make their own contributions in a field that is wide and whose effects can be far-reaching.

This study does not proceed chronologically. The fact is that it is at present not possible to write a history, in the conventional sense of this term, of the oral culture of the early medieval West. The evidence for the oral culture, even when it is uncovered, is very uneven. However, the nature of the oral culture is of a kind that certain assumptions can be made which do not require continuous attestation. Thus it is possible to project from certain good evidence to the context of other evidence which is less well documented. Future studies may proceed differently, but at this stage the existing source evidence necessitates a non-chronological approach.

This book has a fairly long history. My interest in communication studies is almost as old as my professional career. At an early stage I established contacts with Michel Banniard which have continued over the years; 1992 at last saw the publication of his Thèse d'État on written and oral communication in the early medieval Latin countries (*Viva voce*). Michel Banniard has been very supportive over the years in a field which is both difficult and undoubtedly

5 Cf. chapter 10. The university of Freiburg im Breisgau has hosted since 1986 a research programme on orality and literacy: 'SFB 321: Spannungsfelder und Übergänge zwischen Mündlichkeit und Schriftlichkeit'. As far as I am aware, there has been no general discussion of either of the two central terms of reference as evidenced in the several dozen volumes which have appeared under the serial title ScriptOralia.

underexplored. In 1987 Professor Leopold Genicot of Louvain-la-Neuve asked me to write on the medieval oral tradition for the series *Typologie des sources du moyen âge occidental* of which he was main editor until 1992. I am most grateful, particularly in retrospect, for the trust contained in that request. Part of the result of the research on this topic is contained in the fascicle of the *Typologie* with the title 'The oral tradition in the early medieval West', which appeared in 1994. The present book builds on the results of that fascicle but also attempts to flesh out the bare bones presented there.

In the secondary literature, I have generally stopped reading in 1992. As of the end of 1993 I am not aware that any other study of the oral culture of the early medieval West is imminent. However, I should stress that the introductory chapters do not aim at comprehensive coverage (which would be a book in itself) but are intended as a general orientation on aspects that are of special relevance to the chapters on oral culture.

My work on this project began shortly after I had taken up my position at the university of Konstanz. The excellent library resources made it feasible to pursue this wide-ranging and ambitious project. The 'Ausschuß für Forschungsfragen' considered the project worth supporting financially over six years. I gratefully acknowledge this support, as indeed that of my colleague Alexander Patschovsky, which enabled me to employ temporary research assistants. Without their dedicated help this work could not have been done. I thank each of them warmly.

I am in the debt of a number of colleagues and friends for help, not all of which is acknowledged in the notes or in the bibliography. It is a special pleasure to thank here Jane Inglis, who has been supportive of my English language publications for the last twenty years and more, and Michael Enright, for their willingness to read the manuscript and very tactfully help to make it more readable. They were very generous with a commodity which they have in short supply—time.

During my work on the project, I took every opportunity to discuss aspects of it with colleagues and friends all over the world. Here I should like to mention several visits to Dublin and continued fruitful contracts with the members of the Board of Medieval Studies at University College Dublin to which I myself belonged for a dozen years and where I learned to cooperate with colleagues from neighbouring disciplines.

I gratefully acknowledge the opportunity I had to work at the School of History of the Institute for Advanced Study at Princeton in the autumn of 1988 with its characteristic stimulating atmosphere and exceptionally good working conditions. I was very honoured by an invitation to the École des Hautes Études en Sciences Sociales in Paris in the spring of 1993 where I gave lectures on the Carolingian and on the Celtic material; I should like to thank my friend Jean-Claude Schmitt in particular. The medievalist who helped me most all along was Aaron Gurevich, whose friendship and generosity I have had the privilege to enjoy in Moscow, Princeton and Konstanz since 1985.

Finally, I should like to thank Michael Adams and his staff at Four Courts Press, Dublin, for seeing the book through the press so efficiently.

Konstanz,
January 1994.

ABBREVIATIONS

AA SS	Acta Sanctorum
AHR	American Historical Review
AFM	Annals of the Four Masters
AU	Annals of Ulster
BBCS	Bulletin of the Board of Celtic Studies
CCCM	Corpus Christianorum Continuatio Medievalis
CCSL	Corpus Christianorum, Series Latina
CIH	Corpus Iuris Hibernici
CMCS	Cambridge Medieval Celtic Studies
CSEL	Corpus Scriptorum Ecclesiasticorum Latinorum
CSSH	Comparative Studies in Society and History
DIL	Dictionary of the Irish Language
EHR	English Historical Review
FS	Festschrift
HZ	Historische Zeitschrift
IE	Indo-European
MGH	Monumenta Germaniae Historica (with sub-sections)
Ml	Milan-glosses
NL	Nibelungenlied
OHG	Old High German
PBA	Proceedings of the British Academy
PL	J.P. Migne, Patrologia Latina
PMLA	Proceedings of the Modern Language Association
PRIA	Proceedings of the Royal Irish Academy
RC	Revue Celtique
RS	Rolls Series
SBB	Sitzungsberichte
SS	Steinmeyer, Sievers, Althochdeutsche Glossen
Stud. Celt.	Studia Celtica
WHR	Welsh History Review
ZCP	Zeitschrift für Celtische Philologie
ZRG	Zeitschrift der Savigny-Stiftung für Rechtsgeschichte

PART I
THE TRANSFORMATION OF THE ROMAN WORLD

I

POLITICS

While it is true that the past is complete and unchangeable, the same cannot be said about the presentation of the past by the historian. This is due to the perspective from which the individual historian writes, the terminology he uses[1] and the issues he chooses to discuss. All this applies to the subject of this book, the formation of the medieval West. This topic will be dealt with here from a perspective which differs in certain respects from that used in previous treatments.

When do the Middle Ages begin; what justifies our regarding this epoch as different from that which preceded it? Naturally, the term 'Middle Ages' is a post-medieval creation and in its application strictly European. It was intended to refer to the period between the end of the Roman Empire and the Renaissance. However, there are a number of European societies to whose history Rome made little or no direct contribution; for these, therefore, the term 'Middle Ages' is merely a borrowed chronological concept.[2]

There is an established tradition of marking off the Middle Ages from antiquity by reference to political events. One key event is the fate of the Western part of the Roman Empire, which ceased to exist in 476 when the last emperor, Romulus Augustulus, was deposed. There is another tradition, also well established, according to which the event of 476 should be regarded as symptomatic and symbolic rather than as causal or highly significant. There is wide consensus among scholars that the demise of the Western empire was a gradual process, the visible beginnings of which stretch back at least as far as the early fifth century.

It has been argued (less frequently) that even the concept of an even

---

1   It has been well said that 'the use of language is very influential in how we perceive the world', Gill, S.D., *Beyond 'the primitive'. The religions of nonliterate peoples*, Englewood Cliffs 1982, xvi.
2   In Irish historiography, 'medieval' traditionally, although not invariably, means the time between 1169 and 1534; the earlier period is referred to as 'early Christian', which is very problematical since it suggests a formative influence of Christianity on Irish society, a suggestion which is by no means applicable throughout these centuries.

gradual transition from antiquity to the Middle Ages is meaningful only with regard to the territory of the Roman Empire. This empire, however, was not co-terminous with 'the West', which is what we are studying. Those peoples that had not been part of the empire in Europe had their own history—one which is often exceedingly difficult to analyse due to the nature of the historical information available. Some of these peoples were directly involved in the demise of the Western Empire, but others remained outside the Romania.

To view the events in the fifth century as either the 'Fall of Rome' or the 'time of the barbarian invasions' is a legitimate approach. However, one needs to remember that this perspective is eminently Rome-centred. To take this stand (as is commonly done) and to make use of written sources produced mainly within the Empire is to put oneself at the mercy of information of an extremely slanted kind. This is the case with respect to the issues discussed in this book more generally, and it will be necessary to recall from time to time the partiality of the available sources.

There is, by contrast, an equally established tradition of getting away from such a Rome-centred position. This other approach may best be characterized as viewing the period under discussion as a time of 'the transformation of the Roman world' in the West.[3] This approach is, in essence, dynamic and forward-looking in that it focuses on the constructive forces that contributed to the formation of the medieval West.

The position taken in this book is to approach the western half of Europe in these terms of transformation. It sees the West as composed initially of two types of societies, Roman on the one hand, barbarian on the other. In the Roman sources the term *barbarus* has a prominent place and, since we depend on these sources, it might seem that we have adopted the Roman perspective.

The term *barbarus*,[4] which the Romans took over from the Greeks, has many shades of meaning which have to be elucidated wherever possible from the context in which it occurs. It is a highly flexible term. It allows us also to dispense at this stage with describing the barbarians, for example, as 'Germanic', a term that would have to be defined at length in order to avoid misunderstandings. Of course, the various barbarian groups differed one from another, but they also shared a number of features which will be of particular interest here. Be that as it may, there is one fundamental dimension to the

---

3 For a recent application of this concept see Geary, P.J., *Before France and Germany. The creation and transformation of the Merovingian world*, New York and Oxford 1988. For the Roman Empire of Byzantium, the term now commmonly used is 'late antiquity', which puts a welcome emphasis on continuity there.

4 For a recent summary with further references see Rugullis, S., *Die Barbaren in den spätrömischen Gesetzen. Eine Untersuchung des Terminus barbarus*, Frankfurt 1992, esp. 21-51. See also Jones, W.R., 'The image of the barbarian in medieval Europe', *CSSH* 13, 1971, 376-404; Luiselli, B., 'L'idea romana dei barbari nell'età delle grandi invasioni germaniche', *Romanobarbarica* 8, 1984-85, 33-61.

term *barbarus*: it denotes otherness from the point of view of the person who uses it. This otherness need not imply qualitative difference,[5] although that is often the case where 'barbarian' denotes a person or people of a purportedly lesser culture than the subject that so labels them.[6]

The central meaning of 'otherness' associated with *barbarus* is of the greatest value for us, for it invites examination, wherever possible, of the nature of the culture which 'made the others'. In this respect one needs to remember that, generally speaking, the barbarians are described in categories and terms familiar to the commentators which more likely than not fail to do justice to the 'others' even when that is the intention. It is thus necessary to decode the information that has been transmitted.

It must be pointed out that *barbarus* covers a very wide semantic field which cannot be discussed here. We shall come back to some of its meanings at a later stage. For present purposes, it is enough to single out one factor: in the political terminology of late antiquity, 'barbarian' was synonymous with 'hostile', thus underlining the confrontation of the two types of society.

Before the fifth century, there were fairly neat boundaries between the Romans and the barbarians.[7] Thereafter, those boundaries became blurred. Roman society was encroached upon by barbarians, and thereby transformed. It may be helpful to approach the subject in terms of acculturation, for this implies that in the meeting of the two cultures both parties were affected and transformed.[8] By adopting this approach, one can do more than merely present the Roman perspective, even though one has to draw on the available Roman terminology.

Our treatment of the formation of the medieval West, while using the contemporary accounts and their terminology, must not limit itself to making a distinction between Romans and barbarians. A bird's eye view of the political

---

5 For Herodotus' neutral use of the term see Nippel, W., *Griechen, Barbaren und Wilde. Alte Geschichte und Sozialanthropologie*, Frankfurt 1990, 16f. Einhart describes himself as *homo barbarus et in Romana locutione perparum exercitatus*, Preface to *Vita Karoli Magni*, Holder-Egger, O., ed., MGH SS in us. schol., p. 2. For another neutral use of the term by him see below, chapter 4. I have the impression that the term *barbarus* is used less often in a pejorative sense among people whose native language was not Romance.

6 For a classic statement see Prudentius: 'Tantum distant Romana et barbara, quantum quadrupes abiuncta est bipedi vel muta loquenti.' *Contra Symmachum* II, 8, 16-17, CSEL 61, 276.

7 For a different emphasis see Christ, K., 'Römer und Barbaren in der hohen Kaiserzeit', *Saeculum* 10, 1959, 273-88.

8 This point has been emphasized by Hsu, F.L.K., 'Rethinking the concept "primitive",' *Current Anthropology* 5, 1964, 169-78, at 175. See also Fortes, M., 'Culture contact as a dynamic process. An investigation in the Northern territories of the Gold Coast', *Africa* 9, 1936, 24-55, esp. p. 53.

order of the West at some key dates can be helpful. The political map of the western half of Europe between, say, AD 350 and 750 shows very substantial changes. Whereas in 350 the Roman Empire was still intact within boundaries which kept the barbarians out, by 500 there were a number of barbarian *regna* on the territory of the Western half of the former Empire; by 750 hardly any of these *regna* had survived; new political entities had become dominant. One has to approach the barbarians from a variety of perspectives.

Among the barbarians, one can distinguish those who, when they met the Roman world for the first time, already professed Christianity (albeit of the Arian variety as against Roman Catholic orthodoxy), and those which were not Christians at all when they met the Romans. A third category of barbarians were those who did not even encroach upon the Roman world in the period under discussion.

The entry of these different kinds of barbarians into the historical record is uneven; there has been the understandable tendency to give most attention to those that have left most traces. In this manner, however, the Rome-orientated perspective is perpetuated with unfortunate results. The discussion in this chapter serves as a background to the theme of the book and is for this reason rather selective in its presentation of problems. I have not considered it necessary to review the scholarly literature on this subject; the notes will identify those recent accounts which I consider to be of importance.

There were indeed barbarian invasions in the late fourth and early fifth centuries. Thus in 378 the Roman army under the emperor Valens was defeated by the Goths near Adrianople, inside the Empire. In the winter of 406/407, Sueves, Vandals and Alans breached the Rhine frontier and poured into Gaul; in 410 Rome was sacked by the Visigoths under Alaric. These were only the most spectacular events to occur within one generation.

The events from 378 onwards had been set in motion by the arrival of Asiatic Huns in Eastern Europe in 375. These became the dominating force north of the Empire for almost one century until their final defeat in 453. The search for safety from the Huns was one of the reasons why the barbarians invaded the Empire.

The barbarians had invaded the Empire before, but the difference was that this time they came to stay. They settled, but, unlike previous foreigners, were not quickly absorbed and neutralized. Some of these peoples, like the Anglo-Saxons or the Franks, were the founders of medieval nations and states. Others did not survive, but they deserve attention nonetheless because they played a part in the transformation of the ancient world. Those peoples that settled in the Empire in the fifth century—Goths, Burgundians, Franks, Saxons—had, prior to that, been neighbours of the Romans.

It has been suggested more than once that the invaders had undergone *préassimilation*,[9] that they were not as foreign to the Romans as the term *barbarus* suggests. This issue will be examined from various angles; it can be considered as a *leitmotif* of this chapter as well as of the entire book. However, one should guard against emphasizing assimilation too much, although the existing sources deal mainly with this aspect. After all, the fact is that the Western Empire ceased to exist, and in its place barbarian *regna* emerged.

We are concerned with a late sequence of political events which have long been known as *Völkerwanderung*, 'migration', the movement of various peoples from their alleged homelands in southern Scandinavia ('officina gentium aut certe velut vagina nationum'[10]) over much of central and Eastern Europe. *Völkerwanderung*, a calque on *migratio gentium*, although in use for three centuries, is a problematical term. On the one hand, it suggests rather peaceful affairs whereas one should think instead of confrontations, dislocations and certainly a good deal of fighting. Secondly, and equally important, *Volk*, 'people' or 'tribe', suggests an internal coherence and homogeneity of the political entities in question which is belied by the available evidence. By the time these 'peoples' arrived in the Empire, all of them were ethnically mixed groups—groups, however, which believed that they belonged together and which acted on this assumption.[11] The persistence of this belief will also form a significant theme of the present work.

In more recent historiography, another term has been adopted from anthropology for this complex of problems—*ethnogenesis*. This term is used to avoid the pitfalls associated with the previously current terminology (*Volk*, *Stamm*, tribe etc.). Genesis at least implies a certain dynamism and variability even though it also suggests a directional process; on the other hand, *ethnos* is neither better nor worse than *gens* or *natio*, because all three terms carry connotations of biological affinity which may have existed in the imagination of the members of the group even where it had no factual basis. 'People' recommends itself at least by implying a community of human beings. In the treatment that follows, this problem is of minor importance, for we shall be using the names that these political groups had. A name can continue to be used even when the group identified by it changes in composition and appearance, sometimes very substantially. *Ethnogenesis* in this sense is a suitable

---

9   For this see most recently Banniard, M., *Genèse culturelle de l'Europe*, Paris 1989, 71. A similar idea, with reference to Christianity, is found in Momigliano, A., 'Christianity and the decline of the Roman Empire', in id., ed., *The conflict between paganism and Christianity in the fourth century*, Oxford 1963, 1-16, at 15.
10 Jordanes, *Getica* IV, MGH AA 5, 1, p. 60.
11 This is the main theme of Wenskus, R., *Stammesbildung und Verfassung*, Köln 1961, a book of exceptional quality. For a recent summary discussion see Wolfram, H., *Das Reich und die Germanen*, Berlin 1990.

term to deal with the transformation of the Roman world because it directs the attention to the barbarian successor states of the Roman Empire.

One must furthermore bear in mind that the barbarian peoples that became active at the expense of the Empire in the late fourth and fifth centuries were the survivors (in some cases) and the new products (in others), of very substantial political changes in Europe outside the Empire during the life of the Empire. At best the political formation of most of them can be reconstructed only in outline. But those barbarian peoples that became the partners of the Empire brought with them a history of successful survival which would have contributed to their inner cohesion.

While the Romans had always felt intellectually inferior to the Greeks, they took pride in their achievements in at least two spheres: the army and the law. The poet Claudian put it in a nutshell in the late fourth century when he referred to Rome as *armorum legumque parens*.[12] It is extremely instructive, sometimes pathetic, to see how the Romans came to terms with the settlement of barbarian peoples within their Empire by means of arrangements that respected Roman legal sensibilities yet which seem to the modern observer as pious deceptions.[13] But there were, in any case, always two partners to each of these arrangements; while the participation of the barbarian leaders has always received adequate attention from the historians, since it was part of the legal arrangements, it has tended to be forgotten that there was more to the barbarian peoples than meets the eye in the Roman sources. For example, the Roman sources rarely refer to the success of the barbarians as such. Also, the success of the barbarian leaders was also that of their followers, their *populus* or *exercitus*. One needs to highlight the survival of the barbarian peoples within the Empire as recognizable separate political entities side by side with the Roman population. Their behaviour was somewhat ambivalent: they were attracted by Roman culture yet they nevertheless resisted assimilation.

The Romans were ill prepared for the reception of entire peoples in their midst; therefore, means of accommodation had to be found that would be acceptable to both sides. This question is of central importance to our topic and has received much attention, even though it remains very elusive. In 382, after the victory of the Goths, the barbarians dictated the terms; in the course of the next three generations, the Roman contribution to the arrangements was—at least formally—considerable, and it is their contribution that is most prominent in the sources. It can be studied in constitutional and legal terms, but one must not forget that the Romans were no longer fully masters of their action.[14] No text of the many treaties between the Roman government and

12 Claudianus, *Liber tertius de consulatu Stilichonis* v. 136, MGH AA 10.
13 Ladner, G., 'On Roman attitudes towards barbarians in late antiquity', *Viator* 7, 1976, 1-26, at p. 9: 'legal fiction'.
14 For some relevant thoughts in this respect see Faussner, H.C., 'Die staatsrechtliche

barbarian peoples has survived, but it has been established that eventually two institutions were combined that had a place in Roman public life, even though their content was imperceptibly changed: *foedus* and *hospitalitas*.

Foedus had a long tradition.[15] It was a pact between Rome and a foreign power initiated by Rome with the intention of ensuring peaceful coexistence. *Foederati* were expected to behave towards the Romans in specified ways, while being paid an agreed amount of money on a regular basis and retaining their independence and freedom of action. Occasionally, political leaders, who were often at the same time military leaders, were given high Roman military titles (for example, *magister militum*).

The other element which plays a part here is the settlement of foreigners within the Roman Empire. This also had a long tradition, and from 212 onwards such foreigners attained Roman citizenship without much difficulty; they could be and were easily assimilated. This was the case of individuals, small groups of people, and, in the fourth century, even larger groups. A guiding principle was that this should take place without disadvantage to the Romans.

In this respect the consequences of the Gothic-Roman battle in 378 marked a new departure. Before the battle, the Goths had demanded permission to settle in the Empire, and they were refused.[16] After their victory, they got what they wanted: a *foedus*. This arrangement, the first of its kind, lasted only from 382 to 391 when the Visigoths left the places assigned to them; but essentially this policy was continued with other barbarian peoples that came into the Empire.

Hospitalitas of the kind that became customary in the fifth century is found in the technical sense first in a law of 6 February 398 (*Cod. Theod.* VII, 8, 5),[17] regulating the quartering of Roman troops on private estates. These estates were to be divided into two parts, one third for those *qui militant*, and two-thirds to be kept by the owner for his own use. It was a step by which the state resigned part of its responsibility for the upkeep of the army. This

---

Grundlage des Rex Francorum', *ZRG germ. Abt.* 103, 1986, 42-103. A different presentation—subtly Rome-centred—is that of Goffart, W., 'Rome, Constantinople and the barbarians', *AHR* 86, 1981, 275-306.

15 On the following see Wirth, G., 'Zur Frage der föderierten Staaten der späteren römischen Kaiserzeit', *Historia* 16, 1967, 231-51; Wolfram, H., 'Zur Ansiedlung reichsangehöriger Föderaten', *MIÖG* 91, 1983, 5-35 ; Wolfram, H., 'Die Aufnahme germanischer Völker ins Römerreich: Aspekte und Konsequenzen', *Settimane di Studio . . . Spoleto* 29, 1983, 87-117; Chrysos, E.K., 'Legal concepts and patterns for the barbarian settlement on Roman soil', in: *Das Reich und die Barbaren*, Chrysos, E.K., Schwarcz, A., ed., Wien/Köln 1989, 13-23. Cf. also Faussner, esp. 68ff.

16 Ammianus Marcellinus, *Historiae* XXX, 12.8.

17 Demougeot, E., 'Une lettre de l'empereur Honorius sur l'hospitium des soldats', *Revue Historique de Droit Français et Etranger*, Quatrième Série 34, 1956, 25-49.

kind of *hospitalitas* came to be applied to the barbarians,[18] who were thus paid for military service performed under their own leaders and to their own benefit as much as that of Rome. While it may be difficult to see how the Romans benefited from such a *foedus* other than by saving face,[19] it should be remembered that their consistent policy of *divide et impera* ensured that the control of the West would not fall into the hands of a single ruler.[20] The barbarians, on the other hand, obtained substantial areas of land as well as an income at the expense of the Romans. At the same time, various factors operated to the effect that a merging of the barbarians with the Romans did not come about.

This policy can be observed, more or less clearly, throughout the fifth century. We shall deal briefly with particular manifestations of it later. Here, it is the overall picture which matters: almost imperceptibly, domination of the West slipped out of Roman hands. The balance changed gradually, so that it is difficult to decide at what time the different parts of the West ceased to be part of the Empire.[21] Yet as far as the law of the Romans was concerned, the transition was amazingly smooth. This is why the deposition of Romulus Augustulus in 476 hardly caused a ripple on the surface, as far as contemporary observers could see; in the preceding years other political forces had become more important than an emperor in the West.

In what had once been the Roman Empire, there were, by the year 500, kingdoms under the leadership of barbarians (Vandals, Visigoths, Ostrogoths, Burgundians, Franks, Anglo-Saxons), most of them apparently on good terms with the rulers of Constantinople.[22] It was not then clear whether this situation would continue and what would be the long-term implications. In fact, there was no uniform development in the various *regna*; because each of the barbarian peoples had its own history that continued to shape it, the long-term consequences varied regionally.

We shall be dealing separately with some aspects of these societies in the subsequent centuries, and particularly with their cultures. Before doing so,

18   Goffart, W., *Barbarians and Romans. A.D. 418-584. The techniques of accommodation*, Princeton 1980, is highly sceptical about the importance of official Roman *hospitalitas* in this context.
19   Goffart, 'Rome, Constantinople and the barbarians' presents this as the solution most advantageous to the Empire.
20   See most clearly Faussner, 1986, p. 58.
21   The year 474 has been suggested for the Vandal kingdom, 475 for that of the Visigoths: Wolfram, 'Aufnahme', 101. Faussner writes: 'Es stellt sich für uns die Frage, ob das römische Reich staatsrechtlich tatsächlich untergegangen ist', 44.
22   'Der unregierbar gewordene Westen erhielt so eine reduzierte, jedoch berechenbare Staatlichkeit mit festen interregnalen Grenzen', Wolfram, 'Aufnahme', 1983, 102, and identically in id., 'Gotisches Königtum und römisches Kaisertum von Theodosius dem Großen bis Justinian I.', *Frühmittelalterliche Studien* 13, 1979, 1-28, at 28.

other components of these societies have to be carefully considered. The following factors have to be taken into account: the Romans had failed to fend off the barbarians; the latter settled in the Western Empire; they were numerically in the minority, yet politically they dominated, which means that they acquired part of the Romans' wealth. This dominant position of a minority is very difficult to understand.

The political leaders not only availed themselves of Roman structures and institutions; some were outspoken in their desire to become as Roman as possible. It is widely believed that that is what mattered most to them, which is a decidedly Rome-centered view. The diachronic perspective shows another picture. For, in their endeavour to survive as political groups, the barbarians kept apart from the Romans and continued to cultivate their separate identity, as is noticeable most clearly in the survival of their ethnic names. Intermarriage was forbidden by Roman law (*Cod. Theod* III, 14.1), but also by the barbarians. There was, furthermore, the religious divide: most of the barbarians were Arians, not Catholics. Also, while barbarian kingship, making use of Roman institutions and became gradually different from earlier political leadership among those peoples,[23] it did not develop into a known Roman institution but instead became an institution *sui generis*.[24] This was the result of a blending in various degrees of the barbarian and the Roman elements.

We shall look at the implications of the emergence of these barbarian kingdoms. How did they manage to survive in this form? Here the Roman sources are of little direct help, while the oral culture of the barbarians does shed some light. For now it must suffice to state that Romanization of the barbarians and their institutions is only part of the overall structure, albeit an important one and the part most easily visible. It is difficult to imagine how the Roman individuals accepted the substantial reduction of their wealth, status and income, unless one takes note of the shift in the balance of power away from the Romans in favour of the barbarians.[25]

So far we have looked at the events in the fifth century mainly in terms which would have been familiar to the Romans. We have mentioned partial Romanization of the barbarians. It is now necessary to look more closely at

---

23 'Indem der Kaiser ein barbarisches Königreich auf römischem Boden zuließ, . . . stärkte er dessen monarchische Gewalt auf Kosten der gentilen Führungsschicht', Wolfram, 'Aufnahme', 98.
24 A useful discussion of this problem, more wide-ranging than the title suggests, is provided by Faussner, 'Die staatsrechtliche Grundlage'. However, his use of feudal terminology in describing the relationship between the emperor and the individual kings (see 55f and 69) is unacceptable.
25 Wolfram, 'Aufnahme', states factually: 'Es entstanden Königreiche lateinischer Prägung, die ohne die vollständige und bereitwillige Kooperation der Römer keinen Tag hätten existieren können.', 114.

the barbarians. Who were those people who so successfully embedded themselves in Roman society? Their military success is beyond question; the results of the invasions speak for themselves. In view of the pride the Romans took in their armies this is all the more remarkable. Furthermore, the various barbarian peoples did not act in a concerted manner, yet neither were the Romans in a position to confront them with all their power.[26] There is no easy way to explain what happened, but, certainly, these peoples who were so instrumental in the transformation of the Roman world in the West deserve a closer look. One has to start prior to the fourth century.

Their pre-history has to be studied with the help of authors from within the Roman world. Caesar and Tacitus in particular provide exceptionally important information, the perspective of which is, however, very problematical. The details they provide for a particular period cannot be generalized (a mistake often made). In addition, other disciplines must be called upon, in particular prehistory, linguistics, archaeology and anthropology. We need to look at various stages of *ethnogenesis* among a number of peoples.

The peoples we are dealing with are distinguished by names, names which they either gave themselves or were given by others. The names provided a group identity and were therefore of the greatest importance.[27] Some of the names are ethnocentric, being the equivalent of 'men' ('Goths'), implying 'real' human beings to be identical with one's own group.[28]

The names of some peoples who were to play a major role appear rather late in the sources: Alamans, Saxons and Franks are not mentioned until the third century AD; Bavarians are not attested before the sixth. It is not clear whether these peoples' history stretched back much beyond their first appearance in the sources, or whether they were relatively recent political formations combining a variety of ethnic groups under a new name. What can be said, however, is that there were other political groups east of the Rhine who had been Rome's neighbours and who did not survive into the fourth and fifth centuries. Thus one has to reckon with very substantial political changes in the lands east of the Rhine in Roman times, developments that are insufficiently documented.

All the barbarian peoples appeared in their contacts with the Roman

26 A decline of the combat force of the Romans in the fourth century has been suggested by Bernardi, A., 'The economic problems of the Roman Empire at the time of its decline', in: Cipolla, C., ed., *Economic decline of empires*, London 1970, 16-83, at 67-9. For a pointed summary see Jones, A.H.M., 'The decline and fall of the Roman Empire', *History* 40, 1955, 209-26 who suggests a Roman technological inferiority against the barbarians. For a Rome-friendly presentation see Goffart, 'Rome, Constantinople and the barbarians', who is not much interested in the barbarian peoples as such.
27 See Wenskus, *Stammesbildung*, esp. 59ff., 90, 141, 242.
28 This phenomenon also applied to the Roman concept of their own name.

Empire as politically and militarily organized entities. They must be regarded as organized warbands of a kind that survived due to their success as warbands. Unsuccessful warbands would have disintegrated and joined successful groups. Such warbands needed leadership, a leadership which their members in turn freely accepted. In their confrontation with Rome the fighting strength of those peoples would have amounted to several thousands, occasionally tens of thousands. In Roman sources, an *exercitus* of this kind is sometimes equated with the *populus*, a term which therefore denotes all those barbarians who were politically and militarily active, all who guaranteed the survival of the people.

Nearly all the barbarian peoples were organized under the leadership of 'kings', though the Latin terminology can be deceptive, suggesting as it does an institutional uniformity that had no basis in reality. Some native terms are recorded. One can distinguish at least two types of kingship as far as origin and functions are concerned. In Gothic, we find the term *thiudans*, containing the element *theod*, 'people', possibly cognate with *Latin, totus*, 'all', and therefore possibly ethnocentric.[29] The *thiudans* would originally have been regarded as the incarnation of his people, with a religious (sacral) as well as a military quality. The other term which occurs is *reiks* (Latin *rex*), a term probably borrowed by Germanic from Celtic. It is possible that this term places greater emphasis on the military dimension (*Heerkönigtum*). However, one should not think in terms of mutually exclusive concepts. Sacral kingship linked the physical well-being of the people to the king, while the king as leader in battle benefited from the success often attributed to supernatural benevolence. So, the barbarian peoples identified themselves by their common name, were internally strongly organized under a leadership, stayed together as long as they were successful, and gloried in the heroic achievements of their ancestors whom they sought to emulate. Mentally they were anchored in an idealized past on which they looked with reverence.

In the account that follows we shall look at particular areas of the *Romania* to see what happened to the barbarians who settled there. This is not intended as a general presentation of the barbarian invasions; it will include only those barbarian peoples who contribute to our study of oral culture and will thus exclude groups (such as the Vandals or the Visigoths) whose oral tradition did not leave traces in the sources. Our main purpose is to elucidate the manner in which the barbarian groups were or were not affected by the Roman elements which they encountered; we shall be particularly interested in assessing how far they maintained their traditional culture. Due to the nature of the available

---

29 Wenskus, *Stammesbildung*, 45ff, 284. For more detailed discussion see Szemerényi, O., 'Studies in the kinship terminology of the Indo-European languages', in *Textes et Mémoires*, vol. VII, Varia 1977 (= Acta Iranica), 101f.; Benveniste, É., *Indo-European language and society*, Coral Gables, Florida 1973, 297f. I am indebted to Dr Verá Čapková, Dublin, for these references.

information this analysis has to range over a wide period and will form the subject matter of subsequent chapters. The present chapter aims to sketch the political and social framework within which the two types of culture, Roman and barbarian, came to co-exist. We can confine ourselves to fairly short time-spans. The barbarians who established themselves on Roman territory demonstrated by the mere fact of their survival as separate groups in this environment that the environment was no longer as influential on outsiders as it had been previously. One may imagine an accelerating process of transformation after the establishment of the barbarian kingdoms. The longer they survived, the less the Roman content became.

Let us first look at Britain. The island had been the last addition to the Empire in the West (it was not even fully conquered) and was the first to be lost. Here the concept of 'the end of Roman Britain' is entirely appropriate.[30] Britain was the only major area in the West where Latin had not become the mother tongue of the population; however, one has to reckon with widespread bilingualism, in Celtic British and Latin.[31] The information available about the end of Roman rule is remarkably concise even though it is not easy to interpret.

In the early fifth century, Jerome referred to Britain as *fertilis provincia tyrannorum*.[32] In fact, there had been a number of usurpers in Britain during the decades prior to his remark. The end of Roman rule in Britain took place between 407 and 409. The barbarians who had breached the Rhine frontier on New Year's Eve 407 spent some time the following year in northern Gaul. Constantius, one of the usurpers in Britain, crossed over to Gaul in 407, taking with him a large part of the Roman garrison. Neither he nor the troops he took with him were ever to return. In 408 or 409 there was an invasion of Britain by Saxons; this must have been on a major scale since it is referred to in a rather laconic Gallic chronicle of 453: 'Britanniae ... in dicionem Saxonum rediguntur.'[33] However, the Britons fought back and expelled the Saxons. Soon afterwards there appears to have been an insurrection of Britons (possibly from among the lower classes of the population) against Roman officials.[34] The Romano-Britons appealed to the emperor for help. Honorius replied in 410

30 For a recent summary by an archaeologist see Cleary, E., *The ending of Roman Britain*, London 1989. A number of relevant essays are contained in *Britain 400–600: language and history*, Bammesberger, A., Wollmann, A., ed., Heidelberg 1990.
31 See Jackson, K.H., *Language and History in early Britain*, Edinburgh 1953 (repr. Dublin 1994); Hamp, E.P., 'Social gradience in British spoken Latin' *Britannia* 6, 1975, 150-62. See further, chapter 9.
32 *Ep.* 133,9, CSEL 56, 1918, p. 255.
33 MGH AA 9, 660.
34 In this interpretation I follow Thompson, E.A., 'Britain A.D. 406–410', *Britannia* 8, 1977, 303-18.

that the cities of Britain should look after their own defence. Those who warned very soon afterwards that Britain would be lost to Rome forever turned out to be correct.[35] There are no written records attesting to the political organization of the country after the departure of the Roman troops. However, according to the archaeological evidence, the distinguishing features of Roman culture attest to negative consequences of the collapse of Roman presence surprisingly clearly and quickly.[36]

Britain was newly attacked by the Saxons[37] as well as by the Picts and the Irish, and this time the invaders were more successful. When Britain appears in the sources twenty years later, in the context of Germanus of Auxerre's mission to the Christians there as described by Constantius of Lyon, the Saxons were an established force in the island, and the Britons were on the defensive. However, this mission also shows that contacts between Britain and Gaul had not been ruptured as a result of the Saxon invasions.

For this early stage of Saxon activity in Britain, no names of any of their military and political leaders are known. These leaders apparently saw no reason to notify the Roman authorities of their actions.[38] In fact, they did not arrive as one political group under one leader despite those later Anglo-Saxon sources which name Hengist and Horsa as leaders of an invasion (dated in these later accounts to 449). The Germanic barbarians came as separate peoples[39] and in the course of time established strongholds at various sites along the east coast. These groups fought among themselves as well as against the Britons; their descendants gradually widened their areas of control in a westward direction. Under the pressure of the Germanic barbarians from the east, and the Irish barbarians from the west, a sizeable number of Britons emigrated to Gaul to settle in *Britannia minor*, or *Aremorica*, modern Brittany.

There must have been a deep hostility between British and Saxons even though there is scarcely any evidence of it. The long-term thoroughness of the imposition of Saxon rule can be gathered from the fact that over large parts of the eastern half of Britain they imposed their own language at the

---

35 Thompson, 1977, 316; Thompson, E.A., 'Zosimus 6.10.2 and the letters of Honorius', *Classical Quarterly* 32, 1982, 445-62.
36 Cleary, *Ending*, states p. 140: 'The great majority of the Roman features of Roman Britain (towns, villas etc.) had passed out of use by *c*.430, that is to say in the course of about one generation.'
37 For early medieval use of this name see Richter, M., 'Bede's *Angli*—Angles or English?', *Peritia* 3, 1984, 99-114.
38 I differ in this respect from recent suggestions made by Wood, I., 'The end of Roman Britain: continental evidence and parallels' in *Gildas: New approaches*, Lapidge, M., Dumville, D., ed., Woodbridge 1984, 1-25, and taken up by Wolfram, H., *Das Reich und die Germanen*, pp. 336-40.
39 This makes their ethnogenesis different in quality from that of the Goths or Burgundians; the closest parallel is provided by the early Franks before Clovis.

expense of British. This suggests thorough subjection or expulsion of the Britons, or, at least, major confrontations. The strength of the Saxon settlement is further shown by the fact that the Saxons were successful in destroying Christianity in those areas which they controlled, imposing instead their traditional cults.

The fifth and sixth centuries are generally referred to as 'dark' because of the dearth of written information. For, as well as Christianity, literacy was another element of the Roman legacy in Britain which the Saxons dispensed with. Neither did they adopt the Roman monetary economy (which apparently had generally broken down in Britain shortly after 400).

The traditional view of this period of British history is the one just outlined, a presentation cast in negative terms, stressing how the barbarians were culturally inferior to the Romans. But it is easy as well as dangerous to underrate the achievements of the barbarians simply because they are poorly documented.

It is true that one cannot follow the various stages of *ethnogenesis* of the Germanic invaders in Britain in the fifth and sixth centuries. What one can say in view of later evidence is that kingdoms developed with apparently hardly any resort to Romano-British institutions. When these kingdoms appear in the historical records in the course of conversion to Christianity, from the late sixth century onwards, they appear as fairly solidly established territorial entities. These kingdoms were by no means at peace either internally or among one another, yet it may be assumed that the political situation of the Germanic groups had gradually stabilized. According to Bede (HE II, v), there existed even the institution of an 'overking', otherwise known as *bretwalda*, reaching back into the sixth century.[40] In the early seventh century light is shed on the high level of culture reached by at least some of those Germanic societies by the Sutton Hoo ship burial in East Anglia of *c*.625. Less widely known, but similarly significant, are the royal buildings excavated at Yeavering in Northumbria and identified as King Edwin's *Ad Gefrin* mentioned by Bede. The excavations unearthed remains of a great wooden hall, ancillary buildings and a structure that has been tentatively called a theatre providing seating for about 300 people.[41]

Bede's by no means factual or balanced account of these societies gives insight into their prevailing warrior ethos. He even allows glimpses of an organized paganism. But more important is the implicit message conveyed by his work, though not perceived by him in these terms: kingdoms had been set up, maintained, enlarged and held together without recourse to a written

40 For a general survey see Campbell, J., ed., *The Anglo-Saxons*, Oxford 1982.
41 Hope-Taylor, B., *Yeavering*, London 1977. For more findings since then see the survey by Hodges, R., *The Anglo-Saxon achievement. Archaeology and the beginnings of English society*, London 1989.

administration, and that in an area which had been exposed to Roman culture for several centuries. That culture had been largely shunned by these new arrivals, an attitude which had probably worked to their disadvantage.

For several centuries after the fall of Roman Britain, the island was divided into a number of political entities with different languages and different cultures, Saxon and pagan in the south and east, British and Catholic in the west and north of the former Roman province. Saxons and British had in common, however, that both had a culture that was transmitted largely orally.

The Burgundian development was different.[42] These barbarians encroached upon the Western Roman Empire in the wake of the collapse of the *limes* in 406/7; in the decade that followed they are attested as settled on both banks of the Rhine, obviously tolerated by the Romans.[43] Orosius, following Jerome's account from the late fourth century, gives a figure of 80,000 warriors who settled on the Rhine.[44] For the period immediately prior to that, Ammianus Marcellinus reports the names of their secular leaders in the present tense and tells us that they were not as firmly established as their high priests.[45]

The 'first kingdom of the Burgundians' lasted from *c.*413 to 435/7. According to Orosius, the Burgundians became Catholics in 417—evidence of strong Roman cultural influence. The historical sources do not specify where on the Rhine their kingdom was situated. It is not clear whether there had emerged a Burgundian monarchy under a single ruler. A political leader named Gundahar is attested as early as 411, and he is most likely the same as Gundicarius, whom Prosper names for 435 as the Burgundian leader who suffered a devastating defeat, most likely by Aetius in alliance with Hunnic units, an event that heralded the end of the 'first Burgundian kingdom'.

The chronicler Prosper Tiro reports the complete destruction of Gundahar's people,[46] but the Burgundians survived as an organized group of

42 For a very recent assessment see Amory, P. 'The meaning and purpose of ethnic terminology in the Burgundian laws', *Early Medieval Europe* 2, 1993, 1-28.
43 Prosper Tiro, s.a. 413: '. . . Burgundiones partem Galliae propinquam Rheno obtinuerunt' (MGH AA 9, 467). See Altheim, F., *Geschichte der Hunnen*, 5 vols., Berlin 1959-62, vol. 4, 194f; cf. also Wolfram, *Das Reich und die Germanen*, 352-63.
44 'Burgundionum quoque novorum hostium nouum nomen, qui plus quam octoginta milia, ut ferunt, armatorum ripae Rheni fluminis insederunt'. Orosius, *Historia adversus paganos*, VII, 32, 11, CSEL 5, 514.
45 Ammianus Marcellinus XXVIII, 5: 'Apud hos generali nomine rex appellatur Hendinos, et ritu veteri potestate deposita removetur, si sub eo fortuna titubaverit belli vel segetum copiam negaverit terra, ut solent Aegyptii casus eiusmodi suis adsignare rectoribus. Nam sacerdos apud Burgundios omnium maximus vocatur Sinistus et est perpetuus, obnoxius discriminibus nullis ut reges.' This is a most valuable reference to the non-Latin political terminology which underlines their individual qualities.
46 (The Huns) 'illum (Gundicharium) Chuni cum populo suo ab stirpe deleverint'. MGH AA 9, 475. This is frequently repeated by modern historians as a statement of fact rather than a partial account from a decidedly Roman perspective.

considerable importance and strength. This is evident from the fact that they were allowed to settle in Savoy in what was subsequently known as 'the second kingdom of the Burgundians' (443-534). The *Lex Burgundionum* (*c.*508) mentions that the Burgundians were settled there according to the terms of *hospitalitas*, which entitled them to a share of the land that had been previously in Roman hands.[47] The single chronicle reference that we have for this event contains basically the same message.[48]

One is thus dealing with a new *ethnogenesis* of the Burgundians in Savoy. Politically they were in the dominating position *vis-à-vis* the indigenous Roman population. While the information about Burgundy is rather thin, it is known that the Burgundian king Gundowech was made *magister militum Galliarum*.[49] The mere fact that a high Roman political office was conferred on him indicates that he was recognized as a legitimized partner by the Roman imperial administration. This was the Roman dimension of the accommodation of the Burgundians within the territory of the Empire.

In 534 the kingdom of the Burgundians was annexed by the Franks. It became, along with Austrasia and Neustria, one of the *tria regna* ruled over by Merovingians. This subsequent development does not, however, detract from the way in which, in contrast to Britain, the case of the Burgundians shows clearly and concisely the ways and means by which Germanic kingdoms came to be established on Roman territory.

The case of the Burgundians is relevant to us for additional reasons. The 'first Burgundian kingdom' was the stage in the political development of the Burgundians which formed the core of the saga material which was to be passed on orally for many centuries before being transformed into written epic in the twelfth century. It is from the epic, not from previously written documentation, that the 'first Burgundian kingdom' is located not just 'on the Rhine' but centered on Worms. The epic furthermore elucidates periods of amicable relations with the Huns for which no historical sources from late antiquity can be quoted. It is archaeology which attests the historical existence of such peaceful cultural contacts.[50] Also, it has to be noted that oral traditions relating to the Burgundians did not die when Burgundy came under Frankish control. The saga material, originally essentially Burgundian, was continued

---

47   *Lex Burg.*, LIV: 'Licet eo tempore, quo populus noster mancipiorum tertiam et duas terrarum partes accepit, eiusmodi a nobis fuerit emissa praeceptio, ut quicumque agrum cum mancipiis seu parentum nostrorum sive nostra largitate perceperat, nec mancipiorum tertiam nec duas terrarum partes ex eo loco, in quo ei hospitalitas fuerat delegata, requireret'. MGH LL I, II, 1, 88f.

48   'Sapaudia Burgundionum reliquiis datur cum indigenis dividenda'. *Chronica Gallica*, MGH AA 9, 660.

49   He is mentioned as such in a letter of Pope Hilarius to the bishop of Arles, *Ep.* IX, PL 58, 27, of AD 463.

50   See below, chapter 10.

in Frankish times as well, which must be taken as a sign of its continued relevance to all those susceptible to such material.

We shall now turn to the Franks, not in their role as masters of the Burgundians, but in their own right.[51] The Franks appear in the Roman sources in the third century. However, they penetrated into Gaul only in the fifth century, and this is the time when they are relevant to our study. The man to whom we owe most of our information about the Franks, the Gallo-Roman bishop Gregory of Tours, writing in the late sixth century, reports that in earlier times the Franks were ruled by a number of kings. It was Clovis who made himself sole king of the Franks and became the ancestor of the Merovingian dynasty which ruled the Franks for two hundred and fifty years. Clovis is one of Gregory's great heroes.

To the historian interested in the transformation of the Roman world by the barbarians Clovis's father, Childeric, although not yet sole ruler of the Franks, is of almost equal relevance. He does not figure as much in the written sources as his son, but archaeology has a good deal to tell us about him.

Among many thousands of early medieval burials that have been excavated, there are only few which can be assigned to historically attested personalities. One of these is the burial of king Childeric who died in 482. Childeric's grave at Tournai was discovered in 1653; by the standards of the time the richly endowed grave was quite thoroughly documented at the time of its discovery,[52] which is very fortunate, because much of the content has since disappeared.

One of two rings found in the grave is a signet ring. It shows the frontal bust portrait of a man and is inscribed with the words CHILDIRICI REGIS. The fact that the king carried a signet ring shows him to belong to a civilization which had use for such an artefact, although no document authenticated by this ring has survived. It bespeaks Roman, not Frankish, civilization.[53]

The portrait on the ring, however, shows an interesting mix of Roman and non-Roman, that is, Frankish, elements. The man is portrayed beardless, with long hair parted in the middle; the long hair was the totem associated with the Merovingian dynasty, the *reges criniti*. What can be recognized of Childeric's dress has been identified tentatively as a Roman military cloak, a *chlamys* or a *paludamentum*. Whichever of the two it was meant to represent,

51   The most recent synthesis of the early history of the Franks by James, E., *The Franks*, Oxford 1988, does not, unfortunately, take into account the works of either R. Wenskus or H. Wolfram.
52   Cf. Kazanski, M., Perin, P., 'Le mobilier funéraire de la tombe de Childéric I. Etat de la question et perspectives', *Revue archéologique de Picardie* 1986, 13-38. For a recent general synthesis see James, *The Franks*, esp. 58ff.
53   This point is all too briefly touched by McCormick, M., 'Clovis at Tours. Byzantine public relations and the origins of medieval ruler symbolism', in Chrysos, E.K., Schwarcz, A., ed., *Das Reich und die Barbaren*, Wien/Köln 1989, 155-80, at 170.

such a dress symbolized an office conferred, the visible sign of belonging to the Roman military hierarchy. In his right hand Childeric holds a lance which leans against his shoulder. This weapon, a *Herrschaftszeichen*, can be associated with either Roman or Frankish leadership.

Roman as well as Frankish elements, detectable on and in the signet ring, are confirmed in other goods contained in the burial. The body, of impressive stature (179 cm), was dressed in a precious brocade cloak. It was fastened with a gold buckle in the Roman fashion. Thus the dress and the presentation on the signet ring both show the Roman side of Childeric.

The weapons found in the burial—long sword (*spatha*), narrow ax (*Schmalsax*), ax for throwing (*francisca*)—are typical Frankish arms even though they were fastened on the dress in Roman manner. Also of importance are the coins contained in the burial: over 100 gold solidi contained in a leather bag and over 200 silver coins. These are believed to represent the payment of the *foederatus* by Constantinople.[54]

Reference should be made, finally, to a horse buried nearby whose harness was richly decorated. This burial signals Germanic tradition. The horse's head harness included a pendant showing the head of a bull. The decorations associated with the harness were of Eastern European inspiration (the northern shore of the Black Sea and the lower Danube area). However, bulls were essential to the Merovingian Franks. The dynasty was allegedly descended from the union of a queen with a *qinotaurus*;[55] oxen were part of the Merovingian kings' trappings as late as the eighth century.[56]

The burial of Childeric thus shows this leader bearing features of Frankish-Germanic as well as of Roman authority. The latter are particularly significant if one takes into account that Childeric was as yet one of several kings of the Franks.

Childeric's son Clovis ruthlessly eliminated all his Frankish rival kings; confining royalty to his descendants only, he thereby became the founder of the Frankish Merovingian dynasty. Late in his reign, in 508, he assumed the Roman title of 'consul', the exact significance of which remains disputed.[57]

---

54 I have used in this summary the account by Böhner, K., 'Childerich', *Reallexikon der germanischen Altertumskunde* 4, 1981, 440-60.
55 Fredegar III, 9, MGH SS rer. Merov. 2, 95: 'Fertur, super litore maris aestatis tempore Chlodeo cum uxore resedens, meridiae uxor ad mare labandum vadens, bistea Neptuni Qinotauri similis eam adpetisset. Cumque in continuo aut a bistea aut a viro fuisset concepta, peperit filium nomen Meroveum, per eo regis Francorum post vocantur Merohingii.'
56 Einhart, *Vita Karoli Magni*, c.1.
57 See Zöllner, E., *Geschichte der Franken bis zum Beginn des 6. Jahrhunderts*, Köln 1970, 67f.; Hauck, K., 'Von einer spätantiken Randkultur zum karolingischen Europa', *Frühmittelalterliche Studien* 1, 1967, 3-93, here 30-3; important new points are made by McCormick, M., 'Clovis at Tours.' Cf. also Faussner, 'Staatsrechtliche Grundlage', esp. 77ff.

Igitur ab Anastasio imperatore codecillos de consolato accepit, et in basilica beati Martini tunica blattea indutus et clamide, inponens vertice diadema. Tunc ascenso equite, aurum argentumque in itinere illo, quod inter portam atrii et eclesiam civitatis est, praesentibus populis manu propria spargens, voluntate benignissima erogavit, et ab ea die tamquam consul aut augustus est vocitatus.[58]

Gregory of Tours, to whom we owe this information, naturally would have stressed the Roman features particularly. In the discussion of this event it is hardly ever taken into account that Gregory wrote almost a century after the event, and one does not know how he obtained his information and consequently how literally it should be taken. It is also unclear whether Clovis had ruled without recognition from Byzantium for the previous sixteen years.

In any case, it can be argued that there are important elements of rulership which were shared by Clovis and his father Childeric which show that they combined Roman and non-Roman features. In this respect they are particulary telling examples of barbarian kings on Roman territory whose kingship had been influenced by their careers.

The Ostrogoths are the group of barbarians who settled the most prestigious part of the Western Empire—Italy.[59] It is exceedingly difficult to arrive at a balanced assessment of them, simply because the information about them is infinitely richer than for any of the other contemporary barbarian peoples. There is a real danger of being dazzled by the blaze of information and thereby of losing sight of the fact that the Ostrogothic kingdom survived for not much more than half a century.

The first half is dominated by the towering figure of Theodoric (king 493-526), while the second half is a drawn-out agony showing that Theodoric had failed to ensure an appropriate succession. To take Italy required particular political skill; to survive there recognized by Constantinople while still remaining a Gothic king was a great challenge to which Theodoric rose masterfully.[60]

The historical information about these aspects is exceptionally rich, both because there was much continuity with previous Roman government and because the Ostrogoths had in their service a well-educated Roman, Cassio-

---

58 *Libri Decem Historiarum*, II, 38, MGH SS rer. Mer. 1, 88-89.
59 The best modern account is that by Wolfram, H., *History of the Goths*, Berkeley, Los Angeles and London 1988 (German original 1979).
60 This is clearly articulated in Anonymi Valesiani pars posterior, MGH AA 9, 322: 'sic gubernavit duas gentes in uno Romanorum et Gothorum, ... ut etiam a Romanis Traianus vel Valentinianus ... appellaretur, et a Gothis secundum edictum suum, quo ius constituit, rex fortissimus in omnibus iudicaretur'.

dorus, who was consul in 514, having been in Theodoric's service between 507 and 511. He held office again under Athalaric and Witigis (c.533-8). His collection of state correspondence, called by him *Variae*, has no parallel elsewhere and provides considerable insight into the government of the Ostrogoths.[61] This collection does not contain all state correspondence from the periods Cassiodorus held office with the Ostrogoths, and there is no document that depicts the Gothic rulers in a negative light.[62] Furthermore, it is difficult to determine to what extent certain formulations originated in the mind of the secretary rather than with his masters.[63]

Since settlement on Roman territory was the precondition for *rex* and *gens* of a new quality,[64] these changes deserve our special interest. Theodoric's kingship can be studied in some detail because it has left good traces in the records; these, however, need to be handled carefully.

Theodoric's establishment in 493 of the Ostrogothic kingdom of Northern Italy, centered on Ravenna, marked the start of a long and quite successful reign. Theodoric had lived for ten years in Byzantium as an adolescent; he later boasted that during that time he had learned how Romans could be ruled.[65] He certainly showed that he could fit into the Roman world with remarkable panache. In the year 500 he celebrated, with 'bread and circuses', that is, in imperial Roman manner,[66] the thirtieth anniversary of his kingship. This must have referred to his kingship of the Goths, and it has been shown to refer to his first independent activity as Gothic war leader after his return from Constantinople and his victory over the Sarmatians; three years later he had been designated by Thiudimir as his successor as king of the Goths.[67]

Theodoric had entered Italy with Constantinople's approval and with the clear aim of deposing the man who then ruled Italy, Odoacer, who had deposed Romulus Augustulus. He succeeded, and assumed the kingship of Italy himself. It was recognized that he owed his kingship to the achievements of his supporters: 'Gothi sibi confirmaverunt Theodericum regem non expectantes

61 *Variae*, ed., Fridh, A.J., CCSL 96, Turnhout 1973. For a sound assessment see O'Donnell, J.J., *Cassiodorus*, Berkeley, Los Angeles and London 1979.
62 O'Donnell, *Cassiodorus*, pp. 75, 80, 84, 100.
63 This problem has been recently well discussed by Scheibelreiter, G., '"Vester est populus meus". Byzantinische Reichsideologie und germanisches Selbstverständnis', in *Das Reich und die Barbaren*, 203-220, esp. 208f. See also O'Donnell, 96.
64 So Wolfram, passim.
65 *Variae* I, 1, 2: 'divino auxilio in re publica vestra didicimus, quemadmodum Romanis aequabiliter imperare possimus'.
66 *Excerptorum Valesianorum Pars II*, 60: 'exhibens ludos circensium et amphitheatrum ... dona et annonas largitus ... suo labore recuperavit et opulentum fecit'. MGH AA 9, 322.
67 Claude, D., 'Zur Königserhebung Theoderichs des Großen', in *Geschichtsschreibung und geistiges Leben im Mittelalter* (FS Heinz Löwe), ed. Hauck, K., Mordeck, H., Köln/Wien, 1978, 1-13 for details.

iussionem novi principis.'[68] Nevertheless he needed recognition of his rule from Constantinople. From the emperor he received as a gift a *vestis regia*;[69] his acceptance of that gift was considered as an explicit legitimation of his rule by Constantinople as well as an implicit recognition on Theodoric's part of the imperial overlordship. The *Variae*, which begin in 507, fourteen years after Theodoric had established his position in Italy, open with a letter to the emperor Anastasius. In this the Gothic king once again seeks accord (*concordia*) with the emperor; the letter contains what must be considered programmatic statements, for example, 'regnum nostrum imitatio vestra est, forma boni propositi, unici exemplar imperii: qui quantum vos sequimur, tantum gentes alias anteimus'.[70]

Theodoric thus combined in his person two positions with two different ways of legitimation, giving him authority over, or perhaps better, making him acceptable to, both Romans and Goths.[71] These positions were essentially different from each other. Gothic kingship signalled him as the integrating leader of his *exercitus*, while recognition by Constantinople created a degree of distance between himself and his subjects. These two dimensions can be distinguished, but the festivities of the year 500 show that they can also be merged. The Gothic kingship which resulted from this merging was substantially different from the traditional one; it elevated the king over his people. Theodoric's kingship has received ample attention and sufficient analysis for the reasons referred to earlier. It has been suggested that his barbarian kingship had assumed imperial functions and even imperial dimensions.[72] This aspect is more apparent in his policy towards the barbarian kingdoms around him than in his dealings with Constantinople.[73] He attempted to set up a system of alliances with his Western European fellow kings in which he saw himself as rather more than a *primus inter pares*.[74] However, his success in this area was decidedly limited. One could also argue that since the emperor created the circumstances which made it impossible for Theodoric to usurp the imperial office in the West he retained some control over events in Western Europe.

68 *Excerptorum Valesianorum Pars II*, 53, p. 316.
69 *Excerptorum Valesianorum Pars II*, 60, p. 322.
70 *Variae* I, 1. This famous passage is interpreted differently by Claude, D., 'Universale und partikulare Züge in der Politik Theoderichs', *Francia* 6, 1978, 19-58, at 42f., and Wolfram, H., 'Gotisches Königtum und römisches Kaisertum von Theodosius dem Großen bis Justinian', *Frühmittelalterliche Studien*. 13, 1979, 1-28.
71 *Excerptorum Valesianorum Pars II*, 60, see above, n. 69.
72 'Das gentile Königtum nahm nicht nur imperiale Funktionen, sondern auch imperiale Ausmaße an', Wolfram, 'Gotisches Königtum', p. 16. However, see Faussner 1986, p. 58.
73 But see *Variae* I, 1, above.
74 Cf. Claude, D., 'Universale und partikulare Züge in der Politik Theoderichs', *Francia* 6, 1978, 19-58.

There is one area in which the Roman dimension of Theodoric's rulership becomes particularly evident. In the traditional Roman manner he sponsored, for the sake of his Roman subjects, the Roman theatre. This was expressed in one place in rather pompous terms which highlight the Roman ethos of the theatre: 'spectacula voluptatum laetitiam volumus esse populorum'.[75] With this phrase the nature of the Roman theatre is nicely epitomized. What needs to be stressed is that the theatre was highly objectionable to serious Christians for this very reason. In 526 the emperor Justinian, by ordering the closure of the hippodrome in his capital, made a gesture in the direction of promoting Christian values in his society. Thus Theodoric can be said to have been in this respect 'more Roman than the Romans'.

By way of contrast, there is one passage in his correspondence addressed to his Gothic subjects in which he articulates traditional Gothic values: 'You Goths need not be persuaded to go to battle but merely be told to go because a fighting crowd like you takes pleasure in being put to the test. He who thirsts after the glory of bravery does not shun the efforts involved.'[76] It is somewhat incongruous that these sentiments should be expressed in writing and in Latin addressed to the Goths, who were expected to uphold their own, non-Roman, values,[77] which did not include education in Latin.

Few people manage to maintain sufficient distance from Theodoric precisely because so much is known about him. J.J. O'Donnell, for one, does not hold Cassiodorus in high regard either as a royal official or as a Latinist. His verdict is summed up like this: 'Whether it was Theodoric who got the kind of propaganda he deserved, or whether it was the propaganda that was as ineffectual as the government, we do not know.'[78]

The second half of the *Variae* contains documents from the time when the reconquest of Italy from Constantinople (533-54) was under way; however, if one had only the *Variae*, this would not be known. This fact underlines another danger which rich one-sided documentation may hold for the researcher.

---

75 *Variae* I, 31. For other references to the theatre see ibid., I, 20; VII, 10. See further IV, 51, a letter in which Theodoric 'explains' to the patrician Symmachus function and structure of the Roman theatre. Chrysos, E.K., 'Die Amaler-Herrschaft in Italien und das Imperium Romanum. Der Vertragsentwurf des Jahres 535', *Byzantion* 51, 1981, 430-71, underlines the political as well as entertainment function of the Roman theatre, p. 465f.
76 *Variae* I, 24. This translation is rather free and therefore I quote also the original: 'Innotescenda sunt magis Gothis quam suadenda certamina, quia bellicosae stirpi est gaudium comprobari: laborem quippe non refugit, qui virtutis gloriam concupiscit.'
77 In like manner, King Witigis explained the nature of his kingship and its Gothic rather than Roman origins on the occasion of his accession in 536 in Latin to his Gothic subjects, *Variae* X, 31.
78 *Cassiodorus*, 100.

Given the information available about the political events during the sixty-year period when the Ostrogoths dominated Italy, there is a temptation to concentrate on the political developments at the top. One easily loses sight of the fact that the Ostrogoths wished to rule a society that in many respects retained features of the past. It is symptomatic that this period saw some of the great cultural achievements of late antiquity in Italy—the works of a Boethius, a Dionysius Exiguus or a Benedict of Nursia. One can argue that the termination of late antiquity in Italy came about, not with Gothic rule, but with the 'reconquest' from Constantinople initiated by the emperor Justinian. In those twenty years (533-54) Italy suffered physical damage of a lasting character which made for a poorer quality of life for all in the long term.

To contemporaries the situation may well have seemed somewhat different, even though one is not bound to share the explanations they offer. It is appropriate to end this section of our study by quoting a lament by Gregory the Great at the close of the sixth century:

> Ecce cuncta in Europae partibus barbarorum iuri sunt tradita, destructae urbes, eversa castra, depopulatae provinciae; nullus terram cultor inhabitat; saeviunt et dominantur cotidie in nece fidelium cultores idolorum.[79]

Here the bishop of Rome depicts the barbarians as dominating the whole of Europe; he also presents them as still essentially pagan. He thus presents a dichotomy from one side, which he felt was that of the losers. It should be noted that Gregory does not explicitly state that the barbarians had actually caused the destruction of civilized life, but this conclusion is easily drawn. It must be added that this is the only place where Gregory links this destruction with the barbarians in general; elsewhere he links it with the settlement of the Lombards in Italy (568),[80] while in yet another place he presents it as God's punishment for unrepenting sinners.[81] However, *destructae urbes, eversa castra, depopulati agri*—these words had hardened into stereotypes which signal the awareness of a very substantial deterioration of the quality of life for the Romans.

The main purpose of this chapter on politics has been to stress that the barbarians who settled on Roman territory and who thus were hereby subject

---

79 *Reg.* V, 37.
80 *Dialogi* III, xxxviii. PL 77, 316C.
81 *In Hiezech.* I *Homilia* IX, 9, and *In Hiezech.* II, *Homilia* VI, 22, CCSL 142, 128, 310. See also *XL Homiliarum Evangelia in Lib. I*, XVII, PL 76, 1147, and *Reg.* III, 29. This phrase is not attested from those other early Christian Latin authors whose works are available in the current data bank.

to Roman influence more intensively than they had earlier been, retained also important aspects of their previous culture, enough to safeguard their identity as a political group different from the Romans. Since our sources come overwhelmingly from the Roman side, the barbarian dimensions tend to get obliterated. But they did exist and there is good reason to argue that in the course of time they gained again in strength in those political communities that survived.

Having drawn attention to the most important aspects of the political changes that were brought about by the barbarians in the course of the fifth century, events which are regarded as highly significant in most accounts of the period, it is necessary to draw attention to certain continuities outside the field of everyday politics. For example, we have seen in the section on the Ostrogoths that the barbarians had little interest in effecting changes in the everyday life of the Roman society they dominated. They had a vested interest in benefiting from that society, which for this reason they would tolerate as long as it tolerated them.

In the light of these considerations it is both unsurprising and profoundly significant that the most important continuity that prevailed is to be found in the sphere of language.[82] Latin, the language of the Roman Empire, remained the language of the former parts of the Empire in most areas—in Italy, Spain and Gaul (it was to take at least three centuries before the Latin language in these regions developed into distinct separate languages).[83] The barbarians did not impose their own language in the Romania; in due course their descendants would become speakers of Romance.

The case of Britain, where Latin did not survive the end of Roman rule as the everyday language of the population, shows that this result was not a foregone conclusion. In Britain, the current British Celtic language, which survived throughout the Roman period even though it had been influenced by Latin to a considerable extent,[84] was largely superseded in the course of the following centuries by the Germanic language of the invading Anglo-Saxons, who thus left a stronger stamp on the island than the Romans had done.

---

82 Cf. Augustine, *De Civitate Dei* XIX, 7: 'At enim opera data est ut imperiosa civitas non solum iugum, verum etiam linguam suam domitis gentibus per pacem societatis inponeret'.
83 The latest authoritative treatment of this subject is that by Banniard, M., *Viva voce. Communication écrite et communication orale, IVe–IXe siècle*, Paris 1992.
84 Jackson, K.H., *Language and History in early Britain*, Edinburgh 1953.

2

RELIGION

There is no need to justify a treatment of religion in the context of this study. In most accounts of the period, Christianity is considered as the most important institution linking the Middle Ages to antiquity.[1] Furthermore, Christianity was intimately tied to writing and therefore produced a large portion of the relatively scant documentation available to the historian.[2] We shall see that this fact is a mixed blessing.

Here, as with politics, the kind of initial approach one takes affects the problems that are posed and the treatment they receive. Even the essential terminology is fraught with difficulties. 'Religion', 'conversion', 'belief' and the like are abstractions which have to be used with great care. In our account 'religion' applies not merely to the Christian religion. The latter, however, is assessed in astonishingly varying fashion by different authors; apparently, there is no common ground on which to build.[3] This is why we have to sketch our own working position for subsequent discussion.

Here we shall concentrate mainly on Christianity in the late Roman Empire. We shall discuss briefly some aspects of the complex issues often referred to as 'Christianization'. While there are similarities in this process within and outside the Empire, there are also differences. The 'Christianization' of the barbarians will be dealt with later. Unlike the barbarians, the

---

[1] For an interesting overview of the study of medieval Christianity see Engen, J. v., 'The Christian Middle Ages as an historiographical problem', *AHR* 91, 1986, 519-52. Very different approaches are taken to one and the same subject by Flint, V.I.J., *The rise of magic in early medieval Europe*, Oxford 1991, and Angenendt, A., *Das Frühmittelalter. Die abendländische Christenheit von 400 bis 900*, Stuttgart 1990. Yet a different perspective is provided by Herrin, J., *The formation of Christendom*, Oxford 1987.

[2] For more on this see chapter 3.

[3] As far as the Roman Empire goes, one may refer to Rousselle, A., 'Histoire ancienne et oubli du christianisme', *Annales E.S.C.* 47, 1992, 355-68. With regard to the early medieval centuries, it has been rightly pointed out that the major protagonists of the debate on continuity, H. Pirenne, and A. Dopsch, did not treat extensively of Christianity: see Momigliano, A., 'Introduction', in id., ed., *The conflict between paganism and Christianity in the fourth century*, Oxford 1963, 1-16, esp. 5-6.

Romans had a written culture before the rise of Christianity in their midst; as a result the encounter of Christianity and Roman culture produced statements from both parties involved, albeit in an uneven manner. So, the Christianization of the Roman Empire will bring up general issues which may have had parallels among the barbarians (for whom the information is brutally one-sided).

Christianity in the late Roman Empire is a topic which for a number of reasons is extremely difficult to handle. In the form of Catholicism, which eventually won out, it developed as highly intolerant of other forms of belief. The sources depict this victory as being due to Catholicism's inherent superiority. It needs to be said (for it is often not stressed enough) that the Christian sources are inevitably very biased.

The eventual victory of Catholic Christianity in the fourth century was achieved due to a number of factors; moreover, the victory itself must be called a highly qualified one. Christianity grew up within the Roman Empire; this was a society which had known and accommodated a great variety of religions, but Christianity posed special problems. The stubbornness of the Christians, their refusal to integrate with other religions, was already remarked upon by Pliny and Trajan at the end of the first century.[4] It was the Christians who in the course of time drew a dividing line between themselves and all others, whom they called pagans.[5] Their patent unwillingness to compromise with other forms of religion tends to obscure the fact that Christianity, as it developed, was nevertheless heavily influenced by other manifestations of culture in its environment. To take just two examples: Origen (c.185-254) made a grandiose attempt to produce a synthesis of Christianity and Platonism;[6] Augustine's theology is inseparable from the philosophical training he had received as a young man.

The policy of the state seems to provide clear signposts. Thus in the course of the fourth century the Christian religion made steady advances in the Empire, from the edict of toleration in 313[7] to the declaration of Christianity as the only legitimate official religion of the empire around 391.[8] (In 391 and 392 the emperor Theodosius forbade all pagan cults, in public as well as in private: *Cod. Theod.* XIV, 10. 10. and 10. 12.) But these signposts provide only a very rough orientation. What historians of fourth-century religion discuss most often is the struggle of Catholicism against Arianism.

---

4 See O'Donnell, J.J., 'The demise of paganism', *Traditio* 35, 1979, 45-88, esp. 49f.
5 O'Donnell, 'Demise', 48f.
6 See Dodds, E.R., 'The dialogue of paganism with Christianity, in id., *Pagan and Christian in an age of anxiety*, Cambridge 1965, 102-36, at 127.
7 For a recent summary see Bleicken, J., *Constantin der Große und die Christen* (*HZ*, Beihefte, NF 15), 1992.
8 For a concise discussion see MacMullen, R., *Christianizing the Roman Empire, A.D. 100–400*, New Haven and London 1984.

It is difficult to penetrate beyond the highly tendentious, often triumphalist, Catholic sources. Since Arianism eventually lost out to Catholicism, its records were for the most part destroyed, its memory despised. There are good reasons to suspect that within the Empire Catholicism was not immediately as victorious as the decisions of the council of Nicaea in 325 should have ensured.[9] The record is uneven: it is as difficult to gauge the depth of Christian belief among the Catholics as among the Arians.

It has to be emphasized that the emperors from Constantine to Theodosius I had themselves strong Arian sympathies; also, even after the legislation of 391 the government did not immediately act vigorously in favour of Christianity against the traditional pagan religion.[10] It is only after 391 that the Christian divide between Catholicism of the Romans and Arianism of the barbarians emerges as a fairly clear mark of difference.

By the time that Christianity became the Roman state religion it had already taken on important features of the society in which it existed. It had become a Roman religion in the Empire; its universalist claims rested indeed on biblical inspirations but were also ethnocentric in the same manner and partly for the same reasons as Romanitas had been considered as civilization *par excellence*.[11] This was achieved so successfully that many historians have failed to recognize it in its true light. If we bear in mind this element of acculturation when studying developments within the Empire, we shall be more alert to the fact that Christianity faced similar problems of adaptation in other societies. This element of 'localizing' Christianity, as it has been called,[12] is not sufficiently appreciated in the traditional histories of the Church because of the general bias of the sources;[13] but the signs are that it was a very widespread, if not general, characteristic and a virtual prerequisite for Christianity's success, which therefore needs to be re-evaluated.[14] There is no reason why the 'localization' of Christianity need be seen as diminishing its

9 For a recent discussion of the delicacy and complexity of the issues involved see Elliott, T.G., 'Constantine and "the Arian reaction after Nicaea",' *Journal of Ecclesiastical History* 43, 1992, 169-94.
10 The imperial policy has been characterized as one of 'weary pragmatism': see Fowden, G., 'Bishops and temples in the eastern Roman empire, A.D. 320-435', *Journal of Theological Studies* NS 29, 1978, 53-78, at 73. The first imperial decree ordering the destruction of pagan temples dates from 435, ibid., p. 65.
11 See below at n. 63.
12 Mbiti, J.S., 'Christianity and traditional religions in Africa', *International Review of Missions* 59, 1970, 430-40, esp. 431: 'Localization means translating the universality of the Christian faith into a language understood by the people of a given region.'
13 This was repeatedly brought up in the summary by Kloczowski, J., of the Spoleto conference of 1980, see *Cristianizzazione ed organizzazione ecclesiastica delle campagne nell'alto medioevo: espansione e resistenze*, Settimane di studio . . . Spoleto 1982, 1205-21.
14 This phenomenon has been aptly called 'a cultural compromise in matters of religious emotions', Flint, *Rise*, 4.

achievements: it can be interpreted positively, as a sign of vitality. Christianity's lack of uniformity was, indeed, to become one of its most marked features in the early medieval West.

This brings us to the concept of conversion. Here it is possible to draw on the experience of people who are actively involved in this area, both as scholars and as missionaries. The encounter between Christianity (and other world religions) and local or regional religions takes place in our own time in many parts of the world; it can be observed and the process analyzed. While historians of Christianization nowadays tend to see things in Pauline terms of 'replacement' or 'substitution' of one set of beliefs by another, studies of the contact of Christianity with other cultures in our own time place greater emphasis on the fact that 'conversion happens within the context of a rich traditional culture and cosmology in which continuity is as likely to be present . . . as the changes in belief and practice'.[15]

For a long time religions other than world religions were described by Western scholars in terms such as 'primitive' and thus, by implication, innately inferior to the world religions. Since we do not know what terms, if any, the people concerned had for this side of their life,[16] there is a danger in applying a conceptualization which does not do justice to them.[17] Recently there have been efforts to deal with this issue less ethnocentrically—by using terminology that does not prejudge the issue, terminology that would be acceptable also to the people described.[18] The term 'primal religion' has been suggested and will be adopted here.

The term 'primal' underlines the anteriority of the phenomenon and basic, elemental status in human experience.[19] Primal religions are characterized as being ethnocentric and non-missionary.[20] They exist in the interplay between revelation of the transcendent and the human response. In most primal societies religion is interwoven with wider social and political institutions. It is a part

---

15 See Schreuder, D., Oddie, G., 'What is conversion? History, Christianity and religious change in Colonial Africa and South Asia', *Journal of Religious History* 15, 1989, 496-518, at 506.

16 J. Goody points out that 'in African languages I find no equivalent for the western word 'religion' (or indeed 'ritual')', *The logic of writing and the organization of society*, Cambridge 1986, p. 4.

17 It may be pointed out that scholars of religion of any kind are often themselves agnostics 'who find it difficult in conceiving of people who really did look out on the world through religious spectacles.' Horton, R., 'Ritual man in Africa', *Africa*, 34, 1964, 85-104, at 87.

18 Turner, H., 'The primal religions of the world and their study', in *Australian essays in world religions*, Hayes, V.C., ed., Adelaide 1977, 27-37, at 27.

19 See Turner, 'The primal religions of the world',28; cf. also Walls, A.F., 'Primal religious traditions in today's world', in *Religion in today's world*, Whaling, F., ed., Edinburgh 1987, 250-78, at 252.

20 Turner, 28.

of almost all aspects of life.[21] It is orientated towards the past, not in an abstract manner, but with reference to the exemplary deeds of gods or ancestors. These stand for the ideal pattern of society, and acceptance of one's relationship with them comes to stand for this ideal pattern.[22]

Modern observation of the encounters of primal religions and world religions suggests that primal religions underlie all the other faiths and often exist in symbiosis with them.[23] This is an indication that primal religion answers profound human needs. The widespread assumption that primal religions were fragile and, as it were, naturally inferior to world religions like Christianity, has repeatedly been proved to be wrong.[24] What one sees time and again is that the 'incoming faith must suffer a shaping by its receptors at least as substantial as the new shaping which they themselves (its transmitters) hope to effect. Hence it is to the primal, in the concrete form that particular places give it, that permanent shaping influence belongs.'[25]

With these considerations in mind some features of Christianity among the Romans are better understood. 'Christianizing the Roman Empire' is a theme with many variations. Thus one needs to remember that in the fifth century the Roman Empire was not as effectively governed as it had been previously. This has implications for Christianity as well: the imperial religious policy (if such terminology is permissible) could be implemented only where the emperor's writ ran. The way Christianity was adopted in the Empire varied greatly over time and space; due to a number of factors the successes are better documented than the failures and therefore too favourable a picture tends to be painted. There was no uniformity of Christian practice in the Empire.

Many historians of the period are willing to grant that there was notable opposition to Christianity, particularly among the articulate groups of Roman society. Yet different evaluations are made of this opposition, even when drawing on the same sources.[26] However, in the case of Rome at least the affected party itself left some marks on the record which enable scholars to dispute the relative strength of non-Christian Roman culture. Within the Empire, Rome and Athens, for example, retained a pronounced pagan physiognomy compared with Christian Constantinople.[27] The opposition is

21 Gill, *Beyond 'The primitive'*, 8.
22 Horton, R., 'Destiny and the unconscious in West Africa', *Africa* 31, 1961, 110-16, at 110.
23 For this see Walls, 'Primal religious traditions', 250, and again 270.
24 Turner, 34.
25 Mackey, J.P., 'Christian past and primal present. The Scots-Irish connection', in FS D.W.D. Shaw (forthcoming).
26 This is particularly notable as regards Bloch, H., 'A new document of the last pagan revival in the West, 393-394', *Harvard Theological Review* 38, 1945, 199-244 and O'Donnell, J.J., 'Demise'.
27 Herrin 32, 73, and ibid. 116: 'Old Rome continued to look like a pagan capital for centuries . . . there were few major Christian sites in the centre.' But see also Harl, K.W., 'Sacrifice

quite well documented as far as the Roman senate is concerned;[28] the extent of resistance among the lower classes is disputed. We are also quite well informed about the strength of opposition to Christianity in fifth-century Egypt due to the intellectual radiance of places like Alexandria.[29] St Augustine gives us to understand that in North Africa a great number of people could not be persuaded to become Christians.[30] There is no sign that Christianity had been, or was, forced upon the population of the Empire generally, either by the secular powers or by the Christian leaders. It can be suggested that both lacked the means to do so.

It seems to be too facile an approach to maintain that 'Christianity replaced' the traditional Roman religion which, for its part, 'had been decaying'. To use terms like these would be to take some of the Christian apologists as reliable informants.[31] No general statements will do justice to a most complex situation; however, some local and regional insights will help to make this point clear.

It is true that the fourth and fifth centuries witnessed the work of some of the influential personalities in Catholic Christianity—men like St Ambrose (c.340-397), St Jerome (c.348-420) and St Augustine (354-430), whose writings were to be of lasting importance to posterity and to the development of the Christian religion in Europe.[32] But how much is known about the religious belief of their contemporaries? The record is highly unbalanced and the writings of these exceptional personalities can certainly not be considered as representative of their times.

The situation of St Augustine may illustrate some aspects of this issue. His field of action was the deeply cultured Latin North Africa. Augustine's concerns come into focus best in his sermons. While it is true that sermons are a very problematical source for assessing depth of Christian belief, one

and pagan belief in fifth- and sixth-century Byzantium', *Past and Present* No. 128, 1990, 7-27.

28 Cf. Fowden, G., 'Bishops and temples in the Eastern Roman Empire'. For a recent summary see Thrams, P., *Christianisierung des Römerreiches und heidnischer Widerstand*, Heidelberg 1992, especially the second half of the book.

29 See Rémondon, R., 'L'Égypte et la suprème résistance au christianisme (V^e–VIIe siècles)', *Bulletin de l'Institut Français d'Archéologie Orientale du Caire* 51, 1952, 63-78. For a more recent discussion with other aspects see Harl, K.W., 'Sacrifice and pagan belief'.

30 Cf. Chadwick, H., 'Augustine on pagans and Christians: reflections on religious and social change', in *History, Society and the Church* (FS Owen Chadwick), Cambridge 1985, 9-27, at 23.

31 This is maintained here even against the otherwise largely accepted views put forward by O'Donnell, 'Demise'.

32 Jones, 'The decline and fall of the Roman Empire', makes the point that personalities of their calibre were not working for the Roman state, which showed a notable lack of civic spirit. A similar point was made by Momigliano, A., 'Introduction': 'The best men were working for the Church, not for the state.', p. 11, and see p. 9.

simply cannot afford not to use them.[33] One can take it that the sermons which have been preserved were mostly delivered before baptized Catholics.

Augustine's numerous sermons, transmitted often without subsequent revision and therefore breathing everyday life,[34] take the reader into congregations that were highly appreciative of rhetorical brilliance (which Augustine had), more so perhaps than of theological subtlety (which was particularly important vis-à-vis the schismatic Donatists). Augustine certainly could draw an audience and manipulate it. There are also indications that the audience could be extremely well informed: in a letter to St Jerome, Augustine states that a fellow bishop faced riots when, in reading from Scripture, he used the then still unfamiliar translation of Jerome instead of the accustomed version.[35]

While it is impossible to estimate how many people Augustine did not reach, his writings attest that even those whom he did reach were far from being model Christians. This emerges from the way he criticizes the failings of his audience, their unwillingness to forego traditional ways of life and pleasures. This is an aspect which illustrates the continuous maintenance of traditional values even by baptized Christians. I shall concentrate on one particular sign of this.

Augustine was not exceptional among outstanding Church leaders in regarding the theatre as a form of entertainment highly unsuitable for Christians;[36] in fact, the theatre was anathema to every serious Christian and was frequently legislated against.[37] But Augustine's concern in this regard is particularly well documented. Not only does he discuss it frequently but he brought to the subject perhaps more sensitivity than others because he himself had been drawn to the theatre in earlier life and had been highly appreciative of it.[38]

33 See Chadwick, 'Augustine on pagans and Christians'; an important source is also Augustine's *De catechizandis rudibus*, CCSL XLVI, 1969, 115-78.
34 Cf. Deferrari, R.J., 'St Augustine's method of composing and delivering sermons', *American Journal of Philology* 43, 1922, 97-123; 193-219. See also Dolbeau, F., 'Nouveaux sermons de saint Augustin pour la conversion des paiens et des donatistes', *Revue des Etudes Augustiniennes* 37, 1991, 37-78.
35 'Movit quiddam longe aliter abs te positum apud Jonam prophetam, quam erat omnium sensibus memoriaeque inveteratum, et tot aetatum successionibus decantatum. Factus est tantus tumultus in plebe . . .', *Ep.* 71, 3, PL 33, 242.
36 Richter, M., *The oral tradition in the early medieval West*, Typologie des sources du moyen âge occidental, Turnhout 1994. See further Weismann, W., *Kirche und Schauspiele. Die Schauspiele im Urteil der lateinischen Kirchenväter unter besonderer Berücksichtigung von Augustin*, Würzburg 1972; Jürgens, H., *Pompa diaboli. Die lateinischen Kirchenväter und das antike Theater*, Stuttgart 1972.
37 Cf. the Council of Laodicaea (precise date unknown, s. IV/2) c. LIV: 'Quod non oporteat sacerdotes aut clericos quibuscumque spectaculis in scenis aut in nuptiis interesse, sed antequam thymelici ingrediantur, exsurgere eos convenit, atque inde discedere', Mansi, *Concilia* 2, 582.
38 'Veniebamus etiam nos aliquando adulescentes ad spectacula ludibriaque sacrilegiorum,

The Roman theatre had cult functions originally; this aspect lost some of its prominence in the course of time, but Augustine brought it up again: 'Ludi scaenici, spectacula turpitudinum et licentia vanitatum, non hominum vitiis, sed deorum vestrorum iussis Romae instituti sunt . . . Dii propter sedandam corporum pestilentiam ludos sibi scaenicos exhiberi iubebant.'[39] Theatre continued to be associated with the pagan gods and therefore their cult. A compromise was not possible. Besides this religious dimension there was also the immoral quality of the theatre, its lasciviousness and obscenities: this was another reason why the theatre should be shunned by Christians.[40] The condemnation was expressed vigorously and decisively in what appears by this time standardized terminology: *turpis, obscoenus, pompa diaboli*. Since music too was an integral part of the theatre, it was likewise strongly condemned. Christians who continued to go to the theatre were threatened with excommunication. However, Augustine himself conveys the idea that the theatre remained very popular. Once, while preaching in Carthage, he asked rhetorically what would be the situation if people went to church instead of the theatre. Carthage would not be the same city.[41]

The wrath of the Christian leaders extended to the actors of the theatre, called by Augustine *publicae turpitudinis professores*. This profession was judged to be incompatible with being a Christian.[42] However, as Augustine was pained to admit, these professionals were often richly rewarded for their work,[43] while the poor, who were more deserving, did not receive anything.

Hence Augustine's strong language, epitomized in a phrase like: 'Audeo

---

spectabamus arrepticios, audiebamus symphoniacos, ludis turpissimis, qui dis deabusque exhibebantur, oblectabamur.' *De civitate Dei* II, 4. On the art of the actors he writes: 'et quidam motu manuum pleraque significant: et histriones omnium membrorum motibus dant signa quaedam scientibus, et cum oculis eorum quasi fabulantur; . . . et sunt haec omnia quasi quaedam verba visibilia.' *De doctrina Christiana* II, iii.

39   *De civitate Dei* I, xxxii.
40   It must be pointed out that the emperor Julian the Apostate (d. 363), who had himself been a Christian earlier in his life, forbade the Roman priests to attend shows at the theatre; he wrote in terms not unlike those of the Christian teachers: 'No priest must anywhere be present at the licentious theatrical shows of the present day, nor introduce one into his own house; for that is altogether unfitting. Indeed if it were possible to banish such shows absolutely from the theatres. . . . I should certainly have endeavoured with all my heart to bring this about. . . . But I do demand that priests should withdraw themselves from the licentiousness of the theatre and leave them to the crowd. Therefore let no priest enter a theatre or have an actor or a chariot-driver for his friend; and let no dancer or mime even approach his door.' Letter to a priest, Fragm. epistolae 304, *Works of the emperor Julian*, II (Loeb Classics), London 1913, p. 335.
41   *Enarrationes in psalmos* 50, 11: 'Nonne diceremus: ubi est illa Carthago? Quia non est, quod erat, eversa est'. PL 36, 593.
42   See Weismann, 156ff. for references.
43   'Donare quippe res suas histrionibus, vitium est immane'. *Tractatus in Iohannem* 100, 2, CC 36, 589.

prohibere spectacula? Audeo prohibere, audeo plane.'[44] In another place he pleaded instead of threatening: 'Ecce ludi sunt: non eant Christiani . . . hoc vobis praestete vos, Christiani: theatra nolite intrare.'[45]

The conciliar legislation from fifth-century Carthage[46] makes it clear that theatre performances continued to be held in North Africa and continued to be highly popular. The normative sources (such as conciliar prohibitions or threats of severe punishment[47]) do convey an idea of real life, but rarely more than that. In combination with other information, such as sermons, they support the idea that even in an overtly Christian society traditional forms of entertainment continued to be available and to have a following.

As we saw earlier, the theatre was still an essential part of Roman life a century later in Italy; the Ostrogothic rulers considered it desirable to patronize it. There is the formal title for the official in charge, the *tribunus voluptatum*.[48] In this field Christian norms had not ousted traditional culture. To what extent the relevant policy of the emperors was effective in the other parts of the Empire is impossible to say.

We now turn to the situation in southern Gaul in the first half of the sixth century. Caesarius of Arles (bishop 502-42) was a prolific preacher whose sermons give a good idea of how Christianity was faring in this part of the Roman world (they were widely used in later centuries, surely because they dealt with issues that continued to be relevant; they were often attributed to Augustine to give them extra weight). Caesarius' congregation consisted of Romans (rather than Franks) who would understand sermons delivered in Latin,[49] albeit probably not as well as the North Africans. There was no threat of heresy at that time in Gaul; the congregation reached by Caesarius was Catholic.

One of his sermons is particularly illuminating in this respect. That it seems to have been addressed to a rural congregation can be gathered partly from his language, since he plays rather extensively with imagery taken from agriculture.[50] In this sermon he refers to some objections to his demands

---

44 Serm. Denis XIV, 68 = *Sancti Augustini sermones post Maurinos reperti*, Morin, G., ed., in *Miscellanea Agostiniana*, vol. 1, Rome 1930.
45 Serm. Denis XVII, 88.
46 III Carthago, c. xi: 'Ut filii episcoporum vel clericorum spectacula saecularia non exhibeant, sed nec spectent, quandoquidem a spectaculo et omnes laici prohibeantur. Semper enim Christianis omnibus hoc interdictum est, ut ubi blasphemi sunt, non accedant'. Mansi 3, 882.
47 IV Carthago, a. 436, c. lxxxviii: 'Qui die solenni, praetermisso solenni ecclesiae conventu, ad spectacula vadit, excommunicetur'. Mansi 3, 958.
48 Cassiodorus, *Variae* VII, x. Cf. above p. 24.
49 For this aspect see chapter 3.
50 See e.g. 'Animae nostrae cura, fratres carissimi, maxime terrenae culturae similis est . . .

apparently raised by his flock, as excuses for insufficient observance of Christ's teaching. We read:

> Quam multi rustici et quam multae mulieres rusticanae cantica diabolica et amatoria et turpia memoriter retinent et ore decantant! Ista possunt tenere atque parare, quae diabolus docet: et non possunt tenere, quod Christus ostendit?[51]

In fact his demands were quite modest as regards what the congregation was expected to know, namely the Creed, the Lord's Prayer, a few hymns and psalms 50 or 90. He even begs them:

> Nemo ergo dicat: Non possum aliquid de id quod in ecclesia legitur retinere. Sine dubio enim, si velis, et poteris: incipe velle, et statim intelleges.[52]

This *incipe velle* rings ominously. The congregation that Caesarius is addressing is not uncultured; in fact, he makes reference to their culture. While the preacher refers to it in derogatory terms there is every indication that they held it in high regard. Christian ethics were unattractive to them. There is a weary ring to the sermon; Caesarius even says openly that there are people in his audience who are totally indifferent to the message he has to offer; they do not think that the word of God will benefit them in any way: 'omnino non credit quod inde aliquid boni possit adquirere'.[53]

If this attitude towards Christianity causes little surprise, it is all the more remarkable to find it included in a sermon which was meant to have relevance beyond the time it was delivered. Certainly, I know of no other sermon from those times where the subject is treated so concisely and explicitly. Caesarius shows in this sermon that among his congregation there was widespread indifference to the Christian message.[54] Instead, older customs are shown to

---

duo genera agrorum sunt: unus ager est Dei, alter est hominis'. Sermo VI, Morin, G., ed., CCSL 103, 1953, 32, 33. On this sermon see also Gurevich, A., *Medieval popular culture*, Cambridge 1988, 25.
51 Ibid., p. 32.
52 Ibid., p. 32.
53 Ibid., p. 31. This crucial phrase was not taken up by Ferreiro, A., 'Frequenter legere. The propagation of literacy, education and divine wisdom in Caesarius of Arles', *Journal of Ecclesiastical History* 43, 1992, 5-15.
54 A similar attitude is articulated in the late eighth century by Paulinus of Aquileia, *Liber exhortationis ad Henricum Forojulianum*, ch. 38: 'Praecepta Dei ad omnes Christianos pertinere: Grandis namque confusio est animabus laicorum, qui dicunt: "Quid pertinet ad me libros Scripturarum legendo audire vel discere, vel etiam frequenter ad sacerdotes et ecclesias sanctorum recurrere? Dum clericus fiam, faciam ea quae oportet clericis facere",' PL 99, 240.

have been deeply entrenched, particularly familiarity with secular songs of dubious content. If that kind of entertainment was as widespread as Caesarius seems to imply, it should cause little surprise that the demands of a Christian life did not meet with enthusiastic response. However, it is true that Caesarius at least reached those who bothered to attend his sermon, though we do not know what effect his words had on them.

Elsewhere Caesarius shows a more constructive attitude when he tells his congregation that it was not sufficient to be called a Christian; one also needs to live a Christian life.[55] In several places he also refers to pagan practices still being observed among the people. Of these he singles out banquets as occasions for mindless heavy drinking, and he admits that this was by no means unusual even among clerics: 'quotienscumque vobis invicem convivia exhibetis, illam foedam consuetudinem, per quam grandi mensura sine mensura tres homines aut volentes aut inviti solebant bibere, tamquam venenum diaboli de vestris conviviis respuatis: quia ista infelix consuetudo adhuc de paganorum observatione remansit'.[56] Caesarius was very conscious that Christianity in his society was far from being taken to heart even by those who professed it.

Mention must also be made of the way in which the Roman pre-Christian cultural legacy was handled. The influential *Statuta Ecclesiae Antiqua* (*c.*5)[57] from the late fifth century explicitly forbade the reading of pagan works. This was upheld by Caesarius of Arles, who was generally very much influenced by the ethos expressed in these *Statuta*. Likewise, Isidore of Seville inveighed against pagan writings.[58] By contrast, St Augustine, that most learned man in the early Western Church, who was deeply marked by his early education in rhetoric, maintained the need for a full study of secular learning.[59] Not quite as openly in favour, but certainly not outspokenly against this position was another outstanding Christian teacher, Gregory the Great (d. 604). It has been rightly said that Christianity 'tended to strengthen the forces which operated against secular literacy';[60] however, due to the ambivalent attitude of Christian leaders as well as to the limited influence of the Christian Church in early medieval society, the legacy of the pre-Christian past was indeed transmitted into the Middle Ages and beyond, first in the Romania, and eventually also outside it.

The extent to which Christianity had adapted earlier to Roman society and its ideology is best recognized in the widespread view that Christianity

55 See esp. sermo XVI: 'Quales sint Christiani boni, et quales mali', p. 76ff.
56 Sermo XLVI: 'Ammmonitio ut ebrietatis malum totis viribus caveatur', 205-11, at p. 210f. Further references to pagan practices are found in sermo XIII, esp. 67.
57 Concilia Galliae A.314–A.506, Munier, C., ed., CCSL 148, 1963, p. 167.
58 See Riché, P., *Éducation et culture dans l'occident barbare, VIe–VIIIe siècle*, Paris 1962, 135, 137, 342.
59 Riché, *Education*, 171, 199.
60 Harris, W.V., *Ancient literacy*, Cambridge, Mass., and London 1989, 331.

was providentially linked with the Roman Empire.[61] In this way the *orbis Romanus*, the world, could now be claimed to be Christian, and the Christian goal of peace could be seen as having been attained in the *pax Romana*. St Augustine was one of the earliest authorities to question this presentation,[62] and his experience of the Vandal invasion of his country would have confirmed him in this view. However, Romans found it extremely difficult to rid themselves of the idea that they were mankind incarnate; they scarcely conceived that there were other nations to be won for Christ. Prosper of Aquitaine was exceptional in the way he overcame traditional attitudes and stated that Christ's grace extended to where Roman arms had failed to conquer.[63] In a way, the Roman claim to leadership in the Christian Church can be seen to derive its authority from, among other elements, the 'Romanizing' of Christianity in late antiquity.

This is evident in the record concerning the expansion of Christianity outside the area of the Romania which extends deep into the Middle Ages. Here one encounters again the term *barbarus*, used not only in the sense of 'non-Roman' but also quite frequently as a technical term for non-Christians.[64] This term thus could be doubly derogatory. Likewise, there are at least some cases recorded in which at a fairly early stage *Romanus* is used as an equivalent of 'Christian'. This usage is attested in the fourth century in Prudentius when he states: 'tantum distant Romana et barbara, quantum quadrupes abiuncta est bipedi vel muta loquenti, quantum etiam, qui rite dei praecepta sequuntur cultibus a stolidis et eorum erroribus absunt'.[65] The same usage is attested in

[61] See, e.g., Origen, *Contra Celsum*, II, 30, translated by Chadwick, H., Cambridge 1965, 92; also Jerome, *Commentarium in Michaeam*, PL 25, 1187f; Paulus Orosius, *Historiae adversum paganos*, CSEL 5, 1882, esp. VI, 20ff. More generally see Peterson, E., *Der Monotheismus als politisches Problem*, Leipzig 1935, esp. 59ff.

[62] See, e.g., *Enarratio in psalmum* XLV, 10, PL 36, 523: 'Nondum ergo completum est, "Auferens bella usque ad fines terrae": sed fortasse complebitur. An et modo completum est? In quibusdam completum est: in tritico completum est, in zizaniis nondum completum est.' More generally Straub, J., 'Christliche Geschichtsapologetik in der Krisis des römischen Reichs', *Historia* 1, 1950, 52-81.

[63] See Prosper of Aquitaine, *De vocatione omnium gentium* Liber II, c. xvi, PL 51, 704: 'credimus providentia Dei Romani regni latitudinem praeparatam: ut nationes vocandae ad unitatem corporis Christi, prius Iure unius consociarentur imperii: quamvis gratia Christiana non contenta sit eosdem limites habere quos Roma; multosque iam populos sceptro crucis Christi illa subdiderit, quos armis suis ista non domuit'.

[64] For an explicit example see Ambrose, *Ep.* XVIII: 'Hoc solum habebam commune cum barbaris, quia Deum antea nesciebam'; PL 16, 974. Possibly the term is also to be interpreted in this way when used by St Patrick writing: 'Inter barbaras itaque gentes proselitus, Epistola ad Milites Corotici', ch. 1, Bieler, L., ed., 'Libri epistolarum sancti Patricii episcopi', *Classica et Mediaevalia* 11, 1950, 5-150, at 91. For further attestations see Acker, L. v., 'Barbarus und seine Ableitungen im Mittellatein', *Archiv für Kulturgeschichte* 47, 1965, 125-40, esp. 137ff.

[65] *Contra Symmachum*, II, 816-19.

Gaul in the later sixth century, by Gregory of Tours who wrote: 'Romanos enim vocitant nostrae homines relegionis';[66] it is also attested in Ireland, perhaps from the seventh century, where one finds in one of the *Dicta Patricii*: 'ut Christiani ita ut Romani sitis'.[67] It is very likely that the term *Romanus* is also to be understood in this sense in the seventh-century *Vita Eligii* which reports how natives refused to accept the new faith: 'Numquam tu, Romane, ... consuetudines nostras evellere poteris ...'.[68] It is indeed possible to detect this ideology already in the Letter to the Soldiers of Coroticus written by St Patrick some time in the fifth century:

> Manu mea scripsi atque condidi verba ista danda et tradenda, militibus mittenda Corotici, non dico civibus meis neque civibus sanctorum Romanorum sed civibus daemoniorum.[69]

So far, we have considered some aspects of Christianity internal to the Romania and to the Christian sphere. We have seen that there were considerable variations in the way in which Christianity developed; the best way to account for these variations is by reference to the opposing forces that Christianity encountered in each society, the problems that it had to deal with.

We must, then, try to discover the culture of each society prior to the arrival of Christianity. This is, of course, a task which cannot be undertaken equally well for all the societies considered here. Since we gain access to the culture of peoples mainly by way of written accounts, access is most direct in those societies where a written culture existed before the coming of Christianity. In our area of work this was the case only for the Romans. As we have seen, in Roman society Christianity assumed distinct Roman features.

A working hypothesis here would be that the culture which existed prior to the arrival of Christianity in other societies also became an ingredient in what one may call medieval Christianity.[70] Thus 'conversion' should not be

66 *Liber in Gloria Martyrum* c. 24, MGH SS rer. Merov. I, 2, p. 52.
67 *The Patrician texts in the Book of Armagh*, Bieler, L., ed., Dublin 1979, 124; see on this also Ullmann, W., 'On the use of the term 'Romani' in the sources of the earlier Middle Ages', *Studia Patristica* 2, 1955, pp. 155-163, esp. 156 f. Ullmann was of the opinion that the *dictum* was indeed Patrick's. I do not agree with him in some other interpretations of the term in this article.
68 MGH SS rer. Merov. 4, p. 712; this suggestion is also found in Geary, P.J., 'Ethnic identity as a situational construct in the early Middle Ages', *Mitteilungen der Anthropologischen Gesellschaft in Wien* 113, 1983, 15-26, at 24.
69 Bieler, 'Libri epistolarum ', 92. See also ch. 14: 'Consuetudo Romanorum Gallorum Christianorum', p. 98.
70 This concept has been underlined also in the meeting of Christianity and African societies, see Mbiti, 1970: 'The localization of Christianity cannot be carried out effectively without reference to traditional religiosity', 437, and see above p. 29.

thought of as the substitution of one set of beliefs by another but rather as the acceptance and importation of new ideas and ways of life into previously existing modes. Barbarian culture, however, is accessible to us only in a condition already affected by Christianity.

Although it is impossible to encounter pre-Christian barbarian culture in its pristine form, an attempt to give it an unprejudiced hearing may help us to elucidate its place in barbarian societies. Indeed, in this task one can take encouragement from the fact that Christianity spread slowly in the early medieval West and that it manifests itself in noticeable regional variations.

It is helpful to keep these thoughts in mind when dealing with the encounter between the barbarians and the Christian religion in the early Middle Ages. This encounter is usually discussed in terms of 'mission' and 'conversion', of replacement of the old faith by the new one, just as proclaimed by St Paul: 'The old has passed away, the new has come' (2 Cor 5:17). When one keeps in mind how closely integrated traditions were among the barbarians, if one thinks in terms of conversion one would expect a complete transformation of these societies, with one religion substituting another.

In some respects, the problems that Christianity encountered among the Romans were not substantially different from those it met with the barbarians. The new religion required the abandonment of traditional values which had been held from time immemorial because they were considered essential. Christianity was notoriously intolerant towards other beliefs, and Catholicism especially intolerant towards deviations in belief.

All the information which we have about the barbarians in the early medieval centuries, filtered though it be largely through Christian informants, contradicts the idea of complete substitution. Thus the connotations associated with 'mission' and 'conversion' in the traditional historical accounts are misleading. Similarly, the fact that Christianity spread exceedingly slowly among the barbarians likewise needs to be accounted for.[71]

As far as the early medieval centuries are concerned, the existing source material can be extremely misleading if taken at face value, because the bulk of the written sources originated among the institutions of the Church and were connected with Christianity. They are largely either normative or didactic, rarely narrative and hardly ever without a strong Catholic bias. There are reasons to believe that the sermons which have survived from the early Middle Ages were generally addressed to a clerical audience.[72] The Christian religion

---

[71] 'The beliefs and practices of the so-called world religions are only accepted where they happen to coincide with responses of the traditional cosmology . . . it explains why both Islam and Christianity, operating by themselves, produce very meagre results.' Horton, R., 'African conversion', *Africa* 41, 1971, 86-108, at 104.

[72] Richter, M., 'Kommunikationsprobleme im lateinischen Mittelalter', *HZ* 222, 1976, 43-80, at 70.

was the only institution which consistently cultivated writing during those centuries.[73] The vast areas of popular culture continued to be practised orally and at best were noted by the clerical writers, who certainly did not do them justice.

All barbarian rulers within the Romania eventually went over to Christianity. It has been claimed in this respect that the western Empire found its most significant continuation in the Church rather than in the Germanic *regna*.[74] The Frankish king Clovis figures in all general accounts as the first of the barbarian rulers to become a Catholic (sometime around 500). Most of the other barbarian peoples were Arians; the Ostrogoths perished in the mid-sixth century without converting to Catholicism. Catholicism eventually prevailed in the West (although this was not foreseeable around 500); this process empitomizes the transition from antiquity to the Middle Ages.[75]

However, this statement (frequently made) only describes the surface. It is the purpose of the present study to show that the barbarians already had a culture of their own when they encountered the Romans; it was an essential part of their identity. We shall see that they continued for centuries to cultivate their own traditions, their culture, which was in almost every way incompatible with strict Christianity.[76] If one labels these barbarian societies 'Christian', it is important to bear in mind that they were, more often than not, both Christian and traditional.[77] This then would explain the diverse manifestations of Christianity in the early Middle Ages. Due to the technology associated with writing, due to writing being inextricably tied to Christianity, and finally due to the propagandist nature of much of Christian literature, the Christian dimension is much more prominent in the sources than the traditional one.

The history of the spread of Christianity in the early medieval centuries is of interest to us primarily as a coming together of traditions long cherished and a new, often aggressive, faith.[78] Again, the record is quite unbalanced in that the new faith was connected with writing, but the native traditions were not and therefore are recorded, if at all, from a partisan, often hostile

---

73 For this see chapter 3.
74 Herrin, *Formation of Christendom*, 126. For a very different interpretation see Chadwick, H., 'Augustine on pagans and Christians'.
75 See e.g. Chadwick, H., 'Augustine on pagans and Christians', esp. 26f.
76 This term is understood here to characterize those people who took the New Testament message seriously, people like Ambrose, Augustine or Columbanus. The last of these shows that Christianity could be of intrinsic attraction to barbarians as well as Romans. On him see Richter, M., *Medieval Ireland—The enduring tradition*, Dublin, London and New York 1988, 56-9.
77 This has been dealt with, more explicitly than before, by Flint, *The rise of magic*.
78 In a different context, not irrelevant here, however, the term 'missionary assault' has been used, see Diamond, S., 'The search for the primitive', in *Man's image in medicine and anthropology*, Galdston, I., ed., New York 1963, 62-115, at 88.

perspective. And even the record that exists needs to be interpreted carefully.

Despite Christ's command to 'go out and teach all nations and baptize them' (Mt 28:19), there is little evidence that this command was taken to heart. Perhaps this was so because fundamental work remained to be done at home;[79] another explanation may be sought in the continuing ethnocentricity of Roman Christianity. Certainly, the mission to the Angles initiated by Pope Gregory the Great in the late sixth century, was exceptional in those times.[80] It resulted in a particularly strong attachment to the see of St Peter shown by Anglo-Saxon Christians later.[81]

On the continent, the spread of Christianity was exceedingly slow and largely associated with physical force (as, for example, in the case of the Saxons), which gives this chapter of European history a particularly unpalatable appearance. The Christian martyrs are witnesses to the violence that was sparked off during the encounter of the barbarians with Christianity. Many there must have been who left no trace in the sources; others, like St Kilian (d. 689), were later commemorated in written accounts when Christianity was established in the area of the martyr's activity.[82] The forced conversion of the continental Saxons by Charlemagne in the late eighth century is exceptionally well documented; the violence used was questioned even by contemporary Christian dignitaries like Alcuin.[83]

Surely the main reason for the slow spread of Christianity was its unattractiveness to people who had their own way of life which had served them well and which zealous Christians demanded be given up. Perhaps 'way of life' is too banal an expression and should be replaced by terms like ethos, tradition or cosmology. On the other hand, it has been recently pointed out in the discussion of the issue of 'conversion' that to think of religion 'as a belief rather than a practice, as consisting of creeds rather than codes of behaviour'[84] is a modern concept which is unsuitable for many earlier situations. Conflicts between missionaries and non-Christians are frequently recorded in the sources, though as a rule this tends to happen only where

---

79   Hillgarth, J.N., ed., *Christianity and Paganism, 350-750. The conversion of Western Europe*, Philadelphia 1986.; also idem, 'Modes of evangelisation of Western Europe in the seventh century', in *Ireland and Christendom—The Bible and the missions*, Ní Chatháin, P., and Richter, M., ed., Stuttgart 1987, 311-31.

80   Cf. Fritze, W., 'Universalis gentium confessio. Formen, Träger und Wege universalmissionarischen Denkens im 7. Jahrhundert', *Frühmittelalterliche Studien* 3, 1969, 78-132.

81   The outstanding representative is St Boniface. However, the secular leaders in England did not necessarily share this attitude: see Pepperdene, M.W., 'Bede's Historia Ecclesiastica. A new perspective', *Celtica* 4, 1958, 253-62, esp. 261. This is generally less emphasized than the Roman-Saxon links.

82   See *Würzburger Diözesangeschichtsblätter*, vol. 51, 1989, dedicated to the memory of Kilian on the 13th centenary of his death.

83   *Epp.* 107, 110, MGH Epp. IV.

84   Mackey, J.P., 'Magic and Celtic primal religion', *ZCP* 45, 1992, 66-84, at 74.

Christianity was eventually victorious.[85] It is more surprising to find accounts recorded in the Christian sources where Christianity was regarded—mostly temporarily—as unacceptable.[86]

In face of much discussion of the 'conversion of the barbarians' to Christianity in the early Middle Ages, it is well to heed the assertion that 'before the conversion of Constantine and for centuries after, the Church should never be seen . . . as a single wash of color spreading evenly and inexorably across the orbis terrarum: it was an archipelago of little islands of "centrality" scattered across an "unsown sea" of almost total indifference.'[87]

We must, in this context, refer to Ireland, which in many respects represents an exceptional case. We know nothing about how Christianity came to be established in Irish society in the fifth and sixth centuries.[88] All that can be said is that Christianity gained a place in Irish society. There was no central institution like the governmental authority of the Empire to decree adherence to Christian belief; there was no outside authority to impose it. There was not even any need to become 'Roman', as had been the case with some of the barbarians on the continent. What is known about St Patrick, the 'apostle of the Irish', from his authentic writings shows a determined and charismatic Christian whose success, although impossible to measure accurately, is unquestionable. However, the reputation of Irish spirituality in the early Middle Ages is built on material which can hardly be considered representative. For it draws on very few—albeit impressive—sources like the writings of St Patrick, the works of Columbanus, or works about early martyrs like the *Passio Kiliani*.[89]

The special feature of Irish society in the early Middle Ages lies in the

---

85 Cf. Richter, M., 'Practical aspects of the conversion of the Anglo-Saxons', in *Ireland and Christendom*, 362-76.
86 A good example of this can be found in the Vita Eligii, ch. 20, MGH SS rer. Merov., 4, 711f. (see above note 68) Somewhat different in kind is the detailed account of the failure to bring the Frisian duke Ratbod to baptism: he withdrew from it at the last moment, so the dramatic account says, when he learned that baptized and with God he would not enjoy the company of his ancestors: '. . . dicens, non se carere posse consortio praedecessorum suorum principum Fresionum et cum parvo pauperum numero residere in illo caelesti regno'. *Vita Vulframni episcopi Senonici*, ch. 9, MGH SS rer. Merov. 5, p. 663-70, quotation p. 668. A shorter account of the failure to make Ratbod a Christian is contained in Alcuin's *Vita Willibrordi*, ch. 9, MGH SS rer. Merov. 7, 123f.
87 Brown, P., 'The saint as exemplar in late antiquity', *Representations* 1, 2, 1983, 1-25, at 9.
88 I have labeled it 'an enigma': see Richter, M., 'The introduction of alphabetic writing to Ireland: implications and Consequences' (FS Brendan Ó Hehir) (forthcoming).
89 See Scheele, P.-W., 'Motive altirischer Spiritualität in der Passio Kiliani', *Würzburger Diözesangeschichtsblätter* 51, 1989, 181-219. In this respect the case of early medieval Ireland is comparable to that of Rome in the fourth and fifth centuries.

fact that Christianity within a very vibrant traditional society is exceptionally well documented.[90]

We have seen that some of the barbarians, including the Franks, Alamans or Saxons, can be traced back only a few hundred years as political entities. Their first ethnogenesis is to be situated within the range of the third century AD. In absolute terms, this is not a long history, but these peoples did not have absolute time reckoning nor our linear concept of time. What matters here is the fact that they succeeded as political groups; they showed internal cohesion against possible external pressures. Theirs was a history of viability. It is certain that each of these peoples possessed their own traditions, distinctive conceptions of the world, the self, and the relations between them.[91]

Barbarian culture was vital and viable. This is evident in the sources. Those who wanted to bring Christianity to the barbarians found that where they wanted to sow there was a plant already growing. Christian accounts from the early medieval West rarely make more than passing mention of the previously existing beliefs. But we must assume that these peoples held beliefs that answered their spiritual needs and had served them adequately in the past. Some of these beliefs will be encountered in the central chapters of this book.

The 'Christian Middle Ages' can be seen in many different ways: when using the available (Christian) sources, one needs to be aware of their Christian focus and look beyond it. While it is impossible to do full justice to the ontology of the barbarians, they should at least be granted as fair a hearing as possible.

---

90 See chapter 9.
91 Geertz, C., 'Religion as a cultural system', in *Anthropological approaches to the study of religion*, Banton, M., ed., London 1966, 1-46, at 40.

3

LITERACY

There are two important reasons why literacy has to be discussed in this book: 1. it is through the medium of written sources that the oral culture, the principal channel of cultural transmission among the barbarians, has to be studied; hence it is imperative to know who provides this information and how reliable the informant is; 2. writing is a specific method of storing what is worth preserving and tends to be regarded as innately superior to oral culture. As we shall see, oral culture—which we can study only where some kind of literacy exists—held its own alongside literacy. The relation between these two cultural manifestations requires our attention.

In the continental West in the period under discussion, writing took place predominantly, even though not exclusively, in the Latin language and in the Latin alphabet.[1] It is thus necessary, indeed imperative, to view the question of Latin in the early medieval centuries from philological as well as from socio-linguistic angles. The main issues to be discussed with reference to literacy in Latin apply *mutatis mutandis* to other languages once these come to be used in written form.

In view of the fundamental importance of written sources to the historian, it is surprising how inadequately the whole complex area relating to literacy has been studied, particularly for the early medieval period. Here I shall provide an overview of the subject for the early medieval centuries in which I draw on several of my earlier publications although my views have changed to some extent over the years. Recently there has been additional work in this field by other scholars,[2] yet, as we shall see, much remains to be done. It is arguably

---

1 See Gordon, A.E., 'On the origins of the Latin alphabet: modern views', *California Studies in Classical Antiquity* 2, 1969, 157-70. We can exclude here writing in the Greek alphabet, in Glagolitic or Cyrillic, in Celtic ogam as well as in runes. Celtic Britain and Ireland present a somewhat different case and are dealt with in chapter 9.

2 See McKitterick, R., *The Carolingians and the written word*, Cambridge 1989. For a critique see Richter, M., '. . . *quisquis scit scribere, nullum potat abere labore*. Zur Laienschriftlichkeit im 8. Jahrhundert', in Jarnut, J. et al., ed., *Karl Martell in seiner Zeit*, Sigmaringen 1994, 393-404. Cf. also McKitterick, R., ed., *The uses of literacy in the early Middle Ages*, Cambridge 1990; McKitterick, R., 'Frauen und Schriftlichkeit im Frühmittelalter', in

just as difficult to come to terms with the role of writing in past societies as with that of the oral tradition—for two simple reasons: in the first place, there is an enormous danger of projecting onto the past our own experience of a society built on the written word (that this in fact happens is evident from a general lack of discussion of the concept of literacy in medieval society; it has rightly been stated but insufficiently heeded that 'literacy is not a civilizing force in itself').[3] Secondly, by focusing exclusively on written documents one tends to neglect to investigate the other means of cultural transmission current in a society, especially when they are not explicitly and prominently referred to in the written sources. This is why the place and function of written material has to be discussed here in some detail in order to give it its overall place in the early medieval West.

Alphabetic writing is one of the great legacies of antiquity to Western civilization. Writing in the Latin alphabet was mediated to us through the Middle Ages. However, there was no continuous development between the ways in which alphabetic writing was used in antiquity and the ways it was used in subsequent centuries; rather, what we find are fluctuations in literacy, particularly so in the medieval centuries.[4]

Along the lines pursued in the previous chapters, the subject is treated in terms of the transformation of the Roman world. The Roman legacy was literacy in Latin as a prominent element in the organization and functioning of society.[5] Literacy was a cultural accomplishment that carried high social prestige.

Weibliche Lebensgestaltung im frühen Mittelalter, Goetz, H.-W., ed., Köln/Wien 1991, 65-118; Keller, H., 'Die Entwicklung der europäischen Schriftkultur im Spiegel der mittelalterlichen Überlieferung', in *Geschichte und Geschichtsbewußtsein* (FS. K.E. Jeismann), Leidiger, P., and Metzler, D., ed., Münster 1990, 174-204; Keller, H., ed., *Pragmatische Schriftlichkeit im Mittelalter. Erscheinungsformen und Entwicklungsstufen*, Münster 1992; Saenger, P., 'Literacy, Western European', *Dictionary of the Middle Ages*, vol. 7, 597-602; Richter, M., 'Les langages en pays celtiques', in *La voix et l'écriture*, ed. Banniard, M., *Médiévales*, 25, 1993, 53-60. Since this book was begun, the university of Münster has initiated systematic research of literacy in the Middle Ages, but mostly for the period after 1100 and is thus of little relevance here. See *Frühmittelalterliche Studien* 22-25, 1988-1991, and in more detail 26, 1992, 440-66.

3 Clanchy, M.T., *From memory to written record. England 1066-1307*, London 1979, 7.
4 Illich, I., Sanders, B., *The alphabetization of the popular mind*, San Francisco 1988, contains quite an extensive bibliography which, however, is much shorter than that on literacy in antiquity provided by Harris, W.V., *Ancient literacy*, 339-67.
5 It has to be taken into account that Roman society itself had had a strong and formative oral tradition before it became geared to literate culture; see e.g. Timpe, D., 'Mündlichkeit und Schriftlichkeit als Basis der frühromischen Überlieferung', in *Vergangenheit in mündlicher Überlieferung* (Colloquium Rauricum Bd. 1), Ungern-Sternberg, J.v., Reinau, H., ed., Stuttgart 1988, 266-86; Wiseman, T.P., 'Roman legend and oral tradition—Review article', *Journal of Roman Studies* 79, 1989, 129-37; Momigliano, A., 'Perizonius, Niebuhr and the character of early Roman tradition', *Journal of Roman Studies* 47, 1957, 104-14.

In their characteristic ethnocentric world view, the Romans regarded literate learning as an accomplishment that distinguished them from the rest of mankind (which therefore deserved the label 'barbarian'): 'Barbari . . . qui totius litteraturae ac scientiae ignari' (Salvian of Marseilles);[6] or 'hac grammatica non utuntur barbari reges' (Cassiodorus).[7] One may well be dealing with topoi which did not do justice to reality, but this was the way the Romans liked to see the world. We meet here the term *barbarus* in the sense of 'uneducated'.

However, such a global division of mankind within the range of Roman experience into Romans (who were literate) and barbarians (who were not) does not correspond to the facts even in the fourth and fifth centuries. It applies only to some peoples—in the West, for example, the Franks, Alamans, Bavarians, Saxons and Frisians before they received Christianity. These peoples had no use for alphabetic writing before they encountered the Romans. In contrast, those barbarians who confessed Arian Christianity—the very peoples that made the greatest short-term contribution to the transformation of the Roman world—were familiar with alphabetic writing at least in the sphere of religion. One of the most impressive records in this field is the bible translated from Greek into Gothic by Wulfila in the fourth century. When these barbarians converted to Catholicism, as all eventually did, most of their records connected with Arianism were destroyed; because of this it is impossible to get a balanced view of Arianism among them, nor is it clear to what extent these peoples used writing for other purposes besides religion. We have seen that when these barbarians were established within the Romania they could avail themselves of existing institutions that practised writing.

The subject of literacy in the early medieval centuries is a complex one in which continuities and changes must be treated with reference to particular issues. It has been argued that the Germanic *regna* could not have survived for a single day had not the Roman system been in place.[8] This makes sense at least as far as the early stages of these *regna* are concerned; but it is equally apparent that the existing Roman system did not continue unchanged into the early medieval centuries, because those who became dominant in the barbarian *regna* had different ways of running their societies than Romans did. Literacy is an area of central rather than marginal importance in this respect where the transformation has to be carefully evaluated.

There are political dimensions to the issue: those barbarians who had known writing did not survive as political groups; those who did survive and came to make up the physiognomy of the early medieval West acquired literacy only gradually, usually along with Christianity. Thus, as with politics, so with

6 *De Gub.* V, 2-8; MGH AA I, 56.
7 *Variae* IX, 21.
8 See Wolfram, H., 'Aufnahme', 114 and above, p. 11.

literacy: gradually, the *regna* developed their own features in the field of cultural transmission which gave the early medieval societies their very distinctive appearance. These features may be highlighted by the co-existence of two types of learning, one associated with literacy, the other characterized by oral culture.

THE CONCEPT OF LITERACY[9]

At its most basic, to be literate today is to be able to handle letters, to be able to read. It is a skill the acquisition of which demands considerable effort and motivation. The ability to read is taught or acquired wherever the results seem to justify the effort involved and when one has the means to afford the cost of the exercise.

In a celebrated and oft-quoted article by Jack Goody and Ian Watt, 'The consequences of literacy',[10] it was stated that 'the notion of representing a sound by a graphic symbol is itself so stupifying a leap in the imagination that what is remarkable is not so much that it happened relatively late in human history but rather that it ever happened.'[11] The authors maintain, on the other hand, that the alphabet is rather easy to learn; they suggest, on the authority of Plato, that it took about three years to learn it in Greek antiquity.[12] While this may indeed be an acceptable estimate, there is a danger of underestimating the obstacle of a three-year apprenticeship, especially since learning to read also requires an appropriate social and educational environment. It is the evaluation of the environment of the early medieval West which will help us come to terms with the issue.

In our civilization it is customary to twin reading and writing; for the period investigated here, the two skills must initially be treated separately, and it remains to be seen to what extent they can be twinned.[13] It is not clear

---

9 'McKitterick and her contributors write in the English empiricist tradition, avoiding the jargon of continental and American linguists and literary theory'; so approvingly Clanchy, M.T., in his review of *Uses of literacy* in *EHR* 107, 1992, 678-80, here at 680. The lack of any discussion of the concept of literacy in early medieval Europe is one of the greatest drawbacks of this collection. The same is true of McKitterick, *The Carolingians and the written word*, see further below in this chapter.

10 *CSSH* 5, 1962-3, 304-45, reprinted in Goody, J., ed., *Literacy in traditional societies*, Cambridge 1968, 27-62 from which I shall quote. For a later stage in Goody's work in this area see Goody, J., *The domestication of the savage mind*, Cambridge 1977, esp. ch. 2. His later works, e.g. *The logic of writing and the organization of society*, Cambridge 1986, have not produced new insights.

11 Ibid., 38.

12 Ibid., 41; cf. also Williman, D.: 'an alphabetic script is so easy for young children to learn', art. 'Schools, grammar', *Dictionary of the Middle Ages*, vol. 11, 1988, 63a.

13 Cf. Riché, P., 'Apprendre à lire et à écrire dans le haut Moyen-Age', *Bulletin de la Société nationale des Antiquaires de France* 1978-79, 193-203.

whether people learned to read without acquiring at least minimal writing skill; however, what is more important to us here is *how* they wrote and read. In medieval as in earlier centuries, people who had learned to write and could even do so with ease did not necessarily themselves write as a matter of course. Instead, they often left the chore of writing to professional scribes or notaries. This is rarely mentioned explicitly for the very reason that it was a very widespread phenomenon; but it epitomizes the special features of that culture and has to be taken into account.

Let us first look at writing. In Roman education what was aimed at was to be able to write 'clearly and fast', as Quintilian formulated it.[14] One wrote on wax tablets or papyrus, both surfaces that were rather easy to use for this purpose. From the first century AD onwards, gradually parchment came to be used side by side papyrus;[15] this material was more durable than papyrus, but it was also more difficult to write on. Parchment was also very much more costly than papyrus;[16] on the other hand, the raw material was readily available everywhere in Western Europe, whereas papyrus was produced mainly in Egypt and its easy availability depended on efficient long-distant trade.

Parchment was also more difficult to prepare as a surface suitable for writing; however, it is more resistant to the humid climate of western and northern Europe than papyrus and thus ultimately a superior material. Writing on parchment tended to take the form of calligraphy rather than cursive script. On the positive side, the average content of the parchment codex was perhaps as much as six times that of the papyrus roll.[17] For various reasons writing became a more exclusive skill in post-Roman times in the West. On the one hand, the changing political environment reduced the demand for it. On the other, a higher degree of professionalism was required.[18] Wax tablets continued to be used for learning how to write or for writing drafts.[19] While papyrus retained prestige and continued to be used for specific purposes,[20] it was

14   *Inst. Or.* I, 28: 'cura bene ac velociter scribendi'.
15   See Roberts, C.H.I., Skeat, T.C., *The birth of the codex*, London 1983; Rück, P., ed., *Pergament. Geschichte, Struktur, Restaurierung, Herstellung*, Sigmaringen 1991.
16   For this issue see McKitterick, R., *The Carolingians and the written word*, esp. 135ff.
17   Roberts, C.H.I., 'The codex', *PBA* 40, 1954, 169-204, at 202.
18   See also Bischoff, B., 'Elementarunterricht und Probationes pennae' (extended version of the 1938 original in ed.), *Mittelalterliche Studien*, I, Stuttgart 1966, 74-87.
19   Specimens of wax tablets from about AD 600 have survived from Ireland, the Springmout Bog tablets, for which see Lowe, E.A., *Codices Latini Antiquiores*, Supplement, Oxford 1971, no. 1684. Their use in Irish monasteries is attested by Adomnán, abbot of Iona, *De Locis Sanctis*, ed. Meehan, D. (= Scriptores Latini Hiberniae 3), Dublin 1958, 38 and 46. Einhart reports that Charlemagne attempted to learn to write with the help of wax tablets, *Vita Karoli Magni*, c.25.
20   Bischoff, B., *Latin palaeography. Antiquity and the Middle Ages*, Cambridge 1990, 7f. See especially the Merovingian royal chancery and the papacy.

associated more and more with secular business.[21]

In the Roman Empire as well as in medieval times there were people who specialized in writing.[22] However, statements to the effect that the physical act of writing was considered hard labour, which have survived from the early medieval centuries but for which there is no parallel from Roman times, convey the idea of a profound cultural change:

> Qui nescit scribere, putat hoc esse nullum laborem. O quam gravis est scriptura: oculos gravat, renes frangit, simul et omnia membra contristat. Tria digita scribunt, totus corpus laborat.[23]

This was written in the eighth century. The last sentence (including *totus corpus*) is found more than once.[24] Thus a scribe in Italy wrote in the tenth century: 'Tria digita scribunt, totus corpus laborat. Dorsum inclinat, costas in ventrem mergit, et omne fastidium corporis nutrit.'[25] One is obviously dealing with a widespread professional complaint which had found an appropriate formulation and had become a commonplace. This highlights the general view taken of the physical act of writing; it seems significant that even in Italy, where the Roman legacy remained more prominent than in other Western countries, difficulties of this type were experienced.

In fact, in the early Middle Ages the Latin verb *scribere* was not as unambiguous a term as might appear at first sight. Take the following statement of Rabanus Maurus from the ninth century: 'Nam et nos cum scribimus, scripturam ipsam non calamo, quo litterae caraxantur, sed scriptoris manui deputamus.'[26] The physical act of writing was expressed by verbs other than

21   Cf. Gregory the Great, *Moralia in Iob* XIII, 10: 'per papyrum . . . saecularis scientia designatur', PL 75, 1024A.
22   Not to write personally, as had been customary in Rome for centuries, can be observed from the time around AD 400 onwards.
23   Wattenbach, W., *Das Schriftwesen im Mittelalter*, 3rd. ed., Leipzig 1896, 283.
24   Wattenbach, W., 279-84. For a ninth-century example (*totum corpus*) see Meyer-Marthaler, E., ed., *Die Rechtsquellen des Kantons Graubünden* (Lex Romana Curiensis), Aarau 1959, 656; for a twelfth-century example see Bischoff, B., *Die südostdeutschen Schreibschulen und Bibliotheken in der Karolingerzeit*, vol. I, 3rd ed., Wiesbaden 1974, 77 (Clm 6 297, f. 146v). Generally see also Beckmann, G.A., 'Aus den letzten Jahrzehnten des Vulgärlateins in Frankreich. Ein parodistischer Zusatz zur Lex Salica und eine Schreiberklage', *Zeitschrift für Romanische Philologie* 79, 1963, 305-34, esp. 322f.
25   Wattenbach, 284.
26   Wattenach, *Schriftwesen*, 262; and see 421. A formulation to the same effect from Ireland is quoted below, chapter 9, n. 194. For *caraxare* as a term for 'writing' before 800 see Herren, M., 'Insular Latin *C(h)araxare (Craxare)* and its derivatives', *Peritia* 1, 1982, 273-77. One could add to his material two references in a letter by Lull written to England c. 738, *Bonifatius-Briefe*, ed. Tangl, M., MGH no. 98, p. 220. Further attestations of *scribere* in this sense are given in Hoffmann, H., *Buchkunst und Königtum im ottonischen und frühsalischen Reich* (Schriften der MGH 30. 1), Stuttgart 1986, 42-49.

Literacy 51

scribere, such as here *caraxare*; another term that is used is *depingere*.[27] The person who wrote was called *scriptor* by Rabanus Maurus; this term was used very widely for the scribe in the early medieval West, including Ireland.[28] Thus *scribere* was often used for literary creativity rather than the physical act of writing.[29] Isidore of Seville's statement that 'ab scribendo autem scriba nomen accepit'[30] can thus be taken to apply to the early medieval West if *scribere* does not denote the physical act of writing and if *scriba* is taken to denote a scholar.[31]

All this is not meant to suggest that clerical scholars like Rabanus could not write. Apparently the copying of Holy Scripture was a type of work regarded as not beneath the dignity of even eminent clerics.[32] St Boniface, writing a vision of the other world by a monk, may have personally performed the physical act of writing when he uses the term *scribere*.[33] But leading clerics often left to others the physical labour, which was regarded as considerable.[34] However, since being able to write necessarily implied the ability to read, educated people could monitor the work of their scribes and make sure that what they wanted to be written was in fact written. This was what ultimately mattered to literate people in the Middle Ages.

27 See Bischoff, *Die südostdeutschen Schreibschulen*, 123 (Clm 17011); in eighth-century Ireland one finds *discribere* in the sense of 'to copy', see the colophon of *Adomnan's Life of Columba*, Anderson, A.O., Anderson, M.O., ed., Edinburgh 1961, 542.
28 Some references to *scriptor* in colophons: Codex Sangallensis 6, 143, 1019. One finds written in the Book of Durrow: 'Rogo beatitudinem tuam sancte praesbiter Patrici ut quicumque hunc libellum manu tenuerit meminerit Columbae scriptoris qui hoc scripsi . . . met evangelium per XII dierum spatium', quoted in Reeves, W., *The Life of Columba*, Dublin 1857, 242 n. For a Carolingian instance see MGH Capit. II, no. 260 p. 274 additional note: 'scriptorem cum pergamene'. For an early eleventh-century reference see Notker Labeo: 'Si scriptor est oportet eum scribere'. Piper, P., ed., *Die Schriften Notkers und seiner Schule*, vol. I, Freiburg/Tübingen 1882, 594.
29 'Si scribam queris, qui me penna coloraret/Ruathelmus devotus Otgarii fieri iussit'. MGH Poet. IV, p. 1062, no. XIII, Hoffmann, *Buchkunst und Königtum* I, 45. See also *Continuatio Fredegarii*, MGH SS. rer. Merov. 2, c. 34, p. 182: 'Usque nunc inluster vir Childebrandus comes, avunculus praedicto rege Pippino, hanc historiam vel gesta francorum diligentissime scribere procuravit.' The same usage is found in Einhart's *Vita Karoli Magni*, e.g. ch. 29; see chapter 6.
30 *Origines* VI, 14, 9.
31 For *scriba* and related terms see Richter, M., 'The scholars of early Christian Ireland', in the press (Australian Celtic Studies Conference 1992, forthcoming) and below chapter 9.
32 See, e.g., *Adomnan's Life of Columba*, 59a-60b; also Bischoff, B., Hofmann, J., *Libri Sancti Kyliani: die Würzburger Schreibschule und die Dombibliothek im 8. und 9. Jahrhundert*, Würzburg 1952, 5, 154f.
33 *Ep.* 10, p. 15; cf. Richter, M., 'Die Symbiose von Christentum und archaischer Gesellschaft in Irland, 400-800', in Tristram, H. L. C., ed., *Studien zur Táin Bó Cuailnge*, Tübingen 1993, 158-72, esp. 166, n. 19.
34 Bede underlines the situation where this is not so: 'ipse mihi dictator simul, notarius et librarius existerem'. *Letter to Bishop Acca*, Migne, PL 92, 304.

An important result of our investigation is that learning connected with written material was practised without being inextricably linked to writing. It may be suggested that the connotations of *scribere* indicated here epitomize the difference in literate culture between Roman antiquity and the early medieval West.

We now turn to reading. Reading was done aloud in the Middle Ages by people of all levels of erudition;[35] this had been customary already in Roman times among all classes.[36] This fact has to be explored in as many of its manifestations and repercussions as possible if its cultural implications are to be fully appreciated.

The practice of reading aloud in the Middle Ages must not be regarded as evidence of a poor level of education. Since it was so widespread, explicit references to it are rather incidental.[37] Einhart, for example, reports about Charlemagne: 'legebantur ei historiae et antiquorum res gestae'.[38]

In any case, it was noteworthy when somebody read without uttering sounds. In a famous passage, St Augustine described how he observed St Ambrose reading silently:

> Cum legebat, oculi ducebantur per paginas et cor intellectum rimabatur, vox autem et lingua quiescebat. Saepe, cum adessem, . . . sic eum legentem vidimus tacite et aliter numquam.[39]

Thus Augustine associated written words with sound and concluded correctly: 'Cum enim est in scripto, non verbum, sed verbi signum est'.[40] In treating of the manner in which children learn to read, Quintilian commented perceptively on the difficulty of coordinating seeing and speaking in the act of reading aloud when the voice trails behind the eyes: 'The attention of the mind must be

---

35 For a rare different view see Riché, *Education*, 518; but see Banniard, *Genèse*, passim and id., 'Le lecteur en Espagne wisigothique d'après Isidore de Séville: de ses fonctions à l'état de la langue', *Revue des Etudes Augustiniennes* 21, 1975, 112-44.

36 The comprehensive study remains Balogh, J., 'Voces paginarum', *Philologus* 82, 1927, 84-109, 202-40. See also Bonner, S.F., *Education in ancient Rome*, London 1977, esp. 212 ff. That this was not invariably so was argued by Gavrilov, A. (lecture at Konstanz university, May 1992, which will be published in the near future).

37 See below at p. 63f. For this subject see also Zumthor, P., *La lettre et la voix. De la 'littérature' médiévale*, Paris 1987, and chapter 10 below.

38 *Vita Karoli Magni*, c. 24, p. 29. Reading aloud is also implied in ch. 26 where Einhart writes about Charlemagne: 'Legendi atque psallendi disciplinam diligentissime emendavit. Erat enim utriusque admodum eruditus, quamquam ipse nec publice legeret, nec nisi submissim et in commune cantaret', p. 31. In this manner in which Einhart presents Charlemagne it is difficult to assess the ruler's mastery of the two skills. Cf. generally Richter, M., 'Die Sprachenpolitik Karls des Großen', *Sprachwissenschaft* 7, 1982, 412-37.

39 *Conf.* VI, 3; Balogh, 86.

40 *De dialect.* V, 11; Balogh, 225.

Literacy

divided, the eyes and the voice being differently engaged, which is most difficult.'[41]

The act of reading aloud must be related to the high esteem which the Romans accorded to rhetoric, the aims of which were, according to Cicero, *docere, delectare, flectere*.[42] In these ideals, as in the practice of reading aloud, one can see remnants of Roman cultural traditions prior to the age of writing. One should note especially the pleasure that was to be communicated by the reader which he would share with his audience. Pliny adduced non-verbal elements as important factors when justifying why he personally read out his poems to chosen audiences: 'the air of a countenance, the turn of a head or eye, the motion of a hand, a murmur of applause, or even silence itself': 'ex vultu, oculis, nutu, manu, murmure'.[43]

The custom of reading aloud can likewise be gathered from some metaphorical phrases like *verbositas paginae*,[44] *loquax pagina*,[45] as used by Roman authors. In Gregory the Great's correspondence, one finds the phrase: 'Audisti quod volo, vide quid agas.'[46]

The medieval material shows up analogous expressions: *pagina sacra canit*;[47] *scriptura canit*;[48] *carta canebat*;[49] *cronica canit*;[50] *littera canit*.[51] Expressions like these indicating sound are apparently not very frequent, but the repeated use of the verb *canere* in such a context suggests an agreed meaning[52] in different parts of the early medieval West. We shall later present more manifestations of reading aloud.

In view of these considerations, it emerges that the modern concept of literacy is of little relevance for the Middle Ages because of the different cultural and educational contexts. Thus in important respects modern statements about implications of literacy are in need of modification for the early medieval West.[53] On the other hand, it has been rightly stated that 'the

---

41 *Inst. Or.* I, 1, 34: 'quod difficillimum est, dividenda intentio animi, ut aliud voce, aliud oculis agatur'.
42 *De oratore* 2, 27, 115. See Banniard, *Genèse*, 63, and *Viva Voce*, 85, and Augustine, *De doctrina christiana* 4, 12, 27.
43 Pliny, *Letters* V, 3.
44 Augustine, *Ep.* 236.
45 Martianus Capella, Balogh, 204.
46 *Reg.* I, 42.
47 Walahfrid, MGH Poetae Latini II, 297, L. 8.
48 Rabanus Maurus, *Carmina XIII*, 40, MGH Poet. Lat. II, 176.
49 *Ratperti Casus s. Galli*, ch.14, Meyer von Knonau, G., ed. (= Mittheilungen zur Vaterländischen Geschichte 13), St. Gallen 1872, 25.
50 *Chron. Gelr.*, *Gelderse Kronik*, ed., Mocy, A.J.de, Amsterdam 1950, 168.
51 Ibid., 170.
52 *Canere* has a fairly wide semantic field; it seems to refer here to a kind of solemn recitation, a special language register; see also chapter 5.
53 Goody, *Domestication*: 'Writings make speech objective by turning it into an object of visual

introduction of writing did not at once change the habits of the people and displace the method of oral tradition. We must always distinguish between the first introduction of writing and its general diffusion.'[54] These diachronic variations are essential to our investigation.

While literacy is usually taken to denote, in the Middle Ages, a person's ability to read and write, we may now state that wherever the Latin language was spoken and understood,[55] it was not necessary to be able to read, let alone to write, in order to partake in information written in Latin. The general practice of reading aloud made it possible to share written material with people who could not read. This was the case in most of the continental part of the Western Romania for centuries after the transformation of the empire when writing was done in Latin.[56] Thus Latin written material was immediately accessible in many parts of the early medieval West as it had been in Roman antiquity.[57] When other languages came to be written, like Old High German from the eighth century onwards, the same mechanics applied to spread the information written in these languages.[58]

Therefore, every written text from the early medieval West must be taken as having required oral performance. This is why the problem has to be formulated, not 'Who was literate?' or 'How literate was a given society?', but, instead, 'What was produced in written form, and what were the linguistic barriers, if any, of this written material to the intended addressee? What are the indications that such barriers were faced and dealt with?' Within this framework of questions, we shall see that changes in the cultural and political environment that characterize the transformation of the Roman world have their repercussions in the area of written products.

Based on these considerations, where the act of reading appears as an act of oral communication among individuals in groups,[59] it is important to take

    as well as aural inspection; it is the shift of the receptor from ear to eye', 44, and see further 44-50. Also: 'writing ... shifts language from the aural to the visual domain, writing alters the nature of verbal communication', 78.

54 Goody and Watt, 40.
55 For the generally neglected importance of 'understanding' rather than 'speaking' Latin in the early Middle Ages see Richter, M., 'A quelle époque a-t-on cessé de parler Latin? A propos d'une question mal posée', *Annales, E.S.C.* 38, 1983, 439-48.
56 The most thorough discussion is that of Banniard, M., *Viva voce*. Reference should also be made to the publications of Roger Wright and Marc van Uytfanghe quoted therein.
57 In the act of reading concessions could be made to the language registers of the audience present, for manifestations of which see n. 109 below.
58 While this is noted in passing e.g. by Bäuml, F.H., 'Varieties and consequences of medieval literacy and illiteracy', *Speculum* 55, 1980, 237-65, at 245 (with reference to Crosby, R., 'Oral delivery in the Middle Ages', *Speculum* 11, 1936, 88-110), its implications are not really applied and therefore Bäuml's concept of literacy remains on the whole traditional. See further, chapter 10.
59 This is a point where I differ sharply from B. Stock, and his 'textual communities', as

into account that sound rather than sign spread information throughout the period considered here.[60] In this respect, there was no fundamental difference as far as the conveyance of information is concerned between cultures that did not resort to writing and those that did.[61] It would also seem that in reading aloud the speech was modulated in a manner which would produce a kind of language different from everyday conversation. The same holds for the articulation of oral culture, and it is possible to see in the special articulation of written material a legacy of non-literate times.[62]

It is thus of vital importance to clarify the place of written material in the period investigated here, to highlight the transformation of the Roman world in the field of written culture. Only when this is done, can other forms of cultural transmission be properly appreciated. It is equally vital to keep in mind that the written word must be imagined having been transposed into sound according to criteria which were also followed in societies that did not have writing.

LITERACY IN LATE ROMAN SOCIETY

The cultural ideal of education and literacy had been dear to the Roman élite since classical times.[63] We shall now look at some aspects of how the written word was part of the public life of the late Empire, how it was used by the government. This is at the same time an indication of the levels of participation in the *res publica* outside those circles that dictated Roman cultural ideals.

It can be stated as a matter of fact that the Roman Empire in late antiquity was the way it was and functioned the way it did on account of its recourse to writing, although it is extremely difficult to specify the precise contribution

> discussed in his *The implications of literacy. Written language and models of interpretation in the eleventh and twelfth centuries*, Princeton 1983.
> 60 This is also the main subject, although for a later period, of the study by Zumthor, *La lettre et la voix*. This will be further discussed in chapter 10.
> 61 This opinion is shared by scholars who study nonliterate societies live, e.g.: 'We find that the simple view of two basically different types of society, characterized by radically different communication media, just does not accord with the facts.' Finnegan, R., 'Literacy versus non-literacy: the great divide? Some comments on the significance of 'literature' in non-literate cultures', in Horton, R., Finnegan, R., ed., *Modes of thought. Essays on thinking in Western and non-Western societies*, London 1973, 112-44, at 138, but see also chapter 10 below.
> 62 This complex of ideas was suggested to me by the article of Treitler, L., 'Reading and singing: on the genesis of occidental music-writing', *Early Music History* 4, 1984, 135-208; see also chapter 5 below.
> 63 In Roman society, to qualify for the epithet *litteratus* required much more than being able to write. See Grundmann, H., 'Litteratus — illiteratus', *Archiv für Kulturgeschichte* 40, 1958, 1–65, at 21. This highly acclaimed article is otherwise of little relevance here since it deals mainly with a later period.

literacy made to the Roman body politic.[64] However, this is only a technical aspect of larger social and cultural problems.[65] This issue has to be approached from various angles.

In view of the extensive use made of writing in late Roman society it is very surprising that it is impossible to obtain precise information concerning the institutions for teaching Latin, the environment of written learning. There is no evidence that the state provided an institutional infrastructure for teaching the skills of reading and writing. There was no comprehensive system of state schools.[66] It may well be that the state reckoned with the high social prestige of learning among the Roman élite and relied on private initiative to provide schooling. Among the wealthy, senators or aristocrats, teaching was organized on a private basis, often by employing slaves at home. It is difficult to establish how the poorer people fared in this respect. Let us look at some manifestations of the way Rome dealt with public matters which may throw some light on that issue.

Since the times of the early Empire, public announcements were displayed in writing and were set up in such a way that they could be easily read: 'unde de plano recte legi possit(ur)'.[67] Plutarch (died *c.* AD 120) reports that this was done in places that were much frequented and that sometimes such notices were read out of sheer boredom.[68] In view of the general practice of reading aloud one can see how the contents of public announcements would reach even people who themselves were unable to read. This must have been intended, and it shows the practical streak of the Roman mind.

One witnesses here possibilities of participating, albeit passively, and perhaps only marginally, in a body politic that had come to make much use of writing in administration as well as in the field of justice. In this area, the interest of the state seems to have taken precedence over the humanizing aspect of education. However, one should not underestimate the effect of the cultural prestige of literacy in making such a system work more or less well without extensive state investment in schooling. The kind of participation in the written culture outlined above occurred more in towns than in the country. Thus the

---

64 This has been well put by Harris: 'Each society achieves the level of literacy which its structure and ethos require and its technology permits.' *Ancient literacy*, 331.
65 By analogy, e.g. the US 'society functions' despite high and growing adult illiteracy, for which see Kozol, J., *Illiterate America*, New York 1985.
66 This has been recently restated by Harris, *Ancient literacy*, 333. It is imperative to take into account that the modern concept of 'school' does not apply either to the Roman or the medieval term *schola*. See also Kaster, R.A., 'Notes on primary and secondary schools in late antiquity', *Transactions of the American Philological Association* 113, 1983, 323-46.
67 Fröschl, J.M., 'Imperitia litterarum. Zur Frage der Beachtlichkeit des Analphabetismus im römischen Recht', *ZRG romanistsische Abteilung* 104, 1987, 84-155, at 153, and see 105.
68 *De curiositate* 11, quoted Fröschl, 105.

poor and the country people were the most disadvantaged groups in this respect; hence *rusticitas* as a term for lack of education.

The phenomenon of inscriptions is often taken as indicative of widespread literacy, as most recently commented upon by Michel Banniard: 'L'antiquité tardive est ancrée dans le monde de la communication écrite.'[69] Other scholars have warned against drawing far-reaching conclusions about literacy from the existence of inscriptions or graffiti.[70] Indeed, modern experience teaches that pungent graffiti will become known by word of mouth well beyond the circle of people who actually read them, and this may also have been the case in late antiquity.

We have here further indications that the literate/illiterate dichotomy loses much of its usefulness as far as late Roman society is concerned. This is not to say that being or not being literate could not have had important implications, for late Roman society was unthinkable without writing. But it has also been suggested that 'the weakening of the educational system and of the system of written communication hastened the decline of the late Roman Empire'.[71] There is a good case for taking into account regional differences; thus Egypt and North Africa show a greater vitality than other areas. Thanks to the literary work of Ausonius (*c*.310-92) we are exceptionally well informed about educational institutions in Bordeaux.[72]

It has been rightly said that 'the Roman empire, that had sprawled so dangerously far from the Mediterranean by 200, was held together by the illusion that it was still a very small world'.[73] Originally the law of the Romans was declared orally in the public assembly; if it was written down, this was a secondary phenomenon of no legal relevance. That people were ignorant of the laws in their society at their own peril is obvious; yet only as late as AD 391 was it laid down that 'constitutiones nec ignorare quemquam nec dissimulare permittimus';[74] ignorance of the law was not accepted as an excuse. In a similar manner, specific legislation concerning testation by illiterates was made only as late as AD 439: 'Quod si litteras testator ignoret vel subscribere nequeat, octavo subscriptore pro eo adhibito servari decernimus'.[75] This must

69 Banniard, M., *Genèse*, 25, see also 27, 46; a similar view is taken by Riché, *Education*, 60.
70 Harris, W.V., 'Literacy and epigraphy', *Zeitschrift für Papyrologie und Epigraphik* 52, 1983, 87-111; see also more fully id., *Ancient literacy*. However, the extremely sharp decline in inscriptions or graffiti in the early medieval centuries must surely be seen as indicative of less widespread literacy as well.
71 Harris, *Ancient literacy*, 333.
72 Kaster, 331.
73 Brown, P., *The world of late antiquity*, London 1971, 14.
74 Cod. Theod. 1.1.2, quoted Mayer-Maly, T., 'Rusticitas', *Studi in onore di Cesare Sanfilippo* I, Milan 1983, 307-47, at 315
75 Nov. Theod. 16.3, Fröschl, 114f. For one particular area of the empire, Egypt, see in this field Youtie, H.C., 'Ipographeus. The social impact of illiteracy in Graeco-Roman Egypt', *Zeitschrift für Papyrologie und Epigraphik* 17, 1975, 201-21.

not be taken as indicating that the problem had been non-existent before, nor does it present late Roman society *in nuce*.

However, all that should not suggest that being literate in the sense indicated above was a distinctive advantage in Roman society, even though it made it possible for a person to engage more fully in the *res publica*.

The establishment of the barbarian *regna* on the territory of the Western Empire brought about changes in literacy in the public sphere; previously many kinds of written documents had been produced in the service of the state. The extent of this decline is difficult to uncover because in the field of literate culture in the public sector the barbarian kings are visible at their most Roman, as is particularly the case with the Ostrogoths in Italy under Theodoric and his successors. Since the highly articulate Roman aristocrat Cassiodorus worked for them,[76] they come across as deeply imbued with Roman culture and ethos, possibly more so than they were in fact[77] (we have mentioned earlier that this is only one side of their culture, though the one that comes into focus particularly strongly). However, they did want to appear to some extent as Roman rulers, and this is reflected in the documents issued in their name and with their authority.

'Romanus miser imitatur Gothum, et utilis Gothus imitatur Romanum.'[78] This saying attributed to the Ostrogothic king Theodoric does not apply to the field of education. With few exceptions (to be mentioned later), the barbarian aristocracy apparently remained loyal to the traditional values in which Roman culture had only a small place. There are indications, albeit vague ones, that this was deliberate royal policy;[79] indeed, this would make good sense since the cohesion of the barbarians and their segregation from the Romans was the best guarantee of maintaining their separate identity. In this field in particular the concept of 'assimilation' should be used with greatest care after a review of the situation on the ground.

We shall turn to the education of the Romans. Generally speaking, the traditional ideals of the ennobling character of education remained in force. They were clearly formulated by Cassiodorus not long before he quit the public service:

> Grammatica magistra verborum, ornatrix humani generis, quae per exercitationem pulcherrimae lectionis antiquorum nos cognoscitur iuvare consiliis. Hac non utuntur barbari reges: apud legales dominos manere cognoscitur singularis. Arma enim et reliqua gentes habent: sola reperitur eloquentia, quae Romanorum dominis obsecundat. Hinc oratorum pugna

---

76 For a stern evaluation of Cassiodorus' style in the *Variae* see O'Donnell, *Cassiodorus*, 96-100.
77 O'Donnell, *Cassiodorus*, and see also chapter 1 above.
78 *Anon. Val.* XIV, 59; MGH AA IX, 322.
79 Procopius, *Bellum Gothicum* I, 2, quoted by Riché, *Education*, 104, n. 78.

civiliz iuris classicum canit; hinc cunctos proceres nobilissima disertitudo commendat.[80]

These ideals were certainly further pursued, at least partly because Roman institutions, many of which required education, continued to function, albeit often on a reduced level. By the fifth century, rifts became noticeable between Byzantium and the West in the field of learning. The traditional Roman educational ideal *utriusque linguae*, for example, in Greek as well as in Latin, was gradually abandoned in the West. Whereas in Byzantium Latin was kept as the official language of the state into the sixth century,[81] in the West a knowledge of Greek became a rare accomplishment; furthermore, it brought few advantages. Roman education was trimmed down to its literary aspects with scant regard for either science or philosophy.

In this society, two great mediators between East and West in the cultural area stand out in the early sixth century: Boethius and Dionysius Exiguus. Both worked as translators from Greek, Boethius on Aristotle's philosophical corpus, Dionysius in the field of canon law. The work of both is remarkable by any standard, and, in the long term, it was of seminal influence. But during their lifetime they were isolated in what they did, exceptional, without immediate resonance.[82]

The ways in which education was organized among the Romans in the sixth century are largely hidden from view. Schools of some kind are thought to have existed in North Africa as well as in Spain.[83] In this context, a document from the 530s is of exceptional interest. The Ostrogothic king Athalaric wrote to the Roman senate notifying it that he had heard that the customary fees for teachers of things dear to Romans were being cut. He mentions the *grammaticus*, the *orator* and the *iuris expositor*, conveying thereby an idea of what remained of Roman education. The king urged the senate to ensure that the customary fees continued to be paid. Unfortunately he does not mention the places where such teaching was carried out nor who ultimately met the cost. However, this is the case of a barbarian king attempting to maintain Roman learning:

> Nuper siquidem, ut est de vobis cura nostra sollicita, quorundam susurratione cognovimus doctores eloquentiae Romanae laboris sui constituta praemia non habere et aliquorum nundinatione fieri, ut scholarum magistris deputata summa videatur imminui . . . Qua de re, patres

80 *Var.* IX, 21.
81 Dagron, G., 'Aux origines de la civilization byzantine: langue de culture et langue d'Etat', *Revue Historique* 241, 1969, 23-56.
82 Riché, *Education*, 84.
83 Riché, *Education*, 76ff.

conscripti, hanc vobis curam, hanc auctoritatem propitia divinitate largimur, ut successor scholae liberalium litterarum tam grammaticus quam orator nec non et iuris expositor commoda sui decessoris ab eis quorum interest sine aliqua imminutione percipiat et semel primi ordinis vestri ac reliqui senatus amplissimi auctoritate firmatus, donec suscepti operis idoneus reperitur, neque de transferendis neque de imminuendis annonis a quolibet patiatur improbam quaestionem.[84]

These masters possibly taught in their own houses; there was also the custom of education being imparted in the homes of affluent citizens.

We shall now look at the same source to see what it contains about the Ostrogoths more particularly. For a number of reasons the Amalung dynasty of the short-lived Ostrogothic kingdom of Italy requires attention. Of that dynasty, the limelight is taken by Theodoric; he will be considered here only as far as education is concerned.

It matters little whether or not Theodoric himself could write.[85] The person who acted as his *amanuensis* was Cassiodorus. More important, and to my knowledge never discussed, is the question how well Theodoric knew Latin; I assume that he knew this language. One associates Theodoric with his wide-ranging correspondence contained in Cassiodorus' *Variae* (a most happy survival, but in so far as possible one needs to distinguish the king's political ideas from the formulation his Roman secretary gives them).[86] The following examples will highlight some of the problems arising from the *Variae* which also add colour to the overall picture.

The wide range of subjects discussed in the *Variae* apparently speaks for itself. However, the stylishness of some of these letters belies the assertion in the same collection that 'barbarous kings do not use Latin'.[87] Was Theodoric not a *rex barbarus* according to Roman ideology? It is mostly impossible to say where in that collection we encounter Cassiodorus, where Theodoric. However, there are passages which seem to point to Theodoric's mind even though they may have been formulated ultimately by his eloquent secretary. Among these must be reckoned the claim that *regnum nostrum imitatio vestra est*, in all its ambivalence. Here one can perceive the Ostrogothic king resident in Ravenna seeing himself of a different class from the other barbarian kings, as shown in

---

84 *Var.* IX, 21.
85 See the discussion in Riché, *Education*, 96f.
86 See O'Donnell, *Cassiodorus*, esp. ch. 3. The same problem is brought up by Scheibelreiter, G., 'Vester est populus meus. Byzantinische Reichsideologie und germanisches Selbstverständnis', in Chrysos, and Schwarcz, ed., *Das Reich und die Barbaren*, 203-20.
87 *Var.* IX, 21 *hac grammatica non utuntur barbari reges.*

the continuation of the above assertion: *qui quantum vos sequimur, tantum gentes alias anteimus.*[88]

There can be no doubt that as far as resorting to writing in government is concerned the Ostrogoths were exceptional; they must not be taken as representative of barbarian kings in this respect. In the case of the Ostrogoths the meeting of Roman and barbarian cultures has received a particularly 'thick' description.

There are those passages which show that Theodoric as king was delighted with what Italy offered to him; in a touchingly naive way he showed off to his fellow rulers. When sending his daughter to become the wife of the Thuringian king Hermanafrid, the following ideas were formulated: 'Habebit felix Thoringia quod nutrivit Italia, litteris doctam, moribus eruditam, decoram non solum genere, quantum et feminea dignitate.'[89] Not unlike his daughter, a product of Roman civilization, Theodoric praised the civilizing effect of a water clock which he was proudly sending to the Burgundian king Gundobad: 'Discat sub vobis Burgundia res subtilissimas inspicere et antiquorum inventa laudare: per vos propositum gentile deponit ... Beluarum quippe ritus est ex ventris esurie horas sentire et non habere certum, quod constat humanis usibus contributum.'[90] More than once the idea was ventilated that written law was visible proof of true humanity; this was at the same time a subtle attempt to associate kingship with written law, elevating it above traditional kingship and also elevating the king above his people: 'Custodia legum civilitatis indicium et reverentia priorum principum nostrae quoque testatur devotionis exemplum ... Hoc enim populos ab agresti vita in humanae conversationis regulam congregavit. Haec ratio a feritate divisit, ne arbitrio casuali vagarentur, quos regi consilio divina voluerunt.'[91] These are Roman values, but the need to express them so explicitly suggests that they had not been internalized.

In contrast, Theodoric felt it necessary to admonish his Goths that to attain glory required toil and that they should show that they still possessed the qualities of their ancestors.[92] To put this into writing, moreover in Latin, seems utterly incongruous, although one is grateful for this clear formulation of traditional values, particularly the *gaudium* associated with fighting.

There is, finally, Theodoric's attempt to establish correspondence in Latin with other barbarian kings where he sent along interpreters (presumably

88   *Var.* I, 1. On this see also chapter 1 and Faussner, 1984.
89   *Var.* IV, 1.
90   *Var.* I, 46.
91   *Var.* IV, 33. Cf. Rom. 2 : 14: 'gentes quae legem non habent'. See the caustic comments by Wormald, P., 'Lex scripta and verbum regis: legislation and Germanic kingship from Euric to Cnut', in *Early medieval kingship*, Sawyer, P.H., Wood, I.N., ed., Leeds 1977, 105-38.
92   *Var.* I, 24: 'Innotescenda sunt magis Gothis quam suadenda certamina, quia bellicosae stirpi est gaudium comprobari: laborem quippe non refugit, qui virtutis gloriam concupiscit.'

messengers at the same time) to explain the contents of the letters in the language known to the addressee.[93] Literacy in this situation appears as little more than a pretentious symbol.

The documents in the *Variae* (a few items of which I have discussed) show impressively what late Roman culture stood for in the eyes of one of its accomplished representatives. The children of Theodoric were likewise educated. However, the Amal dynasty was exceptional in this regard; they may be regarded as hybrids. There is no point in speculating about what would have been the subsequent course of history if the culture of the Amalungs had been more widespread. Besides, one cannot gainsay the fact that the Frankish king Clovis, who was in no way Theodoric's equal in terms of supporting literate culture, was the ancestor of a dynasty that was to rule Gaul for a quarter of a millennium.

I would like to close this section with reference to the Pragmatic Sanction of Justinian of 554. In this decree the emperor referred to the need for teachers of various professions to be adequately remunerated.[94] For all its vagueness this pronouncement conveys the impression that learning and literacy were facing much harder times, so much so that the authorities were concerned about the situation.

What from a Roman perspective would appear as a deterioration may appear in quite a different light from the point of view of the barbarians in the Empire. Certainly, it is a signal of change, an aspect of transformation. Apparently other values had gained the upper hand; the *regna* were gradually being run in ways different from that of Empire. The written material which was produced in this world in transformation will be assessed from various angles.

CHRISTIANITY IN THE EMPIRE AND BEYOND

Christianity, a religion of The Book, based on Holy Scripture, which had to be taught and expounded to its adherents, required literacy as a prerequisite for its proper functioning. Whatever may be said about limitations of literacy in Roman society, it was a general enough phenomenon for the Church's purposes. Above all, there was no linguistic barrier to be overcome. By the second half of the fourth century, Western Christianity had adopted Latin as the language of the liturgy in the place of Greek. The New Testament, originally written in Greek, was also available in Latin versions by then, and early in the fifth century St Jerome's Vulgate was completed. The Christian religion was mediated through the Latin language. Literacy was required only

93 *Var.* IV, 2.: 'Salutantes proinde gratia competenti reliqua per illum et illum legatos nostros patrio sermone mandamus, qui vobis et litteras nostras evidenter exponant et ad confirmandam gratiam quae sunt dicenda subiungant.'
94 Riché, *Education*, 115, 182.

of such people as took an active part in the celebration of the rites, the clergy. It is noteworthy that in the fifth century no educational institutions of a specifically Christian character emerged.[95]

In the Western *regna* literacy was less widespread than it had been in the Empire. Since literacy in Latin, institutionally linked to Christianity, was present in all medieval societies that encountered Christianity, it can now be suggested that every medieval society used writing according to its requirements and this accordingly has to be studied. Those social and political areas where writing did not manifest itself were catered for by cultural activity that did not involve writing. So, to assess the literacy of medieval societies the first thing to be done is to describe the use made of writing.

One has to reckon, of course, with loss of material, and perhaps more so with regard to evidence not related to the Church. However, the overall impression remains that in the course of the transformation of the Roman world in the West education in reading and writing became increasingly the domain of clerics and monks. In the course of the following centuries, the question whether dedicated Christians should be allowed in the study of Latin to use classical literature (texts of non-Christian orientation), was to surface periodically. It was treated in a variety of manners; those who claimed to be able to dispense with Latin pagan authorities were in the minority.

THE LAITY

The Roman population of Italy, Spain and Gaul in the fifth century spoke Latin as their mother tongue. This was to remain so in subsequent centuries. It is a matter of debate as well as of definition when to place the beginning of the Romance languages; however, there can be no doubt that in the sixth, seventh and eighth centuries Latin was still understood by the Romance population in all those areas,[96] which means, by the overwhelming majority of the population. (This can be taken, incidentally, as an explanation as to why the barbarian laws were codified on mainland Europe in Latin.)[97] Thus, the language of the Church—the Bible, the liturgy and exegesis—was within easy reach of most Christians in those centuries. No special education was required even though there were different registers of Latin, formal and informal.[98]

95 Ibid., 47-49.
96 The importance of understanding rather than speaking was first raised by Richter, ' A quelle époque a-t-on cessé de parler latin en Gaule? A propos d'une question mal posée'. For recent work in this area see esp. Wright, R., *Late Latin and early Romance*, Liverpool 1982; see now the magisterial monograph by Banniard, *Viva voce*.
97 See Stacey, R.C., 'Law and order in the very old West: England and Ireland in the early Middle Ages', in *Crossed paths. Methodological approaches to the Celtic aspects of the European Middle Ages*, Hudson, B.T., Ziegler, V., ed., Lanham, Maryland 1991, 39-60, at 43.
98 See p. 65f.

In fact, by employing Latin as the language of worship, and (in the case of clerics) of learning, the Church contributed most in the long term to the maintenance of learning in that language, in a variety of ways. However, the conduct of Christian worship in a reasonable manner did not require the congregation to be literate or educated. Reading aloud a language accessible to the congregation as a whole made adequate participation of the community possible. Reading passages from the Bible, and talking about of such readings in the homily that followed, was part of the divine service. Correct reading was a task for professionals, especially since this also affected the correctness of the faith of the recipients of the message.[99] The intellectual or theological content of such homilies was probably rather low,[100] but the main point is that in Latin-speaking societies comprehension was no problem. Gregory the Great complained that his *Moralia* had been read before an audience insufficiently educated, an audience who understood the language but not the theology:

> . . . quod . . . Marinianus legi commenta beati Iob publice ad vigilias faciat, non grate suscepi, quia non est illud opus populare et rudibus auditoribus impedimentum magis quam provectum generat.[101]

Let us look at a specific example of the kind of problems discussed. A sermon by Caesarius of Arles addressed to a rural lay congregation deals with this issue in an illuminating manner: inability to read is no excuse for ignorance of the word of God.

> Nec dicat aliquis vestrum: Non novi litteras, ideo mihi non imputabitur quidquid minus de dei praeceptis implevero. Inanis est et inutilis excusatio ista, fratres carissimi. Primum est, quod lectionem divinam etiamsi aliquis nesciens litteras non potest legere, potest tamen legentem libenter audire.[102]

It is here taken for granted that the texts which are read aloud would be understood by the listeners—that there was no linguistic barrier.[103] Caesarius refers to the case of illiterate merchants who hired literate people to assist them in their business:

---

99 Cf. Banniard, 'Le lecteur en Espagne wisigothique d'après Isidore de Séville', 133.
100 This I suggested in my article 'Kommunikationsprobleme im lateinischen Mittelalter', *HZ* 222, 1976, 43-80, at 58f.
101 *Reg.* XII, 6.
102 *Sermo* VI, ed. Morin, CCSL 103, 1953, 31. This sermon is also quoted under a different perspective in chapter 2 at n. 50.
103 The same can be said to apply in late sixth-century Sicily: see Gregory the Great, *Reg.* I, 42: 'scripta mea ad rusticos quae direxi per omnes messas fac relegi'.

Novimus enim aliquos negotiatores, qui cum litteras non noverint, requirunt sibi mercennarios litteratos; et cum ipsi litteras nesciant, aliis scribentibus rationes suas ingentia lucra conquirunt.[104]

Caesarius informs us about people who earned their living by being able to read and write in a society whose language was Latin. If it is surprising to find that there should have been merchants who were illiterate yet whose business involved writing, they apparently could without difficulty employ professionals who mastered the skill.

Caesarius' suggestion that his flock should become acquainted with Holy Scripture in order to attain eternal salvation, as merchants sought literacy for worldly gain, was not unusual. There is a story reported by Gregory the Great of a paralytic, Servulus, who, though himself illiterate, managed to gain access to the text of the Bible. He acquired the necessary manuscripts, and then he invited 'religious people' into his home who read from these texts to him:

Nequaquam litteras noverat, sed scripturae sacrae sibimet codices emerat, et religiosos quosque in hospitalitatem suscipiens, hos coram se studiose legere faciebat. Factumque est ut iuxta modum suum plene sacram scripturam disceret, cum, sicut dixi, litteras funditus ignoraret.[105]

This case has been called exceptional insofar as lay people's familiarity with biblical material is concerned.[106] It is difficult to know how such a conclusion can be drawn. Gregory presents the case twice; perhaps it should be considered as an *exemplum*, a model proposed for imitation.[107] Be that as it may, we have already found in Augustine's North Africa a congregation very familiar with the biblical text.[108] Since there was no linguistic barrier, frequent exposure to the text of Scripture would have made lay people familiar with it.

We have evidence that the audience was able to distinguish various registers of spoken Latin which were all accessible to them. This can be gathered from Bishop Gregory of Tours in the late sixth century who reports a personal experience: one Sunday he had been too tired to say Mass; he asked a priest to stand in for him. Obviously Gregory's substitute, though literate, was not very educated, for many of the congregation ridiculed him for using inappro-

---

104 Caesarius, *Sermo* VI, 31. The same point is made in *Sermo* VIII, p. 41. See briefly Banniard, *Viva voce*, 139.
105 *Dialogi* IV, xiv, PL 77, 341; also *Hom.* 15, PL 76, 1133f. Cf. Banniard, *Viva voce*, 138f.
106 Riché, *Education*, 539.
107 The need for the bible to be read to lay people is also referred to in the *Liber Exhortatonis* by Paulinus, patriarch of Aquileia, from the late eighth century where he articulates the attitude of the layman: 'quid pertinet ad me libros Scripturarum legendo audire vel discere?', PL 99, 240.
108 See chapter 2, n. 35.

priate uneducated speech for the solemn occasion. So, the congregation expected certain standards in particular circumstances:

> Die dominico ad missam veniens, nolens me fatigare, uni presbiterorum gloriosa solemnia caelebrare praecepi. Sed cum presbiter ille nescio quid rustice festiva verba depromeret, multi eum de nostris inridere coeperunt, dicentes: 'Melius fuisset tacere quam sic inculte loqui.'[109]

This text tells us something about audience expectation. The solemnity of the occasion required appropriate diction. Thus, for example, St Benedict had laid down: 'cantare autem et legere non praesumat nisi qui potest ipsum officium implere ut aedificentur audientes'.[110]

It was not easy to find an acceptable position that would do justice to the solemnity of the occasion while at the same time being in line with the fact that Christ's message was addressed to sinners rather than rhetors, and had been spread originally by simple fishermen rather than sophisticated elders.[111] To achieve the one while avoiding the other was close to attempting to square the circle.

Public reading was more than just speaking words to convey a message. The audience had to be attracted emotionally. That this could go quite far can be gathered from Isidore's warning against excessive body movement as part of the performance of the lector in church: 'neque cum motu corporis, sed tantummodo cum gravitatis specie. Auribus enim debet consulere lector, non oculis'.[112] One is reminded of Cicero's *docere, delectare, flectere*.[113]

Thus public reading emerges from these ecclesiastical circles as a complex act of communication in which reader and public were expected to interact, and where the messages were conveyed verbally, but also by non-verbal means which heightened participation. St Augustine, for example, expected to see the effect of his words on his audience by bodily reactions; he freely admitted that much effort could be required to achieve this.[114] There was an art in

---

109 *De virtutibus S. Martini*, II, 1, MGH SS rer. Merov. I, 2, 159. See also Riché, *Education* 241, note 136; Banniard, 'Lecteur', 136f; Banniard, *Viva voce*, 230, n. 180.
110 *Regula* 47, 2; see Banniard, 'Lecteur', 116. It is possible that here *cantare* and *legere* were used as synonyms.
111 For some references see Riché, *Education*, 129f.
112 *Eccl. off.* 2, 11, 51, Banniard, 'Lecteur', 136. See also *Eccl. off.* 2, 11, 5: 'porro vox lectoris simplex erit et ad omne pronuntiationis genus accommodata, plena succo virili . . . nihilque femineum sonans'.
113 See above, n. 42.
114 *De catechizandis rudibus*, CCSL XLVI, 1969, 115-178: XIII, 18: 'multum est perdurare in loquendo . . . cum moveri non videmus audientem: quod sive non audeat, religionis timore constrictus, voce aut aliquo motu corporis significare approbationem suam . . .', p. 142

Literacy

reading aloud publicly; the effect depended—in part at least—on the level of artistry.

Education remained alive among the Roman lay population into the seventh century, albeit on a reduced scale. In the late sixth century Gregory of Tours laments the current trend—learning leaving the cities and losing out to barbarian wildness: 'Decedente atque immo potius pereunte ab urbibus Gallicanis liberalium cultura litterarum . . . feretas gentium desaeviret, regum furor acueretur.'[115]

If this is more than a rhetorical flourish, it attests that the *cultura litterarum liberalium* had survived in some form,[116] that it was a characteristically urban phenomenon, and that it had not been adopted by those whom Gregory called *gentes* and to whom he attributed the conventional characteristics of wildness. So, here we have evidence supporting the view that, by and large, Romans and non-Romans, even when living side by side, maintained their specific cultural orientation. The Roman adage that *victi victoribus leges dederunt*[117] did not apply.

In the field of education the disappearance of the Empire in the West, the gradual dwindling of public sectors, certainly had negative consequences. In a telling way, Pope Agatho responded to condescension expressed from Byzantium on poor standards of learning in Italy around 680:

> Nam apud homines in medio gentium positos, et de labore corporis quotidianum victum cum summa haesitatione conquirentes, quomodo ad plenum poterit inveniri Scripturarum scientia, nisi quod quae regulariter a sanctis atque apostolicis praedecessoribus et venerabilibus quinque conciliis definita sunt?[118]

The times were highly unfavourable for the luxury of learning, and this had been so for quite a while.

As has been shown, the issue of literacy needs to be viewed quite differently from the way this has been done traditionally. People who were illiterate were not necessarily for that reason excluded from culture expressed in written form.[119] This is one point. The other, however, which is just as important, is that the early medieval Western societies could live with contracting literacy.

---

115 *Libri decem historiarum*, Pref., MGH SS rer. Merov. 1, p. 1; quoted in Riché, *Education*, 251, n. 214.
116 According to Bede, *HE* III, xviii, there were schools in early seventh-century Burgundy; see also below, n. 130.
117 Seneca, *De superstitione fragm.* 42.
118 PL 87, 1164.
119 This point is briefly made by Banniard, *Viva voce*, 140.

As a rule, societies continued to function without writing as they had done in the past (and done successfully); in fact the use of writing became exceptional. The early medieval societies of the Romania were not as inextricably tied to literate culture as had been that of imperial Rome. Since writing was available, but was less widely used than before, this was obviously because there was less demand for writing than formerly. The absence of writing in a society should not be seen, as it generally is, in Roman terms, as a deficiency.

Turning to the societies that existed in Europe outside the Romania we find that they received writing only in the wake of Christianity. For a long time literacy was required there only for the purposes of religion, and only in Latin. This meant that the culture associated with writing was not immediately accessible to the people concerned when it was read to them: Latin had to be translated into their own language. Since all these societies had their own culture, including religion, which had served them well in the past and continued to thrive, it is not surprising that Christianity and literacy made slow advances among them.

Finally, we need to look at the barbarians who moved into the Romania. There they encountered a society which was accustomed to written culture. The barbarians were the new masters; all of them eventually adopted the Christian religion. Literacy had in Christianity its most obvious outlet.

The majority of the population of the Romania had been accustomed to an organization of society that used the written word, but there is no doubt that writing was less widely used under the new masters in the early medieval centuries. The typically Roman custom of inscriptions declined sharply—good evidence of a change in the cultural environment.

From the way the barbarian rulers used writing, they showed themselves to be becoming Roman, at least in some respect.[120] But there were others, particularly the Saxons in Britain, who shunned this legacy of Romanization. There can be no doubt that a political environment developed which was generally less dependent on literacy; literacy increasingly became the reserve of the Church, especially the monasteries.[121] It is not surprising that Christian ethics attempted to bring its influence to bear on learning.

Furthermore, there are clear indications that written material was produced on a smaller scale in the political life of early medieval societies than had previously been the case. The skill of writing had not been lost, so the reason

120 The Frankish king Chilperic (561-84) is reported as having decreed the adoption of three new graphemes in order to write sounds in his own language since there were no suitable equivalents in the Latin alphabet. See Gregory of Tours, *Libri Historiarum* X, V, 44. Cf. also Sanders, W., 'Die Buchstaben des Königs Chilperich', *Zeitschrift für deutsches Altertum* 101, 1972, 54-85. There is no independent evidence that his language (Frankish) was written at the time.
121 I cannot accept the continuity of lay literacy on a rather broad scale as postulated by McKitterick, *Carolingians*; cf. Richter, '... quisquis scit scribere'.

for the decline in its use probably lies in the nature of these societies: they were structured in an essentially different way from the Empire. One could say that every medieval society had as much written culture as it needed.

Having looked earlier at some of the most influential Christian minds, we must turn briefly to the basic situation. There are vague indications (nothing more) that from the sixth century onwards bishops saw a particular need to train clerics. To speak of 'bishops' schools', of parish schools, in the sixth and seventh centuries, is to use the term in a very loose sense[122] (in the Roman world, where worship was performed in the language common to all members of society, and were education earned social respect, the Church was able to use secular channels of education).

Organized monasticism took shape in the West in the fifth century. In its early stages, there was little emphasis on learning; however, learning was to become the hallmark of communal living in the subsequent centuries, especially where the Rule of St Benedict was followed. Communal prayer, singing of the Psalter, reflection on the word of God—these regular occupations of monks required learning. The community provided the framework for the acquisition and the continuation of a learning which was completely Christian in orientation. In this restricted sense one can speak of 'monastic schools'. Book learning was geared to a specific end.

We shall finally look at some aspects of education towards literacy in the Frankish kingdom under the Carolingians and determine function as well as purpose.[123] It is important in this context to keep in mind that the Frankish realm, although comprising Romance-speaking peoples as a majority (especially when one includes, as must be done, the *regnum Langobardorum*), included a considerable portion of German-speaking peoples. And perhaps more important even than that was the fact that Charlemagne was German-speaking by upbringing.[124]

---

122 All the efforts of P. Riché, *Écoles et enseignement dans le haut moyen-age*, Paris 1979, have failed to provide a clear picture about the institutions associated with education. Perhaps the term 'schools' tends to be misleading by its modern connotations; see also notes 133ff below.

123 Surprisingly, McKitterick, ed., *Uses of literacy* does not contain an account of the times of Charlemagne and Louis the Pious, traditionally considered to be of exceptional importance, nor does McKitterick, *Carolingians and the written word* deal with these rulers specifically but with the Carolingian epoch in an undifferentiating manner. It is truly disarming to read the author's admission that 'I have only scraped the surface of this potentially rich lode, so that my comments perforce are of a preliminary kind', 227.

124 The extent to which Charlemagne himself mastered Latin is uncertain. I stick to my interpretation of *orare* in ch. 25 of Einhart's *Vita Karoli Magni* as first put forward in 'Sprachenpolitik', esp. 418f. It has not been taken up by Banniard, *Viva voce*, who, however, does not provide a convincing alternative.

For German-speaking people, learning to read and write in Latin meant acquiring a foreign language as well as the technical skills of the craft. Thus the barriers against literacy were higher; greater motivation was required here than in the Romania with its accessibility of Latin when read out aloud. This means that the educational reform brought about by Charlemagne from the last decade of the eighth century onwards necessitated a new approach. What in the Romance parts of the realm could indeed be viewed as a reform,[125] indicating that he considered standards to be too low, was, in the eastern part of the realm, more the implementation of an ambitious new policy.

In this context one thinks in the first place of the so-called Carolingian renaissance, which resulted in a more intensive cultivation of Latin literature, as a by-product of which more written documentation was produced in the administration of the kingdom and later the Empire. There is no modern treatment of the Carolingian reforms as a whole, but recent studies of particular aspects have provided enough material for discussion. More documentation has been preserved from the reigns of Charlemagne and Louis the Pious than from those of their predecessors.[126] This is a sign of increased resort to the written word. What needs to be investigated is the political context within which the educational reform of Charlemagne arose, how it was carried out, and who it was primarily aimed at. However, it must be admitted that it is very difficult to obtain a balanced picture of the place of written material in Carolingian society.[127]

Recently, it has been claimed (though not adequately documented) that literacy continued to be quite widespread among lay people in the Frankish kingdom. It can be stated as a fact that the one lay institution which continuously needed people who could read and write was the royal court, where written documents were produced.[128] However, we do not know very much about the *referendarii* and *cancellarii*, the notaries, and it is impossible to maintain categorically that they were laymen.

As regards the educational policy of the Carolingians, the available evidence

---

[125] McKitterick, *Carolingians and the written word*, in my view assumes too high a standard of written culture in the times before Charlemagne, see pp. 67f., above and my own 'qui scit scribere'.

[126] McKitterick, *Carolingians* maintains that, as far as literacy is concerned, 'there was no dramatic break between the Merovingian and Carolingian periods', 213; however, elsewhere she writes of a 'prodigious output of the written word at every level of Carolingian society', 3, and see 33, which appears as remarkable only when compared with a different situation earlier.

[127] McKitterick, *Carolingians*: 'the Franks had indeed passed from memory to written record', 134. In using the title of Michael Clanchy's book on England in the twelfth and thirteenth century and applying it to the Carolingians the author suggests similarities between the two societies which are far off the mark. See, further, chapter 6 below.

[128] Illmer, D., *Formen der Erziehung und Wissensvermittlung im frühen Mittelalter*, München 1971, esp. ch. 6.

can be interpreted in different ways. There is no reason to assume that the policy of Louis the Pious in this field was in line with that of his father. In several areas Louis made efforts to establish his own standards, to implement ideas other than those advocated by Charlemagne.

But what precisely did Charlemagne advocate? The information is rather scant. There is, in the first place, the circular letter called *Epistola de litteris colendis* addressed at the end of the eighth century to the secular and regular clergy of the Frankish realm[129] which outlines the ideas and motivations of Charlemagne in this respect. This royal letter was addressed to those circles that in the past had been obliged to foster reading and writing as part of their profession. According to Charlemagne, there was much that needed reform in that area.

There is, in addition, his project to establish schools.[130] The term 'school', apparently simple enough, is fraught with problems when one tries to determine what connotations it had at particular times. Perhaps it would be better to think in terms of 'schooling' in the sense of formal learning which can be done without a school as an institution.[131] Whatever the meaning of the term in a given context of the ninth century, it is nevertheless noticeable that the available texts imply the establishment of educational structures which had not existed in this form in the immediate past. This is indeed a sign of policy-making rather than continuing inherited institutions. The new departure in this field is what most interests us here.

The text of his legislation in this field, in the *Admonitio Generalis* of 789, looks deceptively straightforward:

c.72 Sacerdotes. . . . Et ut scolae legentium puerorum fiant.[132]

The concept of *schola* here is as vague as it was in Roman times and in the centuries that followed.[133]

129 Brunhölzl, F., 'Fuldensia', in *Historische Forschungen für W. Schlesinger*, Beumann, H., ed., Köln/Wien 1974, 536-47.
130 He was not the first medieval ruler to aim in this direction. Bede reports that King Sigibert of the East Angles in the early seventh century had planned the establishment of schools in his kingdom: 'qui dudum in Gallia, dum inimicitias Redualdi fugiens exularet, lavacrum baptismi percepit, et patriam reversus, ubi regno potitus est, mox ea, quae in Galliis bene disposita vidit, imitari cupiens, instituit scolam, in qua pueri litteris erudirentur'. *HE* III, xviii, p. 162; see Riché, *Education*, 362. It is not known how Bede came across this information; the political instability in Sigibert's kingdom, however, was highly unfavourable to such ambitious projects.
131 This has been argued recently by Akinnaso, F.N., 'Schooling, language and knowledge in literate and nonliterate societies', *CSSH* 34, 1992, 68-109.
132 MGH Capit. I, p. 60.
133 Hildebrandt, M. M., *The external school in Carolingian society*, Leyden 1992. In a capitulary of 825 Lothar aimed at establishing nine schools in Northern Italy. What these were like

It should be kept in mind that this is all that we have from Charlemagne about education. A recent detailed investigation of the 'external schools' in Carolingian society has come up with novel insights and new suggestions.[134] It has been shown that the legislation in the *Admonitio Generalis* did not envisage the schooling of lay people in and for lay society; it had to do with the education of the oblates of monasteries. Thus Charlemagne here was also concerned with the monasteries as centres responsible for furthering literacy in Latin. His enthusiasm was not sustained. It has been suggested that 'the emperor's monastic policy after 800 was one characterized by benign neglect'.[135]

It has been well said that 'Louis the Pious . . . inherited not only the policies of his father but also the results of those policies.'[136] As far as monasteries and education are concerned, he felt a need to implement a restrictive policy (one can see this in his legislation of 816 and 817). Take, for example, the brief and clear admonition:

> ut schola in monasterio non habeatur nisi eorum qui oblati sunt.[137]

This engimatic ruling could be read as meaning that monasteries were by that time 'schooling more people than oblates; however, the evidence for the existence of (external schools) is thin on the ground. Only St Gall can be considered as a possible candidate for such an 'external school.'[138]

It should be noted that Charlemagne referred to notaries as a matter of course.[139] It can indeed be argued that the huge empire he had cobbled together required, in order to function properly, a literate laity at least in the administrative sector. It is therefore necessary to have a closer look at this side of his policy. To what extent were his plans implemented?[140]

is unclear, only in one case is a school associated with one teacher, Dungal. MGH Capit. I, no. 163, p. 327. It is not known what became of his plans. There is no critical assessment of the concept of schools in this context in McKitterick, *Carolingians*, 220.

134 Hildebrandt, *The external school*.
135 Hildebrandt, 62.
136 Hildebrandt, 63.
137 C. v, *Synodi secundae Aquisgranensis decreta authentica*, Semmler, J., ed., *Corpus Consuetudinum Monasticarum*, Hallinger, K., ed., Siegburg 1963, 474. Cf. also Concilium Aquisgranense of 816, c. cxxxv: 'Ut erga pueros, qui nutriuntur vel erudiuntur in congregatione canonica, instantissima sit adhibenda custodia.' MGH Conc. II, 1, 413.
138 Hildebrandt, ch. 4.
139 Ganshof, F.L., 'Charlemagne et l'usage de l'écrit en matière administrative', *Le Moyen-Age* 57, 1951, 1-25 at 19, n. 62.
140 This has been discussed at length by McKitterick, R., *The Frankish Church and the Carolingian reforms, 789-895*, London 1977; the texts quoted below are not included in Riché, *Ecoles et enseignement*, where they would have belonged to the material gathered under Texts 11.

There are at least some indications that his plans as regards schools were put into effect. There is one relevant text from the German-speaking area, from the synod of Riesbach in 798:

> Episcopus autem unusquisque in civitate sua scolam constituat et sapientem doctorem, qui secundum traditionem Romanorum possit instruere et lectionibus vacare et inde debitum discere. . . .[141]

All the other evidence comes from the Romance part of the Frankish realm. Thus Theodulf, bishop of Orleans (c.760-821) decreed:

> Presbyteri per villas et vicos scolas habeant. Et si quilibet fidelium suos parvulos ad discendas litteras eis commendare vult, eos suscipere et docere non renuant.[142]

This is at once more general and more far-reaching than the rulings from Riesbach. Schooling was to be available in towns and villages. It was left to parents to decide whether or not to send their children to the priests for education.[143] There are other synodal decisions which refer to the subject in a variety of ways. One is, thus, not dealing with mechanical repetition, and this shows that there was indeed action taken by some bishops in this area.

Thus Riculf of Soissons (870-90) felt it necessary to spell out that girls should not be admitted at priests' schools under any circumstances, implying that the local clergy had not only done what had been decreed but cast the net of candidates more widely than Charlemagne had envisaged: 'puellas ad discendum cum scholariis suis in schola sua nequaquam recipiant'.[144] More references to lay children at schools in towns and villages would be needed before one could evaluate the success of Charlemagne's ambitious project; as it is, we have only some sparse evidence that the ideas spelled out in the *Admonitio* did not remain dead letters. In this poorly documented field we also

---

141 MGH Concilia II, 1, p. 199. This text was previously associated with the Synod of Neuching of 771 held under Duke Tassilo III. This legislation quoted as such was published in Scholinger, H., 'Synodus Nivhingana sub Tassilone Bojariae duce anno DCCLXXIIII celebrata, in Westenrieder, L.V., ed., *Beiträge zur Vaterländischen Historie, Geographie und Statistik*, München 1785, vol. I, 1-30, at 26, and referred to by Riché, *Education*, 497 and n. 573 who provided the reference to this publication. For the dating of the synod to 771 (instead of the traditional year 772) see Berg, H., 'Zur Organisation der bayerischen Kirche und zu den bayerischen Synoden des 8. Jahrhunderts', in Wolfram, H., Pohl, W., ed., *Typen der Ethnogenese unter besonderer Berücksichtigung der Bayern*, Wien 1990, 181-97.
142 1. Kapitular, MGH Cap. Episcoporum. I, 116.
143 For a discussion see Brommer, P., 'Die bischöfliche Gesetzgebung Theodulfs von Orleans', *ZRG kanon. Abteilung* 91, 1974, 1-120, esp. 57-62. Theodulf's decree reappears verbatim in the synodal legislation of Atto of Vercelli in the mid-tenth century, c. LXI, PL 134, 40.
144 PL 131, 21.

need to reach beyond the reign of Charlemagne to identify traces of schools which may have had their roots in his initiative.

The references to priests' schools from the mid-ninth century show that the envisaged attainments were modest: 'Si habeat [presbyter] clericum qui possit tenere scholam, aut legere epistolam, aut canere valeat, prout necessarium sibi videtur.'[145] Even zealous bishops had low expectations of educational standards at parish level.

Finally, it should be mentioned that in 829 the bishops urged Louis the Pious and Lothar 'morem paternum sequentes saltim in tribus congruentissimis imperii vestri locis scolae publicae ex vestra auctoritate fiant'.[146] This statement from the Council of Paris can be read as indicating that Charlemagne had brought about the establishment of *scolae publicae* (which are otherwise unattested) and that they had lapsed, most likely as a result of a lack of patronage. The bishops believed in their usefulness; hence their admonition to revive them.

It may be a coincidence of transmission, but there is no reference in the ninth century that such priests' schools for potential clerics or for lay children were available in the German-speaking parts of the Frankish realm. There, the barriers against education in Latin were certainly higher than in the Romance-speaking lands: Latin was a truly foreign language.

There is more information from the early ninth century about the way that material written in Latin, communicated to speakers of Romance, was to be dealt with. A famous and often quoted decree of the reform synod of Tours of 813 ruled:

> *c*.17   ut quilibet episcopus habeat omelias continentes necessarias ammonitiones . . . et ut easdem omelias quisque aperte transferre studeat in rusticam Romanam linguam aut Thiotiscam, quo facilius cuncti possint intellegere quae dicuntur.[147]

While translation from Latin into German was obviously a necessity if the audience was German-speaking, the case is less clear for speakers of Romance. Here the words *aperte, facilius* and *cuncti*, when taken to apply to speakers of Romance, suggest that Latin would have been accessible to some when read out, even though with difficulty.

---

145 Hincmar of Rheims, c. xi, PL 125, 779; cf. Herard of Tours c. xvii: 'ut scholas presbyteri pro posse habeant et libros emendatos', PL 121, col. 765.
146 MGH Capit. II, 37; also MGH Conc. II, 2, p. 675.
147 MGH Conc., II, 1, 288. See Richter, 'A quelle époque a-t-on cessé'; and cf. Uytfanghe, M.v., 'Le latin des hagiographes mérowingiens et la protohistoire du français', I, 288, *Romanica Gandensia* 16, 1976, 5-89, esp. 54ff, Banniard, *Viva Voce*, 410f.

There is another text with a similar message but it is hardly ever quoted because it comes from Raetia, a Romanophone area that is not normally dealt with in this context. In the early ninth century, Bishop Remedius of Chur, who drew up additional rules to the *Lex Romana Curiensis*, supplemented these with the following advice:

> Statuimus enim, ut omnis presbiter habeat brevem istum semper haput se, et in unoquoque mense duas vices legat eum coram omni populo et explanet eum illis, que illi bene possint intellegere, unde se debeant emendare vel custodire.[148]

The crucial terms in this text are *legere* and *explanare*. In combination these would ensure that people would understand material formulated in Latin when read out to them, even the fine details (as necessary because the material concerned them in their daily lives).

So, here we have further cases where people who were illiterate were on that account not necessarily excluded from the products of written culture—for two reasons: Latin was still intelligible to them (though some fine points might pass them by); secondly, reading aloud as a general phenomenon facilitated the spread of written material.

The way in which Charlemagne catered for the needs of his German-speaking subjects comes into focus in some places where it is laid down that material written in Latin should be read to the people concerned and translated. *Tradere* is the term which occurs in this context several times, even where the recipients of the material were regular clerics whom one would suspect to be fairly familiar with Latin. Charlemagne seems to have been a realist at least in this field. It is this activity which I consider as a systematic *Sprachenpolitik*.[149]

We should take note of the fact, brought out clearly in these texts, that communication of material written in Latin was envisaged as taking place orally, and that it was often considered advisable that this be accompanied by explanation, elucidation, clarification. In this respect it may be said that the metaphor of the 'dead letter' is particularly appropriate even in the period of the Carolingian reform.

So far we have dealt only with material written in Latin. As a by-product of the spread of Christianity in the area east of the Rhine, the German language began to be used in written form from the mid-eighth century onwards. By the end of the century, it was used for translations from Latin as well as for original material. It can be said that by then the technical preconditions for

---

148 MGH LL V, 444. For a better edition see Meyer-Marthaler, E., ed., *Lex Romana Curiensis*, 649. On this material see further ead., 'Die Gesetze des Bischofs Remedius von Chur', *Zeitschrift für Schweizerische Kirchengeschichte* 44, 1950, 81-110, 161-88.
149 See 'Sprachenpolitik' esp. 424ff.

writing German without major difficulty had been mastered. Given what we have said about the spread of written material through its being read out loud, this could have been a very useful cultural vehicle.

It has often been suggested, and now it has been thoroughly presented by Michel Banniard, that the transition from Latin to Romance in France was brought about in a very short period in the closing years of the eighth century. Texts written in French become available from the ninth century onwards.

Thus the Carolingian period ushered in the epoch of new written vernaculars in continental Europe. However, when one considers the corpus of available material in Old French and Old High German (down to the eleventh century) it certainly is remarkable how small it is. One must of course reckon with losses on an incalculable scale, but the same applies when one considers Anglo-Saxon England or early medieval Ireland, both of which have much more material to offer.

In the Carolingian realm there was no rush to use the newly available means of writing the vernacular. In studying what has survived, one needs to bear in mind the type of public for whose benefit it was produced. One should not lose sight of the fact that these texts were not primarily (if at all) for private reading but as an aid to oral performance. It would take us too far from our theme to investigate this subject; suffice it is to say that only very little vernacular literature is of a kind that can be even remotely associated with the oral tradition such as the *Hildebrandslied*.[150] The new technology of writing the vernacular obviously did not sweep the ground and replace traditional ways of transmitting cultural values. This is an instance of the ambivalence of the Carolingian achievements which has to date never really been made the subject of study. Looking at what was produced in the period, particularly what was produced in Latin, one tends to lose sight of what could have been written but was not. This category of material is the subject of later chapters.

It is exceedingly difficult to get an adequate perspective of the changes in education of the laity in the Romance and the German-speaking parts of the Frankish realm under Charlemagne. One needs, I think, to take a medium-term view of Charlemagne's intentions, their implementation and their repercussions. Thus one reason why his empire failed to prove politically viable may be linked with the issue of lay literacy. There were indeed apparently more literate laymen in his circle than those of his predecessors, and he attempted, with their help, to govern by way of the written word (as well as by other methods), but the project appears to have been too ambitious.[151] According to one of these educated laymen, Einhart, Charlemagne felt himself drawn to

---

150 See further, chapter 10.
151 See now Nelson, J., 'Literacy in Carolingian government', in McKitterick, R., ed., *Uses of literacy*, 258-96, who, however, deals more with the later period.

Literacy

learning, though the manner in which Einhart deals with the subject is not without its ambiguity.[152]

On the basis of the available written documents from the Carolingian period, it has been claimed that this was 'a society to which the written word was central'.[153] This statement can hardly be upheld in view of what can be known about the oral culture of the Carolingians.[154]

---

[152] Richter, 'Sprachenpolitik', 422-24.
[153] McKitterick, *Carolingians* 273.
[154] See chapter 6.

PART II
APPROACHES TO ORAL CULTURE

4

APPROACHES TO MEDIEVAL ORAL CULTURE

'Quod loquimur transit, quod scribimus permanet.' These words of Gregory the Great[1] are either trivial or misleading. On the assumption that the former was not intended, Gregory's statement reveals the attitude of somebody who sees writing as the only possible form of cultural transmission.[2] As a Roman and as a man of the Church, Gregory was doubly conditioned to such an attitude. His view would appear to be shared in our own culture, which is built firmly on writing.[3] However, many societies today do not, and many more in the past did not have writing, or had it only in a limited form, and yet managed to keep and transmit traditions. Indeed this was the situation of mankind for most of its existence. One could thus turn Gregory's statement into its negative and maintain that 'non omne quod loquitur transit, non omne quod scribitur permanet'. This study is concerned above all with the first half of that statement.

In the previous chapter we put forward some ideas about literacy in the environment of the early medieval West; we must now confront the concept of orality. This is arguably as difficult a task, simply because our own culture is so steeped in the civilization of the written word that orality is largely seen

---

1 *Moralia in Iob* XXXIII, PL 76, 672; see also *Moralia in Iob* XI, 45 and *Enarrationes in Psalmos* XLIV, 6.
2 The same attitude is expressed by Isidore of Seville in writing about 'history': 'Haec disciplina ad grammaticam pertinet, quia quidquid dignum memoria est, litteris mandatur', *Etymologiae* I, xli, PL 82, 122. It is again referred to in quite some detail by John of Salisbury in the twelfth century in the prologue to his Policraticus. It is epitomized by the phrase: 'Eadem est asini et cuiusvis imperatoris post modicum tempus gloria, nisi quatenus memoria alterutrius scriptorum beneficio prorogatur.' *Ioannis Saresberiensis episcopi Policratici sive de nugis curialium et vestigiis philosophorum libri VIII*, Webb, C.C. I, ed., London 1909, vol. I, 13.
3 It has been well said that it is 'characteristic of a literate culture that if it is ever confronted with the habit-patterns of a non-literate culture, it tends to underestimate their efficiency', Havelock, *Preface to Plato*, 139.

as auxiliary and marginal or trivial compared to reliable, palpable written products. Great efforts are required to open oneself to the possibilities and potential of oral culture, which are far less obvious than its weakness and its disadvantages. This applied no less to the literate people of the Middle Ages than to modern Western man.

Thus we find in the twelfth century an apologia for resorting to information transmitted for more than a generation in oral form yet still regarded as valuable. This attitude is articulated in the prologue to the *Historia Tornacensis* which maintains: 'neque enim penitus a nobis discredenda sunt que maiores nostri sive antiquiores oculis perspecta vel a suis predecessoribus accepta memoria tenere potuerunt'.[4]

In this chapter we shall be dealing with approaches to the study of the culture of the early medieval barbarians. Their most salient feature was that they did not resort to writing for transmission and preservation of their culture. Societies characterized by oral culture may be called non-literate rather than, as is more usually the case, pre-literate.[5] It is important to approach non-literate cultures positively when examining how they functioned without resort to writing; their lack of literacy is not a defect and they do have something to teach us. There is no evidence that literacy is a precondition for a rich life of individuals or of societies. Non-literacy simply means the usage of an 'oral and nonverbal rather than literary means by which to bear culture'.[6]

There is to date no study of oral culture in the medieval West even though most people are aware that an oral culture predominated in the Middle Ages.[7] Presumably the attitude of Gregory the Great—that because of the transitory nature of the spoken word the oral tradition simply cannot be studied—is shared by modern scholars of the Middle Ages.

To study oral culture of the past it is first necessary to open oneself to what oral tradition is all about. It is, above all, a form of culture alien to our own and this 'otherness' needs to be treated sensitively. While the spoken word is at the centre of oral tradition and as such is, of course, transitory, it forms part of a greater whole; it is process as well as product. The products are oral messages based on previous oral messages, at least one generation old.[8]

4 MGH SS XIV, 327. The author further maintains that 'possunt (ea) tamen ... nichilominus memoria conservari'. Ibid.
5 This point is made emphatically by Gill, *Beyond 'the primitive'*, esp. 6f. See also Ong, W.J., *Orality and literacy: the technologizing of the word*, London and New York 1982, 13f. For the more traditional attitude, see e.g. Goody, *The domestication of the savage mind*, esp. 19ff.
6 Gill, 30.
7 Vollrath, H., 'Das Mittelalter in der Typik oraler Gesellschaften', *HZ* 233, 1981, 571-94 discusses oral societies, but does not give any concrete manifestations of them in the Middle Ages.
8 Vansina, J., *Oral tradition as history*, London 1985, 3; cf. also 29.

It is important to note that oral tradition is more than the words that make up the oral messages. Also, one needs to distinguish casual, ephemeral oral communication in daily transactions from significant communication, which is what the oral tradition represents.[9] As will be seen, different registers of language are used for these different kinds of oral communication.

The characteristic feature of any oral culture inevitably means that no documentary evidence is available. 'One must reconstruct it by use of inference, intuition and even imagination, and draw on what seem to be principles of human psychology and behaviour. With the help of these one can postulate a situation in which orally preserved communication was operating at three levels or in three different areas: 1. the area of current legal and political transactions, the issuance of directives which would accumulate as precedents; 2. the continual retelling of the tribal history, the tale of the ancestors and their role as models for the present; 3. the continual indoctrination of the young in both tale and precedent through recital.'[10]

Numerous accounts of oral societies are available, for it is the occupation of the modern anthropologist to study such societies and to report on what they find. We shall see to what extent their insights can be of help here. I shall discuss some of the features of the work of modern anthropologists as they appear relevant to a historian. I hope to indicate the degree to which their research results can widen our grasp of oral traditions, and then I shall go on to discuss in what way some sort of anthropological approach to the early medieval barbarians is possible, what the difficulties and the gains are.

In the course of writing this book my views about oral culture have changed substantially. As a medievalist I started out with a vague notion of orality having to do with heroic poetry, so I read widely in that area. However, I came to realize that I had become trapped in a circular movement. Most scholars dealing with heroic poetry treated it (rightly, as I later discovered), as texts, as literature, very rarely taking account of a possible oral background.[11] Eventually I decided that a more fruitful approach would be to expose myself, albeit at second hand, to the study of non-literate cultures.

I have no personal experience of non-literate cultures of the kind studied by anthropologists, and this is undoubtedly a handicap. However, I have benefited greatly from familiarity with Irish traditional music. In this field I have learned much about audience expectation and appreciation as well as repertoire and the musicians' indebtedness to the tradition which they see themselves as part of and feel they have a duty to maintain at the highest possible standard.

9 Cf. Havelock, *Preface to Plato*, 134.
10 Cf. Havelock, *Preface to Plato*, 120f.
11 For this see chapter 10.

However, my greatest gain has been the revision of my own preconceptions (tacit assumptions, for the most part) concerning barbarians or primitives, in short, non-literate societies. Having been conditioned along Eurocentric lines that 'European civilization' (characterized by a culture based on writing) is clearly superior to other cultures, I have come to acquire profound respect and admiration for these other cultures, for the degrees of complexity and sophistication evidenced in them, for their sense of identity, purpose and responsibility as well as humaneness. It was enriching to learn that 'literacy is not a civilizing force in itself'.[12] In the light of this the present study should not be taken as a pursuit of a romantic illusion[13] but rather as an effort to extricate ourselves, to some extent at any rate, from the self-celebrating tendencies of our early medieval sources.

It is with this new awareness—that the barbarians of the early Middle Ages should be approached by attempting to do justice to them on their own terms, not primarily as culturally inferior to either Romanitas or Christianitas and being gradually civilized, but rather as encountering Romanitas and Christianitas as communities in their own right, with their own ethics and traditions which had served them well and had made them as they were—that we may begin.

ANTHROPOLOGY

'Historians can benefit from the insights and experiences of anthropological research . . . they can learn a great deal about the interpretative benefits that come from looking at thought-patterns in the context of the total social, cultural and economic background of the times.'[14]

Anthropology is concerned mainly with the study of man living in societies remote from Western society, uninfluenced by it and thereby providing alternatives to Western ways of life. Many societies studied by anthropologists this century have since disappeared, and the reserve of societies available for study is close to exhaustion.

Over the course of this century anthropologists have taken various approaches to remote societies; one of the attractions of the subject to the outsider is its highly developed sense of reflection on the nature and difficulties

---

12 Clanchy, M.T., *From memory to written record. England 1066-1307*, London 1979, 7. Finnegan, likewise alludes to the widespread attitude that 'the presence or absence of literacy is of absolutely crucial significance for the quality of thought in a given culture', 'Literacy versus non-literacy: The great divide? Some comments on the significance of "literature" in non-literate cultures', 112.

13 The utmost importance of truth for the maintenance of the fabric of a religiously divided community has been well described by Glassie, H., *Passing the time. Folklore and history of an Ulster community*, Dublin 1982, esp. 57f., 144f.

14 Finnegan and Horton, *Modes of thought*, 75.

of the subject. Where the term 'primitive' is used in association with these societies, it acquires a quality of its own and has no pejorative associations.

Anthropology is in a profound way a discipline engaged in cross-cultural study.[15] This is its intrinsic attraction, but here also lie its snares. It has been called a typically Eurocentric exercise.[16] However, the individual anthropologist always brings to the object of his studies more than a European cultural background more or less common to all. His personality and his attitude towards his own cultural background are bound to leave their mark on his work. In some studies it is possible to detect the anthropologist's own national characteristics.[17]

The anthropologist's work may be divided into two main activities: field work on the one hand, and the presentation of his findings on the other. These two activities may be looked at separately.

One can work on the assumption that the anthropologist is on the whole empathetic towards the society which he is studying. 'To reach out into otherness and know, to reach out into otherness and embrace—these are the mainsprings of anthropology.'[18] The field worker has to immerse himself in a culture that is profoundly alien to him.[19] It is his task to acquire an 'exceedingly extended acquaintance with extremely small matters'.[20] He seeks to understand how the society he is studying is made up, how it works. In other words, he is interested less in development and history than in structures.

Collecting material and information, field work *par excellence*, 'reaching out, embracing', actively involves the natives as well. The field worker is expected to do everything he can to meet these peoples on their own terms.[21] In addition to observing what presents itself to him, the field worker can ask what the natives think of what they are doing. More than that: in these societies oral tradition is of paramount importance, and acquaintance with oral tradition is essential to the anthropologist's work. In other words, in addition to assessing how his subjects appear to him he wants to know how they see themselves,

---

15 See Hsu, F.L.K., 'Rethinking the concept "primitive"', *Current Anthropology* 5, 1964, 169-78, here 175b. Kohl, K.H., *Exotik als Beruf*, Wiesbaden 1979, 21.
16 Kohl, K.H., 'Abwehr und Verlangen. Das Problem des Eurozentrismus und die Geschichte der Ethnologie', in id. ed., *Abwehr und Verlangen*, Frankfurt 1987, 141.
17 Geertz, C., *Works and lives. The anthropologist as author*, Stanford 1988.
18 Burridge, K., *Encountering aborigines. A case study: anthropology and the Australian aboriginal*, New York 1973, 84 and see ibid., 150 'pushing ourselves into otherness and incorporating otherness into ourselves, are the very stuff of anthropology'.
19 'An anthropologist's first field research should bring him into close contact with a system of values so unlike his own that it gives him a mental and emotional jolt: it should force him to take a new look at assumptions that he formerly regarded as natural and inevitable', Berndt, C.H., and Berndt, R.M., *The barbarians*, Harmondsworth 1973, 37.
20 Geertz, *The interpretation of cultures*, New York 1973, 21.
21 Gill, *Beyond the primitive*, 4.

what they think, what they make of their place in the world. Their ontology is an essential aspect of anthropology.

This means that it is essential for the researcher to be acquainted with the language of the people he is studying. It has long been seen in these terms;[22] yet that has not always been the case. Earlier this century visitors to remote societies often resorted to interpreters from within the societies they were studying. Frequently these interpreters had an insufficient command of the language of the outsider, and thus information about the society under investigation was often transmitted in crude distortions. This is one reason why remote people were initially and for a long time considered primitive and simple.

The need for a thorough acquaintance with the language of the natives was felt first and most strongly by Christian missionaries. Anthropologists eventually benefitted from this. A good case in point is T.G.H. Strehlow, the son of the missionary Carl Strehlow, who grew up among the Aranda in Australia and became thoroughly acquainted with their language. In due course he came to collect their traditions, wrote a grammar of their language and made their culture accessible to the outside world. The justification for his impassioned plea to anthropologists that they acquire languages[23] is fully demonstrated by his *oeuvre*. Exposing oneself to the language of the natives very soon shows that different languages entail different concepts. The anthropologist is not able to do full justice in his own language to the language of the natives.[24] They need to be appreciated on their own terms, in the literal sense of that phrase. When this is attempted, one gets a completely new idea of what language can do, what non-literate culture can achieve. A good example is the Aranda language of the Australian aborigines which, according to Strehlow, could express no less that 95 tense forms in the verb.[25] This is evidence of the great treasure which language represents to the natives; it makes possible the expression of extremely complex phenomena. However inadequately one may become acquainted with the culture of non-literate peoples, it can be a humbling but also deeply enriching experience.[26]

The remote peoples studied by anthropologists are generally self-sufficient, existing in isolation. This means that they have developed forms of social life

22 Kohl, *Exotik*, pointing already back to Boas.
23 Strehlow, T.G.H., 'Anthropology and the study of languages' (a lecture), Adelaide 1947.
24 See Gellner, E., 'Concepts and society', in *Transactions of the fifth world congress of sociology* vol. 1, Louvain 1962, 153-83: 'the anthropologist's language has its own way of handling the world, which may not be those of the native language studied, and which consequently are liable to distort that which is being translated', 159.
25 Strehlow lecture 1947, 24.
26 'It is very hard to believe that people very different from us can really have anything approaching the depth of understanding or grace of expression that we know in our own society and literature', Finnegan, *Modes of thought*, 142.

Approaches to medieval oral culture 87

that worked, that were most suitable for their environment.[27] Their way of life, their culture was in keeping with their needs and made them into what they were.[28] This caused them to have a deep sense of responsibility for their world and their environment.[29]

Anthropologists have succeeded, more than once, in giving their readers a sense of 'having been there'.[30] It is their declared aim 'to reduce the puzzlement to which unfamiliar acts emerging out of unknown backgrounds naturally give rise'.[31] However, one has to keep in mind that the presentation of the culture studied by the anthropologist is ultimately his own construct, his perception of how the world of the natives is ordered.[32] It must be taken as such. Geertz mentions that 'the inadequacy of words to experience, and their tendency to lead off only into other words . . . is a rather new discovery so far as ethnographers are concerned.'[33]

Here it is important to mention two technical points relating to field work: one is that the anthropologist normally works on his own; this has the effect of deepening his perception of the culture under examination.[34] The other point is that his fieldwork is unique and unrepeatable.[35] This has also a historical dimension to it: a number of societies studied by anthropologists no longer exist.

I have found accounts about the Australian aborigines particularly helpful. In

27 'Primitive man's view of nature is neither merely theoretical nor merely practical; it is sympathetic', Cassirer, E., *An essay on man. Introduction to a philosophy of human culture*, New Haven and London 1944, repr. 1972, 82.
28 'The object of anthropological inquiries are precisely human groups persisting over time. Their very persistence entails that they are reasonably viable', Gellner, 'Concepts and society', 172. Horton gives a different slant when writing about small-scale traditional African communities: 'they have achieved equilibrium with their diseases', 'African traditional thought and Western Science', *Africa* 37, 1967, 50-71, at 56.
29 Eliade, M., *Australian religions. An introduction*, Ithaca and London 1973, 53, 55, 62, 66.
30 Geertz, *Works and lives*, 16.
31 Geertz, *Interpretation*, 16.
32 Geertz, *Works and lives*, 1988, 'the inescapable fact that all ethnographical descriptions are homemade, that they are the describer's descriptions, not those of the described', 145f.
33 Geertz, *Works and Lives*, 138. Similar ideas are expressed by Turner, D., *Life before Genesis. A conclusion. An understanding of the significance of Australian aboriginal culture*, 2nd ed., New York 1987, 105: 'In describing the terms of this theory I have been very careful in my choice of words. But it is inevitable that ambiguities should remain. This is partly due to the nature of the reality at issue. But it is also because conventional English is inadequate to convey my meaning, particularly the meaning of the terms of the dialect of pluralism. In this domain, English usages are particularly impoverished.'
34 This is one of the main themes of Geertz, *Works and lives*. It is at variance with the requirement that 'ethnographers need to convince us . . . that had we been there we should have seen what they saw, felt what they felt, concluded what they concluded.', ibid., 16.
35 This point has been made by Kohl, *Exotik*, 1979, xi.

addition, I have read about traditional African societies. It has emerged that in essential points these different societies have important features in common that are factors of their common non-literate backgrounds. The single most important feature is the value assigned to language, to speech, to words, to oral tradition.[36]

In Australia one encounters a culture[37] that persisted over thousands of years without visibly affecting its environment. Perhaps the aborigines are too different from us to understand them fully,[38] but reading about them has given me a new understanding of what language can achieve, what non-literate culture can entail, how it relates to the people who possess of it.[39]

In the belief that their forms of life were of a kind which had always existed, these peoples looked to their past for orientation; they had a sense of living in harmony with the past, of there being no cultural break between present and past. One of the preconditions for such attitude is the frequent recalling of the past as being still valid for the present. This normally takes place through their oral culture.

Dreamtime (or The Dreaming) is the English term commonly used to refer to how the aborigines conceive of a sacred heroic age when man and nature came to be as they are. 'It was and is everywhen.'[40] 'Man, society and nature, and past, present and future, are at one together within a unitary system. Dreaming is a cosmogony, an account of the begetting of the universe, a story about creation.'[41] The Dreaming entails the ethical precepts which

36 Horton, R., 'The Romantic illusion: Roger Bastide on Africa and the West', *Odu* N.S. 3, 1970, 87-115, 'African cultures are founded on an immense confidence in the power of ordinary, literal speech ... the very luxuriance of African symbolism is a product of the general confidence in the power of such speech', 91.
37 'Within Australia it is possible to distinguish over 200 languages and several varieties of culture, yet in the wider context it is the homogeneity of language and culture that becomes significant', Burridge, K. *Encountering aborigines. A case study. Anthropology and the Australian aboriginal*, New York 1973, 64.
38 'Perhaps the gap between they and us—leading such different lives—is too wide to bridge', Burridge, 139.
39 I have read in detail about the Aranda, the Pintupi, the Murinbata and the aborigines in the Groote Eylandt area (D.H. Turner).
40 Stanner, W.E.H., 'The Dreaming', in Hungerford, T.R.G., ed., *Australian signposts*, Melbourne 1956, 51-65, at 52. Also Eliade, *Australian religions*, 1ff; Myers, F.R., *Pintupi country, Pintupi self. Sentiment, place and politics among Western Desert aborigines*, Berkeley 1986, this edition 1991, 51, 219, 297. For a devastating critique of the concept see Wolfe, P., 'On being woken up: the Dreamtime in anthropology and in Australian settler culture', *CSSH* 33, 1991, 197-224. While I am in no position to decide to what extent the views proposed here are appropriate, for me the cultural manifestations of it are more important than the blanket term used for it. In any case, Wolfe's discussion epitomizes the fundamental problem of cross-cultural studies and the inadequacy of the anthropologist's language to do justice to the culture under investigation.
41 Stanner, 'The Dreaming', 54.

everyone is meant to live up to. 'Only that which was effected *in illo tempore* is real, meaningful, exemplary, and of inexhaustible creativity.'[42]

This creates a fundamental sense of continuity. It has been well formulated that the aborigines 'are not simply a people "without a history", they are a people who have been able, in some sense, to defeat history, to become ahistorical in mood, outlook and life.'[43] The task is to ensure the continuity of their way of life, its balance. Everybody is required to take part in this, everybody lives continuity. This gives the members of the community their sense of purpose and their sense of responsibility. It gives them shared values, and their identity. It is extremely difficult to get a proper grasp of the demands of the community on the individual against the possibilities of establishing one's individuality within the community.[44] The weight of the past lies very heavily on the present of aboriginal life.[45] They bow to it as an unalterable fact: 'the rituals of sorrow, their fortitude in pain, and their undemonstrative sadness seem to imply a reconciliation with the terms of life.'[46] 'The Murinbata, like all the aborigines, gave the impression of having stopped short of, or gone beyond, a quarrel with the terms of life.'[47]

Shared values do not imply that the individual is submerged in the group.[48] On the contrary, in the course of life the individual's responsibilities evolve as the knowledge about The Dreaming deepens. Among the Pintupi, there is a strongly developed sense of personal dignity and freedom, as well as an emphasis on consideration for others.[49] Indeed, one becomes complete and autonomous only through sustaining relations with others.[50] There is no great respect for material goods; instead, pronounced asceticism is highly valued.[51]

However, it would be wrong to imagine such a way of life to be bereft of its lighter sides[52] even where there may be a deeply resigned acceptance of life

---

42 Eliade, *Australian religions*, 40.
43 Stanner, 'The Dreaming', 62.
44 'In the tribal community you must accept the prevailing norms of conduct and manner of life, in the last resort for want of alternatives.' Fortes, M., 'Culture contact as a dynamic process. An investigation in the Northern territories of the Gold Coast', *Africa* 9, 1936, 24-55, at 51. Against this must be balanced the high esteem extended to prowess in individuals.
45 Stanner, W.E.H., *On Aboriginal religion* (Oceania Monograph 11), Sydney 1966, 83.
46 Stanner, 'The Dreaming', 61.
47 Stanner, *On Aboriginal religion*, 170.
48 Aboriginal life was and is intensely personal: Burridge, 81.
49 Myers, *Pintupi*, 18, 159, 161, 257.
50 Myers, *Pintupi*, 110.
51 Turner, D.H., personal communication. See also id., *Tradition and transformation. A study of aborigines in the Groote Eylandt area, northern Australia* (Australian Aboriginal Studies no. 53), Canberra 1974, esp. 162-65.
52 Horton, R., trained as a psychologist before he turned to social anthropology (see *Man* 63.6, p. 8), reflecting on why he chooses to live in a still heavily traditional Africa confesses

as it is. There is every indication that the enactment of song, dance and ritual gives them great pleasure as well as being performed with passion.

It is in the light of these considerations that the oral culture must now be faced squarely. It is what holds these societies together in this life and ties them to their past. It is of central importance, it is the epitome of their culture. It has been called 'the product of a continuous art of making the past consistent with an idealized present'.[53] It is common property and everybody's responsibility. As such it is woven into the very existence of each individual. Oral traditions are normally very extensive, complex in form, and sophisticated and imaginative in thought, content and style.[54]

It is of central importance, and very widely attested, that oral tradition is much more than spoken words. It has been well said that 'sound is a primary medium of the arts and religions of nonliterate cultures'.[55] The oral tradition is sung or chanted, and it is acted; it is a public affair and as such involves many people. There is almost universal consensus that one should think of oral tradition in terms of performace. This conjures up ideas of performers and appreciative audience, a dynamic relationship between them, sound and silences, music, and gestures. The oral tradition in action is an emotive affair; it answers the spiritual needs of the participants.

In view of the central importance of oral tradition among the non-literate peoples it is not surprising to find that the performance is carried out with enthusiasm and devotion. Stanner speaks of the 'aboriginal genius for music, song, mime and dance (which) is applied with skill and passion'; the Murinbata 'celebrate . . . by a rite containing all the beauty of song, mime, dance and art of which men are capable'.[56] Quite appropriately the oral tradition is considered as man's most precious possession, which to cultivate, to treasure, is their greatest task in life.[57]

From the above it is evident that 'oral tradition has to be experienced as performance to be properly evaluated'.[58] While word and sound are of central importance,[59] they are embedded in a wider communal experience. They

    that he appreciates 'an intensely poetic quality in everyday life and thought, a vivid enjoyment of the passing moment.' 'African traditional thought and Western science', *Africa* 37, 1967, 50-71, 155-87, at 179.
53 Stanner, *On Aboriginal religion*, 140.
54 Gill, 69.
55 Gill, 30.
56 Stanner, *On Aboriginal religion*, 20, 56.
57 Stanner, *On Aboriginal religion*, 85 claims, different from Strehlow, that 'the traditions themselves are a continuous inspiration.' Turner, D.H., reports that the aborigines of Groote Eylandt 'sang him back' when they needed his help (personal communication).
58 Gill, 65.
59 'No man can make contact with reality save through a screen of words. Hence no man can escape to see a unique and intimate link between works and things.' Horton, 'African traditional thought', 159.

articulate shared values here and now, which are reinforced with every performance; they also validate the present by reference to the past, and in this they establish a close link with the life and deeds of the ancestors who were guided by the same principles.

I shall now briefly summarize three different accounts of the manifestation of oral traditions, from twentieth-century Australia, Africa and Ireland. These accounts were written without knowledge of each other. Thus where they overlap one detects a common basis due to the nature of the institutions.

Strehlow *Songs of Central Australia* by T.G.H. Strehlow was published in 1971. It is based on field work carried out between 1932 and 1955 in the course of which Strehlow collected 4270 aboriginal songs. By the time the book appeared the oral culture which is its subject had disappeared along with the aboriginal religion.

The songs, traditional narrative poems, were only part of the oral tradition of the Western Aranda people. Strehlow briefly refers to other parts of that tradition but then concentrates on the songs that are the domain of men. Each song is associated with a particular ceremonial centre and with mythical supernatural beings or groups of totemic ancestors. A song in this culture is taken to mean the complete set of verses associated with a given ceremonial centre.

The song forms the central part of a magic ritual. It is closely integrated in the beliefs and is considered to have been inherited from the totemic ancestors. The songs are associated with individuals or small groups of men; they are regarded as private property, not that of the whole tribe. These songs do not use everyday language of conversation; they are part of ritual and show great artistry in composition, exploiting Aranda to the fullest. 'It is a mould in which the untidy scrap material of everyday speech is melted and reshaped' (19).

The songs discussed and reproduced (with musical notation) in this book were the property of the fully-initiated males of the various totemic clans; they were the highest form of poetic art to be achieved among the Aranda. They consist of an unfixed number of verses, each consisting of two lines. The songs were chanted to strong rhythmic measures which made it impossible to retain the normal speech accent of the words. In fact, singing/chanting and instrumental music provide two types of rhythm simultaneously, and the effect on the singer is one of frenzied excitement and fierce exultation. The songs show elaborate structures which fully tax the intelligence of the initiated native.

Each verse of any song is self-contained. The couplet is a structure of the utmost simplicity. It often happens that the second line repeats, with only minimal variation, the message contained in the first line. Each verse may be sung more than once during the ritual. At its best it is a diction of unhurried and measured dignity. The songs were transmitted without the slightest change from generation to generation; as part of the magic ritual, they were scrupulously memorized.

The language of the songs was Aranda, but of a special register. Taken by themselves, the songs would often not be understood by the uninitiated. In fact, there were oral prose explanations attached to individual songs.

The songs contained part of the myth of the Aranda, and in this function they were regarded as historical, religious and also quasi-legal documents, giving a minute account of everything done by the totemic ancestors. They provided glimpses of eternal and unalterable truths. This poetry, in the service of religion, acquired over years, was the greatest treasure an Aranda native could possess (243) and carried supreme social prestige (677). 'Its fullest knowledge and appreciation is the privilege of that section of the fully-initiated men who have toiled hard to learn the sacred songs; who have given liberally of their time, labour and blood during the performance of the sacred ceremonies; and who have been most obedient and generous to the old guardians of the sacred tribal lore' (207-208).

So much for the function of these songs. It is necessary to retain the high quality of the verses as pure poetry in its own right which was uplifting. Characteristic of this poetry is the ever-changing rhythms, the sense of word-weaving into new and stimulating verse patterns, venerability of the archaic diction and of terms rich in legendary association (246).

Finally, as 'legal documents' covering all aspects of the Aranda world, these songs not only combined language, music and movement, but they were also integrated in the physical environment. 'It is this harmony of the story and song with the environment that makes the native sacred traditions so moving. I have always admired the artistic sensitivity of our natives in fitting their myths and songs so splendidly into the geography of their settings that they came to reflect the general mood of the landscape' (674).

Okpewho And what about the performers of these songs? One work, Isidore Okpewho, *The epic in Africa* (1979), deals with the oral tradition in sub-Saharan Africa, the Congo-Niger area. It is based on about a dozen edited epic tales which are regarded as representative of that part of Africa. Those who perform the epic tales are referred to generally as bards; the more common term *griot* is rarely used by Okpewho.

Although there is some connexion between the epic tale and religion, in this account the secular dimension is given more prominence. Artistic playfulness and entertainment are the dominating features here.

The tale is acted out by the bard; the realistic nature of the performance is emphasized by the author. He speaks of the tremendous closeness and empathy which the traditional artist feels with his subject, especially with the hero. The epic is normally built around a kernel of fact, the preservation of which is one of the functions of the tradition; but the fact takes second place, as it were, to the form in which it is cast. Still, there are general ideals considered worth keeping alive. Thus the bard is the imaginative trustee of historic truth. For him, the challenge consists in maintaining general respect for the tradition while at the same time giving vent to the dynamic, creative temper that must be a prominent feature of a successful performance. In each performance the artist handles tradition and its values and in doing so gives it renewed relevance and fresh meaning.

One of the most important features of this study is the analysis of the oral epic within the context of the process during which it is created. Special skill is required to do that, although in the area investigated here the performer rarely lives by his art. Even at court a bard could be a multi-purpose palace-hand. Still, the bards are proud of their skills and boastful of their merits. The creative power which they have is often attributed to divine sources.

Performed at night, the epic tales are well known to their audience. The excellence of a song is not determined by a single performance. In a way, the process of creation is more important than the finished product, the means more important than the end. Not surprisingly, each performance is not a smooth, mellifluous entity.

Field work has made it clear that extra-verbal elements are of crucial importance to a successful performance. 'Every muscle of face and body spoke, a swift gesture often supplying the place of a whole sentence' (52). In addition to often wild gesticulation, even histrionics, there is music. It has been said about the relative role of music and narration in this part of Africa that they constitute the two arms of the balance in a performance (57). Consequently, the importance of the narrative *per se* is not as great as one might assume when reading an edited tale. It is not necessary to have the polish one would expect of a unique piece of poetic expression.[60] The main purpose of the epic appears not to be to convey ideas, but to give the community an occasion to enjoy sound and rhythm. The music is polyrhythmic and characterized as being remarkably suggestive.

Although the epic is known by everybody, each performance is unique in its recreation of the material. The performer does not work according to a preconceived plan but on the spur of the moment. In this way the heroic tale consists of narrative episodes. Repetitions do occur, and they are regarded not as signs of poor craftsmanship but are welcome as tokens of the joy of recollection. There is less emphasis on unity of the story than on its fullness.

60 Okpewho, *Epic in Africa,* refers to the Homeric material that has come down to us as 'our well-manicured texts', 235.

One of the effects of music in these performances is the blurring of the difference between prose and poetry. Prose in the complex environment of music and drama can no longer be considered as prose *tout court*. It has been stated that 'in Bantu literature the difference between prose and verse is one of spirit rather than one of form' (155).

The hero of the epic is exemplary in appearance and behaviour. He embodies the highest ideals to which the society can aspire in the search for excellence and security. In this respect the artist who portrays the hero acts—in the course of the performance—as the imaginative leader of his community. What the bard produces is an imaginative reflection of the aspirations and dreams of his society. In his strong empathy with the hero he becomes 'ideals embodied'.

Okpewho suggests that the performance character of the oral epic is much stronger in Africa than elsewhere.

Delargy Traditional story-telling is the last feature of a rich and complex oral tradition in Ireland which survived into this century. It has been extensively recorded by the Irish Folklore Commission; analysis of the material continues. Here I am concerned with the general aspects of story-telling as presented by J.H. Delargy in his Rhys Memorial Lecture 'The Gaelic story-teller'.[61]

The virtual disappearance of the tradition of story-telling within the last generation or two was one of the results of the gradual replacement in Ireland of the Irish language by English, a process which accelerated in the nineteenth century. Story-telling was done in the Irish language; in fact this was the last medium through which this rich, colourful language was generally transmitted. Story-telling was ubiquitous in Irish society; it took place in the winter months in the evening when people met by the fireside, neighbours gathering. The story-teller (Ir. *sgéaloí* or *sgéaltóir*, from Ir. *sgél* 'story') was generally a man, although the stories were the treasure guarded by everybody, old and young, male and female.

Although not a professional, the story-teller was a creative artist who depended for a successful performance on an appreciative audience. Delargy was so immersed in the tradition that he took for granted what strangers to this culture would need to have spelled out in detail. He reports of a story-teller, Seán Ó Connaill, who, lacking the opportunity to tell his stories, so as not to lose them 'used to repeat them aloud when he thought no one was near, using the gesticulations and the emphasis and all the other tricks of narration' (12).

This passage conveys the information that the stories were more or less fixed[62] and this impression is enforced by the traditional way of ending the

---

61 *PBA* 31, 1945, 177-221. I quote from a reprint which is numbered 1ff.
62 The same is maintained for Scotland, see Bruford, A., *Gaelic folk-tales and romances*, Dublin 1969, p. 20.

story: 'That is my story, if there be a lie in it, be it so. It is not I who have made or invented it.'[63] One should not think of word-for-word repetition, but at least of keeping to the plot and the general form. An Irish proverb says: 'There are seven recensions of a tale and twelve versions of every song' (33-4). Difference in quality of narration could be due to both verbal and non-verbal elements in the performance. The claim of the accomplished story-teller to get a new story in a single hearing (11) need to be taken in its wider (performance) context.

The story-teller generally spoke very fast. Add to this the linguistic richness and one gets the impression of a high standard of this aspect of native Irish culture. 'The thick growth of alliterative adjectives would roll trippingly on the tongue of a practised story-teller and have the effect of impressing his illiterate audience to whom . . . high-flown rhetoric had a charm and an ever-new appeal' (32). While much everyday language would be used, the stories were also store-houses of archaic language. 'One old story-teller friend of mine, speaking of old men whom he had known in his youth, was full of admiration for their "hard Irish" (*crua-Ghaoluinn*), remarking that "they had such fine hard Irish you would not understand a word from them" ' (33). In this way story-telling was a means to keep the language alive and vibrant, to be available also in a dynamic way outside this context.[64]

The stories were transmitted within families as well as neighbourhoods, and, in the nineteenth century at least, wandering people also played a great part in transmission. Social occasions like wakes or 'stations' (religious services conducted in private houses) provided the initiation for story-telling. The repertoire was large: it was said of the best men that they could tell stories all nights of the winter and never have to tell a tale twice.

In our three examples, the carriers of the oral tradition as well as the recipients have been described as illiterate. The cases of oral tradition we have looked at were all, more or less explicitly, ethnocentric, that is, the material that was cultivated orally belonged to the group that cultivated it, and it helped to make the group experience itself by creating common interests, common background and common outlook.

The other message they convey is that the material transmitted from generation to generation must not be reduced to 'mere' words.[65] True, the

63 Bruford, A., 'Recitation or re-creation? Examples from South Uist storytelling', *Scottish Studies* 22, 1978, 27-44: *Ní mise a chum na a cheap é*. 'It is not I who made or invented it.'
64 I have often experienced Irish people commenting on the quality of a speaker's control of the Irish language. A high standard of this is still often held in higher regard than material wealth.
65 The Kirghis author Aitmatov, familiar with the oral tradition of his home area, has stated that 'probably one should not even try to put on paper narrative poetry that is made up by the storyteller in front of his audience. Such poetry withers on paper like a flower that

spoken word is the distinguishing feature of the oral tradition, but it is fully integrated into a wider mesh of sounds, such as musical accompaniment or rhythmic beats,[66] and is not necessarily the dominant element; the word is only one of several media that carry meaning and contribute to the overall event.[67] The oral tradition is, in the process of activation, performed, and a performance is at its best when it brings about a rapport between performer and audience. Nor is it advisable to classify the former as active and the latter as passive: what is conveyed during the performance is already known by the audience; the important experience during the performance is the sharing of the tradition.[68] The contents of the oral tradition are of great importance to everybody concerned. This is why the performance is charged with emotions of various kinds, frequently of great intensity.

The common experience extends to the language in which the tradition is articulated. In several places we have come across the great care which was devoted to the language in which the tradition was expressed.[69] The various kinds of tradition, epic narrative in prose or verse or religious incantations find expression in various registers of language. For this reason one learns most about the nature of a particular oral tradition from those with an intimate knowledge of the language in which it is cast.

Every oral tradition is best appreciated on its own terms and in its own setting, as performance. Transcriptions of the words are the bare bones without flesh, and translated texts are poor seconds because inevitably much is lost in translation and because oral tradition is only partially textual. The highly complex nature of non-literate languages is of paramount importance.

Finally, an issue must be raised that is inevitably related to the research on oral tradition: its reliability. It is often contended that the oral tradition is transmitted accurately over time, and doubts are sometimes raised as to the validity of the contention. From the three descriptions of personal acquaintance with various oral traditions we have learned that such a claim is not made for all kinds of oral traditions. The performed epic lives from its variations within

is dried between the pages of a book.', Aitmatov, C., 'Snow on Manas mountain', in *The time to speak out*, Moscow 1988, 30-47, at 46.
66 Vansina, *Oral tradition*, esp. p. 83.
67 The same phenomenon is very well expressed by Cassiodorus in the early sixth century in his characterisation of the Roman theatre, *Variae* IV, 51: 'loquacissimae manus, linguosi digiti, silentium clamosum, expositio tacita', and further: 'tunc illa sensuum manus oculis canorum carmen exponit et per signa composita quasi quibusdam litteris edocet intuentis aspectum, in illaque leguntur apices rerum et non scribendo facit quod scriptura declaravit'.
68 This has been described particularly well by Glassie, *Passing the time*, esp. 140-45.
69 As regards Africa, Horton, 'Romantic illusion', speaks of 'an immense confidence in the power of ordinary, literal speech . . . the very luxuriance of African symbolism is a product of the general power of such speech,' 91.

the general mould; the same applies to story-telling. The opposite holds good for the ritual songs of aborigines where it is fairly easy to test the claim because the single items of the songs are short and in a deliberately chosen kind of language register.

More generally, however, the question of authenticity, of verbatim repetition, is one which betrays the literate mind of the person who raises this issue. To check verbatim repetition or variations requires the existence of standard texts against which this check can be made. It is a technical issue which is not relevant in the context of non-literate cultures. Significantly, concepts such as accuracy have no equivalent in the native languages. It has been widely remarked by anthropologists that 'truth' is a concept with different connotations in the different cultures.[70] As regards the oral tradition, what matters above all to the people to whom this tradition belongs is their belief in, their conviction of, the authenticity of their tradition and its transmission.[71]

In the context of our work, the main message is that oral tradition is the essence of non-literate cultures. It is of supreme relevance to all members of a society; it expresses the rights and duties of the individual and is accepted as authoritative. Their ontology is articulated in it. We have further noted that oral tradition must be experienced personally to be fully appreciated. Access to the oral tradition of non-literate peoples of our century is mediated to us by anthropologists; the reader of their works can benefit from their personal experience and their translation into their own language of perceptions of different cultures. In this way the mediators contribute greatly to what the reader will learn about non-literate societies, and this 'filter element' must be taken into account.

Whatever details are dwelt upon, one of the main benefits from this survey is the deepened awareness that other cultures should be approached in terms of their autonomy, as viable and tested ways of organizing the life of groups of people, accepted by these groups and passed on from generation to generation. The transmission need not take place in an unthinking way; rather, belief in the validity of the tradition, even passionate attachment to it, seems to be a dominant feature. In the awareness that what one gets from such study is ultimately one's own construct, it must be conceded that in this respect the work of the anthropologist does not differ in principle from that of the historian.[72]

70 See Burridge, ch. 3, 4; Vansina, *Oral tradition*, 13, 83, 129.
71 Burridge: 'it is doubtful whether for any one group, a generation's cultural experience was a replica of the one preceding. . . . On the other hand, it may be taken that such changes in the cycles of cultural experience occurred within fairly narrow limits . . . cultures are never wholly stable, they are in constant flux', 65f. Similarly Gill, 61.
72 Evans-Pritchard, E.E., *Anthropology and history*, Manchester 1961, referring to history and social anthropology says: 'both are trying to translate one set of ideas into terms of another, their own, so that they may become intelligible,' 14.

HISTORY

Between us and oral cultures of the present century the anthropologists are the empathetic mediators. We experience these oral traditions at several stages removed. When we turn to the Middle Ages, the situation is even more difficult. It is true that there were authors in the Middle Ages and earlier whose work can be called ethnographic (for example, Posidonus of Apameia, born *c.*135 BC, or Giraldus Cambrensis, AD 1146-1223) and their writings are valuable for our purposes. Our informants are in general not empathetic towards the cross-cultural phenomena they describe, and this handicap will have to be taken into account repeatedly in our study.

The barbarians of the early Middle Ages are, in many respects, unlike the peoples that are the object of modern anthropological studies. When we meet them, they are not in a state of isolation: they are in touch with the Roman world and contributing to its transformation. We have seen that virtually all the barbarian peoples which we come across in the early Middle Ages were politically fairly recent formations, products of various manifestations of ethnogenesis. However, we have also seen that this objective perspective in some respects differs from the subjective experience. Their pronounced ethnocentrism, combined with a lack of absolute time reckoning, resulted in the conviction widespread among these peoples that they were mankind incarnate, and furthermore, that they were descended from superhuman ancestors, to whom they felt obligations.

Furthermore, we encounter mainly those barbarian peoples that had come into contact with the Roman world and had been able to retain their identity, for several generations at least. Of course they were, over time, marked by their encounter with the Roman world, but the process of acculturation was one which had two partners in each case, and each of the two contributed to the eventual product. What the Romans contributed is much easier to pinpoint since it is linked both to Christianity and to written culture. But the other party also had something to contribute: its past, its success and its traditions.

Thus, what the barbarians of the early medieval centuries have in common with the people studied by the anthropologists in our century is social viability, an internal balance, as well as a non-literate culture. These are characteristics of central importance; for these reasons the concern with the modern anthropological studies can enrich us in our approach of the early medieval barbarians in helping to formulate the appropriate questions to be asked of them.

We have seen earlier that *barbarus* occurs frequently as a synonym of *illitteratus*. In the process of coming into contact with Romanitas (which in due course, could be synonymous with Christianitas),[73] the preconditions

---

73 See chapter 1.

needed to gain access to their culture were created, in however oblique and incomplete way that may have happened. Unlike modern anthropologists those Roman and Christian authors who wrote about the barbarians and their culture were as a matter of course not sympathetically disposed towards the barbarians and this is reflected in their writing.[74]

Because words are of central importance in oral culture, language has to be considered. Each society cultivates the oral tradition in its own language—often in a special register of that language. Encountering the oral tradition in its own language in the medieval centuries is the exception,[75] not the rule. Generally speaking, we are given access to the barbarians and their culture through the medium of the Latin language, which is why attempts must be made to 'decode' the Latin terms in order to draw closer to the barbarian culture.

As recently pointed out, Latin in the late Roman Empire showed a remarkably uniform standard.[76] That language was one of the great achievements of Roman civilization; it has been said that 'dès la fin du Haut Empire, tout est devenu dicible en Latin'.[77] This assessment should be qualified by adding 'everything related to Roman matter'; for our purposes this is a substantial qualification.

For, when Latin, a product of Roman civilization, was used in post-Roman centuries, it was not a suitable language to express non-Roman culture as adequately as had been the case during and within the Empire. In fact, the language itself underwent substantial changes which were no doubt in part the result of the transformation of the Roman world which we discussed earlier. To refer to it, as is often done, as 'medieval Latin', is giving it a deceptively simple label that does not do justice to the reality. There was no longer uniformity; instead, substantial differences developed synchronically as well as diachronically. These changes have not been investigated adequately.[78] They could be substantial especially where Latin was handled by barbarians. In some cases it could be shown, in others not more than suspected, that terms familiar from Roman times underwent semantic changes.[79] Where Latin as the language

74 An exceptionally telling case is that of Otfrid of Weissenburg, writing c.865 about his arduous task of composing a verse account of the Gospels in his own Frankish language which he presents only in terms of deficiency as measured against Latin, see below, chapter 8.
75 See chapter 9.
76 Banniard, Genèse 33, 37.
77 Banniard, Genèse, 45.
78 For a brief survey see Richter, M., 'The reality of the Latin Middle Ages', Montreal symposium 1986 (forthcoming). Michel Banniard's Viva voce deals with the Romance countries from the end of the Roman Empire to the Carolingian period.
79 The term orare is an outstanding case in point for semantic change: Richter, 'Sprachen-

of our sources seems to suggest continuity,[80] it is just as likely that it obliterates discontinuity.

Thus Latin *per se* is unsuitable for granting adequate access to and insight into non-Roman oral culture, generally speaking. This applies even where specific authors writing in Latin were positively disposed towards the oral tradition.[81] Latin was not capable of expressing barbarian culture adequately and thus the available sources contain, inevitably, distortions of the reality to be recovered. In this respect it is of secondary importance how the authors writing in Latin were disposed towards the oral culture.

The continuity of Latin culture from the fifth to the eighth century must be assigned its proper proportion. There were certainly outstandingly gifted authors who mastered the Latin language even though it was an acquired second language (for example, Bede, Alcuin), but these scholars are not representative of their age. Most of those who wrote in Latin had a distinctly poor grasp of it. This can be seen particularly clearly in the sources relating to government and administration. The so-called Carolingian Renaissance is a manifestation of the poor state the Latin language had reached by the eighth century. Its achievements are impressive in view of the starting point.[82]

This is, then, another barrier to easy access to the oral culture through Latin sources: the insufficient mastery of that language by the great majority of those who wrote in it. Incidentally, this state of affairs shows that in the societies where this applied Latin does not appear to have been essential to their functioning.[83]

THE HISTORIAN AND THE SOURCES

While it will always be the main task of the medievalist to deal with the written sources of the period, there remains a suspicion that historians can become slaves to their sources whereas they should be their masters. They particularly need to be in control where the sources are in short supply, as is very much the case in the post-Roman centuries. The scholar should take the very scarcity of written sources as information—as indicating that written sources now had a different function from that which they had, say, in Roman society; in which

---

politik', esp. 418f. See also the discussion of the term *scribere* above in chapter 3 and *cantare*.
80   This is the main theme of Banniard, M., *Genèse*.. The term 'culture' is used here, of course, in association with (Latin) literacy.
81   See chapter 9, n. 103. I have dealt with the problem more generally in 'Is Latin a key to the early medieval world?' (published in Russian) in: *Odysseus—Man in history today*, Moscow 1991, 125-36.
82   A notable by-product of the Carolingian Renaissance was the alphabetization of French, see Wright, R., *Late Latin and early Romance*, Liverpool 1982.
83   Cf. chapter 3.

case it can be highly misleading to take these sources as representative of the societies in which they originated.

It is—merely—a question of perspective. Since literacy was more marginal in post-Roman societies than in Rome, this fall-off in writing demands serious attention. Thus, one must investigate the way in which post-Roman societies went about storing and transmitting knowledge regarded as worth keeping (and it is impossible to imagine a society that does not have such knowledge).

Difficult and incomplete though the study of oral culture in the early medieval West may remain, it can be approached from various angles, each of which provides specific insights. The combination of them results in a picture of considerable detail and even depth.

The most obvious approach is to gather and analyse the information contained in the historical sources (narrative material) about the oral culture. For the decoding and thus a full exploitation of this information the considerations put forward in the previous section have to be applied. Oral tradition as performance always requires a social context; it is communication *par excellence*. In the sources a variety of aspects may be recorded, singly or in combination: accounts of the material transmitted, the guardians of the tradition, the occasion of its performance, the setting, the manner of articulation and the like.

So far we have considered a linguistic aspect of the problem. There are others to be considered as well. One has to take into account the various types of sources from which we obtain our information about those centuries. It may appear paradoxical to maintain that at first sight the oral tradition has left relatively faint traces in the written sources even though, or better, perhaps, because it was an almost universal feature in the early medieval West. This suggestion requires a little elaboration.

In the early medieval centuries those who wrote what one may call, very loosely, historical works, were not concerned primarily with matters of everyday occurrence—those features in their society that were familiar and remained constant. In this respect medieval historians have a different focus from modern anthropologists. For example, it is exceedingly difficult to gauge the importance of feasting in the early Middle Ages—who invited, who was invited, and what normally happened on these occasions. Nevertheless, it is apparent that feasts were a frequent phenomenon and that they functioned as social bonds.[84] Or, take the phenomena of court culture. How was a court composed, who was normally present? Such questions are normally not explicitly reported in the historical sources. These tend rather to record what

---

84 Altenburg, D. et al., ed., *Feste und Feiern im Mittelalter*, Sigmaringen, 1991. Cf. also Althoff, G., *Verwandte, Freunde und Getreue*, Darmstadt 1990, esp. 203-11; Enright, M.J., 'Lady with a mead-cup. Ritual, group cohesion and hierarchy in the Germanic warband', *Frühmittelalterliche Studien* 22, 1988, 170-205.

struck the observers as exceptional, unusual,[85] memorable, events or features which may have brought about change in their society.

Continuity and change are the two poles that mark human society at all times; even in contemporary historiography there are different approaches which vary the emphasis placed on each. While all accounts will have a mixture of these two elements, historians tend to concentrate on change, on development, whereas anthropologists tend to stress continuity. The present study inclines towards historical anthropology.[86]

For the centuries and areas that concern us in this book, we have no works that could be called, even remotely, ethnographic in approach; such works had existed earlier (for example, Posidonius) and were to be produced again later (in the twelfth century, for example, Giraldus Cambrensis, Helmolt of Bosau).[87] The information about oral tradition which we do get comes principally from Latin historical sources, and it will be useful to identify why the particular information is given. One would not expect information about the oral culture to be given for its own sake.

In summary: obstacles to the study of the oral culture in the early medieval West are in two essential respects considerable. There is the obstacle of the Latin language, an unsuitable medium for reporting the oral tradition cultivated in another language, and there is the obstacle of the fact that the oral culture was essentially something unremarkable to contemporaries. Traces of the oral culture in the Latin sources are hardly ever straightforward; when found they have to be carefully decoded in order to yield the maximum of information.

As mentioned earlier, some of the information concerning the oral culture is contained in Latin historical sources of a narrative kind. We also have Latin sources of an explicitly normative kind, especially from the Church. There are likewise further implicit references to normative standards in mainly narrative material. In fact, much of the information about the oral culture derives from a clash of two in many respects mutually exclusive norms: customary lifestyles and Christian demands. We shall also see that many Christians did not view the situation in this way. Since the Christian religion had become established within the Roman Empire, increasing efforts were made by some representatives of Christianity to establish a Christian way of life.[88] Understandably, such efforts met with resistance; therefore they had to be repeated. Christian standards are constantly referred to in the sermon literature as well as in ecclesiastical legislation, sometimes (for better effect) against the foil of everyday reality.

85 Einhart, *Vita Karoli Magni* c.24 'convivabatur rarissime' where Sueton, writing about Augustus, has *assidue*. See chapter 6.
86 See also Richter, *Oral tradition*, ch. 3.
87 This aspect of the works of these men has been highlighted by Bartlett, R., *Gerald of Wales, 1146-1223*, Oxford 1982, esp. ch. 6-7.
88 See chapter 2.

The ethics associated with and expressed in the oral culture were, on the whole, of a very different kind from Christian ethics. The two should have been irreconcilable, given that the oral tradition was concerned primarily with life here and now and its cosmic views were at odds with those of Christianity.[89]

It comes as no surprise to find that the normative sources from the Church do contain references to the oral culture. However, the evidence is uneven, in part at least due to the fragmentary nature of our ecclesiastical sources. It is also evidence expressed in negative terms, an evaluation which the modern observer must not adopt uncritically. In addition to being morally shaded, the information is also uneven; this is, in part at least, a result of the fragmentary survival of even ecclesiastical sources from those centuries. However, it has to be kept in mind that in the Church there were also, at all times, great variations as regards the zeal with which Christian ideals were pursued. We shall see later a number of instances where people in high office in the Church not only tolerated but enjoyed and patronized the oral culture with which they had grown up. Such an attitude gave rise to concern, and hence to information. If this was the case with members of the clergy, one can expect the laity to have been even more inclined towards the oral tradition. The sources are very unbalanced for these centuries, and thus more references to clerics cherishing the oral culture than lay people can be cited.

It is notoriously difficult to relate normative information to reality. This applies strongly to the Christian sources in the early medieval West. It is equally dangerous to generalize from specific information, but a telling case is surely the following account about Rome (shortly before the middle of the eighth century), an account which presents a mixture of Christian norms and reality. Archbishop Boniface complained in a letter to Pope Zacharias about the secular festivities that were celebrated in Rome around New Year. How could he expect his flock, he asked, to abstain from similar feasts when they saw what was happening in Rome? We are fortunate in having the pope's reply in this matter; and it is revealing: Zacharias wrote back to say that he had done his utmost to suppress these festivities,[90] but to no avail.[91]

It is apparent that the oral culture survived in the early medieval West, and it has left traces of various kinds in several societies. With roots reaching deeper than those of Christianity, and surely also because it answered profound

---

89 For particular aspects, especially ancestor worship, see chapter 2 above, esp. p. 43 n. 86 and p. 152 below.
90 A Roman council of 743 forbade these festivities, c. 9, Mansi 12, 384.
91 Tangl, M., ed., *Die Briefe des Bonifatius*, MGH Epp. Sel. 1, 1915, nos 50, 51. Riché, *Education*, 531, n. 21 does not refer to the pope's reply. For a fuller treatment see Schneider, F., 'Über Kalendae Ianuariae und Martiae im Mittelalter', *Archiv für Religionswissenschaft* 20, 1920-21, 82-134, 360-410, esp. 126-33; Meslin, M., *La fête des kalendes de janvier dans l'empire romain*, Bruxelles 1970 (Collection Latomus 115).

human needs in a manner which had stood the test of time,[92] the oral culture persisted even when Christianity had become outwardly established in the various societies of the time. There are reasons to assume that the oral culture flourished: a visible sign of this is that Christianity adopted a number of its features.[93]

For the early medieval centuries, it is important to keep in mind the very unbalanced nature of the available written material. Writing was prominently associated with Christianity, and the vast ranges of life untouched by Christianity leave proportionately too few traces behind. In many respects, the written sources tend to 'obliterate' the existing oral tradition.[94]

It has been well stated that 'the remembered past is unobjective, but it is meaningful and valid to more people because they participate in its transmission. Recorded history on the other hand is more objective and factual, but it is only immediately significant to historians, who have to convince their fellow men of its importance. With one hand writing has given us true history, but with the other it has taken away the past's immediate relevance to society.'[95]

In this difficult situation the researcher can take comfort from the neighbouring discipline of archaeology. In more than one early medieval society, the construction of houses, halls or churches was originally and traditionally carried out in wood. In Bede's Northumbria, building churches in stone was referred to as done *more Romano*.[96] Stone buildings were later often erected on the sites of the previous wooden buildings. But even where that was not the case, wooden buildings leave traces that can be revealing even when they require great expertise for plausible reconstruction.[97] It is an enriching experience to learn what postholes, for example, can tell the archaeologist in this respect. Traces of the oral tradition may well be of a different kind, but they are of a similar quality. With appropriate handling, these traces make possible lofty reconstructions.

---

92 See the concept of congruence, above at n. 38.
93 See chapter 10 below.
94 For this see part III of this book.
95 Clanchy, M.T., 'Remembering the past and the good old law', *History* 55, 1970, 165-76, at 176.
96 *Historia Abbatum* c.5 and elsewhere.
97 I have followed this particularly closely in connexion with the excavation of early medieval Dublin, for which see various publications by Wallace, P.F., e.g. art. 'Dublin', *Reallexikon der germanischen Altertumskunde*, 2nd ed., 6, 215-24.

5

PERFORMERS AND MUSIC

As one moves forward in time from the end of the Western Roman Empire, one finds Romanitas on the wane; the culture of the barbarians continues to be influential. It is a culture accessible almost exclusively by way of information expressed in Latin. If one accepts that a culture is most adequately appreciated in its own terminology, it can be taken as fact that Latin cannot but give a distorted vision of the culture of the barbarians. The almost universal use of the Latin language in writing suggests a degree of continuity which may have no parallel in reality.

Due to political and cultural developments during the early medieval centuries, information about the culture of the barbarians does not flow evenly; for this reason, the culture of the barbarians in the early medieval West can be presented neither chronologically nor systematically. In fact, a cluster of varied information in this field is available from the Carolingian period, allowing us to clarify key terms as well as key issues. On the basis of this material and of the evidence it supplies concerning the barbarian culture of that period, it will be possible to elucidate earlier as well as later stages of that culture, in themselves less fully attested.

Thus in this section chronology takes second place to systematic and thematic investigation. The unevenness of our account is due to uneven reflection of the barbarian culture in the sources. This is itself worthy of comment because it gives insight into various degrees of strength of barbarian culture. This can be gauged from the way in which Christianity manifested itself among the barbarians.

The oral tradition was the property of each political community. When approaching it in terms of 'performance', in its actualization, one has to conceive of it as normally interaction between performer and audience, even though one should not approach it in terms of active and passive participation. The sources can reflect performed oral tradition in a variety of ways; the oral messages themselves are rarely mentioned explicitly. One gets the impression that this was of minor importance to the contemporary observers because these messages were so familiar to everybody. However, it is necessary to begin with a discussion of those people who appear as the performers, the activators of the existing tradition.

THE JONGLEURS[1]

Preliminary remarks The available scholarly accounts present rather uniformly three main features of the jongleurs: they are travelling, non-residential artists of rather dubious repute; they exist on the margins of society; and they come into prominence together with the appearance of epic poetry in the eleventh and twelfth centuries.[2] All three points deserve examination; we shall see that they all have to be qualified substantially.

I shall begin with the last point. There is a type of versecraft which is ascribed by many scholars to the jongleurs, *poesia juglaresca* in Spanish, or *Spielmannsdichtung* in German. Here the jongleurs are associated with written poetry even though scholars differ as to the nature of this poetry. Nor is there agreement on whether the jongleurs are poets or mere performers. The discussion has been conducted on the basis of mainly vernacular poetry in which jongleurs are mentioned.

There is considerable disagreement among the many scholars who have dealt with the issue. Where the present account differs from previous treatment is that I shall look for the jongleurs outside the vernacular poetry, and prior to the eleventh century. This approach produces a different general impression. As far as I can determine no one has ever seriously questioned the view that written vernacular versecraft is to be considered the typical, representative work of the jongleurs. A simple consideration is enough to undermine this view. Jongleurs are referred to, as we shall see, in a variety of terms which are used synonymously, for centuries before the appearance of the written vernacular poetry associated with them. Unless one wants to argue that this had always been the situation and that most vernacular poetry composed by the jongleurs in writing has been lost, one must concede that the jongleurs were for a long time active without their products being fixed in writing. If

---

1 For a concise treatment see Richter, *Oral tradition*, ch. 4.
2 The most relevant studies here are Curschmann, M., *Spielmannsepik. Wege und Ergebnisse der Forschung von 1907-1965*, Stuttgart 1968; Salmen, W., *Der Spielmann im Mittelalter*, Innsbruck 1983; Hartung, W., *Die Spielleute. Eine Randgruppe in der Gesellschaft des Mittelalters* (*VSWG* Beiheft 72), Wiesbaden 1982; Schreier-Hornung, A., Spielleute, Fahrende, Außenseiter: Künstler der mittelalterlichen Welt, Göppingen 1981; Casgrande, C., Vecchio, S., 'Clercs et jongleurs dans la société médiévale, XII et XIII siècles', *Annales*, E.S.C. 34, 1979, 913-28; Menéndez Pidal, R., *Poesia juglaresca: y origenes de las literaturas romanicas. Problemas de historia literaria y cultural*, Madrid 1957; Wareman, P., *Spielmannsdichtung. Versuch einer Begriffsbestimmung*, Amsterdam 1951. Among older studies one should refer to Faral, E., *Les jongleurs en France au moyen-age*, Paris 1910; Moenckeberg, A., *Die Stellung der Spielleute im Mittelalter*, Berlin/Leipzig 1910.

this is the case, the *poesia juglaresca* or *Spielmannsdichtung* cannot be considered as the work typical of the jongleur.[3]

From this it follows that the activity of the jongleurs was not characteristically linked to written poetry. The societies in which they worked used literacy according to their needs.[4] These needs did not include the work of the jongleurs.

In the early medieval centuries, the jongleurs are known by a number of terms, which we shall now discuss.

The terminology The medieval Latin terminology of the performers of the oral tradition derives largely from Latin antiquity. However, as we shall see, Latin was incapable of doing justice to the reality of life in the changed environment of the early medieval centuries.[5] The meaning of a particular term can be recovered only from the context in which it occurs. One must be prepared for the situation that the available context is not always adequately documented.

The term which is used most widely in the medieval sources for such a performer, *ioculator*, is attested already in antiquity, though rarely.[6] It occurs with increasing frequency from the Carolingian period onwards.[7] However, the fact that most Romance languages contain terms derived from *ioculator/iocularis*[8] suggests that this term was already in general use before the various Romance languages evolved from Latin: thus one is dealing with a legacy from late antiquity that makes its widespread appearance in the sources with a considerable time lag. *Ioculator* and its variant form *iocularis* have derivatives in French (*jongleur*, Old French *jogleor*),[9] English *(juggler)* and German (*Gaukler*; German *spilman* is a calque on *ioculator*).[10]

3 For a discussion of the relevant problems see chapter 10.
4 See above, chapter 3.
5 From the early Anglo-Saxon literature one knows of the existence in that society of the *scop*. He is no doubt meant when Latin sources from the eighth century refer to the *poetae vulgares* (Bede, De arte metrica, Keil, H., *Grammatici Latini* VII, reprint Hildesheim and New York 1981, 258 l. 27) or *poetae seculares* (Council of Clovesho, 747, c. 12, Haddan and Stubbs, *Councils* III, p. 366). For the varied vernacular terminology in Irish and Welsh see chapter 9.
6 The Thesaurus Linguae Latinae lists only one attestation, from Cicero, *Ad Atticum* IV, 16, 3.
7 A wide-ranging list of attestations is provided by Faral, *Les jongleurs en France au Moyen-Age*. He does not, however, trace the pre-Carolingian ancestors.
8 This observation was also made by Huizinga, J., *Homo ludens*, ch. 2 (German pbk edition, Hamburg 1956, 42). However, Huizinga uses 'play' in this work in a very narrow sense.
9 See Morgan, R., 'Old French jogleor and kindred terms', *Romance Philology* 7, 1953-54, 279-325.
10 It is revealing that the earliest attestation of *spilman* occurs as a gloss on *istrio*, and it is the only attestation in Old High German: Steinmeyer, E., Sievers, E., ed., *Die althochdeutschen Glossen*, vol. iii, reprint Dublin and Zürich 1969, 319, n. 1.

What reasons may be given for the increasing use of this term of Roman origin in medieval times? We must take a closer look at the meaning of the term. In this respect glosses are a useful tool in that they reveal a semantic range of the term glossed with the help of the glossing term whose meaning is known. In antiquity, *ioculator* is glossed as *scurra*;[11] as it is in later times.[12] Thus *ioculator* was associated with the terminology relating to stage actors, for which the other terms used most widely are *mimus* and *histrio*, and these, in turn, are apparently used interchangeably with *ioculator* as well.[13]

We have seen that the theatre, extremely popular in Roman society, remained attractive into the Christian period in the Romania. How far it continued under the rule of the barbarians is impossible to say. We only know that Justinian ordered the closure of the hippodrome in Constantinople in 526, that the Ostrogothic kings continued to patronize the theatre in Italy, and that, in the last quarter of the sixth century, it apparently was also patronized by the Frankish king Chilperic.[14] It is not clear what one should make of the fact that Isidore of Seville, when discussing the terms *thymelicus*, *histrio* and *mimus*, should use in each case the past tense.[15] In any case, one can take it that in the early medieval centuries there was no culture of the theatre in the Roman tradition.

Thus the terms *histrio*, *scurra* and *mimus* must refer to something else. Nor is it necessarily the case that each term denotes something different. In the knowledge that Latin terminology (with relatively distinct connotations in Roman times) is being used in a transformed world, we must realize that this terminology refers to institutions or functions different from those which obtained in Roman times. This point has to be made in all clarity, for it is a precondition for a fresh approach of the subject.[16]

It is of interest in this respect to find that in late antiquity the verb *ludere* was often replaced by the verb *iocare*.[17] By analogy, it emerges that *iocus* or

11 See ThLL, s. v.
12 *Saeculi Noni auctoris in Boetii Consolationem Philosophiae commentarius*, Silk, E.T., ed., Rome 1935, 129f: 'Scurrae sunt ioculatores pantomini Atellani Thymelici'. The following definition of *thymelici* is that of Isidore, *Etym.* XVIII, 47 (below, n. 15).
13 These terms are discussed at length by Szemerényi, O., 'The origins of Roman drama and Greek tragedy', *Hermes* 103, 1975, 300-32, esp. 314ff.
14 See chapter 1, and Gregory of Tours, *Libri Decem Historiarum*, V, 17.
15 *Etymologiae* XVIII, 47: 'Thymelici autem erant musici scenici qui in organis et lyris et citharis praecanebant'; 48: 'Histriones sunt qui muliebri indumento gestus inpudicarum feminarum exprimebant; hi autem saltando etiam historias et res gestas demonstrabant'; 49: 'Mimi . . . habebant suum auctorem, qui antequam mimum agerent, fabulam pronuntiarent. Nam fabulae ita conponebantur, a poetis ut aptissime essent motui corporis'. Lindsay, W.M., ed., Oxford 1911.
16 For general statements to the same effect see chapter 3 on the unsuitability of Latin and chapter 9.
17 Meillet, A., *Esquisse d'une histoire de la langue Latine*, Paris 1966, 274. Cf. also Wartburg,

iocum and *ludus* are also used interchangeably in the early Middle Ages.[18] It seems therefore justified, when one meets words connected with *iocus*, even when there are no glosses present, to take them in the sense of *ludus* as long as the context does not make this interpretation impossible. Thus terms derived from *iocus* or *iocare* can be associated with performance of various kinds.

The semantic field of *iocare* in late antiquity appears in a condensed form in ecclesiastical legislation first attested from the Fourth Council of Carthage of 436 where it is stated that clerics who involved themselves in the work of stage actors or played their shameful parts were to be removed from office:

> c. 60 Clericum scurrilem et verbis turpibus iocula rem ab offitio retrahendum.[19]

This is an instance of *scurrilis* and *iocularis* being used as synonyms; the activity associated with these terms is condemned.

We have referred earlier to the determined attempts of the Church leaders in North Africa to enforce the ban on Christians attending the theatre. In the light of this the ruling quoted above causes no surprise. In fifth-century North Africa this would have referred to a cleric's involvement in affairs of the Roman theatre which was highly popular but loathed by zealous Christians for its lasciviousness.[20]

However, the theatre was one of those Roman institutions which did not long survive the transformation of the Roman world in the West. Thereafter, and outside the Romania, the activities of the *ioculatores* should not be looked for on the stage as in Roman times. As in the case of the theatre in Roman antiquity, one learns most about the activities of the *ioculatores* from their critics. Furthermore, the language of condemnation is strongly redolent of what Church Fathers had to say concerning the theatre. This language use suggests continuity. It is a very significant instance of terminology remaining rather stable while the terms now refer to different phenomena. In this respect, one is dealing with a clear case of semantic change. The terminology of condemnation coined by Church Fathers remained a very useful arsenal for

---

W.v., *Französisches etymologisches Wörterbuch*, vol. 5, Basel 1950, s.v. *ioca*ri, esp. p. 40, col. 1 and 2, and s.v. *iocularis*, p. 45, col. 1. St Augustine used the two terms occasionally as synonyms: see Richter, *Oral tradition*, ch. 4, n. 8.

18 See the Roman synod of 678: 'episcopi vel quicunque ecclesiastici ordinis religiosam vitam professi . . . nec quoscunque iocos vel ludos ante se permittant'. Haddan and Stubbs, *Councils*, III, 133.

19 Mansi, *Concilia* 3, 956. It has been pointed out by McKinnon, J.W., *The Church Fathers and musical instruments*, New York 1965, 161, that a similar attitude towards the theatre was held by the emperor Julian in the mid-fourth century as far as Roman priests were concerned, Frag. epistolae 304, quoted ch. 2, n. 40.

20 See chapter 1 in several places.

the condemnation of later and different types of performances. This is a paradigmatic instance of the unsuitability of the Latin language for phenomena in post-Roman societies.[21]

The decision of the Council of Carthage concerning the involvement of clerics in stage activities occurs again in the so-called *Statuta Ecclesiae Antiqua* (canon 73) later in the fifth century, which were perhaps compiled under the influence of Gennadius of Marseille. The early sources apparently all have the form *iocularis*, but from the beginning of the sixth century onwards one also finds *ioculator*, as in canon 23 of the council of Agde (Narbonne) of 506.[22]

One finds this text again in the conciliar legislation of Bishop Caesarius of Arles.[23] This ruling was repeated very often in the early medieval Church legislation. It apparently spread from North Africa via southern Gaul to all other parts of Europe[24] and found its way, in the twelfth century, into Gratian's *Concordia Discordantium Canonum* (Dist. XLVI, c.vi). Quite obviously, it catered for very widespread needs. We shall see later what were the objectionable activities that would require the deposition of clerics from their office.

Thus it can be established that the very outspoken criticism of the enjoyment of theatre performances which we have considered particularly in North Africa in the time of St Augustine was mediated to the clergy in subsequent centuries via southern Gaul. The wide distribution of the works of Caesarius, often believed to be works of Augustine, ensured that this attitude remained known. We have seen already that the terms in which this kind of worldly enjoyment was forbidden to serious Christians had hardened into standard phrases; these were to remain astonishingly tenacious. It would appear that the phrases coined in the fourth and fifth centuries were considered particularly apt; after all, they bore the authority of greatly respected men, Augustine in particular.

Aside from the innovation of the *ioculator*, the legacy of antiquity in this field included the established terminology, in particular *mimus, scurra, histrio*. The reputation associated with these people was such that there was no need to qualify them by pejorative terms. Our information is provided almost exclusively by clerical authors or Church synods which are bound to be highly critical of these activities. The almost uniform presentation of them in a negative light must not, however, blind one to the possibility that the contribution of the *ioculator*, the *mimus*, the *histrio* and the *scurra* did command wide popularity and approval, just as the stage did in the Roman world. It is

21 See generally Richter, 'Latein—ein Schlüssel zur Welt des Frühmittelalters?'
22 Munier, C., ed., *Concilia Galliae A. 314–A. 506*, CC SL 148, Turnhout 1963, 228 (= Mansi VIII, 336).
23 C.23, Morin, D.G., ed., *Sancti Caesarii episcopi Arelatensis Opera omnia*, Maretioli 1942, 59.
24 It spread even to Ireland where it is found in the *Collectio Canonum Hibernensis*, Liber X, ed. Wasserschleben, 1885, 28.

possible that the reputation of the jongleurs was as ambivalent as that of the Roman actors. This has to be deduced from specific information about individual incidents. It would be hasty to maintain that the jongleurs were, to the general population, people of ill repute.

MUSIC

The subject of music could equally well have been treated at the end of the section on the transformation of the Roman world as in the section on oral culture. It is placed here because music involves a profoundly oral element, for its cultivation and transmission take place largely outside the sphere of writing. This is the reason why it is quite hard to detect in our written sources in all its repercussions. Isodore of Seville's assertion that sound cannot be written[25] was correct for his time.

In the general histories of the early Middle Ages music is hardly ever mentioned. It is not difficult to see why this should be so: music is attested only in passing and in ways which are by no means clear. And yet there are indications that music held a central place among the barbarians as among the Christians.

At the outset of our enquiry we must point out that the modern term 'music' appears to carry meanings different from its ancestor in late antiquity and the early medieval West.[26] The present state of scholarship may be sketched as follows: there was next to no writing on the theory of music between the death of Boethius (525) and the ninth century. Writing music with neumes begins around AD 800 and spreads gradually.[27] But earlier, and throughout the centuries which witnessed the transformation of the West, music formed a central part of life. It is attested in association with the Christian religion, in ambivalent ways; it is much less well attested outside the religious sphere. One can formulate the hypothesis that music, in the modern sense of the term, found a place in the Christian religion because it had held a central place in human life before Christianity and was considered by the people to be an essential component of their life. It was thus a primal cultural manifestation which, in the process of acculturation, was taken into the Christian religion. For the period between Boethius and the ninth century, the function of music in the Christian religion is currently the subject of research, but no study is being made of secular music.[28]

25 'Nisi enim ab homine memoria teneantur soni, pereunt, quia scribi non possunt'. *Etymologiae* III, xv.
26 Cf. Jonsson, R. and Treitler, L., 'Medieval music and language: a reconsideration of the relationship', in *Studies in the history of music. I. Music and language*, New York 1983, 8.
27 See further below, notes 73ff.
28 For the late antique background, which is important, I found most useful McKinnon, *The Church Fathers and musical instruments*. McKinnon partly builds upon Quasten, J., *Musik*

In the late ninth century, Regino of Prüm, in his *Epistola de armonica institutione*, makes a sweeping statement about the almost universal appreciation of music, which is presented by him as an integral part of the *condition humaine*:

> Omnibus hominibus et omnibus aetatibus, omnique sexui naturaliter musicam esse coniunctam, nulli, qui semetipsum intellegit, dubium est. Quae enim aetas, aut quis sexus musicis non delectatur cantilenis? Proprium quidem humanitatis est, oblectari animum dulcibus modis, exasperari contrariis. Namque infantes ac iuvenes, nec non etiam senes ita naturaliter affectu quodam spontaneo modulationibus musicis implicantur, ut nulla sit omnino aetas, quae expers sit delectatione dulcis cantilenae.[29]

In this section Regino points out more than once that music gives pleasure (*delectatio, oblectari*) to those who are exposed to it. Hand in hand with this goes another assertion of his, namely that melodies (*cantus*) pervade all of human life, are virtually inextricably part of it:

> Ita denique omnis morum habitus cantibus gubernatur et regitur, ut et ad bellum progressui et item receptui canatur, cantu tubae excitante et rursus sedante virtutem animi. Dat cantus somnos, adimitque, nec non curas et sollicitudines inmittit et retrahit, iram suggerit, clementiam suadet, corporum quoque morbis medetur. (*ibid.*)

Earlier in his treatise, Regino had distinguished vocal music (called by him *musica naturalis*) and instrumental music (*musica artificialis*):

> A minus perito musico quaeri potest, quae est distantia inter musicam naturalem et artificialem? Ad quod respondendum est, quia, quamquam omnis harmonicae institutionis modulatio una eademque sit in consonantiarum sonis; tamen alia est musica naturalis, alia artificialis. Naturalis

und Gesang in den Kulten der heidnischen Antike und christlichen Frühzeit, first published 1930, repr. Münster 1973; see also Pietzsch, G., *Die Musik im Erziehungs- und Bildungsideal des ausgehenden Altertums und frühen Mittelalters*, first published in 1932, reprinted Darmstadt 1969; also Hammerstein, R., *Diabolus in musica. Studien zur Ikonographie der Musik im Mittelalter*, Bern/München 1974.

29 Gerbert, M., ed., *Scriptores ecclesiastici de musica sacra potissimum*, vol. I, 1784, 230-47, at 235 (also Migne, PL 132, 485-502). Here I quote from the new edition by Bernhard, M., ed., *Clavis Gerberti*, München 1989, 48f (the reference to this edition was kindly provided by Dr Konstantin Restle, Berlin). Similarly also: 'perspicue et indubitanter apparet, ita nobis musicam naturaliter esse coniunctam, ut ea, nec si velimus quidem, carere possimus. Quocirca erigenda est mentis intentio, ut id, quod naturaliter in nobis est insitum, scientia quoque possit esse comprehensum'. 236 (Gerbert), 50 (Bernhard)

itaque musica est, quae nullo instrumento musico, nullo tactu digitorum, nullo humano impulsu aut tactu resonat, sed divinitus adspirata sola natura docente dulces modulatur modos: quae fit aut in coeli motu, aut in humana voce.[30]

This explanation of Regino has been called typically Carolingian;[31] but it is impossible to agree with this assessment in view of the absence of other comparable material. However, it must be emphasized that the term for instrumental music, *musica artificialis*, often taken to be Regino's original contribution, can be traced back to the sixth century.[32] Thus Regino uses here a technical term that is unattested for several centuries but must have been in common use, having originated in late antiquity at the latest. This term also helps to explicate the term *artifex* in the sense of 'excellent instrumental musician', which occurs more frequently.[33] This term in turn confirms that the concept of *musica artificialis* existed before Regino. Its rare attestation is a result of the lack of any treatise on music in the medieval West between Boethius and the ninth century.[34] All the more is it remarkable that this technical term remained current.

It has been shown that Regino's treatise is largely a compilation of extracts from earlier writings on the subject of music; he relies heavily on the authorities of late antiquity.[35] This use of ancient authorities might seem to be an unremarkable expression of Carolingian learning; what is interesting is his subject: music. The cultural context had changed dramatically; while in Roman times music had been widely accepted, the Christian authorities had for some considerable time tried to minimize its role in religious worship. From this perspective, Regino's work assumes a new importance without being original in its main statements. For it shows that pre-Christian ideas associated with music had found acceptance in the Western Church.

In this context it should also be remembered that Regino lived after the

30   Gerbert 233, Bernhard 50.
31   Bruyne, E.d., *Etudes d'esthétique médiévale*, Bruges 1946, 3 vols., esp. I, 312f.
32   Cassiodorus, *Variae* II, 40. I owe to Dr Konstantin Restle, Berlin, the information that the only other attestation so far traced occurs in Remigius of Auxerre, 73,16, a contemporary of Regino's.
33   Cf. *Bonifatius-Briefe*, no. 116, p. 251 (see chapter 6 below); Gregory the Great, *Regula Pastoralis*, Prologus, PL 79, 49; Cassiodorus, *Variae* II, 40; St Augustine, *Enarrationes in Psalmos* XXXII, 8, PL 36, 283. Ambrose, *Explanatio Psalmi* I, 9, CSEL 64, 1919, 8, line 23-24. For a twelfth-century attestation see Peter the Chanter, *Verbum Abbreviatum*, PL 205, 253C: 'artifices ... instrumentorum musicorum'.
34   Boethius' positive preoccupation with music shows him as a representative of antique culture as yet unaffected by the current Christian ethics.
35   Cf. Bernhard, M., *Studien zur Epistola de armonica institutione des Regino von Prüm*, München 1979 (= Bayerische Akademie der Wissenschaften, Veröffentlichungen der Musikhistorischen Kommission 5), esp. part 2, pp. 34ff.

Carolingian reforms and therefore the state of affairs which he describes as relevant to music can be taken to have the sanction of these reforms. Regino's experience should be taken as representative, and I see no reason to doubt the general validity of his statement which, in this case, provides a most valuable framework which we can fill in with specific instances from other sources. We shall attempt to weave as tight a tapestry as possible, one that validates Regino's assertion for the early Middle Ages.

Before doing so, however, it will be necessary to investigate the place of music in late antiquity. Here, as in the case of the theatre, the Church Fathers provide the richest information. It is very varied. In general, positive information has to be extrapolated from negative assertions. As a result, it emerges clearly that Regino's assertion that music was part of the human condition, including that of Christians, was not to the liking of the great authorities within the Church; or, put another way, the attitude to music articulated by Church Fathers did not find general support in later times.

Obviously, the fourth century is a crucial period in this respect: the Christian religion emerged from hiding and organized itself in many fields, including the celebration of the divine office, the liturgy. Here music was important. The Church had to stake its claim in an environment in which music held an established position and where, therefore, music was charged with deep-reaching connotations. In addition, the Church carried the powerful, at times burdensome, legacy of the Jewish ancestry of Christianity. These topics will have to be considered, however briefly. We shall deal first with singing, then with instrumental music.

The Christian community had slowly developed from the Jewish community of the Synagogue which had practised vocal music, especially in the singing of the Psalms. This is the origin of singing in the Christian service. We know of prayers, songs and readings from the New Testament (e.g. Eph 5:19), but it is not known who led these. The common evening meal was the principal venue of Christian psalmody in the first three centuries of the Christian era.[36] St Paul had warned against excesses at such meals in no uncertain terms: *praecipio* (1 Cor 11:17-34). It was in the course of the organization of the Christian religion that singing in the service became the task of specialists, the *lector* or the *cantor*. These are known from the fourth century onwards.[37] There was some opposition to psalmody in general and to eucharistic psalmody in particular in the late fourth century, but to no avail.[38] With this specialization

---

36 McKinnon, J.W., 'The fourth-century origin of the gradual', *Early Music History* 7, 1987, 91-106, at 93.
37 See Foley, E., 'The cantor in historical perspective', *Worship* 56, 1982, 194-213, esp. 210. A slightly earlier date is posited by McKinnon, 'Origin', 97.
38 McKinnon, 'Origin', 103.

there arose the danger of raising the quality of singing which would then possibly give rise to enjoyment of the melody for its own sake, not in the service of worship. St Ambrose, famous for his composition of hymns, used these songs as means of propaganda against the Arians. It was at Milan that Augustine encountered the hymns and was deeply impressed by them. Pope Celestine I (422-32) introduced psalmody into mass before the sacrifice.[39]

Yet singing remained a problem. Thus St Augustine in his Confessions writes that he sometimes felt like banishing all song from the church but then approvingly quotes St Athanasius that there should be singing, albeit in a modest tone:

> Aliquando . . . erro nimia severitate, sed valde interdum, ut melos omne cantilenarum suavium, quibus Daviticum psalterium frequentatur, ab auribus meis removeri velim atque ipsius ecclesiae, tutiusque mihi videtur, quod de Alexandrino episcopo Athanasio saepe mihi dictum commemini, qui tam modico flexu vocis faciebat sonare lectorem psalmi, ut pronuntianti vicinior esset quam canenti.[40]

A similar attitude is found in St Jerome, who warned against singing in church of a type known from the theatre and demanded instead: 'Sic cantet servus Christi, ut non vox canentis, sed verba placeant quae leguntur.'[41]

Augustine's comment on the passage *Cantate ei canticum novum* (Ps 32:3) is a curious *Cantet canticum novum, non lingua, sed vita*.[42] A similar attitude is found in Jerome who claimed, commenting on Eph 5:19, that 'vel certe psalmus ad corpus, canticum refertur ad mentem. Et canere igitur et psallere et laudare Dominum magis animo quam voce debemus.'[43]

Thus singing hymns and psalms in Church was tolerated, as long as it was done with modesty.[44] Furthermore, the singing was to be in unison, symbolizing the unity and harmony among Christians,[45] and of course unaccompanied by musical instruments. One notes the term *voluptas* used by Augustine for taking pleasure in it, a term of clearly worldly dimensions[46] and

---

39 See Jeffrey, P., 'The introduction of psalmody into the Roman Mass by Pope Celestine I (422-432): reinterpreting a passage in the Liber Pontificalis', *Archiv für Liturgiewissenschaft* 26, 1984, 147-65.
40 *Confessiones* X, 33.
41 *Commentar. in Epist. ad Ephes.* III, V, PL 26, 562. See also earlier: 'nec tragoedorum modum guttur et fauces dulci medicamine colliniendas, ut in ecclesia theatrales moduli audiantur et cantica.'
42 *In Ps. XXXII, Enarratio II*, PL 36, 283.
43 *Comm. in Eph.*, PL 26, 561.
44 Einhart wrote that Charlemagne sang 'submissim et in commune', *Vita Karoli Magni*, ch. 29.
45 Quasten, *Musik und Gesang*, 94, 100-103, passim.
46 See the term *voluptas* associated with the Roman theatre, pp. 24, 35.

one of a respectable semantic range in secular society. Other authors felt free to admit that they took pleasure in singing.[47] Hymn singing was one of the genuine original legacies of late antique Christianity to the Middle Ages, even though it did not succeed in replacing the previous popularity of other kinds of song. There must have been a constant temptation by singers in church to show their skill at their best, thereby giving officially undesirable pleasure to the congregation.[48]

The biblical (mainly Old Testament) background of Christian singing is fairly obvious; less apparent is the contemporary non-Christian context, but this should be considered as one of the factors contributing towards excesses in singing which authorities warned against repeatedly. To Augustine music had also an aesthetic dimension and therefore it was difficult to forego it: 'fluctuo inter periculum voluptatis et experimentum salubritatis ... sententiam proferens cantandi consuetudinem approbare in ecclesia, ut per oblectamenta aurium infirmior animus in affectum pietatis adsurgat'.[49] For Augustine even singing in Church carried the potential of worldly pleasure (*periculum voluptatis*).

It is possible that even the terminology associated with secular singing was regarded as loaded to the ears of fervent Christians;[50] this would help to explain the curious use of terms by Isidore when he wrote: 'Carmina autem quaecunque in laudem Dei dicuntur hymni vocantur.'[51] In a similarly stilted manner,

---

47 The Dacian Niceta of Remesiana, early fifth century, is one of the more enthusiastic supporters of hymn singing which gives him pleasure. Turner, C.H., 'Niceta of Remesiana II. Introduction and text of De psalmodiae bono', *Journal of Theological Studies* 24, 1923, 225-52: 'scio nonnullos non solum in nostris sed etiam in orientalibus esse partibus qui superfluam et minus congruentem divinae relegioni existiment psalmorum et hymnorum decantationem. Ita conlaudo eos qui etiam sono vocis glorificant Deum' (p. 233). He concludes his sermon with the words: 'Iam pleniore fiducia hymnorum ministerium fideliter impleamus ... quid hac delectatione iucundius? Nam et psalmis delectamur, et orationibus rigamur, et interpositis lectionibus pascimur. Et vere, sicut boni convivae ferculorum varietate delectantur, ita nostrae animae multiplici lectione et hymnorum exhibitione saginantur' (p. 239).

48 For this problem see Gratian, D 92, c. 2 ('unde fit plerumque ut ad sacrum ministerium dum blanda vox quaeritur, quaeri congrua vita negligatur, et cantor minister Deum moribus stimulet, cum populum vocibus delectat') where reference is made to a ruling of a council held by Gregory the Great in 595; for the text see PL 77, 1335. This material does not occur, however, in the concordance of the complete works of Gregory issued by Brepols, Turnhout.

49 *Conf.* X, 33.

50 Cf. Isidore, *Differentiae*, no. 98: 'Inter cantare et canere: cantare tantum vocibus vel clamore insonare est, canere autem interdum moddulari, interdum vaticinari, id est, futura praedicere.' PL 83, 21.

51 *De Ecclesiasticis Officiis*, I, 6. CCSL 113, 1989. *Hymni dicuntur* is an expression of Ambrose; see n. 60 below.

Augustine had referred to the official who sang the psalms as *lector psalmi*.[52] Something similar may account for the quite reluctant acceptance of the term *cantor* for the man who was trained to sing; instead he is for long called *lector*.

Again, it was desirable that the singing of hymns should not be the domain of the Church alone but should characterize the homes of Christians generally, as attested by Gaudentius of Brescia (fl. *c*.400).[53] Yet outside the divine service, there was much singing, and it was done for pleasure; people were accustomed to it.

Instrumental music was not a legacy of the Synagogue.[54] In late antiquity instrumental music of any kind for the divine service was condemned by virtually all Christians of authority in the Churches of East and West.[55] This indirectly confirms that music was very widespread and much appreciated, as attested among others by Boethius.[56] The attempt of the authorities to enforce new values in this area was as widespread as it was over-ambitious. Even so, their ambitions in this respect were quite modest; music gave pleasure to those who were exposed to it, and the Church Fathers could not ban it from life altogether however much they disliked its effects.

I shall confine myself to some of their most important statements on this subject. Generally, it can be said that instrumental music as such was not condemned; it was frowned on as being an integral part of certain kinds of social activities from which the Fathers felt Christians should distance themselves.

St Augustine argued that music should be avoided by Christians because of its association with pagan religion:[57] 'nos tamen propter superstitionem profanorum debemus musicam fugere'.[58] Here it must be pointed out that much of the ritual of Roman religion was practised domestically. The other and much more frequent objection to instrumental music was its prominent

52 *Confessiones* X, 33, 50.
53 *Sermo* VIII: 'Sit domus Christiani ac baptizati hominis immunis a choro diaboli, sit plane humana, sit hospitalis; orationibus sanctificetur assiduis; psalmis, hymnis, canticisque spiritualibus frequenter: sit sermo Dei, et signum Christi in corde, in ore, in fronte, inter cibos, inter pocula, inter colloquia, in lavacris, in cubiculis, in ingressu, in egressu, in laetitia, in moerore.' PL 20, 890.
54 McKinnon, *The Church Fathers and music*, 91.
55 See McKinnon, J., *Music in early Christian literature*, Cambridge 1989 (first publ. 1987) who has the richest collection of sources in translation.
56 *De Institutione musica* I, i: 'Ut ex his omnibus perspicue nec dubitanter appareat, ita nobis musicam naturaliter esse coniunctam, ut ea ne si velimus quidem carere possimus'. ed. Friedlein, Leipzig 1867, 187.
57 Quintilian mentioned that music was part of ritual from ancient times: 'quis ignorat musicen . . . tantum iam illis antiquis temporibus non studii modo, verum etiam venerationis habuisse, ut idem musici et vates et sapientes iudicarentur'. *Inst. Or.* I, 9.
58 *De Doctr. Chr.* II, xviii, PL 34, 49.

place at banquets,[59] and thus the Fathers associated instrumental music with inebriation.

Representative of this position is a statement of St Ambrose. He refers to a passage from the prophet Isaiah: 'Vae iis qui consurgunt mane, et sectantur siceram, qui ebrii sunt vesperi; nam vinum eos comburet. Cum cithara enim et psalterio et tympanis vinum bibunt; opera autem Domini non respiciunt, et opera mauum eius non considerant' (5:11). Ambrose comments: 'Praeterieram certe ego citharam, psalteria, tympana, quae cognovimus conviviis huiusmodi frequenter adhiberi, ut vino et cantu excitentur libidines'. He pleads instead that his Christians should turn to Christian hymns: 'Hymni dicuntur, et tu citharam tenes? Psalmi canuntur, et tu psalterium sumis aut tympanum?'[60] Ambrose maintained that fondness for wine could be found among Romans and barbarians alike: 'Habent ergo vinum et barbari; libenter his Romani indulgent.'[61] While the earlier section of Ambrose's account could be taken as relating to the past, here he speaks from experience of his own times.

We find a similar attitude, of slightly later date, in a sermon of Gaudentius of Brescia, who also clearly drew on his own personal experience:

> Cave solum ut aliter non derelinquas fidem. . . . Hoc autem custodire ita demum poteritis, si ebrietatem devitetis, et convivia inhonesta, ubi turpium feminarum colubrini gestus concupiscentiam movent illicitam; ubi lyra sonat, et tibia; ubi postremo genera musicorum inter cymbala saltantium concrepant. Infelices illae domus sunt quae nihil discrepant a theatris.[62]

The passage from Isaiah referred to earlier does present instrumental music in a negative light. In this, however, it is not typical of the evaluation of musical instruments in the Old Testament.[63] In fact, instrumental music played a very prominent part in Jewish religious practice, particularly when psalms were being used. Yahweh was to be praised with music. This is epitomized in Psalm 150, which also lists the instruments used in the Temple:

---

59 This also is presented by Quintilian as an old Roman institution: 'testimonio sunt clarissimi poetae, apud quos inter regalia convivia laudes heroum ac deorum ad citharam canebantur. . . . quibus certe palam confirmat auctor eminentissimus Vergil musicem cum divinarum etiam rerum cognitione esse coniunctam'. *Inst. Or.* I, 10. For a description of such a banquet by Clement of Alexandria see McKinnon, *Music in early Christian literature*, no. 51, p. 32.

60 *Liber de Elia et jejunio*, XV, PL 14, 761-752 (note the term *dicere*); this was later taken up by Isidore of Seville, see 'Carmina autum quaecumque in laude dei dicuntur hymni vocantur', *De ecclesiasticis officiis*, CCSL 113, Turnhout 1989, c.6).

61 PL 14, 751.

62 *Sermo* VIII, PL 20, 890.

63 Another negative statement occurs in the prophet Amos where the Lord says: 'Aufer a me tumultum carminum tuorum: et cantica lyrae tuae non audiam' (5:23).

> Laudate Dominum in sono tubae: laudate eum in psalterio, et cithara.
> Laudate eum in tympano, et choro: laudate eum in chordis, et organo.
> Laudate eum in cymbalis bene sonantibus: laudate eum in cymbalis jubilationis. (3-5)

The important place which instrumental music had held in the Temple, including the figure of David playing the harp in praise of the Lord, posed serious problems to the Christian exegetes.[64] While there were some tentative efforts to grant music, including the harp, a place in Christian worship, the overwhelming attitude was of a different kind. Most authorities in the West, under the influence of the Alexandrian school of exegesis, treated instrumental music and musical instruments in an allegorical manner when relating the decisive passages to their own time.[65] Such treatment of the issue sometimes strikes one as abstruse, particularly in view of the fact that instrumental music was widespread and highly popular in the world in which the Fathers lived and taught. Thus, as in the case of the theatre, their task was to advocate cultural values in opposition to those long accepted and cherished.

One may refer to the way in which Augustine deals with Psalm 150, which lists all the instruments used to praise the Lord. His solution is simple even though it was perhaps not acceptable to his audience: 'Vos estis tuba, psalterium, cithara, tympanum, chorus, chordae, et organum, et cymbala jubilationis bene sonantia, quia consonantia. Vos estis haec omnia: nihil hic vile, nihil hic transitorium, nihil ludicrum cogitetur.'[66] At the same time he sums up what the opinion of proper Christians about the instruments named should be: *vile, transitorium, ludicrum.*

It is not quite clear why the *cithara* appears to have been an instrument which was particularly objectionable. In one sermon St Augustine compares the *cithara* with the *psalterium*: 'Meminerunt qui pridem affuerant, quando quid intersit inter psalterium et citharam. . . . Et nunc non importune repetimus, ut in ista diversitate duorum instrumentorum musicorum diversitatem factorum humanorum, significatam per haec, implendam autem per vitam nostram. Cithara lignum illud concavum tanquam tympanum pendente testudine, cui ligno chordae innituntur, ut tactae resonent . . . hoc ergo lignum cithara in inferioe parte habet, psalterium in superiore. . . . Mementote citharam ex inferiore parte habere quo sonat, psalterium ex superiore. Ex inferiore vita,

---

64 McKinnon, J.W., 'Musical instruments in medieval Psalm commentaries and psalters', *Journal of the American Musicological Society* 21, 1968, 3-20.
65 See McKinnon, *The Church Fathers and music*, esp. ch. 4.
66 *Enarr. in Ps.* CL, PL 37, 1965-1966. Cf. Clement of Alexandria on this passage: '"and praise him on the cithara", let the cithara be taken to be the mouth, played by the Spirit as if by a plectrum', Paedagogus II, IV, quoted McKinnon, *Music in early Christian literature*, no. 52, p. 32, and see also no. 69, p. 39.

id est terrena, habemus prosperitatem et adversitatem etc'.[67]

Obviously the names of the musical instruments which occur in the writings of the Fathers are those which were used in the Latin Bible. For our purposes it is not necessary to specify what these names stood for in late antiquity. The nature of the instrument referred to is debatable especially as regards the *cithara*. Was it a lyre or a harp, and of what kind? It suffices here to note that distinctions are made between wind instruments, stringed instruments which were plucked and percussion instruments.

Here once again the inheritance of Latin in the early medieval West suggests continuity which seems to be more apparent than real. The problem is even greater in the case where Latin terminology is used for musical instruments outside the Latin world. Occasionally, vernacular glosses help explain the Latin source terms which is of some slight help.

In any case, there can be no doubt that instrumental music held a prominent place in all societies of the early medieval centuries. In this area the virtually unanimous views of the great Christian authorities of the early Church were blandly disregarded.

What was the attitude to music in the period between the fourth and fifth centuries and Regino?[68] There is little authoritative information other than that provided by Isidore of Seville, whose brief section on music in his Etymologies (III, xv-xxiii) provides some orientation. Isidore refers to the emotive nature of music: 'Musica movet affectus, provocat in diversum habitum sensus' (III, xvii). Even though he occasionally refers to his own times,[69] most of what he writes about music is expressed in the past tense. This is particularly tantalizing where he writes about the many areas of life which involve music.[70] He ties the origin of music to the gods of the Romans, and, not surprisingly, he refers to the Old Testament.[71] He mentions the great esteem in which music was held in antiquity: 'eratque tam turpe musicam nescire quam litteras' (III, xvi). In the present tense, he refers to music in

67 *In Ps. XXXII, Enarratio II*, PL 36, 279-80.
68 A rare glance at the situation in Ireland around 800 is provided by the Milan glosses where the impression is conveyed that instrumental music was not regarded as inappropriate in the context of the Christian religion. See the gloss on *Confitemini Domino in chithara* Ps. 32:2: 'i. aircech ceneliu ciuil honid techtae molad doe dober som ani as chithara' i.e. he puts *cithara* for every kind of music which is fitting to praise God.' *Thesaurus Palaeohibernicus*, Stokes, W., Strachan, J.J., eds., 2 vols, Oxford 1902, I, 160.
69 (On the tuba): 'Praeceptum enim fuerat Iudaeis ut in initio novae lunae tuba clangerent, quod etiam hucusque faciunt.' III, xxi, 3.
70 'Interponebatur autem non modo sacris, sed etiam omnibus sollemnibus, omnibusque laetis vel tristioribus rebus. Ut enim in veneratione divina hymni, ita in nuptiis Hymenaei, et in funeribus threni, et lamenta ad tibias canebantur. In conviviis vel lyra vel cithara circumferebatur, et accubantibus singulis ordinabatur conviviale genus canticorum.' III, xvi.
71 See III, xvii and xxi.

association with actors and singers (III, xx) while remaining very vague. He is silent on the subject of music and Christians; this may be a heavy silence.

Returning to Regino of Prüm, we can now be more specific: his treatise was addressed to Ratbod, archbishop of Trier. There is no indication that this work had been commissioned. Regino mentions at the outset the types of songs heard in the churches—antiphon, introit and responsoria: he names a number of them. This is the point of departure for his more general discussion in which, skilfully and perhaps not even consciously, pre-Christian views about music are discussed once again,[72] in support of what was actually being done in the churches of the West.

We shall have to look for references, not merely to music, but to vocal music, singing, as well as to instrumental music. While the former had found the grudging approval of the Fathers, as long as it was practised with modesty, the latter had in no way found grace in the eyes of these authorities. However, since, as we shall see, instrumental music was widely enjoyed in society, and not just by lay people, one can take this as an indication of the vitality of pre-Christian norms and values which survived 'Christianisation' and continued to be cultivated.

Writing music Isidore of Seville stated that 'nisi ab homine memoria teneantur soni, pereunt, quia scribi non possunt'.[73] As far as scholarship has established, Isidore was correct here because the attempts to write music in neumes are placed at the earliest in the second half of the eighth century,[74] although another view favours the early ninth century.[75] For our purposes, the difference of half a century is of little relevance, for the scholars who disagree in this respect are of one opinion on another aspect of this issue: the importance of *memoria* in transmission of music alongside with the early notation and certainly before it. Thus Kenneth Levy suggests that 'the minimally pitch-specific, minimally nuance-indicative neumations of the nuance-poor archetype were viable transmitters of the Gregorian melos because that melos was imprinted in all its fullness upon the professional memories.'[76] Leo Treitler points to the cultural context in which the writing of music began and states: 'The script culture of the Carolingians created the general

72 The shifts in evaluation between Boethius and the medieval authors from the ninth century onwards have been highlighted by Reimer, E., 'Musicus und Cantor. Zur Sozialgeschichte eines musikalischen Lehrstücks', *Archiv für Musikwissenschaft* 35, 1978, 1-32.
73 *Etymologiae* III, xv.
74 Levy, K., 'On the origins of neumes', *Early Music History* 7, 1987, 59-90, esp. 89; see also id., 'Charlemagne's archetype of Gregorian chant', *Journal of the American Musicological Society* 40, 1987, 1-31.
75 Treitler, L., 'Reading and singing: on the genesis of occidental music writing', *Early Music History* 4, 1984, 135-208, here esp. 141 and 195.
76 Levy, 'Origins', 86.

background against which the foundation of notational practice becomes understandable.'[77] Earlier he had suggested that 'music writing was introduced into oral tradition, and, furthermore, it must have been used initially in support of that tradition'; he also argued that 'a musical tradition corresponding to the paradigm of literacy is not demonstrable in Europe before the thirteenth century, four centuries after the earliest music writing'.[78]

In the available accounts of music in the early Middle Ages one finds a concentration on Christian music, since this found its way into writing to some extent at least. We must therefore emphasize all the more that music existed in the Church and in the world in many spheres, one may even say in most spheres, outside writing. It took place in the context of oral transmission and cultivation. How high the standards were is impossible to say, but there can be no doubt that music answered profound human needs, and in this respect it was indeed as central to humanity as Regino of Prüm maintains. Its functioning largely outside the sphere of writing, even when the means to write music were available, shows the viability of its oral cultivation and is indicative of a high degree of organisation. The term *artifex* with the connotation of a master instrumental musician recalls the word element *ars*, surely in the sense of 'craft'.[79]

---

[77] Treitler, 'Reading and singing', 141.
[78] Treitler, L., 'Oral, written and literate process in the transmission of medieval music', *Speculum* 56, 1981, 471-91, at 475 and 486.
[79] Cf. for similarities in the Celtic societies see chapter 9 below.

PART III
THE EARLY MEDIEVAL EVIDENCE

6

A CAROLINGIAN CLUSTER (c.790–840)

The Carolingian period offers rich and varied information on oral culture.[1] Two factors seem to combine to produce this wealth of information: firstly, a revival of culture based on the written word, a precondition for a fuller record of societal events (one may refer paradigmatically to Einhart's report that Charlemagne ordered part of the orally transmitted culture to be written down);[2] secondly, and not unconnected with this increase in literacy,[3] a reform movement aiming at deepening the observation of Christianity and its values was implemented. In many respects the oral culture advocated values which were hard to reconcile with Christian ethics: as a result of a clash in this area there arises information about the oral culture.

We may begin with legislation of the great reform synods of 813 which were assembled at Mainz, Rheims, Châlon-sur-Saone, Tours and Arles, thus covering a considerable part of the Carolingian empire, though not all areas.[4] These councils have been called 'Charlemagne's most significant contribution to the reform programme, apart from the *Admonitio Generalis*'.[5] Among the conciliar decrees there are found references to existing oral culture. These are as follows:

---

1 This was also noted by Ogilvy, J.D.A., 'Mimi, scurrae, histriones: entertainers of the early Middle Ages', *Speculum* 38, 1963, 603-19, at 608. As one of the very few works dealing with the topic, this article is quoted frequently although, as will become apparent, it is in many respects unreliable and thoroughly unsystematic.
2 *Vita Karoli Magni* c.29: 'Omnium tamen nationum, quae sub eius dominatu erant, iura quae scripta non erant describere ac litteris mandari fecit. Item barbara et antiquissima carmina, quibus veterum regum actus et bella canebantur, scripsit memoriaeque mandavit'. Note Einhart's use of *describere* for the physical act of writing and of scribere in the sense of 'to have written', for which see chapter 3 at n. 27.
3 See chapter 3 above especially at note at 125ff.
4 On these synods see Hartmann, W., *Die Synoden der Karolingerzeit im Frankenreich und in Italien*, Paderborn 1989, esp. ch. II.6.
5 McKitterick, R., *The Frankish Church and the Carolingian reforms, 789-895*, 12.

MOGUNT. *c.*14

Ministri autem altaris Domini vel monachi, nobis placuit, ut a negotiis secularibus omnino abstineant . . . (non) conductores aut procuratores esse saecularium rerum, turpis verbi vel facti ioculatorem esse vel iocum saeculare diligere.[6]

CABILLON. *c.*9

Ab omnibus oculorum auriumque illecebris sacerdotes abstinere debent . . . et turpium seu obscenorum iocorum insolentiam non solum ipsi respuant, verum etiam fidelibus respuenda percenseant.[7]

REM. *c.*17

Ut episcopi et abbates ante se ioca turpia facere non permittant.[8]

TURON. *c.7*

Quaecumque ad aurium et ad oculorum pertinent inlecebras, unde vigor animi amolliri posse credatur—ut de aliquibus generibus musicorum aliisque nonnullis rebus sentiri potest—ab omnibus Dei sacerdotes abstinere debent, quia per aurium oculorumque illecebras vitiorum turba ad animum ingredi solet. Histrionum quoque turpium et obscenorum insolentias iocorum et ipsi animo effugere caeterisque sacerdotibus effugienda praedicare debent.[9]

The Council of Arles did not legislate on these issues.

As far as I know, these canons have never been the object of discussion,[10] yet they can be considered to provide a key to our investigation and thus deserve close scrutiny. I suggest that all four canons quoted here refer to the same cultural phenomena. As will be seen later, they are not the first of their kind. At this stage, they are of greatest interest in that they attest the existence of these cultural phenomena over many areas of the *regnum Francorum*, both its German-speaking and Romance parts.

Both the terminology employed and the attitudes expressed here indicate that performances involving jongleurs were at stake here[11] and were regarded as unsuitable for clerics. Each of the four synods which legislate on this issue

6 MGH Concil. II, 1, p. 264.
7 MGH Concil. II, 1, p. 276.
8 MGH Concil. II, 1, p. 255.
9 MGH Concil. II, 1, p. 287.
10 Brief reference is made to the subject of this chapter by Haubrichs, *Die Anfänge* (= Geschichte der deutschen Literatur von den Anfängen bis zum Beginn der Neuzeit, Heinzle, J., ed., I, 1), Frankfurt 1988, 81-104, passim.
11 See chapter 5 and Richter, *Oral tradition*, passim.

offers its own wording for such a recommendation, so that one is not dealing with a centrally formulated concept applied mechanically. However, the individual wordings draw on a shared linguistic repertoire as well as on a common outlook in all these cases: *ioculator, iocum, histrio*, associated with pejorative terms like *turpis, obscoenus*. Furthermore, there is some additional phrasing emanating from both Tours and Châlon which suggests that these performances would offend eye and ear (*aurium et oculorum illecebra*), and this formulation strengthens the suggestion that one is dealing with a spectacle (*ante se facere*, REM.).

The terms employed indicate the existence of a common vocabulary of condemnation. The repertoire and the ethics expressed in this synodal legislation of 813 can be traced back to late antiquity and the reaction of ecclesiastical leaders to the Roman theatre.[12] Over the centuries, such usage had acquired a validity and had come to be a widely accepted standard. This is evident especially as regards the very frequent use of *turpis* which, in connexion with *iocum*, has no precursors either in classical or biblical Latin. This ninth-century application of fifth-century language and ethics has to be considered in all its implications, especially in view of the fact that the cultural phenomena referred to were not identical in the two periods under consideration.

The synodal legislation of 813 sought to ensure that clerics, priests and monks, would not indulge in those performances which appealed to ear and eye. At Tours reference is also made to the harmful effect of music. Taking the legislation of all four councils together, including the variations in the wording, it would appear that clerical attendance at such performances was customary. At Châlon, and only there, it is furthermore suggested that such performances should be shunned not only by clerics but also by the general Christian public. This seems to indicate that clerics had shared in the past the same taste in entertainment as the laity and that they had cherished identical culture values. The aim of the legislative initiative was to change this situation.

The legislation of 813 does not spell out what these performances were: apparently everybody concerned could be expected to know that, a point which suggests their widespread existence. The legislation from Mainz stresses their essentially secular nature; Tours adds that they involved music. All texts imply that performances were long established. Hence the reform legislation of 813 conveys a general picture of the state of affairs among Carolingian clergy and society before the reform. No conclusions as to the results achieved by this initiative can be drawn from this material;[13] the Church authorities' desire for reform is, however, a feature of all the synods.

12   See chapter 2, as well as Richter, *Oral tradition*, passim.
13   Not to consider this problem is an essential weakness of McKitterick's *Frankish Church*; after all, a generation had passed since the *Admonitio Generalis*.

The extent to which the reform effort was applied locally has been studied recently.[14] One notices some references to our theme, but they are, for the early period at least, thin on the ground, something which itself deserves notice and which may be due to a number of factors other than indifference. Among the generation of bishops who were active c.813, only Heito of Basle makes reference to the issue in his *Capitula Episcoporum*. Written before 823, when he resigned as bishop, it does not echo the language of 813: canon 11, addressed to the clergy states, 'Nec ullius ludi aut spectaculi licentiam habeant.'[15]

The cultural reality of oral performance emerges from other individual references in this period. An undated capitulary from Italy (prior to 800) forbids all clerics 'ulla iocorum genera ante se fieri'.[16] Clearly this refers to the same issue as the legislation of 813, with the one, significant, difference that the performances in question (*ioca*) are not given here any pejorative adjective. Likewise, another capitulary of 789 declares that bishops, abbots and abbesses should not have, among other items such as hunting animals, *ioculatores*.[17] These clerics had evidently enjoyed the same pleasures as their secular counterparts. The last two items can be considered as secular legislation which appears to antedate the activity of Church reformers although it would be unwise to draw too clear a distinction between the two spheres in Carolingian society. Allusion to the same range of issues can be seen in a capitulary from 802 in which priests were asked to ensure that their clerical companions behaved properly and were not parties to vain performances, worldly banquets and shameful songs.[18]

That this kind of entertainment was regarded as something specifically

14 McKitterick, *Frankish Church*, ch. 2. Some of the statutes have been newly edited in the MGH series since the appearance of her book.
15 MGH Capitula Episcoporum, p. 213. This is possibly inspired by the rulings of the council held in Aachen in 816 which openly referred to the councils of late antiquity, including that of Laodicaea, see esp. c. LVIIII, LXXXX and LXXXIII, MGH *Conc.* II, 1, 364, 367, 368. A similar ruling is contained in a Roman synod of 826, c. 11: (Sacerdotes) 'Quamobrem ludos aliquos coram se fieri non delectetur'. MGH *Conc.* 2, 2, 572, with reference to the Council of Laodicea c. 54, Mansi 2, 582. The undated Capitula Florentina, supposed also to be perhaps ninth century, openly refers to the council of Carthage: c. xvii: 'Ut nullus clericus inter epulas cacinare, id est repercuter e vel cantare presumat et scurrilis, id est iocularis verbisque turpibus, ubique appareat, nisi qualiter in concilio Cartaginensis continetur.' MGH *Capitula Episcoporum*, p. 224.
16 MGH Capit. I no. 92, p. 194f: 'Ut tam episcopi quamque et presbiteri seu diaconi vel abbates et monachi . . . ulla iocorum genera ante se fieri permittant que contra canonum auctoritate eveniunt'.
17 No. 23 c.31: 'Ut episcopi et abbates et abbatissae cupplas canum non habeant nec falcones nec accipitres nec ioculatores.' MGH Capit. I, 64. This earliest medieval reference to a *ioculator* is not listed in Faral, *Jongleur*.
18 Capitulare missorum generale, c.23: 'Presbiteri cleros quos secum habent sollicite praevideant, ut canonice vivant: non inanis lusibus vel conviviis secularibus vel canticis vel luxoriosis usum habeant; sed caste et salubre vivant'. MGH Capit. no. 33, p. 96.

secular is spelled out explicitly in a decision of the Concilium Foroiuliense of 796/797:

> c.6   Item placuit, ut eas prorsus mundanas dignitates, quas seculares viri vel principes terrae exercere solent, in venationibus scilicet vel in canticis secularibus aut in resoluta et inmoderata laetitia, in liris et tibiis et his similibus lusibus, nullus sub ecclesiastico canone constitutus ob inanis laetitiae fluxum audeat fastu superbie tumidus quandoque praesumendo abuti. . . .[19]

It is thus clear that the upper echelons of society of the *regnum Langobardorum* cherished the same cultural values as their counterparts north of the Alps. Allusion is made to the habitual pleasures cherished by lay people. Besides hunting, prominent place is given to *cantica* as well as to instrumental music; this kind of entertainment gave great joy ('resoluta et inmoderata laetitia, inanis laetitia'). Of course, we need not share the ethical evaluation of this ecclesiastical legislation. We may note the use of *ludus*—synonymous with *iocum*—for this kind of activity.

There is further ecclesiastical legislation (*c*.800), unfortunately not precisely locatable, from the Bavarian area in which the laity are asked to pursue a more Christian way of life than hitherto and to shun *inlecebrosa cantica* as well as *lusum saeculare*.[20]

The year 789 marks the beginnings of legislation against the traditional secular entertainment of clerics. By the end of Charlemagne's reign the attempts in this direction broadened. Unfortunately, the normative sources do not provide insight into how the reform efforts fared.[21]

The legislation considered so far is tantalizing in that it provides only allusions to unspecified phenomena. However, Alcuin provides in his correspondence some illuminating information, especially involving the famous courtier Angilbert, alias 'Homer', one of Charlemagne's favourite companions. The letters in question date from about 800. Alcuin writes that 'Homer' was very annoyed about a ban by charter on performances which were associated with devilish figments ('contra cartam prohibentem spectacula et diabolica figmenta').[22] The charter mentioned here has not survived, and it is not quite

---

19   MGH Conc. II, 1, 191.
20   MGH Capit. 112, 'Statuta Rhispacensia, Frisingensia, Salisburgensia', *c*.34: 'Ut omnis populus honorifice cum omnis supplicationibus devotione humiliter et cum reverentia absque praetiosarum vestium ornatu vel etiam inlecebroso cantico et lusu saeculari cum laetaniis procedant et discant Kyrielyson clamare, ut non tam rustice ut nunc usque sed melius discant.' p. 229. The curious formulation *Kyrielyson clamare* should be noted.
21   Further discussion of the subject in the section on the Statuta Episcoporum.
22   MGH Epp. IV, no. 175, 290; no. 237, 381. See *Oral tradition*, ch. 4. The most recent account by Viarre, S., 'Un portrait d'Angilbert dans la correspondence d'Alcuin?', *De*

clear what it referred to. What is remarkable is that here we have evidence that apparently the secular authorities were involved in this issue, which is suggested by Alcuin's use of the term *carta*. Alcuin justified that ban with reference to a saying which he attributed to Augustine: 'Nescit homo, qui histriones et mimos et saltatores introducit in domum suam, quam magna eos inmundorum sequitur turba spirituum.'[23] Obviously, one is dealing with the performers of secular culture and traditions. Angilbert appears to have come to terms with the legislation eventually.[24]

Alcuin makes other allusions to the jongleurs in the form of commonplace references: 'Melius est Deo placere quam histrionibus, pauperum habere curam quam mimorum. Sint tibi honesta convivia et convivae relegiosi';[25] 'melius est pauperes edere de mensa tua, quam istriones vel luxuriosos quoslibet'.[26] These statements allude to the popularity of the jongleurs, their presence at conviviality. The important message here is that everything indicates the widespread existence of jongleurs and their utter social respectability. Referring, as it does, to the same cultural phenomena as the legislation of 813 and the Italian capitulary, in its use of the classical terminology relating to stage actors (*histriones, mimi*) it evidences the re-appearance of this vocabulary in the decades of the Carolingian renaissance.

In this context also belongs a famous admonition sent by Alcuin to Bishop Higbald of Lindisfarne in Northumbria in 797, where he states:

> Verba Dei legantur in sacerdotali convivio. Ibi decet lectorem audiri, non citharistam: sermones patrum, non carmina gentilium. Quid Hinieldus cum Christo? Angusta est domus: utrosque tenere non poterit. . . . Voces legentium audire in domibus tuis, non ridentium turbam in plateis.[27]

Tertullien aux Mozarabes (FS J. Fontaine), Holtz, L. and Fredouille, J.-C., ed., Paris 1992, vol. II, 267-274, at 270f, does not shed further light on this problem.

23 This saying cannot be traced in Augustine's works but is clearly Augustinian in spirit, cf. above, chapter 2, n. 43.

24 Ep. 237, p. 381, esp. lines 31-36. Alcuin took the opportunity to rub in the point: 'Unum fuit de histrionibus, quorum vanitatibus sciebam non parvum animae suae periculum inminere, quod mihi non placuit.' On these references relating to Alcuin see Faral, *Jongleurs*, 19f. who, however, does little to elucidate the problem.

25 Ep. 281, 439.

26 Ep. 124, 183. Cf also Lk 14:13: 'Cum facis convivium, voca pauperes, debiles, claudos, et caecos.'

27 Ep. 124, MGH Epp. IV, 183. One is reminded, in the last phrase, of the NT quotation 2 Cor 6:15: 'Quae autem conventio Christi ad Belial? Autem quae pars fideli cum infideli?' A similar phrase occurs in Tertullian, *Liber de praescriptionibus* VII: 'Quid ergo Athenis et Hierosolymis? Quid Academiae et Ecclesiae? quid haereticis et Christianis?' PL 2, 20. Cf. also the famous sentence written by Gregory the Great to Desiderius of Vienne: 'in uno se ore cum Iovis laudibus Christi laudes non capiunt', *Reg.* XI, 34.

Here Alcuin gives a very good insight into the social context of the performance of the *carmina gentilium*: they were performed as part of conviviality initiated by men in holy orders, and they were possibly performed to musical accompaniment.[28] The performers shared the meal in an unspecified way with their hosts. Alcuin's letter is not quite specific as to whether this was the only kind of entertainment on such occasions or whether it shared pride of place with reading of Christian material. Whatever the situation referred to, Alcuin demanded a ban on all secular songs in that context. In fact, the last phrase of our quotation already occurs four years earlier in a letter by Alcuin to the same Higbald where Alcuin also warned against drunkenness.[29] He appears to have had good reasons to specify particular aberrations even though he did so in standardized terms. Those who provided entertainment at Lindisfarne and caused laughter belonged properly in the streets, in public places. One also gets the impression that Alcuin had reason to believe that in Lindisfarne he preached to closed ears.

Alcuin's references confirm the idea that the performers of traditional culture enjoyed great popularity, that their art was widely appreciated, and, in his opinion, (unfittingly) well rewarded. His last letter shows further that this was the case not only in the Carolingian kingdom but also in England. That the bishop of Lindisfarne had to be admonished in this matter shows how utterly respectable the art of the jongleurs was even in the highest English ecclesiastical circles.

We shall now jump a generation, beyond the reform councils of 813, into the reign of Louis the Pious. His biographer Thegan has the following to report:

> Nunquam in risum exaltavit vocem suam, nec quando in summis festivitatibus ad laetitiam populi procedebant themilici, scurri et mimi cum coraulis et citharistis ad mensam coram eo, tunc ad mensuram ridebat populus coram eo, ille nunquam nec dentes candidos suos in risu ostendit.[30]

In the light of our previous discussion a careful analysis[31] of this sentence will produce rich insights into the court culture of the time. Thegan's purpose in presenting this cameo of court culture was to describe the mental state of the emperor which he does by placing him in a customary environment.

28 See at n. 30.
29 *Ep.* 21 p. 59: 'Audiantur in domibus vestris legentes, non ludentes in platea; et inter seniores consilia salutis, non ebrietatis iniquitas, quae fovea est perditionis et multum Deo servientibus noxia; dicente apostolo: "Ebriosi regnum Dei non possidebunt".' (1 Cor 6:10).
30 Thegani vita Hludowici, c. 19, MGH SS II, 595.
31 Cf. the 'thick description', a term which Clifford Geertz borrowed from the philosopher Gilbert Ryle as meaningful for his own work as ethnologist, *Interpretation*, 7ff.

Thegan refers to a manifestation of culture which marked especially the great feast days, no doubt the feasts of the Christian calendar. The entertainment was provided for the enjoyment of the entourage of the emperor, called here twice *populus*, to be understood as 'nobility'. It was an integral part of a conviviality (*ad mensam*) which brought together emperor and nobles. Thegan shows that Louis did not appear to enjoy the entertainment in the way his table companions did who responded appropriately (*ad mensuram*).[32] One is given the impression that this entertainment was of a traditional kind and an established institution. This valuable information concerning the customary events at court is reported by Thegan incidentally, because he regarded it as noteworthy that the emperor did not respond to it in the appropriate and accustomed manner.[33] However, because of this one also learns what the appropriate reaction to the performances was: one of loud laughter, or perhaps one should call it 'joyful response'. The purpose of the convivial festivity was to provide social equals an opportunity to share enjoyment and edification.[34] One is thus dealing with a manifestation of highly ritualized socialization at court.[35]

As to those who provided the entertainment, three kinds of activity are mentioned—those of actors (*scurrae, mimi*[36]), of instrumentalists (*themilici, citharistae*) and singers (*coraulae*). Words, sounds and movement were part of this entertainment; unfortunately, it is impossible to say whether or how they combined.[37] However, it can be assumed that those who performed were professionals of the highest rank; nothing less would have done for the imperial court. Their contribution was expected on suitable occasions; it is highly likely that they were part of the court personnel although the sources say nothing on this score.

Thegan does not state whether the audience on these occasions consisted of lay people only. However, in view of the fact that this entertainment took

32 'Immoderata laetitia' shown by lay people is criticized by the Concilium Foroiuliense of 796/7, c. vi. See n. 19 above.
33 The attitude would have been the appropriate one for Roman as well as Byzantine emperors (as kindly pointed out to me by Professor Jean Claude Bonne, Paris), but not Germanic kings who were supposed to share the ethics of their nobles. This interpretation is strengthened when taken in conjunction, as I think it has to be, with Louis's reaction to the *carmina gentilia*, for which see below (n. 58).
34 This subject has received excellent treatment by Ostheeren, K., *Studien zum Begriff der 'Freude' und seinen Ausdrucksmitteln in altenglischen Texten*, Heidelberg 1964 and is of relevance beyond Anglo-Saxon England.
35 Althoff, G., 'Fest und Bündnis', in *Feste und Feiern im Mittelalter*, Altenburg, D., ed. et al., Sigmaringen 1991, 29-38. For an important presentation especially of the ritual element see Enright, M.J., 'Lady with a mead-cup'.
36 In the early medieval centuries, *mimus* is nowhere attested in the sense of 'play', as was the case in antiquity.
37 For the problems see chapter 5.

place on high feast days, it would have been most unlikely for clerics not to have been present. From what has been reported by Thegan, the clerics also would have been expected to take pleasure in the festivity of this kind.

Thegan makes it clear that such socializing was taken for granted even if the host did not share the general taste. This is indicative of the vitality of traditional social norms. In this context it is tempting to juxtapose Thegan's account with a fleeting reference to the same issue in Einhart's *Vita Karoli Magni* (which was written, after all, during the reign of Louis and is considered by many scholars as a sort of critical comment on the reign of Louis). Einhart writes of Charlemagne that he gave banquets very rarely; however, on high feast days,[38] when he did so, it was with panache: 'Convivabatur rarissime, et hoc praecipuis tantum festivitatibus, tunc tamen cum magno hominum numero' (ch. 24). Einhart obviously found it remarkable that Charlemagne followed the social norms within rather narrow limits although even he apparently was bound by them. We now have a better idea of what such gatherings consisted of, namely food, drink, music, entertainment and enjoyment.[39]

Charlemagne's reservations about feasts[40] seem to have had other reasons than those of Louis. Whereas his son did not warm to the performances of the jongleurs, he detested inebriation.[41] Here one can only guess that heavy drinking was the norm at court festivities.[42] Again the emperor was the odd one out who did not subscribe to the norm although he could not change it even if he tried.[43] There are plenty of indications that heavy social drinking was very widespread at the time, and that the clergy cultivated it as much as the laity, and not only when they were in mixed company.[44]

38 Cf. Thegan: 'in summis festivitatibus'.
39 Cf. the illuminating though brief account by Vierck, H., 'Hallenfreude. Archäologische Spuren frühmittelalterlicher Trinkgelage und mögliche Wege ihrer Deutung', in *Feste und Feiern im Mittelalter*, 115-21.
40 The remarkable quality of his attitude is underlined by the fact that Einhart's exemplar Sueton reports here that the emperor Augustus feasted *assidue*.
41 Einhart ch. 24: 'ebrietatem in qualicumque homine, nedum in se ac suis, plurimum abhominabatur'. Unlike this statement, another sentence in the same chapter is heavily dependent on Sueton: 'Vini et omnis potus adeo parcus in bibendo erat, ut super caenam raro plus quam ter biberet.'
42 For more evidence see Richter, *Oral tradition*, ch. 6.
43 Duplex legislationis edictum of 789: 'omnino prohibendum est omnibus ebrietatis malum et istas coniurationes, quas faciunt per sanctum Stephanum aut per nos aut per filios nostros prohibemus'. MGH Capit. I, 64.
44 A particularly telling insight comes from the council of Châlon of 813 where it was ruled: c.X 'Ut sobrietatem sacerdotes teneant et hanc habendam fidelibus praedicent, quia non potest libere sobrietatem praedicare qui se mero usque ad alienationem mentis ingurgitat', MGH Conc. I, 276. This is the most explicit statement; that the reformers regarded it as a widespread evil appears from the Annotatio capitulorum synodalium, c. XIII, Conc. 2,

Besides drinking, there was of course also eating. Excess in this respect was anathema to serious Christians; indeed, gluttony held a prominent place among the seven deadly sins. Alcuin defined it as excessive delight in eating and drinking ('intemperans cibi vel potus voluptas'). He further associates gluttony with

> inepta laetitia, scurrilitas, levitas, vaniloquium, inmunditia corporis, instabilitas mentis, ebrietas, libido: quia ex saturitate ventris libido corporis congeritur, quae per jejunia et abstinentiam, et operis cuiuslibet assiduitatem, optime vincitur.[45]

When reading these condemnatory statements in a positive way, one finds that they echo in many respects the information about feasting provided by Thegan from the court of Louis the Pious. We should take note of the great joy (*inepta laetitia*) which such feasting produced.

As to the kind of entertainment provided at the imperial court for the nobility—the art of the jongleurs—one is tempted to think in the first place of the heroic songs which were then current in oral tradition as explicitly stated by Einhart writing about Charlemagne:

> Barbara et antiquissima carmina, quibus veterum regum actus et bella canebantur, scripsit memoriaeque mandavit. (VKM c.29)

This phrase has been much discussed and very variously interpreted.[46] Unfortunately, Einhart does not say what Charlemagne thought of this material; but his familiarity with it and interest in it is beyond doubt.[47]

One notices in the first place the fact that the poetry was sung, which was a form of eminently memorable transmission; the musical element would likewise contribute to the pleasure created by the performance. Einhart's account would not appear to be inappropriate to Thegan's description of the court scene under Louis. In Einhart's opinion the songs were very old, which

---

1, p. 302. See further Richter, *Oral tradition*, ch. 6; also Bischoff, B., 'Caritaslieder', *Mittelalterliche Studien* II, Stuttgart 1967, 56-77.

45 *Liber de virtutibus et vitiis*, c. 28, PL 101, 633.

46 For a recent survey of the broader subject see Haubrichs, *Die Anfänge*, 142f. Cf. also Moisl, H., 'Kingship and orally transmitted Stammestradition among the Lombards and Franks', in Wolfram, H., Schwarcz, A., ed., *Die Bayern und ihre Nachbarn*, vol. I, Wien 1985, 111-19, esp. 117f.

47 A very concrete political use of it has been suggested recently— though not for the first time—by Ebel, U., 'Historizität und Kodifizierung. Überlegungen zu einem zentralen Aspekt des germanischen Heldenlieds', in *Althochdeutsch*, Bergmann, R., ed., Heidelberg 1987, I, 685-714, esp. 709f.

implies that they had for a long time been orally transmitted.[48] It should be noted that the term *barbarus* in this phrase has no pejorative connotations; it may be taken as a technical term best understood in the sense of 'non-Latin'. In this respect, the text of the *Hildebrandslied*, first written *c*.800,[49] attests that heroic verse in the *lingua barbara* was current then.[50] Since its 'historical kernel' is to be placed in the fifth century, the term *antiquissimus* would not be inappropriate either.[51] One may mention in this context that Charlemagne was attracted by the figure of Theodoric; he must have heard of the remarkable achievements of the Ostrogothic king, and he brought about the transfer of an equestrian statue of Theodoric from Ravenna to Aachen.[52]

The information concerning this transfer is remarkably tenuous, which suggests that the emperor's esteem for the Ostrogothic king was not shared by everybody, particularly those who wrote about their times. Theodoric's Arianism would have been a possible explanation[53]—in which case it is all the more remarkable that Charlemagne, himself a champion of Christian orthodoxy, would have placed Theodoric's political stature above his religious preference. While it is impossible to be explicit as to what kind of information Charlemagne had of Theodoric and how it had reached him,[54] it is very likely

48 In this respect, it is not at all valid to take the information provided by the Poeta Saxo on this subject as reliable information about Einhart's *carmina*: 'Est quoque iam notum: vulgaria carmina magnis/Laudibus eius avos et proavos celebrant,/Pippinos, Carolos, Hludowicos et Theodricos/Et Carlomannos Hlothariosque canunt.' MGH Poetae latini IV, 58.
49 See Haubrichs, *Anfänge*, 147ff. For a more general discussion of the issue of oral poetry and heroic literature see chapter 10 below.
50 It should be noted, however, that this poem does not throughout articulate heroic values. For an attempt to relate the poem to the political situation in the empire towards the end of the reign of Louis the Pious see Schlosser, H.-D., 'Die Aufzeichnung des Hildebrandsliedes im historischen Kontext', *Germanisch-Romanische Monatsschrift* 28, 1978, 217-24. For other, more acceptable thoughts on this much-discussed text see Ebel, 'Historizität und Kodifizierung'.
51 For further discussion see chapter 10. Paulus Diaconus in s. viii referring to the killing of the Burgundian king Gundicarius by Attila, Haubrichs, *Anfänge*, 119, appears to draw on oral tradition.
52 Agnellus of Ravenna, Liber pontificalis ecclesiae Ravennatis: 'Karolus rex . . . revertens Franciam, Ravenna ingressus, videns pulcherrimam imaginem, quam numquam similem, ut ipse testatus est, vidit, Franciam deportari fecit atque in suo eam firmare palatio qui Aquisgranis vocatur.' MGH SS rer. Langob., 338. For a modern assessment see Hoffmann, H., 'Die Aachener Theoderichstatue', in *Das erste Jahrtausend. Kultur und Kunst im werdenden Abendland an Rhein und Ruhr*, Textband I, Elbern, V.H., ed., Düsseldorf 1962, 318-35.
53 Cf. Thürlemann, F., 'Die Bedeutung der Aachener Theoderich-Statue für Karl den Großen (801) und bei Walahfrid Strabo (829). Materialien zu einer Semiotik visueller Objekte im frühen Mittelalter', *Archiv für Kulturgeschichte* 59, 1977, 25-65, with references to earlier literature, esp. 34f.
54 See Höfler, O., 'Theoderich der Große und sein Bild in der Sage', *Österreichische Akademie der Wissenschaften, Phil.-hist. Klasse, Anzeiger* 111, 1974, 349-72.

that it was oral tradition in the form of heroic saga.[55]

In fact, there is corroborative evidence for the existence of such heroic material a generation before Einhart, which, curiously enough, is hardly ever discussed. In his *Historia Langobardorum*, Paul the Deacon reports factually and with no negative connotations whatever, that the achievements of the Lombard king Albuin were celebrated in songs among the Bavarians, Saxons and other people in his lifetime:

> Alboin vero ita praeclarum longe lateque nomen percrebuit, ut hactenus etiam tam aput Baioariorum gentem quamque et Saxonum, sed et alios eiusdem linguae homines eius liberalitas et gloria bellorumque felicitas et virtus in eorum carminibus celebretur. Arma quoque praecipua sub eo fabricata fuisse, a multis hucusque narratur.[56]

For Paul the Deacon, the existence of heroic verse was taken as a normal aspect of life among the barbarians.

The collection of heroic verse initiated by Charlemagne has not survived, and so there is not much point in speculating about its size or content.[57] The intiative of Charlemagne should not be taken, as it often is, as an attitude of antiquarianism attempting to preserve in the new medium material whose oral transmission was coming to an end. On the contrary, as will be seen, there is every reason to maintain that heroic verse continued to be orally transmitted,[58] that it remained in demand and continued to find appreciative audiences and occasions of performance. Einhart reports further that Charlemagne had read to him the 'historiae et antiquorum res gestae'.[59]

According to Thegan, Louis had in his youth learned a certain kind of poetry that he came to detest later in his life:

> Ch. 19 Poetica carmina gentilia quae in iuventute didicerat, respuit, nec legere, nec audire, nec docere voluit.

---

55 Cf. Thürlemann 35 and note 25; Graus. F., *Lebendige Vergangenheit. Überlieferung im Mittelalter und in den Vorstellungen vom Mittelalter*, Köln 1975, 39-43.
56 Pauli Historia Langobardorum, MGH SS us. schol., 1878, 81.
57 See Meissburger, G., 'Zum sogenannten Heldenbuch Karls des Großen', *Germanisch-Romanische Monatsschrift* 44, 1963, 105-19 as well as the sharp criticism of this work by Ebel, 'Historizität und Kodifizierung'.
58 However, I have to draw attention to a passage in a letter by Lull of c.738, never commented on, where he states that he sent poetry 'iocistae more caraxatos' (*Bonifatius- Briefe*, Tangl, ed., no. 98, p. 220), which suggests that jongleurs did also avail themselves of the medium of writing. It is uncertain what the meaning of *iocista* is; in Aldhelm's letter it is used synonymously with *scurra*: Ep. 5, MGH AA 15, p. 493: 'iocistae scurraeque ritu dicacitate temeraria loquentium'. Perhaps the term is an insular Latin speciality since it appears to be attested nowhere else.
59 VKM c. 24, p. 29.

It is not clear whether Thegan's *carmina gentilia* are the same as Einhart's *barbara et antiquissima carmina*; they could refer equally to poetry from Latin antiquity. They were available in written form. However, what one can learn from Thegan here is that there were cultural norms current at court to which the prince was initially subjected and against which he turned only later in life. There is confirmation of sorts in this field. We have pointed to the respect which Charlemagne showed to the memory of Theodoric. In a long poem on Aachen written in 829 by Walahfrid Strabo, the Theodoric statue figures prominently,[60] and the king is presented throughout in a negative light. In his treatment of the heroic figure, the poem may be taken to articulate the opinion of the emperor's entourage with its strong emphasis on orthodox Christian norms.[61] Walahfrid's is the second and last reference to this statue; it must remain speculation whether the statue was actually removed at the time of the writing of his poem.[62]

We have now come across several instances in which generally accepted social norms were not appreciated by everybody concerned. Indeed, this is the main reason why the information about these social norms is provided. We can see that even rulers were expected to bow to such norms; the two rulers mentioned here are presented as having done so, albeit with reservation. Their range of choice was limited by tradition.

The widespread custom among lay people (presumably of the higher ranks) of banqueting in grand style with drink and entertainment by jongleurs is also attested by Agobard of Lyon in a letter written in 823/4.[63] Here we learn explicitly what was alluded to only in an imprecise way by Alcuin—that the conviviality which produced hilarity also included the jongleurs being treated to food as well as drink. They were thus considered to be respectable company.

Agobard provides further insights. Leaning on the authority of councils and the writings of Church Fathers—Jerome, Cyprian, Augustine and Gregory—he complains about the way in which singing in church is practised. Even in songs containing the word of God, gesture and sound are used (which are highly inappropriate) and the sweetness of the voice gives unrestrained pleasure.[64] He characterizes a truly free mind as being above the enticements

---

60 MGH Poet. Lat. II, 370ff., Carmen XXIII, see the section 'De imagine Tetrici'.
61 Cf. Thürlemann, 'Bedeutung', esp. 48: 'Walahfrid scheint die Absicht zu haben, ein allgemein verbreitetes positives Theoderich-Bild zu korrigieren. Es ist wohl das gleiche, das schon die Aufstellung der Statue durch Karl den Großen ermöglicht hat.'
62 Cf. Thürlemann, 64.
63 MGH Epp. 5, 178f. PL 104, 249: 'convivia splendida . . . epulatur cum divitibus opulentis gaudens ridensque et opus Domini non respiciens et quasi agens que Deo placeant, iucundatur, satiat preterea et inebriat histriones, mymmos, turpissimosque et vanissimos ioculares, cum pauperes ecclesiae fame discrutiati intereant'.
64 *Liber de correctione antiphonarii*, PL 104, 334: 'eos vero qui theatralibus sonis et scenicis modulationibus, et quamvis in divinis verbis, vocis dulcedine intemperantius delectantur'.

of ear, eye or nose.[65] Apparently he moved among people who had not attained such freedom.

Louis the Pious was not consistent in his policy. One may refer in the first instance to the ambitious reform synod of 816 which was held at Aachen. Its canons made ample, explicit reference to councils of late antiquity, including Carthage, as well as to the writings of the Fathers.[66] How difficult it is to assess the realization of such intentions appears from the other great reform synod held on Louis' initiative in 829 but which breathes severe criticism of his action on the part of the bishops. Two statements epitomize the situation in the empire in a devastating manner:

> c.61   Professio Christiana a multis et in multis propter delectationes carnales et propter diversissimas huius saeculi vanitates et perversissimas consuetudines miserabiliter neglegitur.[67]
>
> c.93   Sacerdotes partim neglegentia, partim ignorantia, partim cupiditate in saecularibus negotiis et sollicitudinibus mundi ultra, quam debuerant, se occupaverint.[68]

These assessments of the actual situation precede the prolonged agony of the reign of Louis; one can be quite certain that the situation described here did not improve over the next decade. This is a devastating comment on the realization of the *societas Christiana* which Louis sought, a policy which he had intended to contrast with that of his father. The utter failure was manifest to his contemporaries some of whom did not hide their disappointment.

We have raised the question earlier whether clerics and lay people cherished the same culture. Virtually all the normative legislation from the reign of Charlemagne strongly suggests that this had earlier been the case. In the eyes of dedicated Christians traditional oral culture was of a kind which was unsuitable not only for clerics but for all Christians; however, the authority of Church leaders extended in the first instance to clerics, who were

> Here one sees very well how Agobard uses the language of the Fathers even though writing from a different environment. The *theatrales soni*, familiar to Jerome, would be merely a metaphorical expression for him.

65   Ibid., 334-335: 'Mens ergo libera, id est, sensibus corporis non succumbens, ita resistere debet vanae ac noxiae delectationi aurium, sicut et delectationibus sensuum caeterorum, visus videlicet et olfactus, gestus, et tactus; quorum perturbationibus anima praegravatur, et capitur.'
66   MGH Conc. II, 1, 307-456.
67   MGH Conc. II, 2, 657.
68   MGH Conc. II, 2, 679.

immediately in their charge. To change their way of life, to make it different from traditional forms, was the first objective of the reformers. Future legislation on the same issues shows that the need for such reforms continued. Thus there is reason to think that traditional culture was deeply embedded in society. This also means that those who most visibly practised this culture were approved of by leading circles in society.

It is difficult to estimate how many clerics saw no need to distance themselves from traditional culture. These clerics are clearly under-represented in the sources, but the legislation of 829 shows that there was considerable scope for reform. However, the political climate necessary to implement the change had deteriorated.

Our source material is such that one is better informed about the upper echelons of society and the clergy than about the rest of the population. However, Jonas of Orleans gives us to understand that feasting of the kind which Thegan described as taking place at the imperial court was quite widespread: 'Nunc autem vix a quibusdam sumitur cibus sine detractione, sine simulatione, sine insultatione, sine histrionum saltatione, et obscena jocatione, et turpiloquiis, et scurrilitatibus, et caeteris innumeris vanitatibus.'[69]

The sources which we have looked at so far give no ground for believing that there was a specific form of culture for clerics and another for the lay nobility. The clerics are encountered in the sources as generally sharing the one and same taste as the *populus* at court.

Here we may also mention information about milieus other than the court. In his Life of St Liudger, written *c.*800, the author describes the saint coming to the Frisians to spread the gospel and continues:

> Oblatus est ei caecus vocabulo Bernlef, qui a vicinis suis valde diligebatur, eo quod esset affabilis et antiquorum actus regumque certamina bene noverat psallendo promere.[70]

In the light of the information provided by Paul the Deacon in the late eighth century this reference to the songs of the ancestors among the Frisians comes as no surprise. The Life of St Liudger confirms that among the Frisians a culture existed similar to that of the Carolingians, Bavarians and Saxons: the deeds of the ancestors and the heroic battles of the kings were commemorated in song, and the person who knew how to do this well was popular in his community. By comparing this Life with the accounts previously discussed,

69 *De Institutione Laicali*, PL 106, I, 20, col. 164.
70 *Die Vita Sancti Liudgeri*. Diekamp, W., ed. (Die Geschichtsquellen des Bistums Münster, vol. 4), Münster 1881, ch. 25, p. 30 (also AA SS Martii III, 647). For a recent discussion see Haubrichs, *Anfänge*, 84, 87. Cf. also Lebecq, S., 'Entre tradition orale et littérature héroique: le cas du *scop* frison Bernlef', *Médiévales* 20, 1991, 17-24.

we see that Christianity among the Carolingians had done little to alter this appreciation.

There were, of course, Christian leaders who saw the situation differently. Paulinus, the patriarch of Aquileia, articulated this attitude particularly well in a brief work written for the benefit of Count Henry of Friaul around 795. From his way of arguing one can glean views generally held, namely that there may well have been particular norms of life appropriate for clerics but that these were considered as being of no relevance to lay people. Paulinus was emphatic that this attitude was wrong, for Christ had shed his blood not only for clerics, but for lay people as well: therefore clerics and lay alike were expected to follow his precepts.[71]

The same point was made in greater detail, a generation later, by Jonas of Orleans in his work *De Institutione laicali* written for Count Matfrid in the 820s.[72] Jonas insisted that the observation of Christian precepts was demanded not only from clerics but from all Christians: 'Lex itaque Christi non specialiter clericis, sed generaliter cunctis fidelibus observanda est . . . sunt alii qui eam (legem evangelicam et apostolicam) sibi datam credunt, hanc tamen intelligere, et secundum eam vivere detrectant.'[73] The same point was made in 829 at the synod of Paris in which Jonas played a prominent part.[74] The bishops pointed out that the implementation of Christian precepts should begin with the clergy, followed by kings and princes and the faithful generally.[75] Likewise, in a long and important letter to the emperor several bishops warned against obscene and detestable songs as suitable entertainment for all Christians.[76] The clergy were to give a good example to the laity in this matter in order to encourage them to follow suit. This letter was written at a time when the relationship between the emperor and his bishops had drastically deteriorated. A similar message is conveyed by Paschasius Radbertus, who wondered why people did

71 *Sancti Paulini patriarchae Aquileiensis Liber Exhortationis*, PL 99, esp. ch. xxxviii 'Praecepta Dei ad omnes Christianos pertinere: quia non solum pro nobis clericis, sed etiam pro omni genere humano . . ., Christus sanguinem suum fudit: nec solum nobis, sed etiam omnibus laicis, eius ex toto corde praecepta servantibus, regnum coelorum promissum est'. 240; and 'Omnis enim clericus et laicus, qui praetioso sanguine Christi redemptus est, qui baptismo Christi tinctus est, debet humiliter ambulare et perseverare in Spiritu sancto,' 241.
72 PL 106, 121-278. See further Scharf, J., 'Studien zu Smaragdus und Jonas', *Deutsches Archiv* 17, 1961, 333-84 for the dating.
73 *De Institutione Laicali*, I, 20, PL 106, 161. The first part of the quotation reappears in Jonas' *De Institutione Regia*, Reviron, J., ed., Paris 1930, ch. 11. See further: 'Necesse est ut unusquisque fidem Christi quam perceperit, operibus exornet', PL 106, 160.
74 c.38: 'non solum sacerdotibus, verum etiam ceteris fidelibus', MGH Conc. II, 2, 637.
75 c. 50: 'primum sacerdotes, postea reges et principes cunctique fideles', MGH Conc. II, 2, 643.
76 Episcoporum ad Hludowicum imperatorem relatio: '. . . noxio assiduoque iuramento et obscenis turpibusque canticis omnibus christianis intellegendum et observandum est, ut summopere ab his se caveant . . .', MGH, Capit. II, p. 45.

A Carolingian cluster

not devote the same attention to the mysteries of Christianity as they did to performances of worldly compositions.[77]

There is, finally, matter of fact reference to oral traditions in the Carolingian period. Thus Paul the Deacon reports in his *Historia Langobardorum* about the Lombards: 'Virtus in eorum carminibus celebretur.'[78] He also refers to Agelmund, first king of the Lombards, who reigned for 33 years, 'sicut a maioribus traditur'.[79] In his Life of Louis the Pious, Thegan mentions Charlemagne's Spanish campaign of 778 in the course of which some prominent Franks died. He does not consider it necessary to mention their names since these are generally known ('Quorum, quia vulgata sunt, nomina dicere supersedi').[80] This is testimony to the oral tradition of history that was considered as vital enough not to need to be written. The historical event referred to here lay two generations in the past.

The references which we have discussed so far are all contemporary with the reigns of Charlemagne and Louis. They have long been known, yet in our presentation they add up to a kind of culture among the Carolingians which appears in none of the current textbooks.[81] It is simply a matter of how one decodes the available information.[82] This needs to be treated in its general social and historical context, and this has in fact not been done previously.

The references are mainly of a negative and a normative kind and are repeated as such by the modern authors. An approach to Carolingian secular culture is made possible by its critics, whose attitudes could range from mild to vehement—which is why the information requires detailed decoding. Taken together the sources reveal remarkable phenomena of a vital oral culture. One should add that the critics like Alcuin, Jonas or Agobard, though prominent in the sources, cannot be taken as representative of Carolingian culture. There

---

77 'Unde miror satis, quid divina eloquia quorundam moribus offendunt, quod non velint mystica Dei sacramenta ea diligentia perscrutari, quo tragoediarum naenias et poetarum figmenta sudantes cupiunt investigare labore et sic per teatralia mimorum plausus hominum excitare', MGH Epp. VI, 142.
78 Historia Langobardorum I, 27, MGH SS us. schol. 48, p. 81.
79 Historia Langobardorum I, 14, p. 61.
80 Vita Hludowici imperatoris, c. 2, MGH SS II, 608.
81 This is apt even for one of the most recent and highly sensitive treatment of the subject, by Haubrichs, *Anfänge*, who writes: '(man muß) vor der Überbewertung von Konzilsbeschlüssen und geistlichen Bußbüchern warnen. . . . Es sollen wohl nur die Auswüchse, die "häßlichen und unkeuschen Tänze und Lieder" getroffen werden', 92. The same applies to the assessment of the reforms of Christian life for which see the account by McKitterick, R., *Reforms*, which seems to be far too positive in its assessment.
82 No decoding was done by Ogilvy, 'Mimi, scurrae, histriones', the only work during the past generation to deal with this material and referred to by later authors uncritically. The same must be stated of Bezzola, R., *Les origines et la formation de la littérature courtoise en occident (500-1200)*, I, Paris 1958, esp. ch. 5, Les Carolingiens. Bezzola's mistake is to view the material with an anachronistic concept of literature for this period. See further, chapter 10.

is enough to indicate that, generally speaking, they failed to impose the ethics they advocated.

We still have to refer briefly to information about Charlemagne concerning traditional culture which is not contemporary with his reign but comes from the 880s. Notker Balbulus of St Gall, author of the *Gesta Karoli*, mentions at the court of Charlemagne a cleric who was outstanding in worldly and divine literature, who composed ecclesiastical and worldly songs and also could sing them excellently.[83] While his information cannot be accepted as factual and was meant to be above all didactic, it does allow insight into what was considered appropriate by the author for the imperial entourage. It suggests that secular song (*cantilea iocularis*) was quite acceptable there even when composed or recited by clerics.

There is furthermore an account from the eleventh century about Charlemagne's Italian campaigns against the Lombard king Desiderius. It is told that a Lombard jongleur came to the court of the Frankish king and drew attention to himself by reciting a little composition to the accompaniment of a harp in which he presented himself as being of potential use for the Franks. Of course his help had its price.[84] This account should be considered again as evidence at best for the time of the chronicler who would have projected his knowledge of the work of the jongleurs into the past.

A reconstruction of court events shows the following features. High Christian feasts of the year saw the gathering of the nobles at the royal or imperial court. Central to the gathering was the banquet at which drink was consumed in large quantities. There was an atmosphere of merriment among peers who shared the same taste as well as the same culture. During the festivities, as an integral part of the occasion, performers and musicians provided entertainment. The performance highlighted the memorable and exemplary deeds of the ancestors. The material was well known to all present, while joyful response to the performance and audience participation regularly confirmed and thereby reinforced approval of the ethos contained in the accounts.

While it remains unspecified what precisely the performance consisted of,

83 I, 33: 'Habuit incomparabilis Karolus incomparabilem clericum in omnibus, de quo illud ferebatur quod de nullo unquam mortalium, quia videlicet et scientia litterarum saecularium atque divinarum, cantileneque aecclesiasticae vel iocularis, novaque carminum compositione sive modulatione, insuper et vocis dulcissima plenitudine inestimabilique delectatione cunctos praecelleret'. MGH SS II, 746.

84 Chronicon Novaliciense III, 10, MGH SS 7, 100: 'contigit ioculatorem ex Langobardorum gente ad Karolum venire, et cantiunculam a se compositam de eadem re rotando in conspectu suorum cantare. Erat enim sensum predicte cantiunculae huiusmodi': (there follows the Latin text: it is implied that the song was not in Latin) '. . . Cumque haec dicta ad aures Karoli pervenissent, accersivit illum a se, et cuncta quae quesivit dare illi post victoriam repromisit.'

A Carolingian cluster

even a lively recitation accompanied by gestures and body movement, by facial expressions as well as by silence, to the sound of music from one or several different musical instruments, would merit the term 'performance'. How established this culture was is shown by the fact that it was cultivated at court even where the host was not showing the appropriate reaction, when he placed himself outside the company, the norm, the expectations.

It has been suggested that not only Louis the Pious, but also his father Charlemagne apparently did not lead the way in traditional culture but instead seems to have submitted, however reluctantly, to existing expectations. Besides Charlemagne's lack of enthusiasm for feasts, one should once more point to the 'cartam prohibentem spectacula et diabolica figmenta',[85] which is most likely to have originated from Charlemagne. Traditional culture had a broad support.[86] In the light of these considerations it is particularly tantalising to find that the one explicit disapproval of the activities of the entertainers that figures in the legislation of the ninth-century Carolingian rulers cannot be dated or allocated with any degree of certainty.[87] Otherwise, the jongleurs and musicians appear as professionals respected and well rewarded by those for whom they worked. At that time they certainly did not exist on the margins of society; there is no indication in the sources that they were itinerants.

There is one place where the expertise of the bearers of the oral tradition and its accompanying skills is presented directly in a positive manner. In the Latin preface to the Old Saxon 'Heliand' biblical poetry it is stated that on the initiative of Emperor Louis a Saxon poet of the best reputation and highly regarded by his people was asked to cast the Old and New Testament into the vernacular language:

> Praecepit namque cuidam viro de gente Saxonum, qui apud suos non ignobilis vates habebatur, ut vetus ac novum Testamentum in Germanicam linguam poetice transferre studeret.[88]

Not only do we encounter here a personality expert in versecraft and popularly respected for this reason, but his skills were considered suitable for being applied to the biblical material, which suggests also respect for his skills by people responsible for religious education.

---

85 Cf. above at n. 22
86 In this respect, it is possible to suggest that Pippin, king of Aquitaine, lived up to the expectations of his entourage even though Regino of Prüm describes his behaviour in a negative light: 'ebrietatibus enim et commessationibus die noctuque vacans', *Chronicon* s.a. 853, MGH SS I, 569.
87 'Hoc sancimus, ut in palatiis nostris ad accusandum et iudicandum et testimonium faciendum non se exhibeant viles personae et infames, histriones scilicet, nugatores, manzeres, scurrae' ... Capit. no. 167, 8. MGH Capit. I, 334.
88 *Heliand und Genesis*, Behaghel, O., ed., 9th ed. by Taeger, B., Tübingen 1984, p. 1.

We have further seen that this type of culture was enjoyed not only by the lay nobility but also by clerics, and one could say clerics of all grades, high as well as low.[89] Where, according to a few strict Christians, there should have been only one Christian way of life for everybody, the available evidence points in the opposite direction: there was, largely, one culture, shared by clerics and lay people, but this was the traditional culture which apparently held infinite enticement. There are also some, though only few, indications that this type of culture was not bound to a particular social class; its attraction went beyond the aristocracy and would thus have functioned as a formidable social cohesive.

The references which we have to this culture stand in no appropriate proportion to its social significance. In fact, this culture can be recovered, almost exclusively, from normative sources which must be considered as permitting insight into affairs of everyday quality which historians rarely report. What strikes me as especially remarkable is that this culture was so deeply entrenched in society that it was cultivated even where the rulers did not gain much pleasure from it. It was cultivated not on the margins of society, but was as central to it as can be imagined. A minority of people appear to have expressed dislike of it, and then to little avail.

To sum up: a variety of sources (predominantly of a normative kind) emanating from Carolingian society in the half-century before the death of Louis the Pious, illuminate, independently of each other, yet confirming one another, various aspects of the barbarian culture of the time. It may be called barbarian in not being articulated in Latin as well as not being of a kind acceptable to strict Christians. We have experienced this culture as deeply rooted in society to the extent that the king and the emperor had to put up with it, in their entourage, even where, as clearly in the case of Louis, less so for Charlemagne, it was not to their liking. In this respect, the ruler was no more than a *primus inter pares*. The barbarian culture was part of tradition and could not be dispensed with.

We have encountered this culture as integrated in social life of lay and clerical peers; they all derived pleasure from it. The tradition was performed before them, sung to musical accompaniment which heightened the pleasure. The terms used for the performers, who were specialists, are in part those of the stage actors of Roman antiquity, a terminology which enjoyed a renaissance under the Carolingians. It is important to note that the terminology of criticism of these performances was likewise inherited from late antiquity and leading patristic authorities. The more recent term, *ioculator*, is found in the sources less frequently than their work, the *ioca*.

There is no indication that the performance of barbarian culture was unusually prominent in the period under discussion. What was unusual was

---

89 Cf. McKitterick, *Carolingians*: 'One should not discount the possibility that Carolingian monks and priests enjoyed heroic lays and fostered their production', 228.

A Carolingian cluster 145

the effort to reduce its accustomed place in society. There are good indications that it was difficult to combat this culture because it was so firmly established, because it was so widely shared, because it was tradition. What was new was a concerted effort to ban this culture at least in clerical circles. In other words, many clerics shared the one taste for barbarian culture with their lay peers. Those who did not share this taste and wanted to impose different norms, had to fight an uphill battle. The dominance of clerical Latin writing from the period has managed quite well to obliterate the vigour of secular culture, which seems to have remained dominant among the Carolingians even against the inclination of some rulers and some clerics. What Alcuin had written to Lindisfarne was no less of a problem in the society in which he worked. The Carolingian reforms would appear to have achieved little in this area.

One final consideration: however one assesses the success of the efforts at Church reform in the reigns of Charlemagne and of Louis the Pious—and I am sure that many people would rate it greater than I have—in the broader historical context these two generations witnessed an exceptionally active reform drive.[90] Councils and synods (important sources for our subject) had not been convened for almost a century before the 740s, and even those scholars very favourably disposed towards the achievements of the Carolingians will grant that the reform policy had waned by the second half of the ninth century. This means on the one hand that it is no coincidence that our information about the secular culture of the Carolingians is uncharacteristically full. Efforts to implement Christian ethics in a society which we refer to as Christian are not in evidence on a comparable scale on either side of the reigns of Charlemagne and Louis the Pious. Thus even such evidence of a negative kind can be turned positively for our issue: apparently the two generations which we have discussed were untypically unfavourable to the secular culture which had been inherited and played an important part in Frankish society.

While it has to be said that we have no single full positive account of the barbarian culture of the Carolingian period, the reconstruction which we have presented of the traditional setting of the occasions on which this culture was activated has given us a number of features any of which, preferably more than one, when occurring in the available sources, could signal this culture alive. With this in mind we can now approach fragmentary pieces of information from other periods in a constructive manner.

---

90 There is another field in which the reform effort was much more effective, that of ecclesiastical and liturgical singing: see chapter 5.

7

BEFORE THE CAROLINGIANS

From the sources emanating from the period of the Carolingian reforms, we have recovered important aspects of the barbarian culture which was deeply embedded in society. We shall now go to the time prior to the beginnings of the Carolingian reforms and in search of manifestations of this culture. We shall also cast our net beyond Frankish society which has been in the centre so far. By going back chronologically we may be able to identify possible cultural continuities.

We shall naturally only be able to deal with those societies which are mentioned in the written sources, and this means almost invariably societies into which the Christian religion had already come. As we have seen, Christianity was a potential rival to barbarian culture; this rivalry could be helpful in providing information about the indigenous culture.

In 748 Pope Zacharias, writing to Frankish nobles and apparently drawing on information provided from within Frankish society, demanded that they should not keep clerics in their entourage, pointing out how unfitting it would be for clerics to be involved in performances or in hunting, both activities of an evil kind.[1]

A very similar message is contained in a letter written around that time by Lull, Boniface's successor, to Gregory, abbot of Utrecht, in which he warns against indulgence in hunting, feasting in the presence of jongleurs, and refinements in food and drink.[2] While he might appear to be using clichés, the chances are that he was voicing criticism of clerical life in his own time.

---

1 *Bonifatius-Briefe* no. 83, ed. Tangl, M., p. 186: 'Detestabilis est enim et iniquum opus clericum in ludis inveniri aut cum acceptoribus vel venationibus degere vitam tantisque scenicis causis sauciatam ad episcopatum aut presbyterium vel quodlibet sacerdotale officium accedere...'. Note especially the term *ludus* being used as synonymous with *scenicae causae*.
2 *Bonifatius-Briefe* no. 92, p. 211: 'Vestimenta preciosa, caballos farre pastos, accipitros falconesques cum curvis unguibus, latrantes canes, scurrarum bacchationes, cibi potusque exquisite dulcedinis sapores...'.

ENGLAND

We may begin with a letter from the abbot of Monkwearmouth and Jarrow, Gutbert, to Lull, written in 764. Among other points mentioned the abbot requests the bishop to send him a man who is competent in playing a *rotta*: to hear the *rotta* played is one of his delights:

> Delectat me quoque citharistam habere, qui possit citharizare in cithara,[3] quam nos appellamus rottae; quia citharum habeo et artificem non habeo. Si grave non sit, et istum quoque meae dispositioni mitte. Obsecro, ut hanc meam rogationem ne despicias et risioni non deputes.[4]

When we recall what Alcuin later wrote to the bishop of Lindisfarne concerning performances involving a *cithara*, we can take it that something of this kind was at stake here as well. Not only did the abbot of the monasteries which Bede has made famous incline to this kind of entertainment: he also reckoned that his compatriot working in the Frankish realm could provide the expert (*artifex*)[5] he desired. His expectations were thus those of a shared cultural taste. However, his last sentence is most revealing in that the Northumbrian abbot seems to have been aware that his request and his taste might be regarded as inappropriate.[6] Unfortunately we do not know how Lull responded to this request. We have seen, however, that fifteen years earlier he had warned against *luxuria*. The Northumbrian abbot freely admitted that music gave him great pleasure, a reaction which in Augustinian terminology would have been called *voluptas aurium*.[7]

From the council of Clovesho, held in 747, one gains more insights into daily life among the English clergy, who were in need of reform. One of the canons requires the priests not to chirp in church according to the manner of secular poets but instead aim at a simplicity in recitation, as was appropriate in Christianity.[8] This is a valuable reference to the fact that there was a special manner in which secular poetry was normally delivered. There must have been a constant temptation to emulate in the divine service the kind of worldly

---

3 Cf. Rev. 14: 2: 'Vocem quam audivi, sicut citharoedorum citharizantium in citharis suis.'
4 *Bonifatius-Briefe* no. 117, 253f.
5 For this term see chapter 5, p. 113.
6 It may be recalled that a Roman synod of 679, the decisions of which were known in England, had ruled explicitly concerning clerics: 'nec citharoedas habeant, vel quaecunque symphoniaca'; Haddan and Stubbs, ed., *Councils*, III, 133.
7 See above chapter 5 at n. 49.
8 *c*.12: 'Ut presbyteri saecularium poetarum modo in ecclesia non garriant, ne tragico sono sacrorum verborum compositionem ac distinctionem corrumpant vel confundant, sed simplicem sanctamque melodiam secundum morem Ecclesiae sectentur ...', Haddan and Stubbs, *Councils*, III, 366.

performance to which the audience was accustomed and which it was brought up to like.[9]

In another canon a warning is uttered that monasteries are no places for actors and musicians, but instead places for people who prayed and praised God: 'ut sint monasteria iuxta vocabulum nominis sui, id est, honesta silentium, quietorum, atque pro Deo laborantium habitacula, et non sint ludicrarum aurium receptacula, hoc est, poetarum, citharistarum, musicorum, scurrorum; sed orantium, legentium, Deumque laudantium habitationes'.[10] As we have seen, in the monastery of Monkwearmouth this command was not followed. As Clovesho ruled further, a sharp line should be drawn between the world and the monastery: 'nam satis nociva atque vitiosa consuetudo est illa laicorum familiaritas'. It was felt appropriate that this warning be uttered particularly in regard to nunneries, places renowned for supposedly inappropriate entertainment, eating and drinking.[11] This canon conveys the impression that the way of life referred to here, a way of life characteristic of lay people, was very widespread in the monastic houses. There was a shared culture between laity and clergy, and this culture was of a secular kind.

A further canon warns against the evil of drunkenness among clerics, especially at banquets, and the custom of encouraging others to drink in an unrestrained manner.[12] It seems that the term *ebrietatis malum*, though not biblical in origin, was widely applicable among clerics in England as well as on the continent.[13]

Returning once again to Monkwearmouth we may point out how Bede (d. 735), in a wide-ranging letter to bishop Egbert of York towards the end of his life, complained bitterly about the unsuitable company chosen by some bishops:

> Ut nullos secum alicuius religionis aut continentiae viros habeant; sed potius illos, qui risui, iocis, fabulis, commessationibus et ebrietatibus,

9   Cf. chapter 5 on music and esp. Augustine.
10 *c*.20, Haddan and Stubbs, III, 369.
11 Ibid.: '. . . maxime in nunnorum minus regulariter conversantium monasteriis. . . . Unde non sint sanctimonialium domicilia, turpium confabulationum, commessationum, ebrietatum, luxuriantiumque cubicula; sed continentium sobrieque viventium, ac legentium, psallentiumque habitacula, magisque legendis libris, vel canendis psalmis, quam textendis et plectendis vario colore inanis gloriae vestibus studeant operam dare.'
12 *c*.21: 'Ut monasteriales, sive ecclesiastici, ebrietatis malum non sectentur aut expetant, sed velut mortiferum venenum, apostolo denuntiante, quod "ebriosi regnum Dei non possident" (1 Cor 6:10) et alibi, "Nolite inebriari vino in quo est luxuria" (Eph 5:18). 'Sed neque alios cogant intemperanter bibere; sed pura ac sobria sint eorum convivia, non luxuriosa neque deliciis vel scurrilitatibus mixta, ne habitus sui reverentia contemptibilis apud saeculares habeatur.' A very similar point is made in c. 20. Ibid., 369.
13 Cf. Oexle, G. O., 'Gilden als soziale Gruppen der Karolingerzeit', in *Das Handwerk in vor- und frühgeschichtlicher Zeit*, I, ed. Jankuhn, H. et al. (Abhandlungen der Akademie der Wissenschaften zu Göttingen, phil.-hist. Klasse, 3. Folge 122), Göttingen 1981, 284-354, esp. 309ff.

ceterisque vitae remissioris illecebris subigantur, et qui magis cotidie ventrem dapibus, quam mentem sacrificiis caelestibus parent.[14]

In another place Bede refers factually and tantalizingly briefly to the poetic compositions of the native poets, highlighting the rhythms used by them without strict metre. In the same place he shows knowledge of the pre-Christian Roman poets even though he claims that because of their paganism their work should be regarded as irrelevant.[15]

However, Bede also reports in his *Historia Ecclesiastica* that in his monastery secular culture was the order of the day among the lay members of the community. This he does in his famous account of the herdsman Caedmon. By divine intervention the layman Caedmon had become a renowned Christian poet in the English language. It should be pointed out that Bede here writes of an event that lay two generations in the past. The story no doubt had in the meantime become part of the collective memory of the monastic community. We are interested particularly in the cultural background to his vocation for which Bede, reporting factually, offers valuable insights:

> Unde nonnumquam in convivio, cum esset laetitiae causa decretum, ut omnes per ordinem cantare deberent, ille, ubi adpropinquare sibi citharam cernebat, surgebat a media caena.[16]

Thus the lay members of the monastic community practised conviviality in the course of which it was customary that songs were sung to the accompaniment of the harp. Bede calls this type of song 'frivola et supervacua poemata'[17] which, however, he does not present as inappropriate for the company concerned. We note that this kind of entertainment was practised *laetitiae causa*, to give pleasure to the company.

As distinct from the conviviality practised at the Carolingian court, the culture here was shared actively by everybody involved. The harp made the round of the table, and virtually everybody was expected to have a song to offer in his native language, and to be able to accompany himself on the instrument.[18] Shared pleasure surely derived also from a shared skill in the

14 *Epistola Bede ad Ecgbertum episcopum, Venerabilis Baedae Historiam Ecclesiasticam*, ed. Plummer, C., Oxford 1896, 407.
15 Bede, *De arte metrica* (*Grammatici Latini*, ed. Keil, H., vol VII, reprint Hildesheim and New York 1981, 258): 'De rhythmo: . . . reperiuntur quaedam et in insigni illo volumine Porphyrii poetae . . . quae, quia pagana erant, nos tangere non libuit. Videtur autem rhythmus metris esse consimilis, quae est verborum modulata compositio, non metrica ratione, sed numero syllabarum ad iudicium aurium examinata, ut sunt carmina vulgarium poetarum.'
16 *Historia Ecclesiastica* IV, xxii, ed. Plummer, 259.
17 Ibid., 259, lines 9-10; yet the term *religiosa poemata* also occurs, ibid., line 5.
18 This is a rare reference for this time suggesting song to musical accompaniment, thus implying poliphony, even though perhaps of a very basic kind; see chapter 5.

execution of the cultural repertoire. Metaphorically speaking, therefore, there could well be, in Bede's view, both lay and religious poetry performed under the one monastic roof as long as each was confined to the appropriate public. It is worth noting that this kind of oral culture was very different from that practised at the Carolingian royal court. There is no suggestion in Bede that the songs were performed in Whitby in the manner earlier discussed; the two occasions may appear to be similar due to the fact that they are described in Latin with its limited vocabulary.

The techincal terminology employed by Bede deserves a closer look. He distinguishes here human versecraft (*canendi artem*) from the gift of Christian poetry divinely granted (*donum canendi*).[19] He also refers to the fact that Caedmon retained in his memory what he had sung in his sleep: 'cuncta, quae dormiens cantaverat, memoriter retinuit'.[20] In this chapter, Bede uses both *cantare* and *canere* for secular and Christian singing, whereas he uses the term *carmina* only for the Christian material.

Bede writes also about the introduction of Roman chant into his own monastery. This is associated with the activities of John, the archchanter of St Peter's in Rome. On the initiative of Benedict Biscop, founder abbot of Monkwearmouth, John came to Northumbria to teach there the Roman manner of singing in Church:

> Accepit et praefatum Iohannem abbatem Brittaniam perducendum; quatenus in monasterio suo cursum canendi annuum, sicut ad sanctum Petrum Romae agebatur, edoceret; egitque abba Iohannes, ut iussionem acceperat pontificis, et ordinem videlicet, ritumque canendi ac legendi viva voce praefati monasterii cantores edocendo, et ea, quae totius anni circulus in celebratione dierum festorum poscebat, etiam litteris mandando.[21]

The terminology in this passage also requires comment. It is more complex than is normally believed. We have seen earlier that church reading was done in the form of chanting from late antiquity on. Thus *canere* and *legere* should be taken as synonyms, as Bede can be taken to use them in the same chapter later on: 'cantandi uel legendi munere'.[22] He also seems to have had no difficulty in using *canere* and *cantare* interchangeably.[23] John taught personally, but he also saw to it that what was to be sung was also written down. However, it was only the words that were written down, for musical notation was as yet unknown in the West. The musical dimension of the rite was still taught

19 Ed. Plummer, 259.
20 Ed. Plummer, 260.
21 HE VI, xvi xviii, Plummer, 241.
22 Ed. Plummer, p. 241, third last line; see also chapter 5.
23 See Isidore, *Differentiae* 98 and chapter 5, p. 116.

exclusively orally; John could draw on familiarity with the oral medium in this field; this did not require special mention, unless one would wish to construe *viva voce* together with *edocendo* rather than *canendi ac legendi*.[24] According to Bede, people came from most parts of the province to benefit from John's teaching.

We have noted earlier that a separation of the different kinds of culture, even though regarded as desirable by zealous Christians, must be considered the exception rather than the rule. Thus it is reported without any note of censure that Aldhelm, abbot of Malmesbury and the outstanding scholar of his time (d. 709) was a recognized expert in Latin culture and also a singularly outstanding expert in songs in the native language. He even composed such songs and sang or recited them in the appropriate manner:

> Litteris itaque ad plenum instructus, nativae quoque linguae non negligebat carmina; adeo ut . . . nulla umquam aetate par ei fuerit quisquam. Poesim Anglicam posse facere, cantum componere, eadem apposite vel canere vel dicere.[25]

This information comes from William of Malmesbury in the twelfth century. There is reason to believe that the community of Malmesbury had cherished particularly the memory of one of their own. William reports further that one of these secular songs, still sung by the folk in his days, was believed to be by Aldhelm.[26] One is thus confronted with a living oral tradition in twelfth-century England which associated Aldhelm with the composition of secular songs which had become part of the popular repertoire.

Finally, mention must be made of a couple of brief references to oral tradition connected with royalty and aristocracy. An anonymous Life of the East Anglian king Ethelbert, a contemporary of Offa of Mercia, reports that the king encouraged the recitation in his presence of songs relating to his royal predecessors, called *carmina regia*. He was very pleased with the results and those who had performed were instantly rewarded with gifts.[27] It must be noted that the versecraft (called here *scienctia canendi*) which the king wished

24 For the more conventional interpretation see the translation by Colgrave, B., and Mynors R.A.B., *Bede's Ecclesiastical History of the English people*, Oxford 1969, 389. However, since both singing and reading were normally done aloud, there is no reason why Bede should have used *viva voce* with these verbs.
25 *Willelmi Malmesbiriensis monachi Gesta pontificum Anglorum*, ed. Hamilton, N.S.E.A., RS 52, 336. Cf. also Riché, *Éducation*, 448, n. 259.
26 'Denique commemorat Elfredus carmen triviale, quod adhuc vulgo cantitatur, Aldelmum fecisse', *Gesta Pontificum*, 336.
27 'Nec mora, duo canendi prediti scientia in cordis leticia psallere ceperunt. Erant carmina de regis eiusdem regia prosapia. Quibus ille delectatus abstracta brachio protinus armilla modulantes carmina donat.' James, M.R., 'Two Lives of St Ethelbert, king and martyr', *EHR* 32, 1917, 214-44, at 238. Nothing is known of the date of this work. For a more

to hear was immediately available. It would have been focused on the line of the royal ancestors. All available Anglo-Saxon royal genealogies ultimately go back to the pagan gods, are thus of pre-Christian origin and have by implication an oral past.[28]

This is all that can be established about secular culture and secular and religious singing in England in the second half of the seventh and the first half of the eighth century. All the sources are from an ecclesiastical context, which means that the light which is thrown on cultural aspects not specifically Christian is sparse and sometimes incidental. For the earlier period there are no references at all. Nevertheless, one can take it that there was an established secular culture of pre-Christian origin, which celebrated values not specifically Christian and which continued to thrive in English society even after the implantation of Christianity.

THE CONTINENTAL BARBARIANS BEFORE 700

Franks or Gallo-Romans The Frankish king Clovis is believed to have become a Catholic in 496 or 497, an event often hailed as of great significance because it meant that the true faith had made an important advance among the barbarians. Gregory of Tours portrays Clovis as a new Constantine, and later historians generally are happy to take over this characterization. Other sources, however, force the observer considerably to modify this assessment and the presentation of the Franks as the most Christian people as they saw themselves in the mid-eighth century.[29]

A letter addressed to Clovis by Avitus of Vienne after the Frankish king had been baptized tactfully alludes to Clovis' apparent refusal to abandon his reverence for his ancestors, having maintained that 'vestra fides nostra victoria est'.[30] Christianity seems to have made more progress in the royal family a century later. This is the message contained in the so-called constitution of King Childebert I of c.581. The king saw it as his obligation to effect the realization of the 'populus Christianus'. If the people failed to follow the commands of the priests, it would be his duty to step in and enforce what was necessary.[31] In the surviving text of the constitution the main emphasis is put upon the abandoning of the *cultura idolorum*. News had reached him that:

> detailed treatment of this text see Richter, M., 'Die mündliche Kultur im früheren Mittelalter: ein Problemaufriß', Prague 1994.

28 On this subject see Moisl, H., 'Anglo-Saxon royal genealogies and Germanic oral tradition', *Journal of Medieval History* 7, 1981, 215-48. On Ethelbert see ibid., 231f.
29 This view finds its classic formulation in the prologue to the Lex Salica, MGH LL I, 4, 2, p. 2ff.
30 MGH AA 6, 2, Ep. 46, p. 75.
31 In a similar manner King Guntram stated in 585 that he derived his authority from God: 'nos, quibus facultatem regnandi superni regis commisit auctoritas', MGH Capit. I, no. 5, p. 11.

multa sacrilegia in populo fieri, unde Deus laedatur, et populus per peccatum declinet ad mortem; noctes pervigiles cum ebrietate, scurrilitate, vel canticis; etiam in ipsis sacris diebus pascha, natale Domini, et reliquis festivitatibus, vel adveniente die dominico, bansatrices per villas ambulare.[32]

This shows that the old customs had survived the establishment of Christianity among the people subject to the Franish king. There is no way of telling whether the king would have had Gallo-Romans or Franks in mind.

In this edict the king presents himself as the promoter of Christianity. It is salutary to have as a counterbalance the assessment of Frankish kingship in the mid-sixth century from the perspective of the Italian poet Venantius Fortunatus. He saw his vocation in the composition of panegyric poetry in Latin, and he took pride in the dynamic use he could make of the language. In his view, the leading circles in Frankish society could not appreciate his art: 'it was just as acceptable for me to drone forth a discordant noise as to sing before an audience incapable of telling the difference between the honking of a goose and the song of a swan, only their harps twanging to the repetitive strains of their barbaric lays, so that, in their company, I ceased to be a musical poet' ('ubi mihi tantundem valebat raucum gemere quod cantare apud quos nihil disparat aut stridor anseris aut canor oloris, sola saepe bombicans barbaros leudos arpa relidens; ut inter illos non musicus poeta)'.[33]

His picture is by no means balanced, and he may well have been carried away by his own verbiage, but he provides insight into the kind of taste that was prevalent among the ruling circles in Frankish society. It is interesting to find him using, for the songs preferred in those circles a term which is a Latinized Germanic term *leudus* (Old High German *liod*, modern German *Lied*). It is possible to intepret this as his acceptance, however churlishly, of the appropriate native terminology for this aspect of barbarian culture. Unfortunately, Venantius does not provide the native terminology for the people who practised this kind of barbarian culture. In another place he gives his reader to understand that this kind of culture, songs and the sound of the harp,[34] was also common among the British peoples.[35] The barbarians of different groups shared comparable institutions.

32 MGH LL I, p. 1.
33 Venantius Fortunatus, MGH AA 4, p. 2. The translation is taken from Godman, P., *Poets and emperors. Frankish politics and Carolingian poetry*, Oxford 1987, 1.
34 As pointed out earlier, there is no indication of the kind of musical accompaniment of this kind of song at this time. Also, it should not be supposed that the instruments named here were of the same kind; at least, they can be taken to belong both to the family of plucked instruments.
35 Venantius, *Carminum* Lib. VII, VIII: 'Romanusque Lyra, plaudat tibi barbarus harpa,/ Graecus Achilliaca, crotta Britanna canat./... dent barbara carmina leudos'. p. 163. This

There is a short letter to an unnamed Frankish king by an anonymous cleric, perhaps from the seventh century, writing about the behaviour appropriate to a king—a sort of early *Speculum Principis*. In this letter, the king is asked to seek the company of wise men rather than that of the *ioculares* with their vain talking.[36] This letter suggests that a *ioculator* was permanently in the entourage of the king.[37]

The Life of Bishop Eligius of Noyon, also from the sixth century, sheds light upon the old religious persuasions among the people of Gaul. It is in the nature of the hagiographic source that non-Christian beliefs should be portrayed in a negative manner, and what is reported is told because eventually the true Christian faith triumphed. However, one is invited to read the negative portrayal as factual information.

St Eligius encountered these 'pagan' customs (which he demanded should be abandoned) not far from the city of Noyon:

> abiciendos dumtaxat atque abhominandos esse cunctos daemonum ludos et nefandas saltationes omnesque inanes prorsus relinquendas superstitiones.

We are fortunate to be given, most exceptionally, the reaction of those under censure by the missionary; even this hagiographical work conveys a sense of the hurt caused by the demand to give up beliefs long and deeply cherished:

> Quam eius praedicationem praestantiores quique loci illius valde aegre ferebant, scilicet quod ferias eorum everteret ac legitimas, ut putabant, consuetudines exinanirent. . . . 'Numquam, tu, Romane, quamvis haec frequenter taxes, consuetudines nostras evellere poteris, sed sollemnia nostra sicut actenus fecimus, perpetuo semperque frequentabimus, nec

---

passage is quite fully treated by Moisl, H., 'A sixth-century reference to the British bardd', *BBCS* 29, 1980-82, 269-73. It is also noted by Riché, *Éducation*, 290, n. 455. It should be noted that he uses the different terms for the accompanying instrument, Latinized *crotta* (Old Irish *croth*, Middle Welsh *crwth*) and the Latinized *harpa* for the Germanic term for harp. See, further, chapter 9 below.

36 MGH Epp. 3, no. 15: 'Et quando tu cum sapientibus locutus fueris aut cum ministerialibus bonas fabulas habueris, ioculares taceant; quia plus opportet recondere sapientiam in cubiculo cordis tui, quam fatuos et stultos sermones loquentes audire,' p. 458.
37 This is attested by Gregory of Tours for King Miro of Galicia where a *puer* at court is characterised as follows: 'Erat enim mimus regis, qui ei per verba iocularia laetitiam erat solitus erat'. In the following sentence the 'praestigium artis suae' underlines his professionalism. Gregory of Tours, *De virtutibis S. Martini* IV, 7, MGH SS rer. Merov. I, 2, 201.

> ullus hominum erit, qui priscos atque gratissimos possit nobis umquam prohibere ludos.[38]

Of course the reader is exposed to the scene from the perspective of the hagiographer. Yet it is notable that the people concerned are credited with regarding their festivities as *sollemnia* which were of great age and formed a frequent and inalienable part of their life. Unfortunately the text does not allow any insight into the possible nature of the *ludi* that made up these festivities.

A more conventional account of a meeting of Christian and pre-Christian culture is contained in the Life of St Amandus. He was called from Flanders to take the Christian message to the Basques. However, his preaching fell on barren ground; the spokesman of the opposing party, called *mimilogus*, maintained that the Christian message was no good. Apparently he was listened to:

> Vir autem domini Amandus eorum miseratus errori enxaeque laborans, ut eos a diaboli revocaret instinctu, dum eis verbum praedicaret divinum atque evangelium adnuntiaret salutis, unus e ministris adsurgens levis, lubricus necnon insuper et superbus atque etiam apta cachinnans risui verba, quem vulgo mimilogum vocant, servum Christi detrahere coepit evangeliumque quod praedicabat pro nihilo duci.[39]

Again the message seems to be that the familiar and traditional culture was preferred.

Lastly, there is an account in the Life of St Radegundis by Venantius Fortunatus which shows what a grip traditional culture continued to have on those who should have left it behind. A nun in the community of St Radegundis recognized secular songs performed outside the monastery which she heard inside. When she told her abbess about this, Radegundis maintained that she herself had not heard any secular song. In spirit, the abbess was not of this world:

> Quadam vice obumbrante iam noctis crepusculo inter coraulas et citharas dum circa monasterium a saecularibus multo fremitu cantaretur et sancta duabus testibus perorasset diutius, dicit quaedam monacha sermone ioculari: Domina, recognovi unam de meis canticis a saltantibus praedi-

---

38 MGH SS rer. Merov. 4, 711-12. We have already referred to part of this passage in chapter 2. This passage is frequently quoted without being turned positively: see Wenskus, *Stammesbildung*, 105; Geary, *Before France and Germany*, 168; Flint, *Rise*, 71f.
39 MGH SS rer. Merov. 5, 444.

cari. Cui respondit: Grande est, si te delectat coniunctam religioni audire odorem saeculi. Adhuc soror pronuntiat: Vere, domina duas et tres hic modo meas canticas audivi quas tenui. Sancta respondit: Teste deo me nihil audisse modo saeculare de cantico. Unde manifestum est, ut care licet in saeculo, mente tamen esset in caelo.[40]

Here then is a case where an ordinary member of a religious community had brought her past, her memories and her preferences with her into the monastery.[41] Once more the enjoyment of this culture is articulated by the term *delectare*. We have seen examples which show that this seems to have been quite common. Not being gullible in this respect showed the abbess up as a saint. And saints were the exception even among the Merovingians.

The Goths Our information about the Ostrogoths is derived from accounts which are more or less directly the products of Roman civilization. These in turn draw on information part of which had until then not been written down. The first known history of the Goths, *Getica*, was written by Cassiodorus, most likely after his first spell in Gothic public service, and most likely as a piece of panegyric.[42] This work has survived only indirectly as part of a Gothic history written by Jordanes, a contemporary of Cassiodorus.[43] It has proved impossible to clarify what each contributed to the work as it has come down to us;[44] thus I shall refer unspecifically to 'the author'. While Cassiodorus was a Roman patrician, Jordanes was of either Gothic or Alan descent, working most likely at Constantinople. In any case, the author does not explicity identify with the Goths, and one gets the impression that what is reported about them was noted from outside, as it were. It is also important to remember that the work as we know it was written after the destruction of the Ostrogothic kingdom in Italy by the Romans under Justinian.

On his own admission, the author prefers written accounts to oral tradition.[45] However, he does refer in several places explicitly to oral traditions of the Goths. Thus he writes that the Goths commemorate in song deeds of their ancestors, songs which he likens to history as he himself understands

---

40 MGH AA 4/2, 47 f.
41 The meaning of the possessive pronoun in the statement by the nun remains unclear.
42 Cf. O'Donnell, *Cassiodorus*, who would place it in *c*.519, 43f.
43 *Iordanis de origine actibusque Getarum*, MGH AA 5,1, 53-138.
44 'What we want most to do is to read the work as though it were the product of Cassiodorus himself; what we are in fact forced to do is to read it as Jordanes produced it', O'Donnell, *Cassiodorus*, 49. '(Jordanes's) contributions are probably minimal . . . In Jordanes's *Getica* we see Cassiodorus the panegyrist through a dark glass, obscured to our view but not obliterated', 53.
45 V, 38: 'Nos enim potius lectioni credimus quam fabulis anilibus consentimus', p. 64.

this term: 'quemadmodum et in priscis eorum carminibus pene storico ritu in commune recolitur' (IV, 28, p. 61).[46] It should be pointed out here that the author uses the present tense; he conveys the idea that this was still happening in his own time. Furthermore he regards the *carmina* as old;[47] even if they were not in fact old, the significant thing is that they were regarded as such. The author further notes that these songs were remembered *in commune*, that is, they formed part of the collective memory. Thus, oral tradition acted as a social cohesive in that it kept alive the deeds of the ancestors. In another place the author refers to the same phenomenon, with the additional information that singing the deeds of the ancestors also involved instrumental music, although the form in which this was done is not specified: 'ante quos etiam cantu maiorum facta modulationibus citharisque canebant' (V, 43, p. 65).

Elsewhere the author refers to the Gothic leader Dicineus, presenting him as a contemporary of Sulla (2nd century BC). He closes the lengthy account of him by stating that his deeds were still recalled by the Goths in their songs: 'adhuc odie suis cantionibus reminiscent' (XI, 72, p. 75). Again the employment of the present tense should be noted.

In the context of another episode of the Gothic past, their victory over the army of the emperor Domitian (emperor AD 81–96), the author informs his readers that the Goths derived their ancestors from demigods rather than ordinary mortals; these ancestors are also referred to as heroes. He gives the seventeen generations of the royal genealogy, which is based on oral tradition: 'Gothi . . . iam proceres suos, quorum quasi fortuna vincebant, non puros homines, sed semideos, id est Ansis vocaverunt, quorum genealogia, ut paucis percurram vel quis quo parente genitus est aut unde origo coepta, ubi finem effecit, absque invidia qui legis, vera dicentem ausculta. Horum ergo heroum, ut ipsi suis in fabulis referunt, primus fuit Gapt.'[48] This is important for another reason not obvious at first sight. Both the reference to the descent from Gapt/Gaut and the fact that the Goths referred to their leaders as 'Ansis' (= 'semidei') point to the Scandinavian origin which continued to be remembered in the sixth century.[49]

We have mentioned that the author of the *Getica* in several places uses

---

46 This statement is frequently noted and commented upon in modern literature, see e.g. Hauck, K., 'Heldensdichtung und Heldensage als Geschichtsbewußtsein', in *Alteuropa und die moderne Gesellschaft* (FS O. Brunner), Göttingen 1963, 118-69, at 125; Wenskus, *Stammesbildung*, 65; Moisl, 'Kingship and orally transmitted *Stammestradition* among the Lombards and Franks' in Wolfram, H., Schwarz, A., ed., *Die Bayern und ihre Nachbarn*, vol. I, Wien 1985, 111-19.
47 See also V, 44, p. 65: 'prisca tradit auctoritas'.
48 *Getica* XIII, 78, XIV, 79, p. 76. The seventeen generations of the Gothic kings are also referred to in *Variae* IX, 25, 4.
49 Cf. Höfler, O., 'Theoderich der Große und sein Bild in der Sage', esp. 352ff.

the present tense when bringing up the subject of the Gothic oral tradition even though the events which are specified as the subjects of that tradition are placed into a fairly distant past. So, it is very fortunate to find a reference to oral tradition among the Goths in 377 being reported by a contemporary, Ammianus Marcellinus. When the Roman and Gothic armies met, according to Ammianus, the Romans shouted in a manner described as *barritum*; and the barbarians shouted about the fame of their ancestors, even though their utterances are reported in derogatory terms.[50]

Why all these references to Gothic oral tradition? The probable explanation lies in the nature of the *Getica*: the history written in Latin was most easily accessible to the Romans, to whom oral tradition of this kind would have been newsworthy. Indeed this is the simplest explanation for the fact that the oral traditions are noted at all.

Finally, we might mention an episode from the time of king Theodoric. One of his letters, addressed to the philosopher Boethius, is dedicated to the subject of music.[51] This is a rather pretentious missive since the addressee was the greatest contemporary expert on music. This letter is important for a technical reason in that it contains the earliest attestation of the term *musica artificialis* (denoting instrumental music). Theodoric claims that the musician can affect the listener ('mutat animos artifex auditus'), and he apparently enjoys the idea of non-verbal communication achieved by instrumental music ('tacitus manibus clamat, sine ore loquitur'). However, the background to this letter is explained briefly at the beginning and at the end. The Frankish king (Clovis) is said to have heard about the banquets held by the Gothic king and urged him to supply a *citharoedus*, who obviously was an integral part of these feasts. At the end of his letter, Theodoric formally asked Boethius to choose such a musician. He expressed his hope that that man would have the effect of an Orpheus and tame the wild hearts of the barbarians ('facturus aliquid Orphei, cum dulci sono gentilium fera corda domuerit').

It is good to have this independent evidence that singing and instrumental music were part of Gothic society before the Goths settled among the Romans; we have seen earlier that the Franks had their traditional form of entertainment which struck Venantius as uncouth two generations after Clovis. So there is no reason to believe that this kind of cultural cross-fertilization fostered by the Gothic king towards the Franks made a lasting impact. On the other hand, this letter provides evidence that music at banquets formed an integral part

50 *Ammiani Marcellini Rerum Gestarum libri qui supersunt* (Teubner, Stuttgart 1967), XXXI, 7, 11: 'Romani quidem voce undique Martia concinentes, a minore solita ad maiorem protolli, quam gentilitate appellant barritum, vires validas erigebant. barbari vero maiorum laudes clamoribus stridebant inconditis, interque varios sermonis dissoni strepitus leviora proelia temptabantur.'
51 *Variae* II, 40.

of society among the Romans just as among the barbarians. Judgments as to its refinement or its roughness, and therefore its cultural value, have to be taken as subjective.

I shall close this section with reference to two sources which are of no more than marginal relevance to our subject but which help to put it into a wider perspective.

There is, in the first place, the description of the oral culture at the court of Attila, from the pen of a Roman observer, Priscus, who reported what he himself had witnessed. Having been received at the court of the Hunnish leader with formal respect, the Roman emissaries witnessed, in the context of a banquet, the following scene: 'When evening fell, torches were lit, and then two Scythians appeared before Attila. They recited verses which they had composed, in which they sang about his victories and strength in war. Those who were present at the banquet had their eyes fixed on them; some took pleasure in the verses, for others the recalling of the wars caused excitement, others again had tears streaming down their faces, namely those whose bodies were weakened by age and whose strength of heart was constrained to remain quiet.'[52] In fact, Priscus is able to convey with a few words the deep effect which this recital of heroic deeds made on the audience as well as obviously on himself.

The second reference is to Tacitus and his famous statement in the *Germania* that 'they celebrate [their descent from gods] in old songs—for this is the only kind of recollection and history they have': 'Celebrant carminibus antiquis, quod unum apud illos memoriae et annalium genus est.'[53] Here is a reference to oral tradition attested among the Germanic peoples at a time prior to their intensive contacts with the Roman world. This statement of Tacitus has been often commented upon.[54] At that time the Germans (it is not clear precisely which groups Tacitus was writing about) had not been confronted with alphabetic writing and written forms of cultural transmission.

However, we have shown that oral culture, including *carmina antiqua*, was something not specifically Germanic but rather a universal feature among the barbarians in the early medieval West. Furthermore, we have seen that oral culture continued to be socially relevant even after the barbarians encountered alphabetic writing, and after writing had found a niche in their society through the activity by the Church. This underlines the strength of the oral culture inherited from the past.

52 *Fragmenta historicorum Graecorum*, Müller, Karl, ed., IV, Paris 1851, 92, which gives a Latin translation along with the Greek original.
53 *Germania* c. 2.3.
54 See in detail Wenskus, *Stammesbildung*, esp. 234-46.

8

AFTER THE CAROLINGIANS

THE JONGLEURS

It has been said that 'modern scholars are agreed that the golden age of the jongleur appeared with the opening years of the thirteenth century'.[1] We have seen that jongleurs were on the scene continuously from late antiquity. However, it is true that information about them becomes much richer in the eleventh and twelfth centuries; thus the increase in their importance is more apparent than real.

The most detailed account concerning the function and position of jongleurs is contained in the works of Peter the Chanter (d. 1197).[2] A moral theologian best known as the author of the *Verbum Abbreviatum* (VA), which he completed *c.*1192,[3] he did not treat the issues that concerned him in a systematic manner but rather by way of associations and digressions. This was also done in his other work, less widely known and left incomplete, his *Summa de sacramentis et animae consiliis*. It is not surprising that the jongleurs should receive negative publicity from Peter the Chanter, and it remains to be seen how representative his views were of his age. Be that as it may, provided one bears in mind his general attitude one can benefit from the more passing information about the jongleurs contained in his writings.

For example, Peter the Chanter used the jongleurs as a negative example when, in criticizing clerics who read more than one mass per day, for monetary gain, he likened them to the singers of tales and stories. When they realized that their first story did not appeal to their audience, they would choose a second, or a third (presumably until they hit on one which brought them the desired reward):

[1] Baldwin, J.W., *Masters, princes and merchants. The social view of Peter the Chanter and his circle*, 2 vols., Princeton 1970, vol. I, 198; the 'modern' scholars the author has in mind are Faral, *Jongleur* of 1910 and Reich, *Der Mimus* of 1903, respectively.

[2] We shall refer here not only to the *ioculatores*, but also to *mimi*, *scurra*, *histriones*: see chapter 5.

[3] For the general points, I draw on Baldwin, *Masters*.

After the Carolingians 161

> Hi tales sacerdotes similes sunt ioculatori vel fabulatori qui videns cantilenam de landerico non placere auditoribus statim incipit cantare de antiocho. Quod si non placuerit de alexandro quo fastidito cantilenam permutat in appollonium vel karolum magnum vel quemlibet alium.[4]

Peter's most detailed account of the jongleurs is found in chapter XLIX of the VA, which is entitled 'Contra dantes histrionibus'.[5] Although in the opening statement, the *histriones, mimi* and *ioculatores* are classed with *meretrices, magici, aleatores* and *tyrocinatores,* in the course of the chapter only the jongleurs are dealt with. As already evident from the chapter heading, the jongleurs are considered unsuitable companions for good Christians.

Significantly, Peter does not directly describe the activity of the jongleurs, apparently because he knew that everybody was familiar with them;[7] but their characteristic features can be gathered from the way he warns against them. Peter was writing a running commentary on the Scriptures; unfortunately for him, one may say, the term *histriones* does not occur in the Vulgate. So his scriptural references warn against *curiosi*[8] or those *ambulantes inordinate*.[9] Their other characteristic feature for Peter was that they did not work properly to earn their living; he gives several quotations from the Old and the New Testament to the effect that one should work like other men.[10] Subsequently he quotes Seneca's warning that one should choose one's table companions with care, and he attributes to Jerome a saying to the effect that 'paria sunt histrionibus dare, et daemonibus immolare'.[11] So far Peter has nothing good to say about the jongleurs.

By far the most interesting account, given in an incomplete form in the shortened printed version of the VA, is that concerning the remuneration of a jongleur. Here a jongleur is presented as behaving in a most edifying manner: it is an instance of *exemplum*, a favourite literary genre at the time. A certain nobleman is said to have paid a jongleur the sum of fifteen pounds. This same

4   This quotation is taken from the unpublished longer version of the *Verbum Abbreviatum*, quoted by Baldwin, *Masters*, vol. II, 143, n. 224; the published version of the same work has a shorter account which opens with the words: 'Hi similes sunt cantantibus fabulas et gesta', PL 205, ch. XXVII, col. 101.
5   PL 205, 153–156.
6   Unlike Baldwin, *Masters*. I take these terms to be vitually synonymous for Peter.
7   However, in another place he described the jongleurs as people 'cantantes fabulas et gesta', see PL 205, 101 (ch. XXVII) which must be taken together with the longer version as given by Baldwin, *Masters*, II, 143, n. 224 where he calls the people in question 'ioculatores vel fabulatores'.
8   Cf. Sir 3:22 and 24 as well as 1 Tim 5:13.
9   2 Thess 3:6: 'Ut subtrahatis vos ab omni fratre ambulante inordinate.'
10   There is here an interesting reference to Tob 4:18 where the Vulgate text does not use the term *histriones*.
11   The above are PL 205, 153–155.

jongleur was present when the nobleman offered a considerably smaller sum to a destitute knight who had escaped from captivity.[12] In fact this sum was proffered only reluctantly after the knight produced witnesses to testify to the truth of his account. The jongleur protested against this behaviour of the nobleman. He argued that the knight, a man of free birth and one who had behaved admirably, deserved a higher reward than himself, an utterly abject person. He handed his own payment to the knight on top of what he had already received. This (most unusual) gesture astonished everybody present.

> Item ad hoc facit quod quidam princeps dedit cuidam histrioni tali xv libras. Interim quidam miles captus in tirocinio venit (vel cruce signatus nescio) et quesivit auxilium a principe illo more solito. Cui respondit princeps cum gravi supercilio dicens: Quis scit si miles es vel quis scit si captus in tirocinio? Tandem productis testibus et quod captus fuerat et de professione militari vel etiam quod peregre profecturus erat, precepit ei dari xl solidos. Contra quem invehens histrio ait: villissime princeps michi histrioni villissimo ludibriose et sine contradictione et probatione dedisti xv libras. Isti honesto et ingenuo ac strenuo viro et eiusdem cuius tu es professionis vel conditionis et forte strenuiori ut utiliori rei publice quam tu si in apice regiminis constitutus esset non dedisti nisi xl solidos vilissime monete cum indigeat nec sine probatione. Indignatusque dedit militi xv libras quas acceperat. . . . Hoc ergo factum omnes circumstantes movit principe valde deluso.[13]

While one is aware that this is an *exemplum*, and the sums mentioned need not be taken literally, it is nevertheless conveyed (and not presented as exceptional) that the work of a jongleur was rewarded generously by the nobleman. The jongleur's description of himself as a *vilissimus* should be attributed to Peter's initial classification of this sort of people.

In his *Summa*,[14] Peter deals with technical aspects of the jongleurs, but also and incidentally provides valuable additional information.

Towards the end of his long chapter *De furto et restitutione*, he discusses how to classify dishonestly acquired gains ('possint licite retinere que turpiter accipiunt'). Here, as in the *Verbum Abbreviatum*, Peter brackets *histriones* together with *aleatores* and *meretrices*; but, in contrast to the earlier work, he now deals with the various professions separately. As in the VA, he quotes the opinion that 'hystrionibus dare est demonibus immolare' (which he earlier

---

12 The accounts vary: the short version has 'sexaginta solidos', PL 205, 156B, the longer version lists twice 'xl solidos', Baldwin, *Masters*, II, 140f, n. 205.
13 Baldwin, *Masters*, II, 140f, n. 205; for a shorter version see PL 205, 156.
14 *Pierre le Chantre, Summa de sacramentis et animae consiliis*, Dugauquier, J.-A., ed., Louvain 1963 (= Analecta Mediaevalia Namurcensia 16).

attributed to St Jerome). Peter tries to distinguish here when the gift was made and for what purpose. If it was made in order to get the *histrio* to perform, then this was evil, but if it was given to the man in the *histrio* it was justified:

> Hystrionibus dare est demonibus immolare. Licet quidam distinguunt dicentes: qui dat aliquid aliquibus ut hystriones fiant demonibus immolat, sed qui hystrionibus iam factis dant, non peccant dummodo non dent propter turpitudinem aliquam, credimus quod quandocumque aliqui dant hystrionibus quia hystriones, non quia homines sunt, demonibus immolant.[15]

According to Peter, one should distinguish between acceptable and unacceptable work of jongleurs. It was acceptable to listen to pleasant verses on decent subjects, even to music, as long as the effect was recreation, not lust: 'Possumus tamen licite audire versus iocundos de honesta materia, vel instrumenta musica ad recreationem sed nullomodo ad voluptatem.'[16] But there are jongleurs who earn money by contorting their bodies, which means distorting the image of God; these are to be shunned. However, those who sing for recreation or information are almost acceptable: 'Distinguendum est modicum in superioribus circa ioculatores. Quidam enim cum ludibrio et turpitudine sui corporis acquirunt necessaria, et deformant ymaginem Dei. De talibus vera sunt que diximus. Sed si cantent cum instrumentis, vel cantent de gestis rebus ad recreationem vel forte informationem, vicini sunt excusationi.'[17]

This indecisive conclusion on the part of Peter was no doubt influenced by the *exemplum* which he adds. He reports an encounter between a jongleur and Pope Alexander (most likely Alexander III, whom Peter knew personally): the jongleur asked the pope whether his soul would be saved since being a jongleur was the only way he could earn his living. The pope is said to have refrained from replying; Peter guessed that he may not have wanted to encourage the jongleur to use his skills extensively:

> Unde quidam talis cum accessisset ad papam Alexandrum, et quesisset ab eo utrum posset salvare animam suam, sic sibi victum queritando cum aliter nesciret, papa nec dedit licentiam ioculandi, nec prohibuit. Et forte dedisset licentiam, nisi quia per consequentiam illius concessio traheret ad ampliorem licentiam.[18]

15 *Summa*, § 211, p. 175f. Note the dual meaning of *hystriones* here for which I know no parallel.
16 *Summa*, p. 176. For *voluptas* associated with music see chapter 5.
17 *Summa*, 176f.
18 *Summa*, p. 177. A shorter version is found in the *Verbum Abbreviatum*, PL 205, 253.

Even as a moral theologian, Peter thus wavered on the brink of accepting the work of the jongleurs in certain circumstances. Certainly, he took for granted that this was a full-time profession that earned people a livelihood. He also was familiar with their declamations, accompanied by instrumental music as well as bodily gestures.

There is one more place in the *Summa* in which Peter deals with the activities of jongleurs.[19] No new arguments are brought to bear; but jongleurs are said to frequent the castles of princes ('qui sequuntur castra principum'). By this time, however, Peter had reached the conclusion that the activities of jongleurs were acceptable as long as they refrained from bodily contortions or effeminate songs.[20] In the light of his general stance, this attitude of this moral theologian shows how even stern ecclesiastics learned in the course of time to accept the realities of the life around them, albeit if grudgingly and with reservations.

The teaching of Peter the Chanter bore fruit in one of his immediate pupils, the English theologian Thomas of Chobham (b. *c.*1158/68, d. *c.* 1233/6). His treatment of the jongleurs in his *Summa Confessorum*[21] (Distinctio IVa, quaestio IIa. De histrionibus) bears clearly the stamp of Peter's ideas. He even includes the *exemplum* about the jongleur and Pope Alexander although in his account the pope gave a positive, if circumspect, response.[22] The main point on which he differs from his teacher is in distinguishing three classes (one with two sub-classes) of jongleurs. One of these consists solely of actors; the second of people who have no domicile, frequent the courts of magnates and talk badly about people not present. Thomas calls them *scurre vagi*.[23] The third class of *histriones* are those who play instruments in order to entertain. Here Thomas knows two types: on the one hand there are those who sing songs of doubtful morality in public gatherings and public drinking places. Since they incite people to lust, they are to be condemned. He distinguishes them from those whom he calls *ioculatores*. The latter sing the deeds of the great and the lives of the saints and thus bring comfort to those in need of it: 'Sunt autem alii qui dicuntur ioculatores qui cantant gesta principum[24] et vitas sanctorum et faciunt solatia hominibus vel in egritudinibus suis vel in angustiis suis'.[25] Chobham has no objections to those professionals.

19 *Summa*, 343, p. 426f.
20 *Summa*, p. 427: 'De ioculatoribus autem qui non exponunt corpora sua ludibrio, nec turpia vel effeminata dicunt, credimus quod sustineri possunt.'
21 *Thomae de Chobham Summa Confessorum*, Broomfield, F., ed., Louvain 1968 (= Analecta Mediaevalia Namurcensia 25).
22 'Permisit igitur papa quod ipse viveret ex officio suo, dummodo abstineret a predictis lasciviis et turpitudinibus.' *Summa Confessorum*, p. 292.
23 *Summa Confessorum*, p. 291.
24 The editor has *principium*, obviously a misprint, cf. six lines further down.
25 *Summa Confessorum*, p. 292.

Otherwise the information on jongleurs is rather patchy and incidental, which is to be accounted for by the fact that they formed an integral part of society and therefore there was generally no reason for mentioning them.

It is significant, however, that the fullest information about the place of jongleurs in society should come from their harshest critics. Thus Peter of Blois (d. 1204) wrote bitterly how people could be moved to tears by the material sung by jongleurs; even the violence that formed part of such compositions reached to the hearts of those who listened. He hoped that Christians would be moved at least as much by the deeds of God as by those of Arthur:

> Saepe in tragoediis et aliis carminibus poetarum, in ioculatorum cantilenis describitur aliquis vir prudens, decorus, fortis, amabilis et per omnia gratiosus. Recitantur etiam pressurae vel iniuriae eidem crudeliter irrogatae, sicut de Arturo et Gangano et Tristanno, fabulosa quaedam referunt histriones, quorum auditu concutiuntur ad compassionem audientium corda, et usque ad lacrymas compunguntur.[26]

It is apparent that here Peter used the terms *poetae*, *ioculatores* and *histriones* as synonyms.

Even more detailed is the information, also of a negative kind, provided by Peter Abelard (1079–1142) towards the end of his *Theologia Christiana*. Pointing out that Plato had banned poets from secular society,[27] he asked why bishops and other Christian teachers did not do likewise. He then described their ordinary behaviour: even on important feast days of the Church they had jongleurs and others at their table, day and night. These were generally remunerated from the goods of the Church. Abelard called these jongleurs 'apostles of the demons', people who preyed on poor souls with words and gestures. He emphasized once again the attention given to the jongleurs with their diabolical sermons:

> Quid ergo episcopi et religionis Christianae doctores poetas a civitate Dei non arcent, quos a civitate saeculi Plato inhibuit? immo quid in solemnibus magnarum festivatatum diebus quae penitus in laudibus Dei expendi debent, ioculatores, saltatores, incantatores, cantatores turpium acciunt ad mensam, totam diem et noctem cum illis feriant atque sabbatizant, magnis postmodum eos remunerant praemiis quae de ecclesiasticis rapiunt beneficiis, de oblationibus pauperum, ut immolent certe daemoniis? Quid enim sunt tales histriones nisi praecones, et, ut ita dicam, apostoli daemonum per quorum ora vel gestus praedari miseras non cessant animas? . . . Totus flagrat et anhelat animus foras ad curiam

---

26 *De confessione*, PL 207, 1088.
27 On this issue see the detailed account by Havelock, E.A., *Preface to Plato*, chs. 1 and 2.

> daemonum et conuentus histrionum, ubi sunt in oblationibus prodigi et cum summo solentio et toto desiderio attenti illi, ut dictum est, diabolicae praedicationi.[28]

Abelard here confirms how deeply rooted in the whole of society was the culture carried by the jongleurs, how generously and appropriately they were sustained by their society, which felt the need for their professional contributions. A contemporary of his, Honorius Augustodunensis, succinctly and categorically declared that jongleurs were beyond hope of salvation: 'Habent spem ioculatores? Nullam: tota namque intentione sunt ministri Satanae.'[29]

Another fairly detailed description of the place of jongleurs in their society, likewise in exclusively negative terms, comes from the pen of Manegold von Lautenbach who, writing about 1085, stated that they are said to endear themselves to princes with lies and adulation by way of verbal barrages by which they manage to seduce the souls of sinners:

> subsecuta est poetarum turba, qui tanquam ioculatores ad nuptias idolatrie concurrentes, figmentis et immodestis laudibus animas vana sectantium oblectati sunt; causa etiam questus ad adulandum et maledicendum parati sceleratos principes et violentos predones deificando et inflatorum verborum tinnitu et sententiarum ornatu nulla veri puritate munito inutili memorie et inani glorie serviendo obscena et turpia quibusdam involucris adornarunt et prout natura singulorum viguit, alii comedi, alii lirici, satirici, tragedi effecti multis fantasmatibus animas peccantium seduxerunt.[30]

However, one can read this text also as testimony to the highly skilled use of language which made jongleurs attractive. This in turn shows that their audience was appreciative of such verbal art.

This negative presentation in the sources is, however, only one side of the coin. There is another factual account of the art of the jongleurs from the late twelfth century. In the Chronicle of the counts of Ghisne the exceptional learning of Count Baldwin is described in great detail. He had numerous works translated for him from Latin into Romance, and then read out aloud before him, but he was also very well versed in the material offered by the best of the jongleurs: 'in cantilenis gestoriis sive in eventuris nobilium sive etiam in fabellis ignobilium ioculatores quosque nominatissimos equiparare putaretur'.[31]

28 *Petri Abaelardi Opera Theologica*, II, Buytaert, E.M., ed., Turnholt 1969 (CCCM 12), 192f.
29 PL 172, 1148.
30 Manegold von Lautenbach, *Liber contra Wolfelmum*, c. IX, Hartmann, W., ed., MGH Quellen zur Geistesgeschichte des Mittelalters 8, Weimar 1972, 62f.
31 *Lamberti Ardensis historia comitum Ghisnensium*, c. 81, MGH SS 24, 598.

Here is positive evidence that skilled jongleurs were highly regarded. As yet another variation, one may mention the jongleur whose public narration of the Life of St Alexis brought about the conversion of Peter Waldes in 1173: 'Is quadam die dominica cum declinasset ad turbam, quam ante ioculatorem viderat congregatam, ex verbis ipsius conpungtus fuit . . . fuit enim locus narracionis eius, qualiter beatus Alexis in domo patris sui beato fine quievit.'[32] This is the most explicit account of the repertoire of the jongleurs including edifying Christian material (as alluded to by Peter the Chanter) alongside the far better attested secular and heroic accounts.

The social acceptance and utter respectability of the jongleurs in their society is best evident from the attestation of their presence in the entourage of rulers. This fact is rarely attested, but one needs to remember how to assess rare attestations of this kind; rare attestation by historians can also be considered as indicative of everyday occurrence.

Thus the splendid court held by the emperor Frederick I at Mainz in 1184, according to the description of a visitor, Gislebert de Mons, included *ioculatores* and *ioculatrices* who were well rewarded.[33] Similarly, the universal chronicler Ekkehard of Aura (d. 1125), describing the splendid marriage feast of Henry V and the English princess Mathilda in 1114, lists the many dignitaries who attended the celebration and presented gifts to their lord. He in turn distributed gifts, and of the recipients the chronicler mentions explicitly only the innumerable crowd of jongleurs: 'innumerabili multitudini ioculatorum et istrionum'.[34] These two references should be taken as exemplary: the royal and imperial court set standards which were worthy of imitation by other groups of society.

By way of contrast, it was worth emphasizing and holding up as an exceptional kind of behaviour (even though approved by clerical writers) that another emperor, Henry III, on the occasion of his marriage in 1043 did not consider it necessary to reward the jongleurs who were present. This is reported by a contemporary, the monk Hermannus Contractus of Reichenau, who in this presentation voiced the official ecclesiastical attitude towards jongleurs: 'Regales apud Ingelenheim nuptias celebravit, et in vano hystrionum favore nihili pendendo, utile cunctis exemplum, vacuos eos et moerentes dimittendo, proposuit.'[35] It should be noted that two other contemporary accounts refer to the great number of jongleurs present on that occasion: 'infinita histrionum et ioculatorum multitudine'.[36]

32 *Ex chronico universali anonymi Laudunensis*, MGH SS 26, 447.
33 *La chronique de Gislebert de Mons*, Vanderkindere, L, ed., Bruxelles 1904, 156.
34 *Ekkehardi chronicon* s. a. 1114, MGH SS 6, 248.
35 MGH SS 5, 124.
36 *Annales Hildesheimenses*, s.a. 1044, MGH SS 3, 104; *Chronicon Suevicum Universale*, MGH SS 13, 72.

These almost identical ways of referring to jongleurs in the presence of rulers at important festivities, separated as they are from each other by nearly a century, have the ring of standardized expressions referring to a social phenomenon regarded as normal: one must note the great number of jongleurs; there is no sign here of their being a marginalized group. This in turn finds confirmation of sorts when one learns, in passing as it were, from a source as sober as the Domesday Book of 1087, of the existence of a *ioculator regis*.[37] And this conveys the idea of an officially recognized position in the king's entourage. The man named here as Berdic may not have been the only jongleur to hold a regular position at the court of the English king; however, the English historians of the time have nothing to say on the subject, not even about Berdic.

This raises the question whether jongleurs held permanent positions at other courts. A possible indication that this was the case can be given in the Life of Queen Mathilda, wife of King Henry I (919-36), which reports that after the death of her son Duke Henry in 955 she ceased to listen to secular songs or performances but turned to Christian subjects instead:

> Posthac neminem voluit audire carmina secularia cantantem, nec quemquam videre ludum exercentem, sed tantum audivit sancta carmina de evangeliis vel aliis scripturis sacris sumpta, necnon in hoc sedulo delectabatur, ut de vita vel passione sanctorum sibi cantaretur.[38]

Generally, the sources are such that for continental Europe this question cannot be answered either way;[39] however, on balance it is more likely than not that jongleurs did hold permanent positions.[40] In view of the social acceptance of the oral tradition we have described, royal courts clearly did not rely on jongleurs being casually available. However, it is significant that such an important topic is not more explicitly dealt with in the sources. Be that as it may, the social acceptance of jongleurs and their contribution in spheres other than the most rigorous ecclesiastical circles is beyond doubt.

37 Domesday Book, 162a (Gloucestershire 1982). An *Adelina joculatrix* is listed in DB Hampshire, 1982, p. 1.
38 MGH SS 4, 294.
39 For Wales and Ireland see chapter 9.
40 Possibly an allusion to a permanent position at court is given in *Anselmi gesta episcoporum Leod*, c. 34 (s.a. 1020): 'mimos caeterosque palatinos canes', MGH SS 7, 208. The derogatory terms used for the *mimi* would reflect ultimately also upon the groups that kept them. Another indication to this effect may be seen in the description of the royal entourage of king Conrad I when he visited the monastery of St Gall whose monks were on that occasion exposed to unfamiliar odours, sights and sounds: 'Nunquam ea domo saporatum monachum odorem farine hauriunt et carnium. Saltant satirici; psallunt symphoniaci.' *Casus Sancti Galli* c. 16, Haefele, H.F., ed., Darmstadt 1980, 44. There is finally the 'mimus regis, qui ei per verba iocularia laetitiam erat solitus excitare', attested for a Spanish king by Gregory of Tours, *De virtutibus s. Martini*, IV, 7, MGH SS rer. Merov. 1, 2, p. 201.

After the Carolingians

There is exceptionally varied information about a jongleur taking part prominently in the battle of Hastings in 1066 on the Norman side.[41] Three Latin accounts have been preserved which have something to say on this subject; but it is not possible to say that they are dependent on each other, and it is more likely that they each draw on different sources, very likely on oral tradition.

The earliest account, *Carmen de Hastingae Proelio*, is by Guy of Amiens, who is believed to have been involved in the battle himself. He refers to the jongleur by two different terms, *histrio* and *mimus*, terms which thus appear again clearly as synonyms.[42] His surname is given as *Incisor-ferri*, which in contemporary French was Taillefer. According to this account, the jongleur admonished the French army with words, then stormed forward into battle, successfully killing the first Englishman, beheading him, and showing his trophy to his own side. He is thus depicted as an example of bravery and courage.

Chronologically the next Latin account to mention something on this subject is that by William of Malmesbury who wrote more than a generation after Guy. He tells us that at the outset of the battle the song of Roland was sung to incite the warriors; God's help was invoked as well: 'Tunc cantilena Rollandi inchoata, ut martium viri exemplum pugnaturos accenderet, inclamatoque Dei auxilio.'[43] One can only infer that the song was performed by a professional singer. This passage is also interesting because it refers to a *cantilena Rollandi* at a time earlier than the oldest preserved manuscript of the *Chanson de Roland*.

There is finally the account of Henry of Huntingdon which names Taillefer without using one of the familiar terms for a jongleur. He is said to have played in front of the English, who were mesmerized by what they saw, and to have killed two English soldiers in quick succession before being killed himself: 'Quidam vero nomine Taillefer dudum antequam coirent bellatores, ensibus iactatis ludens coram gente Anglorum, dum in eum omnes stuperent, quendam vexilliferum Anglorum interfecit. Secundo similiter egit. Tertio idem agens et ipse interfectus est.'[44]

For a complete picture of the jongleur Taillefer leading the lines of the duke of Normandy into battle, reciting heroic verse about Roland and thus

---

41   Sayers, W., 'The jongleur Taillefer at Hastings: antecedents and literary fate', *Viator* 14, 1980, 77-88, has aims different from those pursued here.
42   Morton, C. and Muntz, H., ed., *The Carmen de Hastingae Proelio of Guy of Amiens*, Oxford 1972, lines 391 and 399. The translation of this passage is particularly awkward: *mimus* is rendered as 'mummer'.
43   *Willelmi Malmesbiriensis monachi de gestis regum Anglorum*, ed. Stubbs, W., 2 vols, III, 242, vol. 2, 302.
44   *Henrici Archidiaconi Huntendunensis Historia Anglorum* VI, § 30, Arnold, T., ed., RS 74, London 1879, 202f.

stimulating the troops to emulate Roland's bravery, the three Latin accounts have to be taken together. The subject was still written about several generations after the event in works which are regarded as serious historical works,[45] and since the two twelfth-century Latin prose accounts do not draw on a known written source, it can be suggested that the outline of the story lived in oral tradition in England. More detail about Taillefer is given in Wace's verse epic 'Guillaume le conquérant':

> Taillefer qui mult bien chantout,
> Sor un cheval qui tost alout,
> Devant le duc alout chantant
> De Karlemagne et de Rollant
> E d'Oliver e des vassals,
> Qui morurent en Rencevals.[46]

It is easy to see all three Latin accounts drawing on a pool of information but only partially, presumably because they could rely on general knowledge about this incident.

One is reminded of Regino of Prüm who mentioned song prominently in the context of going into battle: 'omnis morum habitus cantibus gubernatur et regitur, ut et ad bellum progressui et item receptui canatur, cantu tubae excitante et rursus sedante virtutem animi'.[47] In fact, the phenomenon itself is known from antiquity and especially from the Bible, but in the early medieval West it is not often mentioned in the sources, perhaps because it was so widespread.[48]

That such singing was done by experts is reported in a case from France in the late eleventh century, where a band of robbers were so confident of their strength that in roaming the countryside they had a jongleur leading the way, who played an instrument and sang songs about exemplary deeds and wars of the ancients: 'scurram se praecedere facerent, qui musico instrumento res fortiter gestas et priorum bella praecineret, quatinus his acrius incitarentur ad ea peragenda, quae maligno conceperant animo'.[49]

45 Campbell, J., 'Some twelfth-century views of the Anglo-Saxon past', in id., *Essays in Anglo-Saxon history*, London 1986, 209-28.
46 *Le Roman de Rou de Wace*, Holden, A.J., ed., vol. II, Paris 1971, 183.
47 *Clavis Gerberti*, p. 49, see above, p. 112.
48 Two examples may be mentioned here: 1. Alcuin claims to have composed verses for fighting at the request of Charlemagne, *Ep.* 149, 241f; 2. for crusaders singing in battle see Gerhoch von Reichersberg, *Commentarius in psalmos*, XXXIII, MGH Libelli de Lite III, 431: 'in quo Teutonici more suo cantantes et Francigena more suo clamantes tantas in altum voces extulerunt'.
49 *Ex miraculis sancti Benedicti abbatis, Recueil des historiens des Gaules et de la France*, XI, Delisle, L., ed., Paris 1826, 489. Further down the page the term *cantor* is used for the same person. Cf. also the following note.

Similarly, a jongleur is attested in the army of the Dane Waldemar when he faced his enemy and rival Svein in 1157. Recalling the treachery of Svein was supposed to raise the morale of the troop.[50]

While the sources are throughout more informative about the highest echelons of society, there is incidental information that the jongleurs formed also part of social gatherings lower down. This is attested for the feast of the knighting of Arnoldus, son of the count of Ghisne, in 1181. He generously showered with gifts those who acclaimed him, thereby reaping a harvest of lavish praise:

> Arnoldus itaque militaribus vix indutus vestimentis prosiliit in medium et ministralibus, mimis, nebulonibus, gartionibus, scurris et ioculatoribus omnibusque nomen eius invocantibus et predicantibus satisfecit, adeo ut in remunerationis premium laudem eorum consecutus est et gratiam.[51]

This applied to secular society. We may note here three terms used for jongleurs (*mimi, scurrae, ioculatores*), all used in the plural.

It is evident that, as in Carolingian times, the extreme position adopted by strict clerics met with little ready acceptance in society generally, even among clerics. Thus the author of the Life of Archbishop Bardo of Mainz (d. 1051), when mentioning that Bardo was kind even to jongleurs, stressed that this was not because of what these had to offer: 'Miseris ioculatoribus valde fuit benignus, nulla scurrilitartis specie conductus.'[52] Abbot Absalon of Sprinkirsbach devoted himself to the *bella vitiorum* of his time and asked rhetorically: 'Was it not granted to you to play with birds in the sky, to feed jongleurs, to bring up sons or daughters and concubines without number? Certainly not!' ('Nunquid indulsit tibi in avibus coeli ludere, pascere mimos et ioculatores, nutrire filios vel filias et concubinas, quarum non est numerus? Minime)'.[53] Likewise, in the Life of Bishop Otto of Bamberg a distinction is made between two kinds of generosity; the negative kind is that which spends heavily on banquets, gifts to jongleurs, unnecessarily expensive clothes and other vanities: 'Prodigi sunt, qui epulis et viscerationibus et ioculatorum muneribus et superfluo cultu vestium aliisque vanitatibus pecunias profundunt.'[54] These examples may suffice to illustrate that jongleurs were often to

50 Olrik, J., Raeder, H., ed., *Saxonis Gesta Danorum*, 1931, XIV, xix, 13, p. 410: 'Medius acies interequitabat cantor, qui parricidalem Suenonis perfidiam famoso carmine prosequendo Waldemari milites per summam vindictae exhortationem in bellum accenderet'. Saxo's use of *cantor* in this sense is exceptional, but at least he uses it consistently: see below, p. 251.
51 *Lamberti Ardensis historia comitum Ghisnensium*, c. 91 MGH SS 24, 604.
52 *Vita Bardonis auctore Vulculdo*, MGH SS 11, 321.
53 PL 211, 78.
54 *Herbordi Vita Ottonis episcopi Babenb.* L. I, c. 5, MGH SS 20, 707. Note: *prodigus* used in the same sense and the same context by Abelard, above at n. 28.

be found in the entourage of ecclesiastics, and their acceptance by clerics seems to have been more common than their exclusion.

Roger of Howden reports how Hugh de Nonant, bishop of Coventry, who briefly played an important political role in England in 1191 in the absence of King Richard, imported jongleurs from France in order to sing favourably about him in public (as he had previously commissioned): 'Hic ad augmentum et famam sui nominis emendicata carmina et rhythmos adulatorios comparabat, et de regno Francorum cantores et ioculatores muneribus allexerat, ut de illo canerent in plateis.'[55] The chronicler remarks that this was highly exceptional, although he does not specify what was exceptional about it.

In almost all of these accounts jongleurs are depicted as socially accepted, and there is no indication that they were considered to be of a low social standing. The only explicit reference to their being as a rule non-residents comes from Hugh of St Victor, who commented on their unstable nature since they were accustomed to roam the world: 'Illi (ioculatores) vero, qui per diversas regiones discurrere sunt consueti, si taedio claustri fuerint aggravati, citius a claustris exeunt, quia terrarum diversitates norunt.'[56]

It is certainly remarkable how the picture emerging from the narrative sources differs from that given by normative sources.[57] The jongleurs were representatives of what was originally a purely oral and secular culture. We have seen that from time to time references attest their existence in large numbers in socially accepted and recognized positions, and with their work finding adequate remuneration. Some are explicitly referred to as earning their livelihood by this profession. Ambivalence towards them or outright condemnation appears to be over-represented in the sources, especially those deriving from strict clerics. Otherwise, the social position of jongleurs throughout the early medieval West resembles very much that of stage actors in late Roman society: they were very highly respected and well rewarded and thus regarded as essential. The incessant fulminations against them by those who believed it their task to make social and ethical standards conform to Christian precepts, had little effect, as was bitterly admitted at the Fourth Lateran Council in 1215.[58]

We shall now turn to other manifestations of oral culture, the prominent position of which throughout the time to c.1200 can be taken as fact. We can therefore proceed by subject rather than in chronological order.

---

55 Benedict of Peterborough, *Gesta Regis Ricardi*, RS 49.2, 1867, 216.
56 *De bestiis et aliis rebus liber primus*, c. xlv, PL 177, 46.
57 Cf. chapter 5.
58 Cf. above, p. vii.

OTFRID OF WEISSENBURG

Around 865 Otfrid, monk and priest of Weissenburg, wrote to his metropolitan, Archbishop Liutbert of Mainz, on the subject of his recently completed versification of parts of the Gospel (*Liber Evangeliorum*) in his native Frankish language.[59] This work had been undertaken at the request of some brothers and a woman named Judith who had asked him to write on this subject because they felt offended by certain songs and performances (apparently quite common). Otfrid, professing himself a pupil of the famous teacher Rabanus Maurus and visibly proud of his mastery of Latin, the language in which he wrote the letter, felt it necessary to explain the unusual nature of his work and the difficulties posed by the Frankish language, which lacked the polish of Latin. This sounds highly conventional, and it must be taken into account that oral culture placed great stress on artistic use of language.

Of greatest interest in our context is, however, what Otfrid reports about the cultural products which his work was supposed to replace. He refers to 'the sound of useless things' (*rerum sonus inutilium*),[60] and the 'obscene singing of the lay people' (*laicorum cantus. . . obscenus*, p. 166, line 32), as well as 'the performance of secular voices' (*ludum saecularium vocum*, p. 166, line 35). This kind of language is familiar from the first half of the ninth century and recognizable as the negative presentation of oral secular culture current then as in the time of Otfrid.[61] These are references to words, singing and gestures.

The manuscript evidence makes it clear that the text of the *Liber Evangeliorum* was meant by its author to be sung. This is apparent from the musical notation contained in some of the early manuscripts.[62] On the basis of our previous investigation, however, this would have been highly plausible in any case. One can make the point more or less emphatically that, as far as the medium of the work was concerned, Otfrid chose to offer material that would successfully rival the secular culture which, on his own admission, consisted of sung verse.

Later in his letter, having dealt with the qualitative inferiority of the Frankish language *vis-à-vis* Latin, Otfrid stated that there existed no histories written in that language, no accounts of the lives or deeds of the ancestors: 'lingua enim haec velut agrestis habetur, dum a propriis nec scriptura nec arte aliqua ullis est temporibus expolita; quippe qui nec historias suorum anteces-

---

59 MGH Epp. 6, p. 166-9). Rädle, F., 'Otfrieds Brief an Liutbert', in: *Kritische Bewahrung* (FS W. Schröder), Berlin 1975, 213-229; cf. also Haubrichs, *Anfänge*, 321 f., 354-78; Günther, H., 'Probleme beim Verschriftlichen der Muttersprache. Otfrid von Weissenberg und die lingua theotisca', *Zeitschrift für Literaturwissenschaft und Linguistik* 59, 1985, 36-54.
60 P. 166, line 31, and see also line 36.
61 Haubrichs, *Anfänge*, 321, who, however, is unaware of the late antique background of this language usage.
62 Haubrichs, *Anfänge*, 375 f; cf., however, also chapter 5 on music above and the fact that musical performance must be assumed long before the appearance of musical notation.

sorum, ut multae gentes caeterae, commendant memoriae[63] nec eorum gesta vel vitam ornant dignitatis amore' (p. 168, lines 28-31).

Here Otfrid explains what he understands as the appropriate subject of written *historia*. He does not give any indication whether the secular songs mentioned earlier in this letter dealt with the deeds of ancestors, or that there was poetic language available also in Frankish. It is known from other sources that both in fact applied, but Otfrid chooses to ignore this, just as he leaves the reader to wonder whether he was familiar with the Saxon biblical epic created in the two preceding generations.[64]

ENGLAND

There is reason to believe, quite apart from this account of Otfrid, that poetry and music were an integral part of the education of the nobility. There are two reports from England that can be understood in this way, and in each case the information is provided incidentally. In his biography of King Alfred the Great (d. 899), Asser reports that before Alfred learned to read at the age of about twelve, he was an avid listener to poems in English which were recited around him day and night and which he learned by heart: 'Usque ad duodecimum aetatis annum, aut eo amplius, illiteratus permansit. Sed Saxonica poemata die noctuque solers auditor, relatu aliorum saepissime audiens, docibilis memoriter retinebat.'[65] This is only reported as a prelude to Alfred's eagerness to learn to read, which was exceptional in his circle.

Of a similar nature is the information about the musical training of the young Dunstan, the future archbishop of Canterbury and Church reformer (*c*. 910-88). His musical expertise is brought up in the context of a miracle that happened to him and pointed the way to his future career. On one occasion, his harp, his favourite instrument, played on its own the melody of an antiphon: 'cithara, pendens in cubilis pariete, audientibus cunctis, sponte sua sine tactu cuiusquam iubilationis modulum alta voce personuit, et ad finem usque serie cantando perduxit: "Gaudent in coelis animae sanctorum qui Christi vestigia sunt secuti; et quia pro eius amore sanguinem suum fuderunt, ideo cum Christo regnabunt in aeternum".'[66] This account is valuable for trying to describe in words instrumental music of the time.

As background to this miraculous account, it is reported that the young Dunstan was gifted in various arts, in writing, playing the harp (*cytharizandi*, and later 'cytharam suam quam lingua paterna hearpam vocamus'),[67] and

---

63 Cf. Einhart, *Vita Karoli Magni* c. 29: 'scripsit memoriaeque mandavit': above p. 134.
64 See p. 245f.
65 Asser, *De rebus gestis Aelfredi*, ed. Stevenson, H.W., Oxford 1904, repr. 1959, c. 22, p. 20.
66 *Memorials of St Dunstan*, RS 63, ed. Stubbs, W., London 1874, 21; similarly 170.
67 Ibid., 20 and 21.

drawing, all of which were brought to bear in the miracle. What the hagiographer Eadmer (c.1055–1124) has to say about Dunstan's musical activity should be regarded as imaginary and reflecting his own times rather than being applicable to the early tenth century; but even as such it is instructive: 'Super haec instrumentis musici generis, quorum scientia non mediocriter fultus erat, non tantum se sed et multorum animos a turbulentis mundi negotiis saepe demulcere, et in medicationem coelestis harmoniae tam per suavitatem verborum, quae modo materna modo alia lingua musicis modulis interserebat, quam et per concordem concentum quem per eos exprimebat, concitare solebat. Propter haec igitur a multis frequentabatur et ab eo multa fieri petebatur.'[68] The socializing and harmonizing effect of music is well articulated in this account. Nor is familiarity with song in the vernacular presented as something negative, even in the mouth of a future saint.

HISTORIANS AND THE ORAL TRADITION

Widukind of Corvey An outstanding example of the use of oral tradition by a historian is to be found in the work of Widukind of Corvey (b. c.920, d. after 973), *Rerum gestarum Saxonicarum libri tres*.[69] Particular attention is due in this work to the *origo et status gentis*. The author states that he almost completely relies on oral tradition; he vows that the account is uncertain because of its age: 'solam pene famam sequens in hac parte, nimia vetustate omnem fere certitudinem obscurante' (I, ii). At the end of the *origo*-account he disclaims any guarantee as to its reliability when writing: 'Si qua fides his dictis adhibeatur, penes lectorem est' (I, xiii). However, in between he at one stage calls what he has to report *historia*,[70] and this after a digression in which he draws on Bede's *Historia Ecclesiastica*, that is, a written Latin source.

Widukind knew of two different versions concerning the origins of the Saxons: these came either from northern Europe or were descendants of the Greeks; the latter version Widukind had heard in his youth[71] and obviously retained. He explained that the Saxon name derived from their characteristic weapon, the sword: 'Cultelli enim nostra lingua "sahs" dicuntur, ideoque Saxones nuncupatos' (I, vii).

The story of how the Saxons came to obtain the lands which they later had forms the subject of chapters IV-VII and IX-XIII. Quite obviously Widukind drew here on material of oral saga (*Heldensage*) current in his time.[72]

---

68 Ibid., 170.
69 MGH us schol 60, 1935, ed. Hirsch, P.
70 I, viii, p. 10.
71 I, ii: 'ut ipse adolescentulus audivi quendam predicantem, de Graecis, quia ipsi dicerent Saxones reliquias fuisse Macedonici exercitus'. p. 4.
72 Cf. Beumann, H., *Widukind von Korvey*, Weimar 1950, 71ff., 110ff.; cf. also Lintzel, M.,

He offers the most detailed Latin version of this material.[73] The story, reduced to a few personalities as the main actors, deals with the Franks, the Thuringians and the Saxons. The main actors are the Frankish king Theuderic, the Thuringian king Irminfrid and his wife Amalberga, half-sister of Theuderic, and the Saxons who do not have a named leader. It ends with the slaying of Irminfrid[74] and Theuderic by Iring, follower of Irminfrid, and the acquisition by the Saxons of the lands once Thuringian.

In the course of the complicated story there are changes of alliance, there are promises and frauds, there is cunning, fighting and bravery. It is the sort of material that will eventually find its way into written epics.[75] There is even a prophecy of great slaughter resulting from insulted pride.[76]

Some of the names in this account are known from earlier historical accounts; thus there is an historical kernel to the narrative: the Thuringian king Erminfrid did suffer a decisive defeat near the river Unstrut (mentioned by Widukind) in 531 at the hands of the Frankish king Theuderic (and his brother Chlothar, who does not figure in Widukind); he was murdered in 534. He was married to Amalaberga, sister of Theodoric, not, as is also evident from her name, the Frank but the Ostrogoth.[77] The historical accounts in Latin from late antiquity contain nothing about a Saxon connexion with this encounter between Franks and Thuringians.

Thus Widukind drew on accounts which had been current for more than four centuries; the fact that our available written sources from the sixth century contain information not compatible with Widukind's story confirms that he did not draw on these. On the other hand, the essence of Widukind's *origo gentis* account is also found in two other sources, the *Translatio Sancti Alexandri*

'Untersuchungen zur Geschichte der alten Sachsen', *Sachsen und Anhalt* 13, 1937, 28-77, esp. 54ff. For the term in this sense see Curschmann, M., 'Unter 'Sage'—hier natürlich synonym mit 'Heldensage'—verstehe ich zunächst ganz allgemein das Gesamt dessen, was man zu einem gegebenen Zeitpunkt über ein bestimmtes Ereignis oder eine Ereigniskette der heroischen Frühzeit zu berichten wußte.' 'Zur Wechselwirkung von Literatur und Sage. Das 'Buch von Kriemhild' und Dietrich von Bern', *Beiträge zur Geschichte der deutschen Sprache und Literatur* 111, 1989, 380-410, at 383.

73 The Annals of Quedlinburg, Saxony, composed in the early eleventh century, draw on the same *Heldensage*, not on Widukind, as differences in their accounts make clear. It is also much shorter: MGH SS III, 31f. Cf. Robert Holtzmann, 'Die Quedlinburger Annalen', *Sachsen und Anhalt* 1, 1925, 64-125, esp. 74f.

74 'Et ut evaginato gladio stetit, ipsum quoque Thiadricum obtruncavit, sumensque corpus domini posuit super cadaver Thiadrici, ut vinceret saltem mortuus, qui vincebatur vivus. Viamque ferro faciens discessit.' I, xiii, p. 23.

75 See chapter 10. Some scholars suggested that there was a written epic already in existence in Widukind's time, but there is nothing to prove this.

76 'Mallem hoc caput meum tibi tradere quam huiuscemodi verba a te audire, sciens ea multo sanguine Francorum atque Thuringorum diluenda', I, ix, p. 12.

77 Wolfram, *Geschichte der Goten*, 396.

by Rudolf of Fulda from the ninth century,[78] and the annals of Quedlinburg from the early eleventh century.

It has been suggested that Widukind drew on a written source, an epic written in German; this assumed epic is said to have been composed in the first half of the tenth century.[79] While the account in the Quedlinburg annals does not refer to the oral background of the *origo*-story, Rudolf of Fulda does.[80] Furthermore, there are enough differences between the three accounts to exclude the possibility that they all drew on a common written source; nor is it possible to assume that the Quedlinburg annalist drew on Widukind. Instead, all three appear to have drawn on an oral tradition that was current in their time with characteristic variants accompanying a more solid kernel. Widukind makes clear allusions to the oral nature of his source several times: 'Thuringi traduntur fuisse' (I, iv); 'maiorum memoria prodit' (I, xii);[81] 'memorabilis fama' (I, xiii). It is very likely that this tradition was current in verse; it would have beeen normal for such a verse account to be sung.[82] In the present case one sees clearly how historical facts are not transmitted accurately in the course of the oral tradition.[83]

For us this is of less importance than the attitudes contained in the account which were still recalled and regarded as valid by those who cherished the tradition. The warrior ethos of the Saxons is neatly expressed in a speech attributed to the old warrior Hathagat, who reasons why there is no question of not fighting in a difficult situation:

> Hucusque inter optimos Saxones vixi, et ad hanc fere ultimam senectutem aetas me perduxit, et numquam Saxones meos fugere vidi; et quomodo nunc cogor agere quod numquam didici? Certare scio, fugere ignoro nec valeo. Si fata non sinunt ultra vivere, liceat saltem, quod michi dulcissimum est, cum amicis occumbere. Exempli michi paternae virtutis sunt amicorum corpora circa nos prostrata, qui maluerunt mori quam vinci, inpigras animas amittere quam coram inimicis loco cedere. (I, xi)

78 MGH SS II, 674-81, new edition by Krusch, B., 'Die Übertragung des H. Alexander von Rom nach Wildeshausen durch den Enkel Widukinds 851. Das älteste niedersächsische Geschichtsdenkmal', *Nachrichten der Gesellschaft der Wissenschaften zu Göttingen, Phil.-hist. Klasse* 1933, 405-36, text 423ff.
79 See Pelka, W., 'Studien zur Geschichte des Untergangs des alten Thüringischen Königreichs im Jahre 531 n. Chr.', *Zeitschrift des Vereins für Thüringische Geschichte und Altertumskunde* 22 (NF 14), 1904, 165-228, esp. 179ff. This view was taken over by Beumann, see 61-3, 78, 80, who refers to the 'Iring-Lied', 61, 78.
80 Beumann mentions him only once, p. 78, n. 6.
81 Cf. also 'fama prodit' II, xxxii, p. 93 on an event of 941.
82 However, it has to be stressed that such a 'Lied', unlike a written epic, being oral, would have been variable in its content.
83 This is a (although not the) characteristic feature of oral culture, cf. Clanchy, 'Remembering the past', 176, as above, chapter 4, n. 95

A similar ethos is also expressed concerning the Franks, and in this case the exemplary deeds of the ancestors are mentioned: 'In rebus honestis pulcherrimam semper esse arbitror perseverantiam, quam ita coluerunt mariores nostri, ut a ceptis negotiis raro vel numquam deficerent. . . . Indecorum est victoribus victis vincendi locum dare.'[84] We may lastly mention the way Iring is portrayed in rough and clear terms: 'vir audax, fortis manu, acer ingenio, acutus consilio, pertinax in agendis rebus, facilis ad suadendum quae vellet.'[85]

The Latin version of Widukind provides only oblique access to the current oral tradition, but one is grateful for this detailed account.

Archbishop Hatto of Mainz and Adalbert of Babenberg A *cause célèbre* in the year 913 was the betrayal of Count Adalbert of Babenberg by Archbishop Hatto of Mainz. Widukind of Corvey considered it a sensitive subject two generations later. He referred to it only in a late recension, calling it *rumor vulgi*.[86] This clearly refers to an oral account. One gets the impression that Widukind describes the story as being of little reliability in order to be able to include it. About a century later, Ekkehard IV of St Gall alludes to the story again, specifying that it was spread in the form of song by the common people: 'quoniam vulgo concinnatur et canitur, scribere supersedeo'.[87] However, this shows how tenacious such a tradition could be; according to Ekkehard, the existing oral tradition meant that there was no need to write about the story in detail; he just gave the bare facts. One century later again, Otto of Freising gave an account which drew on a written exemplar, the universal chronicle of Frutolf of Michelsberg. But he also mentions specifically that the events relating to Hatto and Adalbert were still topics for discussion at various courts: 'ut non solum in regum gestis invenitur, sed etiam ex vulgari traditione in compitis et curiis hactenus auditur'.[88] It is worth noting that the oral tradition continued alongside written accounts. Otto apparently accepted the information as reliable and included it in his work. It is noteworthy that Otto distinguished the two genres of sources and availed himself of both.

Frutolf of Michelsberg The Bamberg historian Frutolf of Michelsberg, author of a universal chronicle in the first half of the twelfth century, when dealing with the history of the Goths, made explicit use of the Gothic history of Jordanes. However, he also mentions that there were oral accounts current

84 I, ix, p. 14.
85 I, ix, p. 11-12. The fact that Widukind in his Latin account drew on classical authors does not take from the heroic ethos of the barbarians which is at stake here.
86 I, xxii, p. 35.
87 *Casus Sancti Galli*, c. 11, p. 36.
88 *Chronicon* VI, xv, p. 274. Hofmeister, A., ed., *Ottonis episcopi Frisingensis Chronica sive Historia de duobus civitatibus*, MGH SS in us. schol. 45, 1912.

in his time, apparently in prose and in verse ('vulgari fabulatione et cantilenarum modulatione') about Ermanaric, Attila and Theodoric. He also noted that there were accounts in chronicles which suggested that these three personalities had been contemporaries, which was not the case according to Jordanes. Frutolf concludes cautiously: 'Igitur aut hic falsa conscripsit, aut vulgaris opinio fallitur et fallit.'[89] For us it is most important that oral traditions about the history of the Goths were current in the twelfth century, and that some of these had also comparable parallels in written works.[90]

There are other ways in which oral culture is referred to in the sources, predominantly in connexion with an individual whose life or deeds were said to have been transmitted in verse form and/or sung.

Thus the chronicler of Petershausen, reporting the election in 1077 of Rudolf of Rheinfelden at Forchheim as a rival to the emperor Henry IV, claims that Pontius Pilate was a native of Forchheim and that therefore, after the election of Rudolf, 'the people sang of him as another Pontius Pilate' ('tunc vulgus de Ruodolfo concinebat, quod alter Pilatus surrexisset').[91] Under the year 1104, the chronicler Ekkehard of Aura reports the descent of Aerbo and Boto, brothers of noble stock from Noricum; one of their ancestors, also named Aerbo, was remembered in song in the vernacular for the fact that he was killed by an aurochs during a hunt ('quem in venatu a visonta bestia confossum, vulgares adhuc cantilenae resonant').[92]

The exemplary deeds of Benno II, bishop of Osnabrück, in the war against the Hungarians under the command of Henry III in 1051 found their way into popular tales as well as into vernacular verse which were current long after the event: 'ubi quantae sibi utilitati, quanto honori, quanto denique vitae tutamini et praesidio fuerit, populares etiam nunc adhuc notae fabulae attestari solent et cantilenae vulgares'.[93]

Ekkehard of St Gall early in the eleventh century gives a few instances of the heroic deeds of a nobleman by the name of Kuno; because of his small size he was nicknamed Churzibolt, but this did not affect his bravery. He lived

---

89 *Ekkehardi Chronicon Universale*, MGH SS 6, 130. For this and another similar passage see Curschmann, 'Wechselwirkung', 384, n. 11.

90 One is tempted to think of a case like that of the Quedlinburg annalist who wrote around 1025 about Ermanarich, Theodoric and Attila, MGH SS 3, 31, lines 21-28. The phrase on Theodoric 'et iste fuit Thideric de Berne de quo cantabant rustici olim' is unfortunately apparently not eleventh century but the incorporation of a gloss from the fifteenth century, see Robert Holtzmann, 'Die Quedlinburger Annalen', *Sachsen und Anhalt* 1, 1925, 64-125, esp. 95-98. It is presented as being from the eleventh century by Haubrichs, *Anfänge*, 111, and See, K. v. *Germanische Heldensage* 1971, 134.

91 Feger, O, ed., *Die Chronik des Klosters Petershausen* II, 33 (= Schwäbische Chroniken der Stauferzeit 3), Lindau/Konstanz 1956, 112.

92 *Ekkehardi chronicon universale*, MGH SS 6, 225.

93 *Vita Bennonis episcopi Osnabrugensis auctore Nortberto*, MGH SS 30, 2, 874.

under the early Saxon kings, and thus his deeds lay several generations in the past when Ekkehard noted that much was sung about him ('Multa sunt, que de illo concinnantur et canuntur').[94]

One encounters in these four examples explicitly oral traditions carried among the common people; and these traditions were not confined to secular heroes. There is further information, from 1088, concerning the memory of Abbot Angilbert, the renowned Carolingian courtier and founder of the monastery of St Riquier. His reputation was said to have received very wide oral transmission prior to the discovery of his burial place in the late eleventh century ('eius celeberrima memoria in ore universorum Franciscorum vel Pontivorum').[95] Here the oral tradition emerges as a successful and perhaps even superior medium of transmission in a milieu characterized by a written culture.

However, this method of transmission was not limited to dealing with individual personalities even though such cases are mentioned more frequently in the sources. Thus Widukind of Corvey writes that the memory of a remarkable defeat of the Franks by the Saxons in 915 was proclaimed by jongleurs ('ut a mimis declamaretur':[96] note the present tense). Two centuries later, Rahewin, writing in detail about an important diet held by the emperor Frederick I in Italy in 1158, closes his account by reporting that the deeds of the emperor were sung publicly in highly favourable terms: 'Fuere etiam qui ibidem in publico facta imperatoris carminibus favorabilibus celebrarent.'[97]

From these varied incidental references reported obviously independently of each other there emerges the picture of orally remembered 'history' in song as a widespread phenomenon well into the twelfth century. The almost identical way of formulating this phenomenon in Latin, tantalizingly uninformative though it is, suggests a standard sort of terminology for a ubiquitous institution which itself appears to be significant. When taking into account how widespread the institution of oral memory was, alongside history written in Latin, one once again gets a good idea of how unrepresentative of their age most written histories must have been—and how restrictive their potential public, due to the fact that they were written in Latin.

94 *Casus Sancti Galli*, c. 50, 112. In fact Ekkehard uses the same phrase as in his earlier reference to oral tradition. See previous note.
95 Hariulf, *Chronique de l'abbaye de Saint-Riquier*, IV, xxxii, Lot, F., ed., Paris 1894, 264.
96 I, xxxiii, 36; cf. Beumann, *Widukind*, 101.
97 *Rahewini gesta Friderici imperatoris* IV, v, Waitz, G., ed., MGH SS in us. schol. 46, 1912 (1978), 239.

9

THE CELTIC COUNTRIES

In the investigation of oral culture in the early medieval West, the Celtic countries hold a special place and offer rich, varied and valuable insights. It must be said nevertheless at the outset that the picture which can be drawn is neither complete nor free from inconsistencies. As in all other medieval societies, evidence for oral culture is derived from written sources and is thus filtered through literate minds. That must be taken into account. However, in contrast to the sources studied earlier, the Celtic sources were at least for the most part written in the native language, and, where they are written in Latin, one can recognize the great impediment of language switch. Thus in Ireland and Wales the native culture can be perceived, if not exactly on its own terms, then at least through its own terminology. Part of our task will be the eludication of this terminology.

As shall be seen, the attestation is richest for Ireland, with Wales in second position (from Scotland there is not sufficient evidence before the twelfth century to justify inclusion). The societies will be discussed in this order of priority. It is not advisable, however, to treat them separately, for the phenomena to be studied are attested unevenly: sometimes Wales offers better evidence than Ireland, sometimes the other way round. Nevertheless, despite the fact that Irish and British are both part of the Celtic family of languages, by the time the historical period begins they had developed along very different lines; although they shared a number of terms, they were not mutually understandable in the historical period.

In the early medieval centuries, Ireland produced by far the richest non-Latin corpus of literature in Europe, a treasure too little known and appreciated outside the relatively small circle of specialists in Celtic studies.[1] The term 'literature' should be understood here in a very wide sense, for it includes material such as legal texts. Latin was also used, even though less extensively

1 This point has been made recently by McCone, K., *Pagan past and Christian present*, Maynooth 1990, 2; a good survey of this literature has been provided by Zimmer, H., 'Sprache und Literatur der Kelten im allgemeinen', in *Die romanischen Literaturen und*

than Irish.[2] Two phenomena combined to produce this material: alphabetic writing (which came to Ireland with Christianity in the fifth century) and native learning with roots stretching into the distant past and continuing alongside Christianity. This literature is first attested in the sixth century AD and was to continue vigorously for about a thousand years. Naturally, there were changes and developments during that millennium, but in a general overview these appear to be less significant than those features which signal continuity. Native learning was an integral part of society in the Celtic countries; in Ireland it disintegrated when its proper political and social environment was destroyed by outsiders in the seventeenth century. In Wales the Edwardian conquest and settlement in the late thirteenth century had a similar effect.

Celtic scholars have always been aware of the riches of native learning; however, there has been no discussion of the phenomenon of oral culture. There has not even been a comprehensive study of how native learning was organized, yet many conflicting presumptions are made about it. The discussion is based on the written products of Irish learning, and the complex relationship between oral and literate culture is left to one side.

In this respect the present study has no explicit precursors: it does not intend to harmonize existing disagreements nor to present the different views of the various parties. The views presented here are greatly indebted to earlier works and have benefited in no small manner from the discussion of different views, as well as from (sometimes heated) debates. The arguments to be considered are complex, and the various strands of the arguments are intertwined.

A key issue in the discussion is the evaluation of writing in Ireland and Britain in general and its impact on native learning in particular. Here Britain and Ireland have a different history. Alphabetic writing[3] came to Britain with the Romans in the first century AD and continued in Christian circles after

---

Sprachen mit Einschluß des Keltischen, Berlin/Leipzig 1909 (=Die Kultur der Gegenwart, Teil I, Abt. XI, 1). Most recently see Williams, J.E.C., Ford, P.K., *The Irish literary tradition*, Cardiff 1992 (this was originally published in Welsh in 1958 and has been slightly revised in the English version). It is symptomatic that the Celtic countries were left out of the survey by Langosch, K., et al., *Geschichte der Textüberlieferung der antiken und mittelalterlichen Literatur*, vol. 2 (the Middle Ages), Zürich 1964.

2 The opposite relationship between Latin and Irish writing in Ireland has been maintained by Kelly, J.F.T., 'Christianity and the Latin tradition in early medieval Ireland', *Bulletin of the John Rylands Library* 68, 1985-86, 410-33.

3 This is not the place to discuss writing in ogam in Ireland and Britain, for which see recently McManus, D., 'Ogam: archaizing, orthography and the authenticity of the manuscript key to the alphabet', *Ériu* 37, 1986, 1-31; Harvey, A., 'Early literacy in Ireland: the evidence from ogam', *CMCS* 14, 1987, 1-15. See also Thurneysen, R., *A grammar of Old Irish*, Dublin 1946, § 12-14.

the departure of the Romans in the early fifth century. In the early medieval centuries Wales would become the crucial area of the osmosis of alphabetic writing and native learning. Wales is the one area where British culture, in as far as it had survived Romanization, continued after the end of Roman rule;[4] it is possible to account for the rather small corpus of writing in Old Welsh by the established position Latin held as a medium of writing when Welsh first came to be written (apparently not long after AD 600).[5]

Since Ireland was never part of the Roman Empire, it did not receive alphabetic writing as part of Roman secular culture. The lack of a Roman past makes the term 'medieval' strictly speaking unsuitable for Irish history in the centuries after about 400. However, the coming of Christianity is generally to be considered as the dawn of a new epoch in Ireland and, since the chronological framework is not unlike that on the continent, the term 'medieval' is used here for the time beginning with the introduction of Christianity.[6]

Alphabetic writing came to Ireland with Christianity around AD 400; it can be viewed as one of the fringe benefits of the Christian religion to Irish society.[7] However, Christianity offered more than writing: it offered above all a new set of ethics which posed a serious challenge to values traditionally cherished.

In this respect, Ireland epitomizes the whole issue of oral culture. The written sources from Ireland are based in part on material inherited from times when all culture was organized orally. Oral learning of a non-Christian nature continued after the arrival and the establishment of Christianity. Thus Ireland had two systems of learning existing side by side, one originally oral ('native'), the other written (but not exclusively Christian). The former system can be studied only in so far as it has left traces or marks in the written material, in other words only obliquely. These traces have to be analysed carefully.

We shall be dealing with information provided in several languages, particularly Latin and the Celtic languages. It is true that languages are never static, and it has to be said that, like medieval Latin, neither Welsh nor Irish have been sufficiently studied; in some places we shall have to offer our own interpretation of the particular terms or passages. The same applies, perhaps more so, to Latin in these countries, which was an acquired foreign language;

---

4   On this see further chapter 3 above.
5   I have argued this in 'Les langages en pays celtiques'. See also Koch, J.T., 'When was Welsh literature first written down?', *Stud.Celt.*, 20-21, 1985-86, 43-66.
6   Many Irish medievalists refer to the time from the fifth to the twelfth century as 'early Christian'; cf. p. 3 note 2. As will be seen in the course of our discussion, the place of Christianity in Ireland in these centuries needs close consideration.
7   For this see Richter, M., 'The introduction of alphabetic writing to Ireland: implications and consequences' (FS Brendan O Hehir, forthcoming); Stevenson, J., 'The beginnings of literacy in Ireland', *PRIA* 89, 1989, 127-65.

this also needs careful analysis, not least due to its interaction with the native languages.[8]

The civilization of the Celts had dominated much of continental Europe during the first millennium BC.[9] With the expansion of the Germanic peoples from the north and the Romans from the south, it was gradually eclipsed on the continent. Celts came to Britain and Ireland in the last centuries of that millennium, and there they came to be dominant.[10] For the medieval period, only the insular Celts are of concern to us.

Britain was exposed to Roman occupation and civilization for over three centuries. The Romans did not penetrate all parts of Britain with the same intensity, but Celtic civilization was certainly strongly affected by the Romans. Nevertheless, the Britons retained their Celtic languages. It is no evidence that these were written at the time. Of those languages British (Welsh, called also 'neo-Brittonic', Koch) is attested best in written documents from post-Roman times; it shows strong influences from Latin.[11]

Language was only one of several areas in which society in Britain was affected by the Romans; yet it is difficult to gauge the full extent of Romanization because of events after the end of Roman rule. The Roman period was followed almost immediately by the Saxon invasions and settlement from the early fifth century onwards.[12] These Germanic groups brought their own culture to Britain, and they became dominant over Romano-British culture in many parts of the island. The latter had the greatest continuity in the west, particularly in what was later to be known as Wales. This area had been less thoroughly Romanized than the eastern parts of Britain, a factor which would have favoured the survival of British-Celtic elements there.

Ireland had remained outside the boundaries of the Roman Empire. That is not to say that the Irish had had no contact with Roman civilization, but such influences were notably slighter than in Britain. This is the main reason why Celtic civilization managed to thrive there with fewer modifications than in Britain. Nevertheless, substantial changes affected the Irish language between the arrival of the Celtic speakers in Ireland and the arrival of

8   A dictionary of medieval Latin from Celtic sources is in preparation at the Royal Irish Academy, Dublin. After some years of being involved with that work I gratefully acknowledge access to the databank for the dictionary.
9   The most recent summary has been provided in the form of the catalogue for the exhibition in Venice in 1991 *I Celti*. See also Schmidt, K.H., Ködderitzsch, R., ed., *Geschichte und Kultur der Kelten*, Heidelberg 1986.
10 How and when Britain and Ireland received speakers of Celtic is far from clear. Recent summaries of various points of view were published in *Emania* 9, 1991.
11 Jackson, K.H., *Language and history in early Britain. First to twelfth century*, Edinburgh 1953.
12 See also above, chapter 1.

Christianity around 400;[13] it is unlikely that these occurred as an isolated phenomenon in Irish society, but this period has produced no historical sources which would shed light on this problem. The evidence from archaeology has been summarized recently.[14]

It is often argued that the greatest challenge to Celtic culture in Ireland was posed by Christianity. Since there has not yet been a systematic discussion of the pre-Christian culture of Ireland, there has been no way either of properly assessing this challenge. There is the other view that Christianity embedded itself in existing Irish society by making considerable concessions.[15] Indeed, the present treatment will have to be very concerned with this issue, directly and indirectly, in as much as alphabetic writing provided the possibility of recording native traditions.

THE LEARNED ORDERS OF THE CELT ACCORDING TO CLASSICAL AUTHORS

The earliest surviving accounts of the Celts, ancestors of the Irish and the Welsh, come from peoples who themselves had a written culture, the Greeks and the Romans. One is thus faced with description from without, with all the difficulties which this potentially entails, since the information provided may be incomplete, or be distorted, intentionally or unintentionally. Most important, the description is articulated in a language and in terms perhaps foreign to the Celts. For this reason accounts of the Celts by classical authors must be treated very carefully; they must not be taken as comprehensive. For the most part the accounts which have survived belong to a form of ethnographic writing, a literary genre which has its own characteristics: it tends to be shaped by the society and by the value system of the writer. Ethnographic writing is inclined to focus on the unfamiliar. Descriptions by outsiders are liable to be distorted to some extent. However, they also have hidden potential. Implicitly or explicitly they build on comparison, which can be helpful if one

---

13 For a recent statement with further references see Evans, D.E., 'Insular Celtic and the emergence of the Welsh language', in *Britain 400-600: Language and History*, Bammesberger, A., Wollmann, A., ed., Heidelberg 1990, 149-77. It will be sufficient here to refer to the stages outlined by McManus, D., 'A chronology of the Latin loan-words in early Irish', *Ériu* 34, 1983, 21-71, at 21: Primitive Irish, Archaic Irish, Early Old Irish (before the earliest of the Old Irish glosses which are from the eighth century), Old Irish.

14 Edwards, N., *The archaeology of early medieval Ireland*, London 1990.

15 This position was most clearly articulated by Hughes, K., *The Church in early Irish society*, London 1966, esp. 156. See also Hughes, K., 'The church and the world in early Christian Ireland', *Irish Historical Studies* 13, 1962-63, 99-113, at 110, and ead., 'Sanctity and secularity in the early Irish Church', *Studies in Church History* 10, 1973, 21-37, at 21. These interpretations have not been seriously challenged since. See also Mac Cana, P., 'Christianisme et paganisme dans l'Irlande ancienne', in id. ed., *Rencontres de religions*, Paris 1986, 57-74.

knows enough about the society against which another society is being assessed. Thus, the information available to us about the learned orders among the Celts can help us to understand the background of Celtic men of ancient learning in the Middle Ages.

The source for most of the information about the Celts in the classical world is the account by Posidonius of Apameia (135-51 BC) in Book 23 of his History.[16] This work has not survived, but it can be recovered in part from later authors who used it. Caesar's account of the Gaulish Celts draws on it at least in some parts; therefore, his evidence can not be taken as an independent corroboration of Posidonius' account. Generally speaking, what classical authors tell us about the Celts is regarded as reliable,[17] although it is not always pointed out that Celtic civilization even in antiquity was not static and unchanging.

When the Greeks and Romans encountered the Celts, they were tribally organized and politically disunited. However, their bravery in fighting is amply attested. Aristotle remarked in this context: 'We have no word for the man who is excessively fearless; perhaps one may call such a man bereft of feeling, who fears nothing, neither earthquake nor waves, as they say of the Celts.'[18] This 'we have no word' is a good example of the lack of adequate terminology in cross-cultural encounters.

We shall deal only with the subject of learning among the Celts. The Greco-Roman authors were surprised and impressed by the great importance the Celts attached to learning. It was a learning not fixed in writing but transmitted orally. That kind of learning was of central importance to Celtic society, and this was presumably why the Celts were not inclined to disclose their learning to others. For this reason ethnographers have more to say about external matters related to learning than about its content.

Besides the warrior class, there was among the Celts a class of men of learning exempt from military activity and generally enjoying privileged status. According to Strabo (65 BC – AD 24):

> Among all the tribes (of Gaul), generally speaking, there are three classes of men held in special honour, the *bards*, the *vates*, and the *druids*. The *bards* are singers and poets, the *vates* interpreters of sacrifice and natural philosophers, while the *druids* in addition to the science of nature, study also moral philosophy.[19]

---

16 In what follows, full use has been made of Tierney, J.J., 'The Celtic ethnography of Posidonius', *PRIA* 60, 1960, 189-275.
17 See however below at nn. 97f.
18 *Nicom. Ethics* III, 7.7; Tierney 194.
19 Strabo IV, IV, 4, Tierney, 269.

Strabo thus presents learning among the Gaulish Celts as the domain of different groups for which he offers separate terms, two of which (*bard, druid*) were proper Celtic words. These people were highly regarded. It is not certain whether his statements concerning the contents of the various kinds of learning are correct.

From Caesar's account of the Gaulish Celts, we shall only look at the passage relating to the druids. He presents them as arbiters in society as well as priests.[20] He is the only author to refer explicitly to the oral nature of their learning:

> Druides a bello abesse consuerunt neque tributa una cum reliquis pendunt, militiae vacationem omniumque rerum habent immunitatem. Tantis excitati praemiis et sua sponte multi in disciplinam conveniunt et a parentibus propinquisque mittuntur. Magnum ibi numerum versuum ediscere dicuntur. Itaque annos non nulli vicenos in disciplina permanent. Neque fas esse existimant ea litteris mandare, cum in reliquis fere rebus, publicis privatisque rationibus, Graecis litteris utantur. Id mihi duabus de causis instituisse videntur, quod neque in vulgum disciplinam efferri velint neque eos, qui discunt, litteris confisos minus memoriae studere; quod fere plerisque accidit, ut praesidio litterarum diligentiam in perdiscendo ac memoriam remittant.
>
> (The druids are wont to be absent from war, nor do they pay taxes like the others; they are dispensed from military service and free of all other obligations. Attracted by these prizes many join the order of their own accord or are sent by parents or relatives. It is said that they commit to memory immense amounts of poetry. And so some of them continue their studies for twenty years. They consider it improper to entrust their studies to writing, although they use the Greek alphabet in nearly everything else, in their public and private accounts. I think they established this practice for two reasons, because they were unwilling, first, that their system of training should be bruited abroad among the common people, and second, that the student should rely on the written work and neglect the exercise of his memory.)[21]

Caesar raises important points: the profession of the druids entailed substantial material privileges; their training was thorough, which made them into respected specialists; there were considerable numbers of them; they cast their wisdom in verse which they did not allow to be written even though the Gauls were familiar with writing.[22]

20 For a useful sceptical summary see Ross, A., *Pagan Celtic Britain*, London 1976, 78-84.
21 Caesar, *Bellum Gallicum* VI, 14; Tierney,'Celtic ethnography', 243 (text), 272 (translation).
22 It has to be stressed that by the time Caesar wrote the Celts had been in Britian and Ireland

Like Strabo, Caesar conveys the idea that oral learning of the druids had nothing casual about it; the people in charge of learning were well rewarded for their contribution to their society. This fits in with the thorough training the people of learning underwent and the respect with which they were treated.

The last two quotations represent the most abstract as well as the most general features of oral learning among the continental Celts. Athenaeus mentions in addition people who recite praise poetry of chieftains; these he calls them 'parasites', a Greek term which probably glosses a Celtic special term,[23] denoting the eulogist.

Specialists in oral learning, of central importance to their society, are in this capacity also guarding the value system of that particular society. Oral learning was inextricably linked with the cultivation of the language in which this learning was cast and transmitted. The transmission often occurred in verse form, and the cultivated language can be termed *Dichtersprache* for short.

So far we have heard about learning among the continental Celts only through outside observers. There is, fortunately, an account which takes us a step nearer to the Celts themselves, although it is also reported at second hand. Lucian (second century BC) recorded the story of:

> a Celt . . . not unversed in Greek lore, as he showed by his excellent use of our language: 'We Celts do not agree with you Greeks in thinking that Hermes is Eloquence: we identify Heracles with it, because he is far more powerful than Hermes. . . . In general, we consider that the real Heracles was a wise man who achieved everything by eloquence and applied persuasion as his principal force.'[24]

This is an interesting case of an inverted *interpretatio Graeca* which sheds light on the way the Celts considered eloquence (an aspect of oral learning): it was potentially mightier and more effective than physical valour.

THE INSULAR CELTS IN THE MIDDLE AGES

As a consequence of Roman domination in Western Europe, Celtic civilization lost out on the continent. In the British Isles, however, on the western

---

for some time, perhaps prior to the adoption of writing. For the subject generally see Schmidt, K.H., 'Keltisch-lateinische Sprachkontakte im römischen Gallien der Kaiserzeit', in *Aufstieg und Niedergang der römischen Welt*, Temporini, H., and Haase, W., ed., 29/2, Berlin and New York 1983, 988-1018.

23 See Williams, J.E.C., 'Posidonius' Celtic parasites', *Stud. Celt.* 14/15, 1979/80, 313-43.
24 *Lucian, Heracles*. An introduction with English translation by Harmon, A.M., London and Cambridge, Mass. 1960, I, 64-67.

periphery of the Empire, and indeed beyond the Empire, Celtic civilization continued under Roman rule and even more so beyond Roman rule.

In Britain, the Celts became incorporated in the Roman Empire in the first century AD and remained part of it for three centuries. Romanitas was not the only force that affected the Britons. In the course of the fourth century, the Roman Empire was transformed into a Christian society. However imperfectly Christian ethics were practised, they certainly posed a potential threat to the existing social value system of the British Celts.

It is very difficult to establish the extent to which pre-Christian ways of life and social norms retained their strength among the Britons. Roman rule ended in Britain in the early fifth century. Christianized Roman Britain very soon became subject to pagan invasions from west and east, to intruders who themselves had no written culture and aimed at imposing their own way of life. Thus Britain experienced considerable rupture and discontinuity; this is one of the reasons for inadequate documentation. Latin Christianity survived the end of Roman rule in Britain, but even where it thrived it is extremely poorly attested by contemporary documents. The non-Christian aspects of British life are even more poorly documented.

In fact, there is very little written documentation from Wales prior to the eleventh century. This does provide occasional insight into what happened in the previous half-millennium. We shall deal with some aspects of British/Welsh culture at a later stage.

Written documentation arose in Ireland as a by-product of the establishment of Christianity. It was to be abundant; it took place in two languages, in Irish as well as in Latin. The beginnings of documentation in Latin can be traced back to the fifth century, and here Patrick's writings hold a very special place.[25] Documentation in Irish can be taken to have begun in the sixth century. There was no awareness among the Irish of an affinity with their British neighbours or of a relationship with earlier Celts.[26] But this need not affect the modern observer: he can see common elements which are apparently the result of a common culture.

Unlike Britain, which received Christianity when the Romans were in power, Irish society received Christianity without any recognizable outside pressure. The process of the establishment of Christianity eludes the observer. The fifth and sixth centuries, which are when this happened, are very poorly documented; thus it is impossible to follow how exactly Christianity was

---

25 In addition to Kenney, J., *Sources for the early history of Ireland*, vol. I, Ecclesiastical, New York 1929, still indispensable (latest repr. Dublin 1993); see Lapidge, M., and Sharpe, R., *Bibliography of Celtic-Latin Literature 400-1200*, Dublin 1985.
26 See Byrne, F.J., '*Senchas*: the nature of Gaelic historical tradition', *Historical Studies* IX, 1974, 137-59 at 144.

established. That it found a place in Irish society is beyond question.[27] In principle Christianity would have been averse to many aspects of Irish society; in practice accommodation of sorts appears to have been achieved, with each party making concessions to the other.[28] Apparently, arrangements were found that granted some room to new ideals within the established order. It is quite likely that this situation created special tensions; in fact it was responsible for the unique character of Irish Christianity.[29]

This co-existence was particularly sensitive in the field of learning. There had been oral learning among the Celts in pre-Christian times, and now there was introduced a new kind of learning, written in manifestation, Christian in content. Several aspects of this situation will be discussed later; what must be stated here is that traditional Irish learning was not destroyed by Christian learning; the two cultures continued side by side, and they influenced each other.[30]

Native learning was articulated almost invariably in the Irish language; the documentation becomes quite substantial for the Old Irish period, that is, after *c*.750.[31] For the earlier period, the evidence is fragmentary, but it implies at least that the medium which was central to the native 'men of learning' underwent considerable changes in what was perhaps quite a short time.[32]

NATIVE LEARNING

Ireland The medieval Irish language contains a collective term for the 'men[33] of learning', *oes dána*. This is traditionally rendered as 'artists, poets'.[34]

27 I have dealt with the technical side of manuscript production as a sign of that in 'The introduction of alphabetic writing', passim.
28 For my criticism of Bieler's views in this respect see 'alphabetic writing'; McCone's 'triumph of Christianity', *Pagan past* 84, while not original, is hasty.
29 This may be also the clue to distinctive features of Christianity in other societies where, however, the pre-Christian culture is not as amply attested as in Ireland.
30 In this respect there was no potential vital threat to native learning as suggested, e.g., by Meid, W., 'Dichter und Dichtkunst im alten Irland', Innsbruck 1971, 5f.
31 The most accessible collection is *Thesaurus Palaeohibernicus*, which, however, does not include the legal material. See also Thurneysen, R., *Grammatik des Altirischen*, Heidelberg 1909, still the standard work; cf. English version, *Grammar of Old Irish*, Dublin 1946.
32 The phrasing has of necessity to be vague due to the largely hypothetical basis of arguing: see McManus, 'Chronology', *Ériu* 34, 1983. See also Jackson, K.H., 'Common Celtic', *PBA* 37, 1951, 71-97.
33 Learning was not exclusively the domain of men; but when women were involved (which seems to have been rare), the ordinary terminology was used accompanied by a specific statement that a woman was referred to, often by prefixing *ban* 'woman', e.g. *ban-fili*. See e.g. Carney, J., 'Society and the bardic poet', *Studies* 62, 1973, 233-50, at 239.
34 For the following I refer especially to the *Dictionary of the Irish Language* (DIL), Dublin 1913-76, here s.v. *dán* II. See also Vendryes, J., *Lexique etymologique de l'ancien irlandais*, Paris 1959-87 (s.v. *aes*).

However, it is worth looking more closely at the term *dán*.[35] This noun occurs as an equivalent of Latin *ars* and is used, as is indeed also the Latin term, to denote, among other areas of human occupation, 'craft, skill, profession'. In this sense it shares the semantic range of Ir. *cerd*, W. *cerdd*, terms which translate Latin *professio*.[36]

A good illustration of the interchangeability of *dán* and *cerd* is provided in the famous Old Irish poem *Pangur Bán*: In the opening stanza, the author contrasts, in a playful manner, his work with that of his pet cat:

> Messe ocus Pangur Bán. cechtar nathar fria saindan/
> bith a menmasam fri seilgg. mu menma céin im saincheirdd.

> (I and Pangur Bán, each of us two at his special art:/his mind is at hunting (mice), my own mind is in my special craft).[37]

The author conveys the idea that his task is of a kind which can be referred to by the same terms as that of his cat. It is tempting to see this language use not as a personal quirk but as an invitation to regard the occupation of the people of learning in the sense of 'craftsmanship' rather than in modern notions of 'learning', vague though this may be.[38] There is a term in Old English which expresses this very notion: *wordcræft*.[39] I suggest that the men of learning in medieval Ireland (as well as their ancient Celtic predecessors) were concerned with 'wordcraft', that they were handling language as the most important raw material in their professional work. This can indeed be referred to as 'learning', as long as one allows this term a range reaching beyond what is associated with the modern notion of 'learning'. 'Craft' suggests the existence of measurable expertise, and the possibility of acquiring this in the course of

---

35 'The meaning of any word only becomes intelligible when the context in which it has been uttered is taken into account', Vansina, J., *Oral tradition*, 85; 'to ascertain a word's real semantics we must . . . look to the texts,' Watkins, C., 'New Parameters in historical linguistics, philology and culture history', *Language* 65, 1989, 783-800, at 790.

36 For this see most recently Schmidt, K.H., 'Handwerk und Handwerker in altkeltischen Sprachdenkmälern', in *Das Handwerk in vor—und frühgeschichtlicher Zeit*, Teil II, Jankuhn, H. et al., ed., Göttingen 1983, 751-63, at 753.While *kerd-* is attested in other IE languages, it seems to have in the Celtic languages alone the range from 'craft, skill' to 'poem, poet'. See also Gillies, W., 'The craftsman in early Celtic literature', *Scottish Archaeological Forum* 11, 1981, 70-85. We may point further to the medieval Italian *arte*, 'craft, guild'.

37 Text and translation in *Thesaurus Palaeohibernicus*, II, 293.

38 For an awareness of different kinds of learning in early medieval Ireland see the treatise known as the caldron of poesy, Breatnach, L., 'The caldron of poesy', *Ériu* 32, 1981, 45-93; and Henry, P.L., 'The caldron of poesy', *Stud. Celt.* 14-15, 1979-80, 114-28.

39 This term is attested, as far as I could establish, once only, in *Elene* I 1237. It is referred to in passing, with the connotation here suggested, by Bloomfield, M.W., and Dunn, C.W., *The role of the poet in early societies*, Cambridge 1989, 46.

a training process. It also comprises the ability to practise it, once the training is completed, to the satisfaction of those in the society who rely upon expertise in this craft. This does not exclude the possibility of various degrees of accomplishment within the profession, nor that successful training implied some inclination towards this profession from the start. In turn, the end product could be more than just 'craftsmanship'. However, generally agreed criteria seem to have been an important element.

The medieval Irish language contains a considerable number of terms referring to practitioners of wordcraft. This can be taken, on one level, as indicative of a great variety existing in this field, as well as of the importance attached in Irish society to these professions. However, it is not possible to convey the full range of the various terms, partly because this cannot be gleaned in a satisfactory manner from the existing material, but also because of the limitations of modern languages generally, and English in particular.

While the evidence of native learning in medieval Ireland is quite rich, it is also varied and not in all its manifestations consistent. Apparent contradictions or inconsistencies must be accepted without casting doubt on the system as a whole. 'Otherness' can appear in a variety of forms; to press it into the straightjacket of one's own concepts or world view would do damage to it. This is the practical dimension of the need to approach different cultures on their own terms.

As mentioned earlier, the Greco-Roman ethnographers were familiar with three different classes of people among the continental Celts who were dealing with learning: the *bards*, *druids*, and *vates*.[40] The insular Celtic societies in the Middle Ages show some continuity in the terminology but there also occur additional terms. This could indicate that the set-up had changed and become more differentiated, but it is also possible that the reports about the Celts in antiquity did not do full justice to the situation of the people of learning.[41] Let us look at the three terms in turn.

The case is, at first sight, easiest as far as the druids are concerned. These representatives of pre-Christian 'moral philosophy' do figure in medieval literary works, but they are very rarely found in historical works, that is, material dealing with events from the sixth century onwards. Their disappearance is normally regarded as one of the achievements of Christianity, which 'ousted paganism'. However, the situation is not as simple as that. How or to what extent pre-Christian religious ideas and ideals were replaced by Christian ones still is one of the great problem areas of early Irish history. In any case,

---

40 See above at n. 15.
41 In this respect it is important again that the information about the Celts is not as broad and varied as appears at first sight because most authors borrow the information, indirectly or directly, from Posidonius, see p. 185.

the absence of the druids from the historical sources should not be taken as meaning that all functions associated with them had come to an end.

Those people who wrote in early medieval Ireland were professionals in that craft; most of them would have been clerics. It can be assumed that those actively involved with Christianity had a vested interest in the 'obliteration' of the druids in particular. Yet this happened in a most revealing way: the druids occur, mostly in a negative light, rather prominently in Saints' Lives where they are usually referred to by the Latin term *magus*, a term with negative biblical connotations. However, in several prominent works of early medieval Latin hagiography, the exemplary saints,[42] while portrayed as opponents of the druids, are also shown as their rivals whom the saints, at their best, could not always outdo in druidic might.[43] Furthermore, in some of the serious religious writings from early Ireland, even Christ is referred to as 'my druid'—'is é mo drui Crist mac Dé'—,[44] a usage which conveys an undercurrent of continuing respect for the druids.

Let us take the bards next. The term occurs in the medieval centuries in Ireland as well as in Wales. Thus, as regards the 'singers and poets', there is the clearest evidence of continuity from the Celts of antiquity to medieval Celtic societies. However, there are indications that the status of the bard in Ireland was different from that of his namesake in Wales.[45] Unfortunately, considerable confusion is created by modern usage which refers to a certain type of poetry from medieval Ireland as 'bardic poetry',[46] a technical term; in addition, 'bard' is also used in a looser sense for 'poet' in general and 'Celtic minstrel' more specifically. This modern usage is not applicable in the present account.

Finally, there is the *vates*. This term was current in Latin for Roman poets.[47] Among the Irish terms for the men of learning there is one, *fáith*, which derives from the same root as *uates*. There are other Irish terms which cover the same semantic range as *fáith*.[48]

There is, then, some continuity in terminology referring to the men of learning among the Celts from antiquity into the medieval period. In antiquity, these people, explicitly associated with oral learning, were held in great honour

---

42 Brown, 'The saint as exemplar in late antiquity'.
43 For a general discussion of this see Plummer, C., *Vitae Sanctorum Hiberniae*, 2 vols., Oxford 1910, repr. 1968, esp. Introduction; for the phenomenon with regard to early Patrician hagiography see Richter, *Medieval Ireland*, 81f.
44 See Vendryes, J., 'Druidisme et christianisme dans l'Irlande du Moyen-Age', in id., *Choix d'études linguistiques et celtiques*, Paris 1952, 317-32, at 331.
45 See below, n. 86.
46 Bergin, O., *Irish Bardic poetry*, Greene, D., Kelly, F., ed., Dublin 1970.
47 See below, n. 93 for more detail.
48 See below n. 98.

among the Celts. We shall now go on to examine their status, the nature of their work and their training in the early Middle Ages.

MEDIEVAL NORMATIVE SOURCES

A major group of sources for early medieval Irish society are the extensive law tracts, most of which were compiled around 700. D.A. Binchy's edition of the *Corpus Iuris Hibernici* in 1978 constitutes a milestone for their study. The material is extremely complex both in its language and in its content.[49] The law tracts are potentially of the greatest relevance to an understanding of early medieval Irish society generally as well as the subject of native learning more specifically. However, it has to be stressed that the corpus of Irish law which has been preserved, although voluminous, is not complete; it is difficult to assess the degree of its fragmentary nature.[50]

The Irish law tracts present considerable problems on several levels. There is, perhaps most importantly, the language: legal language tends towards archaism or even obscurantism,[51] and this is certainly true of the Irish language of the law tracts. Furthermore, the law tracts are not law in the sense of modern statute law, but instead guidelines for legal experts on particular aspects of the Irish social order.[52] In this manner, they do not even aim to offer systematic treatment of particular issues,[53] nor is the material in general free of internal contradictions.

The law tracts did not come into existence in written form until Christianity brought alphabetic writing to Ireland; within a relatively short time alphabetic writing was also applied to Irish.[54] The Irish law tracts came indeed into existence under the influence of Christianity. The content of this material has traditionally been regarded as of great antiquity.[55] This position

49 Charles-Edwards, T.M., 'Review article. The Corpus Iuris Hibernici', *Studia Hibernica* 20, 1980, 141-62. A useful survey is provided by Kelly, F., *A guide to early Irish law*, Dublin 1988.
50 Plummer, C., 'On the fragmentary state of the text of the Brehon Laws', *ZCP* 17, 1928, 157-166; see also Binchy, D.A., 'Corpus Iuris Hibernici: Incipit or finit amen?', *Celtic Studies Congress Galway 1979*, Dublin 1983, 149-64.
51 For comments on this issue from medieval Ireland see notes 141f below.
52 This has been well argued recently by Stacey, 'Law and order in the very old West: England and Ireland in the early Middle Ages'.
53 In this, however, these sources are in the trend of the time rather than oddities. Roman law was not a close system without contradictions, and the same may be said even about modern legal systems, see Schott, R., 'Die Funktionen des Rechts in primitiven Gesellschaften', *Jahrbuch für Rechtssoziologie und Rechtstheorie* 1, 1970, 107-74, at 167. Likewise, canon law was not systematized before the twelfth century on the basis of Gratian's *Concordia Discordantium Canonum*.
54 See Richter, 'Les langages en pays celtiques'.
55 A leading representative view is that of Binchy, D.A., 'The linguistic and historical value of the Irish law tracts', *PBA* 29, 1943, 195-227; id., 'Linguistic and legal archaisms in the

has recently come under attack;[56] however, it is not yet possible to comment finally on the influence of Christianity on the law tracts that have come down to us.

Independent of that discussion there is the question of how far the legal material, given that it is to be taken as at least partly normative, reflects reality.[57] Here, also, it is too early to state confidently that 'there was an enormous gap between the concept as preserved and elaborated by the literary men, on the one hand, and the realities of political structures in early Christian Ireland'.[58]

Owing to the availability of the *Corpus Iuris Hibernici*, systematic investigation of early Irish law has begun, but it is still in an early stage. The law tracts contain a substantial amount of information concerning native learning in Ireland. Much of it, from the Old Irish period, was collected, along with material less immediately relevant, in the late Middle Ages by the Irish scholar Dubhalthach Mac Firbhisigh (d. 1570), in TCD MS H.2.15B. This material was transcribed and published in 1940 under the title 'An Old-Irish tract on the privileges and responsibilities of poets'.[59] The editor did not live to discuss the material as fully as it needs to be treated. However, this text is the starting point for most of the subsequent discussion in this area, a work that is still going on.

Recently, one particular aspect has been dealt with in depth, that of the so-called poetic grades in early Irish law. The treatise *Uraicecht na ríar*[60] is one of several works dealing with the subdivisions among the *filid*. It is considered to date from the second half of the eighth century.[61] It deals with some aspects concerning the position of the *filid* in the form of question and answer, a feature frequently found in early Irish legal material. Thus it commences:

1. 'Cis lir gráda filed? Ní hansae: a secht'.
(How many grades of *filid* are there? Not difficult: seven.)

Celtic law books', *Transactions of the Philological Society 1959*, 14-24; for a late statement see id., 'A pre-Christian survival in mediaeval Irish hagiography', in *Ireland in early mediaeval Europe* (= Studies in memory of Kathleen Hughes), Whitelock, D., et al., ed., Cambridge 1982, 165-78.

56 Ó Corráin, D., Breatnach, L., Breen, A., 'The law of the Irish', *Peritia* 3, 1984, 382-438; but see also Charles-Edwards, T.M., 'Early Irish Law', *School of Celtic Studies. Fiftieth anniversary report, 1940-1990*, Dublin 1990, 110-12.
57 References from other types of sources are discussed below.
58 Greene, D., 1979, quoted approvingly by McCone, K., *Pagan past and Christian present*, 136; see also further below.
59 Gwynn, E.J., *Ériu* 13, 1940, 1-60; 220-36.
60 Breatnach, L., ed., (Early Irish Law Series vol. II), Dublin 1987.
61 Breatnach, 77.

These grades are subsequently named:

> ollam, ánruth, clí, cano, dos macfuirmid, fochloc. Trí fográd leo, i. taman, drisiuc, oblaire.
> (The terms are given; 'they have three sub-grades' and their names are given.)[62]

The functions of the highest grade of the *filid* are outlined next:

> Dán ollaman cétomus: secht cóecait drécht lais, .i. cóeca cach gráid; is éola i cach coimgniu, ⁊ is éola i mbrithemnacht fénechais.
> (The competence of an *ollam*: he has three hundred and fifty compositions, that is, fifty for each grade; he has knowledge of all historical sciences, and he is knowledgeable in the jurisprudence of Irish law).[63]

The key term in this tract, *fili* (pl. *filid*), was translated in the modern edition, as is normally done, as 'poet'. However, given what the treatise says the expertise of an *ollam* encompassed not only 'composition', arguably (though not necessarily) 'poetry', but also two other areas of learning, history and jurisprudence, areas that are not normally associated with the modern notion of the domain of 'poets'. It would thus appear that in this treatise, *fili* carries a meaning extending far beyond the modern English concept of 'poet'. We are dealing with a legal treatise specifically devoted to the subject, and its terms must surely be taken seriously. Thus, *fili* appears to be used here as a generic term for experts of various branches of native Irish learning.[64] There is material that supports the suggestion that the term *fili* became restricted to 'poet' at a stage somewhat later than the compilation of *Uraicecht na ríar*.[65] In view of

---

62 *Uraicecht*, 102-103. The law-tract *Uraicecht Becc* lists the seven principal grades, in ascending order, but does not name the sub-grades, see Mac Neill, E., 'Ancient Irish law. The law of status or franchise', *PRIA* 36, 1923, 265-316, at 274 V26.-10. It also lists seven grades of the Church V 22.- 8. and the seven grades of government V 24.-9.
63 *Uraicecht* § 2.
64 That at an early stage the *filid* were associated with law has been tentatively suggested by Gwynn, E.J., *Ériu* 13, 9; Binchy, D.A., 'Bretha Nemed', *Ériu* 17, 5f.; also Mac Cana, P., 'The three languages and the three laws', *Studia Celtica* 5, 1970, 62-78, at 66-71. L. Breatnach conceded this after the publication of his edition: see his 'Lawyers in early Ireland', in *Brehons, serjeants and attorneys. Studies in the history of the Irish legal profession*, Hogan, D., and Osborough, W.N., ed., Dublin 1991, 1-13, esp. p. 5. In a similar vein, the Welsh term 'cyfarwydd', normally taken to mean 'poet' (see Ford, P., 'The poet as 'cyfarwydd' in early Welsh tradition', *Stud. Celt.* 10-11, 1975-76, 152-62) perhaps also denoted a legal expert. See Jenkins, D., Owen, M.E., 'The Welsh marginalia in the Lichfield Gospels. Part I', *CMCS* 5, 1983, 37-66, at 53f.: *cimarguitheit* of Chad 3.
65 See below at notes 73ff.

the prominence of the *filid* in every discussion of early medieval Irish society, this interpretation has wide repercussions.

According to another early Irish law-tract, *Críth Gablach*, roughly from the same time as *Uraicecht na ríar*, the seven-fold classification of the men of learning in Irish society mirrored the Christian Church with its seven grades of ordination:

> 2. Cid asa fordailtea grád túaithe ? A aurlunn grád n-ecalsa; ar nach grád bís i n-eclais is coir cia beith a aurlann i túaith, dég fortaig nó díthig nó fíadnaisi nó brithemnachtae ó chách dialailiu.[66]
> (Whence come the divisions of orders of a *túath*? From a comparison with the orders of the Church, for every order that is in the Church, it is just that its like should be in the *túath*, for the sake of declaration or denial on oath, or of evidence, or of judgment, from each of the other.)[67]

This is considered as a very obvious Christian feature in material which had traditionally been taken as particularly archaic. While the Christian element cannot be denied—it is openly referred to—it needs to be assessed in its proper proportions. The editor of *Uraicecht na ríar* himself points out that the seven-fold division of the poetic grades is not a general feature of all the passages in early Irish law which deal with the men of learning.[68] This is an important qualification; but one must go further: even in *Uraicecht na ríar* there were in fact ten, not seven, sub-grades. Rather than mirroring the sacred orders of the Christian Church, there are better reasons for suggesting that in this text the material was cosmetically 'prepared', superficially treated in such a way that a lenient observer might grant a certain similarity between ecclesiastical orders and secular learned grades. Thus we are faced indeed with Christian influence, but a discussion of the Christian element in Irish society must not be terminated at this point.[69]

As for the professions, there is one term used for the highest grade in the oldest law tracts: *ollam*. The etymology of this term is uncertain, but it has been suggested that the term figures in the earliest texts as a superlative of the adjective *oll*, 'vast, mighty'.[70] While at a later stage, *ollam* was to be

---

66 *Críth Gablach*, Binchy, D.A., ed., Dublin 1941 (= Mediaeval and Modern Irish Series XI).
67 The translation is taken from Mac Néill, E., 'Law of status', 282 62.
68 Breatnach, *Uraicecht*, 81ff.
69 In taking over the views of Ó Corráin, Breatnach and Breen (*Peritia* 3), McCone hastily refers to 'Christian' influence while the biblical material quoted is almost completely from the Old Testament. That the Irish men of learning 'recognized' their society in Old Testament accounts has long been acknowledged; it cannot be taken as a sign of Christianity as having marked Irish society.
70 See Binchy, D.A., *Ériu* 18, 1958, 49 and addendum, 54.

used only for the highest grade of the men of learning,[71] in earlier times it was also applied to other professions (for example, smith etc.). This is in broad agreement with what has been suggested earlier about the interchangeability of *dán* and *cerd*. Indeed, all this helps to explain the structure of these professions. They all were organized along agreed criteria of qualification and classification which could, somehow, be measured. People of these professions had to acquire generally recognized skills. Advancement in the profession could be marked by assigning different terms for the individual stages passed through. Ten such names making up the *filid* were given earlier; other law tracts name sixteen grades of the bard culminating in the *rígbard*.[72]

The kind of learning expected from the *filid* can best be gleaned from the so-called 'compositions'. The 350 'compositions' which the *ollam* had to master were the result of cumulative acquisition, each of the seven grades being characterized by a multiple of fifty.[73] Thus, the 'compositions' were not creations of the men of learning; their task consisted in the acquisition and transmission of existing material. This was the essence of oral culture. What applies to the 'compositions'[74] can be taken to hold also for law and 'history': all this was traditional learning; the task of the men of learning was to preserve and maintain these traditions. The acquisition of this knowledge was obviously a lengthy process. Some Middle Irish texts mention between seven and twelve years of training until the required knowledge and expertise was attained.[75] The fact that professional specialists were in charge of this traditional learning shows that it was regarded as indispensable for a functioning of Irish society.[76] It was also very costly.[77]

There is no obvious precursor from the Celts in antiquity for the term *fili* which is very frequent in the Middle Ages. Before thinking that one is dealing with an innovation in terminology,[78] it is worth pointing out that there are other terms besides *fili* in medieval Ireland designating the men of learning which have no ancient ancestor, such as *suí* or *éices*.[79] The attempt to fathom

71 Note the hybrid *ard-ollamh brithemnachta*, *Three Fragments* s.a. 908; another manner to denote mastership was *suí-* + the craft concerned, e.g. *suí cruitirechta*, 'master harpist', AU 1110, cf. McCone, *Pagan past*, 87.
72 Breatnach, *Uraicecht*, 50-56, referring to BN XIII, XIV, XV.
73 *Uraicecht na ríar* mentions elsewhere, §§ 12-17, different figures for the individual grades; the treatise is thus not consistent even in itself.
74 See Mac Cana, P., *The learned tales of medieval Ireland*, Dublin 1980, and 200f. below.
75 For this see Thurneysen, R., 'Mittelirische Verslehren', in *Irische Texte*, Stokes, W., and Windisch, E., ed., Dritte Serie 1. Heft, Leipzig 1891, 1-182, Part II, 110ff. Cf. Caesar's statement on the training of the druids, above, p. 187.
76 See further below 209.
77 See below after n. 109.
78 However, as suggested earlier, the classical authors may well have supplied an incomplete picture. See above p. 185.
79 See further below at n. 98.

the specific meaning of these terms by reference to Irish glosses of Latin texts[80] (these are, after all, part of the earliest existing material in Irish) cannot take one very far. On the one hand, if an Irish author uses Latin, there is the distinct possibility that this Latin has a Hibernian dimension,[81] in which case one would conduct a circular argument. On the other hand, Latin, though for centuries used for literate learning, has a rather restricted vocabulary in this field, mainly *poeta, uates, scriba, propheta*.[82] By contrast, the medieval Irish language has a very varied vocabulary as regards the men of learning,[83] which in itself sheds light on the great importance attached to learning in general; furthermore, it distinguishes Christian and traditional learning by using different terms for the experts.[84]

Wales The Welsh law texts are of more recent date than the law-tracts from Ireland; they are also less varied. Unlike the material from Ireland, which is available only in Irish (with brief passages in Latin), the legal material from Wales is available in Latin as well as in Welsh, thereby testifying to the stronger Roman influence in this field. Also, as distinct from the Irish laws, medieval Welsh law appears to have been transmitted virtually in its entirety. It is much less voluminous than its Irish counterpart.

Modern scholars place the compilation of these laws (which purport to stem from the reign of Hywel Dda, king of the greater part of Wales in the first half of the tenth century), a later time.[85] Be that as it may, they were compiled when Christianity had existed in Welsh society for many centuries; prior to its codification the legal material had been cherished and transmitted orally, and that in a society which professed Christianity. In the Welsh texts, Christian influence is more substantial than in the Irish material.

The Latin redactions of the Welsh laws, while not now believed to be earlier than the earliest versions in Welsh, are sufficient for our purpose: for

80   See, e.g. Mac Mathuna, L., 'The designation, functions and knowledge of the Irish poet', *Veröffentlichungen der keltischen Kommission Wien*, Nr. 2, 1982, 225-38, 228, with reference to Ml 26 b 10 *fili* = *poeta*.
81   For this see further pp. 204f.
82   Marouzeau, J., *Le Latin*, Toulouse/Paris 1923 on *poeta*: 'les Latins . . . se sont instruits à l'école des Grecs, et leur ont volontiers empruntes les mots qui désignent les choses de l'esprit.' See also pp. 200ff.
83   For this and for the separate terminology relating to Christian learning see below, notes 102f.
84   See below at notes 100f.
85   Edwards, J.G., 'Studies in the Welsh laws since 1928', *WHR* Special number 1963: The Welsh Laws, 1-17; also Pryce, H., 'The prologues to the Welsh lawbooks', *BBCS* 33, 1986, 151-87. The view put forward by Emanuel, H.D. (see the following note) that the Latin versions are the oldest stratum, has been revised more recently, see the discussion by Charles-Edwards, T.M., *The Welsh laws*, Cardiff 1989. Cf. also Pryce, H., *Native law and the Church in medieval Wales*, Oxford 1993.

the men of learning they retain the native Welsh terms. Only two terms (which are given here in normalized spelling) occur: *pencerdd*, 'chief of song', and *bard teylu*, 'poet of the warband, *familia*'.[86] We note the term *cerdd* which was also used in Irish. The other element *pen*, 'head', may allude to various grades of men of learning of whom the *pencerdd* was or had at some stage been the most eminent one. However, he stands quite low in relation to the king.[87] He is, in the laws, associated more distinctly with the king than is the *bard teylu*.

Admittedly, the Welsh law texts are several centuries younger than the earliest Irish material, but this is not sufficient reason to explain why native learning in Wales appears to have been less elaborate. Apparently, Irish society had maintained more archaic features in this area.

WORDS AND MEANINGS

The great seventh-century Spanish scholar and antiquarian, bishop Isidore of Seville, was of the opinion that one could find in the components which made up words the essence of the meaning of these words, and that in a comprehensive study of this phenomenon one would acquire a key to the understanding of the world. His encyclopedic work on the *Etymologiae* became highly influential throughout Europe where Latin learning was cultivated. While modern etymology proceeds along lines that differ substantially from those of Isidore, there is nevertheless the conviction that a study of the development of words back into earlier times can yield information about their original meaning. It is useful to do this for the terms concerning the men of learning in the Celtic societies that are being investigated here; we shall also review briefly the Latin terminology since this is relevant at all stages of investigating the early Middle Ages, in the Celtic countries and elsewhere. Furthermore, the investigation concerning Celtic and Latin converges in some cases back in time.

According to Varro (116-27 BC), Old Latin had a term for 'poet' that was also used for another profession: 'antiquos poetas vates appellabant'.[88] He was referring here to a period when the Romans did not yet make much use of writing.[89] *Vates* thus denoted a representative of an orally structured culture.

---

86 Emanuel, H.D., ed., *The Latin texts of the Welsh laws* (Board of Celtic Studies, History and Law Series Nr. 22), Cardiff 1967, Red. A, 110, 113. The other redactions do not differ significantly. See also Parry, J.J., 'The court poets of the Welsh princes', *PMLA* 67, 1952, 511-20.
87 For the comparable situation in Ireland see below at notes 124ff.
88 *De lingua Latina* VII, 36. This statement is discussed at length by Bickel, E., 'vates bei Varro und Vergil', *Rheinisches Museum für Philologie* NF 94, 1951, 257-314, esp. 258-63; 276-78.
89 Although the Greek alphabet was available in Italy since the seventh century, the Romans did not use it to any considerable extent before the third century. For a recent review see

The more common meaning of *vates* had been that of priestly 'seer', 'inspired one'. The term has been derived from an IE verbal stem **vat-*, 'to blow', literally 'to in-spire'.[90] In other words, the *vates* articulated what had been given him by the gods. Here one gets the idea of the early 'poet' in a quasi-priestly function, as a mouthpiece of supernatural forces, a medium rather than an individualistic creator.[91]

After *vates*, the earliest attested term in Latin for 'poet' is *scriba*, a term which recalls the technical aspect of the work.[92] Significantly, the *scribae* of Rome (as indeed later the *poetae*) were organized in the form of guilds.[93] Even at that stage, writing was regarded as a craft, a technical expertise.

The term for 'poet' used most widely in Latin, *poeta*, was borrowed from Greek *poietes*, which also lays stress on the mechanical rather than the inspired side of the occupation. The latter dimension was not, however, altogether lost sight of. It was expressed through a renewed use of *vates*. The most telling usage of this kind is that applied to Virgil: 'maximus vates et veluti divino ore instinctus'.[94] Whereas *scriba* was not to be used for 'poet' in Latin in later centuries,[95] *vates* and *poeta* remained, with *vates* tending to carry somewhat greater prestige than *poeta*. Isidore of Seville may well have got the etymology wrong by modern criteria, but he conveyed the essence rightly when he wrote: 'vates a vi mentis appellatos, cuius significatio multiplex est; nam modo sacerdotem, modo prophetam significat, modo poetam'.[96]

In turning to the terminology in the Celtic languages, we recall that there is greater variety than in Latin. Inevitably therefore a Latin text on learning in Irish or Welsh society cannot do justice to the complex situation there. We have already mentioned *cerd/cerdd*, 'craft', 'profession', 'poetry' occurring both in Irish and in Welsh. The other term these two languages share is *bard/bardd*. This term, which was taken from Celtic into a number of other IE languages, denotes the person that 'sings', 'praises'.[97]

Poucet, J., 'Réflexions sur l'écrit et l'écriture dans la Rome des premiers siècles', *Latomus* 48, 1989, 289-311.

90 That *uates* has an IE rather than a Celtic origin is stressed by Bickel, 'vates', 310.
91 Thieme, P., 'Die Wurzel vat-', *Asiatica* (FS Friedrich Weller), Leipzig 1954, 656-66; also Runes, F., 'Geschichte des Wortes vates', *Beiträge zur griechischen und lateinischen Sprachforschung* (FS Paul Kretschmer), Wien, Leipzig and New York 1926, 202-16.
92 Bickel, E., 'vates', 259.
93 Sihler, E.G., 'The Collegium poetarum at Rome', *American Journal of Philology* 26, 1905, 1-21; I owe this reference to the kindness of Dr Ute Schillinger, Konstanz.
94 Quoted by Dahlmann, H., 'Vates', *Philologus* 97, 1948, 337-53, at 353. Cf. also Tacitus, Dial. 9, 3: 'Saleium . . . egregium poetam vel, si hoc honorificentius est, praeclarissimum vatem.'
95 For the use of *scriba* in Ireland see below, n. 100.
96 *Origines* 7, 12, 15; cf. also 8, 7, 3
97 For a recent summary with further literature see Campanile, E., 'L'étymologie du celtique *bard(h)os', *Ogam—Tradition Celtique* 22-5, 1970-73, 235f. Jones, D.M., 'bardd', *BBCS*

The other terms we have mentioned stress rather the supernatural dimension of the work of the 'poets'. Irish *fáith* is connected with the IE root **vat-* . The etymology of *fili* is not quite clear; apparently the term is cognate with the Welsh verb *gweled*, 'to see'. In a similar manner, Irish *éices* is taken to be related to the Irish verb *ad-ci*, 'sees'.[98] Thus learning is in a variety of ways associated with inspiration, with supernatural powers. Of course, the etymology of the terms is only one of the ways in which the function of the men of learning can be elucidated. Another one is that of observing them in action.

We have pointed out that every oral culture, focused as it is on language, can best be appreciated when approached in its own language, on its own terms; wherever that is not possible (which is the situation for the majority of the societies in the early medieval West), something will be inevitably lost. The different range of vocabulary in Latin and Irish concerning the men of learning makes this problem especially acute. And yet in a curious way some Latin material from early medieval Ireland and Wales can be positively helpful, especially in cases where equivalents in the other languages are available.

We shall now turn to other material which contributes to an assessment of the validity of normative texts like the laws. In the Irish annals we have what appear to be contemporary or near contemporary entries recording the deaths of individual scholars from the seventh century onwards.[99] Between the various annals which for the earlier part draw on common sources, such entries are often available in Latin as well as in Irish. Most of the scholars commemorated in the annals are also associated with monasteries, and many of them held offices in the monastery.

Most of the scholars mentioned in these obituary notices in the annals are referred to by terms not familiar from the terms associated with the *oes dána*. More than three quarters are called *sapiens* or *égna*, *scriba* or *scríbnid* (and variants like *scríbneoir*) or *fer léighinn*. The Latin origin of these terms[100] is obvious, and there is good reason to consider these scholars as experts in Latin and Christian learning. It is not possible to detect the difference between these terms, especially between *sapiens* and *scriba* which are fairly common in the same period. It would seem that *scriba* may have been taken from the Latin bible where the scholars of Scripture are so called.[101] Both *scríbnid* and *fer*

11, 1941-44, 138-40 quotes Festus: 'Bardus Gallice cantor appellatur, qui virorum fortium laudes canit.'

98 More detail in Mac Mathuna, L., 'Designation', 1982; see also further below notes 102ff.
99 For more detail see Richter, M., 'The scholars of early Christian Ireland', Australian Conference of Celtic Studies 1992 (forthcoming). Bieler, L., 'The island of scholars', *Revue du Moyen-Age Latin* 8, 1952, 213-34 refers to the material discussed here in passing, 215f.
100 Lambert, P.Y., 'Le vocabulaire du scribe irlandais', in *Ireland and northern France, AD 600-850*, Picard, J.M., ed., Dublin 1991, 157-67.
101 Such usage is evident in the *Collectio Canonum Hibernensis*; see e.g. XXI, 1: 'scriba interroget

léighinn are terms to be associated with written learning.[102] The terminology is used fairly consistently; since these entries appear to have been originally contemporary entries, they attest a commonly used vocabulary. Thus apparently learning associated with written material, primarily of a Christian nature, had received its own terminology which was established by the time the annals begin to record these entries in the seventh century. This can also be taken as evidence that the type of learning previously practised in Ireland, that of the *oes dána*, was not, essentially, associated with writing, that it had been and continued to be, generally oral.

There are reasons to believe that the obituary notices in the annals refer to only outstanding representatives of their field; this is certainly the case when representatives of the *oes dána* were commemorated which becomes more frequent towards the end of the period investigated. Thus the approximately 400 obituary notices are merely a tip of an iceberg; Christian learning, especially in monasteries, was broadly based in Ireland at that time. Around three quarters of these notices in the annals refer to scholars of the Christian variety. This should not be taken as evidence that Christian scholarship had taken the field previously dominated by the men of traditional learning; instead it should be regarded as indicative of the limited horizon of the annalists to whom apparently Christian scholars were of the greater interest.

This is one instance in which Latin sources, combined with Irish sources, can throw new light on the Irish material. It must be further pointed out that some sources written in Latin are earlier than the material written in Irish or Welsh. The Latin sources can thus elucidate aspects of Irish society at a comparatively early stage.

With this purpose in mind we shall consider a passage from the *Life of St Patrick* by the Irish cleric Muirchú who wrote in the second half of the seventh century. The following sentence describes the appearance of Patrick at the court of Loiguire, king of Tara:

> Adveniente ergo eo in caenacolum Temoriae nemo de omnibus ad adventum eius surrexit praeter unum tantum, id est Dubthoch maccu Lugir, poetam optimum, apud quem tunc temporis ibi erat quidam adoliscens poeta nomine Feec, qui postea mirabilis episcopus fuit.
>
> (As he entered the banquet hall of Tara, none of them all rose in order to welcome him, except one man only, Dubthach moccu Lugir, an

---

scripturam', Wasserschleben, H., ed., *Die irische Kanonensammlung*, second ed., Leipzig 1885, reprint Aalen 1966, 62.

102 For *scriba* see p. 51 where it is emphasized that the term does not refer to a scribe.

excellent poet. With him was then in that place a young poet named Fiacc, who afterwards became a renowned bishop.)[103]

This brief passage merits close analysis. Written two centuries after Patrick's life, this earliest text dealing with him at length,[104] relates an episode that is unknown until then. It may well be fictitious, but even in that case it can be of great interest to the historian, if properly treated. It would not be unusual for a medieval author, in describing past events, to project the world of his own experience onto the past, which he would thus describe in terms familiar to him. In the text quoted above one notes the presence at the court of the king of Tara more than one *poeta*. Of them, one is referred to as *poeta optimus*; this terminology may appear at first sight unremarkable,[105] but in view of the legal material discussed earlier it is likely that Muirchú intended in this manner to designate the highest grade of the *filid*, the *ollam*. Latin did not have an appropriate noun, which is why Muirchú used the combination of a noun and a qualifying adjective. This may be the earliest attestation of what appears as a Hiberno-Latin term; however, there is no need to attribute to Muirchú the creation of this Latinized *ollam*. The earliest comparable attestation in the annals is more than half a century younger: 'Ruman mac Colmain poeta optimus' (AU 747).[106] Very likely Muirchú and the annalist drew on a common stock of Latin which had been developed in Ireland to express specific features of Irish society. After all, there could have been other ways to describe the institution of the *ollam*. A parallel usage occurs in association with another term denoting men of learning: *iudex optimus* (AU 802).[107]

Secondly, there was another *poeta* at the court of Loiguire at Tara who was in some manner (which would have been familiar to Muirchú well as to his audience) associated with the *poeta optimus* (and note the telling Hibernicism *apud quem*). The young man was perhaps professionally attached to the *ollam*, that is, apprenticed to the master and would then have been one of the lower grades of scholar (for which there was no separate Latin terminology).

If there is little doubt that *poeta optimus* in this passage should be taken as the Latin equivalent of *ollam*, what remains to be considered is the meaning of *poeta/ollam* in this text which pre-dates *Uraicecht na ríar* by about half a century. In the terms of *Uraichecht na ríar* Dubthach maccu Lugir would have been considered as having 'three hundred and fifty compositions . . . , a knowledge of all historical sources, and (a knowledge of) the jurisprudence of

103 Text and translation from Bieler, L., ed., *The Patrician Texts in the Book of Armagh* (=Scriptores Latini Hiberniae 10), Dublin 1979, 92-3.
104 Earlier, of course, are Patrick's own works, on which see further p. 205.
105 *Poeta optimus* is, however, very rare in continental Latin texts; see e.g. Orosius VI, 1, 28f, on Lucan.
106 This, but not Muirchú's term, is mentioned by McCone, *Pagan past*, 24.
107 For this see further p. 228.

Irish law'. As will appear later, this is quite close to the manner in which other medieval Irish texts present him.

Finally, Muirchú's text can be taken as evidence, independent of the law tracts and earlier than them, of a recognized hierarchy of the men of learning in early Ireland. Behind the superlative of the *poeta optimus* there probably existed lower grades of an undefined number.

This is as far as Muirchú's text can take us, and it has taken us a long way beyond previous interpretations. There is also another *Life of St Patrick*, which was written, mostly in Irish, about two centuries later. In that text, the *Vita Tripartita*, Muirchú's *poeta optimus* is given as *rigfile ind rig*, 'high poet of the king'.[108] One sees here how the Irish tried various ways to harness Latin to their own society, however clumsy the result may appear. At the same time, it becomes obvious that the 'classical' terminology for the men of learning in the laws was not the only terminology to be used in later centuries.

As far as one can tell, Muirchú's account which has been quoted has no claim to historicity, but this does not diminish its value. What he portrays is the setting at the court of a prominent Irish king as would be customary at his time. In his account the reference to the *poeta optimus* is purely incidental. Muirchú needed him merely to place socially the other man of learning who later on became a bishop. The text conveys, incidentally as it were, that the men of learning at the royal courts were taken for granted in the seventh century.

There is a possible reference to men of learning in Ireland two centuries earlier than Muirchú's *Life of St Patrick*. Patrick himself in his *Confessio* writes:

> 55 Vos autem experti estis quantum ego erogavi illis qui iudicabant per omnes regiones quos ego frequentius visitabam.[109]

> (But you know from experience how much I have paid to those who administered justice in all districts, whom I was in the habit of visiting.)

This passage can be taken to allude to legal experts who enjoyed prominence beyond the confines of a political unit, the *túath*. In the terminology of *Uraicecht na ríar*, these experts would have been referred to as *filid*. Unquestionably, Patrick experienced the traditional Irish society which had legal specialists. At that time Irish society was not familiar with alphabetic

---

108 'Bethu Phátraic', Mulchrone, K., ed., Dublin 1939, 32, lines 531-36. *Rigfile* is not listed in *DIL*. A 'rigfile Erenn' occurs in AU s.a. 887.7, p. 342 (Mac Airt/Mac Niocaill), thus roughly contemporary with Bethu Phátraic. For an analogous *rigeices* see Mac Cana, P., 'Mongan Mac Fiachna and Immran Brain', *Ériu* 23, 1972, 102-42, at 134. This and cognate terms are discussed in Richter, 'The scholars of early Christian Ireland'.
109 Quoted after Bieler, L., 'Libri Epistolarum Sancti Patricii episcopi', *Classica et Mediaevalia* 11, 1950, 1-150, at 86-7.

writing; these specialists were experts in orally transmitted learning.¹¹⁰ Thus there are glimpses at least of Irish society from the fifth and seventh centuries, independent of the law tracts, but pointing in the same general direction as the law tracts.

Fortunately there are also indications of secular learning in Britain in the sixth century. References to poets being active in the entourage of rulers, incidental as they are, reflect the everyday phenomena of institutional life. It must be emphasized that the following two references are independent of each other, which adds to their evidentiary weight.

There is, from Britain, information on the cultural scene at the court of the ruler Maelgwn. Gildas, the autor of this material, writes in the sixth century. He was a cleric who was disappointed with the behaviour of that ruler, behaviour which would have been normative in his society:

> 34 arrecto aurium auscultantur captu non Dei laudes canora Christi tironum voce suaviter modulante neumaque ecclesiasticae melodiae, sed propriae, quae nihil sunt, furciferorum referto mendaciis simulque spumanti flegmate proximos quosque roscidaturo, praeconum ore ritu bacchantium concrepante, ita ut vas, Dei quondam in ministerio praeparatum vertatur in zabuli organum, quodque honore caelesti putabatur dignum, merito proiciatur in tartari barathrum'.¹¹¹

> (Your excited ears hear not the praises of God from the sweet voices of the tuneful recruits of Christ, not the melodious music of the Church, but empty praises of yourself from the mouths of criminals who grate on the hearing like raving huxters—mouths stuffed with lies and liable to bedew bystanders with their foaming phlegm. Hence a vessel that was once being prepared for the service of God is turned into an instrument of the devil, and what was once thought worthy of heavenly honours is rightly cast into the pit of hell.)¹¹²

Gildas wrote about his own times. More than two centuries later, the *Historia Brittonum*, attributed to Nennius, gives in close proximity to a reference to Maelgwn Gwynedd the names of some famous native poets:

> tunc Talhaern Tataguen in poemate claruit et Neirin, et Taliessin, et Bluchbard, et Cian, qui vocatur Gueinth Guaut, simul uno tempore in poemate claruerunt.¹¹³

110 For this see further below pp. 219f.
111 *De Excidio Britanniae*, MGH AA XIII, 46.
112 The translation is that of Winterbottom, M., Gildas. *The ruin of Britain and other works* (= Arthurian period sources 7), London and Chichester 1978, 34.
113 MGH AA XIII, 205. A new edition of this text which is as important as it is difficult, is

Some of the names mentioned here will concern us in a later section.

The other fragment of information is of a different kind. Venantius Fortunatus, the polished Italian poet who was working in the Frankish realm, referred in a poem written in 566 for Lupus to two types of poetry, one civilized, the other barbarous:

> sed pro me reliqui laudes tibi reddere certent, et qua quisque valet te prece voce sonet, Romanusque lyra, plaudat tibi barbarus harpa, Graecus Achilliaca, crotta Britanna canat.[114]

Barbarous songs (line 69 referred explicitly to 'dent barbara carmina leudos') were being performed to the accompaniment of the harp among the Franks and likewise among the Britons. This is factual information.[115] To our inquiry it is irrelevant whether the crucial half-line 'crotta Britanna canat' is taken as 'the *crotta* sings about British matter' or 'the British *crotta* sings'.[116] But it should be noted that Venantius was familiar with the appropriate terminology.

The scant attestations from Ireland and Britain before 700 allow the suggestion of continuity in the sphere of secular learning in those societies from pre-historical times. In all the cases we have discussed, the references are to ordinary institutions, not to exceptions or innovations. This is one of the reasons why the information is so fragmentary: there was little motivation, apart from Christian zeal, to report what was a general and widespread feature. It is necessary to keep in mind the stability and solidity of non-Christian learning in these societies. The attestation improves for later periods, but this is only the visible evidence of institutions that had had a continuous and solidly based existence.

This continuity is particularly noteworthy as regards Britain. The glimpses we get of secular learning or culture there in the sixth century are part of a society that had been exposed to two major forces which, each in its own field, would have been potentially detrimental to native institutions: Romanization

---

being prepared by David Dumville. For some comments see Jarman, A.O.H., *The Cynfeirdd. Early Welsh poets and poetry*, Cardiff 1981, 15ff.

114 MGH AA IV, Nr. VIII, p. 162 f. lines 61-64.
115 Moisl, H., 'A sixth-century reference to the British bardd', *BBCS* 29, 1980-82, 269-73. See also Williams, J.E.C., 'Gildas, Maelgwn and the bards', in *Welsh society and nationhood* (FS Glanmor Williams), Davies, R.R., et al., ed., Cardiff 1984, 19-34. A somewhat different interpretation, which I do not share, is offered by Sims-Williams, P., 'Gildas and vernacular poetry', in *Gildas: New approaches*, Lapidge, M., Dumville, D., ed., Woodbridge 1984, 169-92, esp. 179.
116 For Irish *crott*, 'harp' (a-stem) see Binchy, D.A., *Ériu* 18, 1958, 47; further below p. 220.

and Christianity. That these were not able to suppress native culture is an indication of the strength, of the staying power of those institutions. The work of Gildas must be read as testimony to that state of affairs, one which he deeply deplores. He points to the 'stupidos et ad ludicra et ineptas saecularium hominum fabulas' ('they show alert interest in sports and the foolish stories of worldly men').[117] This section refers to the clergy among the Britons; *a fortiori* this can be assumed for the lay people since the clerics whom Gildas castigated still clung to values of the secular world.

There is a much greater likelihood of continuity in the field of secular culture in Ireland where there was no Roman 'interlude'. The continuity in terminology, at least in parts, points in this direction. In the discussion of Muirchú's *Life of St Patrick* it has already been shown that seventh-century Irish society continued to maintain a number of features from pre-Christian times, including institutions connected with traditional culture. I have referred to the establishment of Christianity in Ireland as an enigma in view of the fact that Irish society had long-tested institutions and that the Christian religion would have had little to recommend it to a traditional society endowed with its own learned orders.[118] The following discussion, in dealing with aspects of Christianity in Ireland, may help to make the enigma somewhat less puzzling. Thus, three centuries after the arrival of Christianity in Ireland there are a number of pointers to the existence, side by side, of Christian culture and a culture characterized by pre-Christian values and institutions. The fact that this traditional or native culture can be studied only with the help of written information is a technical factor which has been raised more than once in this study. But here is the place to discuss the major issue of oral culture and written culture.

In Ireland (and Wales) texts written in the vernacular can report sympathetically about the strength of oral learning. There was available an appropriate vocabulary, and there was the traditional respect for the oral material. The environment that had enabled the oral culture to unfold and to blossom was not, apparently, substantially altered by Christianity to the detriment of this native culture.

We have seen that on the continent, evidence of the oral tradition is found in the early medieval centuries predominantly in normative or narrative sources written in Latin.[119] In these sources the attitude towards the oral culture is frequently negative; the terminology used for the articulation of the attitude was, to some extent at any rate, stereotyped. The oral culture existed there in an environment where some representatives of that society which made use of writing were hostile to it.

117 *De Excidio* 66, text MGH AA XIII, p. 62, line 22, translation Winterbottom, p. 53.
118 Richter, 'Alphabetic writing'.
119 See chapters 6-8.

There is no comparable evidence from Ireland and Wales, which can be taken as a preliminary indication that there the situation could have been in essence very different. Furthermore, the Latin terminology employed on the continent for criticism of the oral culture[120] has left few and only faint traces in the Latin material from Ireland, none from Wales. Thus the treatise *De duodecim abusivis saeculi* (seventh century) contains the maxim: 'Iustitia regis est... impudicos et striones non nutrire':[121] a king who supported jongleurs[122] did not live up to strict ecclesiastical expectations. The *Collectio Canonum Hibernensis* gives the complete legislation from the council of Carthage of 435 including the famous command 'Clericus scurrilis et verbis turpibus iocularis degradetur'.[123] However, the information available shows that kings cherished the company of the men of learning; whether clerics would be deposed if they dealt with secular learning is not known.

In the earliest texts relating to that issue, native learning is mentioned, and it is presented as the domain of an identifiable group characterized by its own terms.

The position of the men of learning in Irish society is referred to in various places, incidentally as well as explicitly. We are interested particularly in early attestations of the phenomenon. The law tracts have always been regarded as important evidence in this matter. In their present form, they must be taken as reflecting at least the situation as it was when they were compiled, namely the eighth century. However, they may also contain older, indeed much older material. Perhaps the clearest statement concerning the men of learning occurs in the collection *Bretha Nemed*:

Ni ba túath túath gan egna, gan egluis, gan filidh, gan righ.
(A *túath* is not a *túath* without an ecclesiastical scholar, a churchman, a *fili*, a king.)[124]

According to this text, there existed two kinds of learning in Irish society, one associated with the Church and one associated with the *filid*. This text assigns precedence to the representatives of Christian learning over the *filid*; however, their existence in a prominent position is acknowledged.

A further point deserves attention. The legal maxim centres on *túath*. While in later centuries this term was to denote a kingdom as a territorial unit, its earlier meaning was 'people' or 'community' (cf. Germ. *theod*, Latin *totus*).[125]

120 For this see chapter 5.
121 Hellmann, S., ed., *Pseudo-Cyprianus De XII abusivis saeculi*, Leipzig 1909, p. 51.
122 For the Latin vocabulary associated with the jongleurs see chapter 5.
123 Book X, ed. Wasserschleben, *Kanonensammlung*, p.28.
124 Gwynn, 'Old-Irish tract', 31.10f.; the translation used here (with modifications) is from Breatnach, *Uraicecht*, 90.
125 See chapter 1, n. 29.

The above maxim may be paraphrased as follows: 'a community will not be a proper community without religious officials, without a political head and without people who guard traditional learning.' I consider *fili* in this text in the same sense as it is used in *Uraicecht na ríar*.[126]

There is another Old Irish maxim that expresses the prominent position solely of the representatives of traditional learning: 'Do-eimh ollamh túath' ('an ollam protects a *túath*').[127] Statements to that effect occur elsewhere in the laws.[128]

While there appears to be general agreement among scholars that law was the preserve of specialists among the Irish from the earliest historical times, what has not been recognized is the fact that the oral background to medieval Irish law can be shown more clearly than such background for other branches of native learning. Whereas there may not be total traditionalism in Irish law, there is good reason to maintain that its core was old; repeated attempts by ecclesiastics to bring the law into line with Christian ideals had remarkably little effect.[129]

The law tracts which have been preserved are held to date from the late seventh and the eighth centuries, that is, from a time when alphabetic writing had been practised for over two centuries, after Christianity had taken root in Irish society. It is from these and other material that evidence can be gathered both concerning the specialists in legal matters and the complex manner in which Christianity was accommodated within the existing social system.

One of the early authoritative compilations of Irish law, *Senchas Már*, 'the great wisdom', has the following opening statement:

> Senchas fer n-Erenn, cid conid roiter? Comchuimne da sen, tindnacul cluaise di araili, dichetal filed, tormach o recht litre, nertad fri recht n-aicnid.
>
> (The legal knowledge of the men of Ireland, what has preserved it? The joint memory of two old men, the transmission from one ear to another, the chanting of the *filid*, the enrichment through the law of the letter, the strong support by natural law.)[130]

---

126 See above at n. 64.
127 Breatnach, 49, 5.
128 See e.g. 'Bretha Déin Chécht' § 2: 'Grande cruthnechtu do ollum rig ⁊ escop ⁊ do olum filed', 'a grain of wheat for a supreme king, a bishop, a master fili ', ed. and transl. Binchy, D.A., *Ériu* 20, 1966, 1-66, at 23. See also Kelly, *Guide*, 46f.
129 Richter, *Medieval Ireland*, passim.
130 Thurneysen, R., 'Aus dem irischen Recht IV. Zu den bisherigen Ausgaben der irischen Rechtstexte', *ZCP* 16, 1927, 167-230, at 175, 177; CIH 346.25-347.17; Binchy, 'Linguistic and historical value', repr. in *Celtic Law Papers*, 83; McCone, *Pagan past*, 99.

This brief section contains a number of relevant points: the people in charge of the law are the *filid*, oral transmission is mentioned three times; the law is made up of two major components: *recht litre* and *recht n-aicnid*.

Recht litre, 'law of the letter', written law, is used in early Ireland for Scripture and more especially for Mosaic law,[131] a usage paralleled by medieval Latin usage of *lex*.[132] One finds this expressed clearly in *De duodecim abusivis saeculi* from the seventh century, where it is written: 'populus sine lege, populus sine Christo est'.[133] The formation of the term shows the phenomenon of writing associated with *recht* as a notable feature of this, by implication distinguishing it from material not characterized by writing even where it is written. Thus we are explicitly told here about a recognizable and recognized biblical element in early Irish law. The other main source of it is *recht n-aicnid*, 'natural law'. It is possible that this term should be understood in the way in which it is used by St Paul when he wrote that the heathens lived *naturaliter*.[134]

There are several other texts that deal with the complex co-existence of *recht litre* and *recht n-aicnid*, as well as with pre-Christian and Christian Irish culture, texts which have not been considered together in the past but which, when looked at as a corpus, convey a quite clear message. It is not possible to establish with certainty their individual dates, but here more important than that is the long-term message which they contain.

There is a brief text traditionally known as the Pseudo-historical prologue to *Senchas Már* which also treats of the two components of Irish law, albeit in a different form. It tells of Dubthach moccu Lugir acting as mediator between Patrick and the old traditions.

> RORAIDE DUBTHACH MAC UA LUGAIR IN FILI BRETHEM FER NEREND A RACHT AICNID 7 A RACHT FAIDE AROFALLNASTAR FAIDSINE A RACHT AICNID I MBREITHEMNUS INDSE HEREND 7 INA FILEDAIB DOTOIRCECH-NATAR DIDHU FAIDE LEO DONICFA BERLA BAN BIAID .I. RACHT LITRE. ATA MARA A RECHT AICNID ROSIACHTATAR NAD ROCHT RACHT LITRE. DOAIRFEIN DI DUBTACH DO PATRAIC NI NA TUDCAID FRI BREITHIR NDE A RACHT LITRE 7 FRI CUIBSE NA CREISEN CONAIRIGED A NORD MBRETHEMAN LA HECLAIS 7 FILIDA ROBO COIR RACHT ACNID UILE ACHT CRETEM 7 A COIR 7 COMUAIM NECALSA FRI TUAITH 7 DLIGED CECHTAR DA LINA UARAILE 7 I NARAILE AR ATA DLIGED TUAITHE I NECLAIS 7 DLIGED NECALSA I TUAITH.

131 *DIL*, s.v. *liter* col. 167; see also Mac Néill, E., 'Ireland and Wales in the history of jurisprudence', *Studies* 16, 1927, 249, n. 2.
132 See Richter, 'Latein als Schlüssel', passim.
133 Ch. VII, ed. Hellmann, p. 59.
134 Rom 2:14: 'Cum enim gentes, quae legem non habent, naturaliter ea, quae legis sunt, faciunt, eiusmodi legem non habentes, ipsi sibi sunt lex.' A substantial number of the attestations of *aicned* in this sense comes from the earliest biblical glosses, see DIL s.v. (a).

(Dubthach moccu Lugair the *fili* declared the judgements of the men of Ireland in accordance with the law of nature and the law of the seers; for divine inspiration had ruled the jurisprudence of the men of Ireland and their *filid*. There are many things covered in the law of nature which the law of the letter did not reach. Dubthach expounded these to Patrick. What did not conflict with the word of God in the law of the letter and (= or) with the conscience of the faithful has been fastened in the canon of the judges by the Church and the *filid*. The whole of the law of nature was right save for the faith and the harmony of Church and tribe.)[135]

This text has received recently much attention, and its date is by no means established.[136] For our purposes this is not of prime importance. It can be taken as an aetiological tale concerning matters Christian and non-Christian in the Irish legal material. The text was written by a *litteratus*, and very likely by a cleric. It testifies to the acceptance of a substantial amount pre-Christian matter in the Irish law as it was when the text was composed, and it 'explains' how this came about. Patrick had ultimately approved of this situation.

Indeed, the message that Irish law contained substantial amounts of material decidedly un-Christian is expressed elsewhere, without reference to Patrick and Dubthach moccu Lugir. These texts are apparently later than either of the two previously quoted; if anything, the pre-Christian material in Irish law is presented here more proudly, perhaps defiantly.

We read in *Lebor Gabála Erenn*:

ar cach ndiamuir ndána ⁊ in cach léire leghis ⁊ in cach amaindse elathan do chúisin is o Thúathaib De Danann atá a bunadh. Ar cia thánic cretim, ní ro dichuirthe na dána sin ar it maithe, ⁊ ni dernai demun maith etir.

(Howbeit they learnt knowledge and poetry; for every obscurity of art and every clearness of reading, and every subtlety of crafts, for that reason, derive their origin from the Tuatha De Danann. And though the Faith came, those arts were not put away, for they are good, and no demon ever did good.)[137]

---

135 The text is given from CIH 528.17-529.5; the translation reproduces Binchy, D.A., 'The pseudo-historical prologue to the Senchas Mar', *Stud. Celt.*, 1975/1976, 15-28, here 23f.

136 McCone, K., 'Dubthach maccu Lugair and a matter of life and death in the pseudo-historical prologue to the Senchas Mar', *Peritia* 5, 1986, 1-35; for some criticism of the intepetation offered there see Carey, J., 'The two laws in Dubthach's judgement', *CMCS* 19, 1990, 1-18, at 8.

137 Text and translation from Macalister, R.A.S., ed., *Lebor Gabala Erenn* (The Book of the taking of Ireland), Irish Texts Society vol. 41, Part IV, 353, p. 164, 165.

And yet another text: the 'Tale of ordeals, Cormac's adventure in the land of promise, and the decisions as to Cormac's sword' treats of the meeting of the men of Ireland before the coming of the Faith at which decisions were made concerning the administration of law:

> 4 7 ised atberat-somh, is í sin comdail is aregdha doronadh a n-Erinn ria creideam, uair is iad na smachta 7 na rechta doronadh sin dail sin merus a n-Erinn co brath.

> (And they say that that convention is the noblest ever held in Erin before the Faith. For the rules and laws which were made in that meeting shall abide in Erin forever.)[138]

What has been maintained concerning the Pseudo-historical prologue applies to the other accounts equally: 'the better we understand the story, the closer we come to glimpsing that culture's vision of itself.'[139] Here we get the message that in the eyes of those who wrote these works native culture prior to Christianity was nothing to be ashamed of. It had the aura of antiquity and thus respectability. It need not be abandoned.

Finally a word on the language of Irish law. Legal material is of a kind which requires authentic transmission rather than innovation or creativity. It best fulfills the expectations brought to oral tradition. The expertise of the guardians of the legal material extended to the language in which it was couched. It was a technical language which cherished obscurity, possibly for its own sake in order to make it inaccessible to the non-specialists and therefore enhance the position of the experts. *Bélre Féne* 'language of the (?) legal scholar' was one of the terms for it;[140] another was *iarnbélre*, lit. 'language of iron', that is, obscure poetic language.[141] Obscurity of the language was occasionally raised as an objection to the discipline generally.[142] This can be taken as a malevolent statement concerning the specific requirements of this branch of learning.

Legal expertise was essential at every stage of society's history. The experts were taken for granted and for this reason are rarely mentioned in the narrative sources. Nevertheless, there can be no doubt that law was an area of prime importance to the internal cohesion of Irish society, before and after the arrival of alphabetic writing.

---

138 'Scel na Fir Flatha . . .', ed. and translated by Stokes, W., in *Irische Texte* III, 1891, 185-229, at 186/204.
139 Carey, 'Two laws', *CMCS* 1990, 18.
140 Binchy, *Ériu* 18, 1958, 45; cf. also Mac Néill, E., 'A pioneer of nations', *Studies* 11, 1922, 441.
141 See Thurneysen, R., 'Le terme Iarmbérla', *RC* 13, 1892, 269.
142 'Obscure to every one seemed the speech which the *filid* uttered in that discussion, and

POETS

Those professionals who are summarily referred to as 'poets' are attested in the sources more fully than the legal experts; even so, their attestation hardly does justice to their social importance. As was shown earlier, there existed several grades of expertise in this field of learning; there was a standard programme of qualification that had to be mastered. The sources tend to mention among the men of learning only the most eminent grade, certainly in the early medieval Irish annals. This is not peculiar to Ireland but is a more widespread tendency: the higher echelons of society are over-represented. As regards the men of learning, the metaphor of the proverbial tip of the iceberg that is visible is particularly apt; much of the expertise and learning associated with the men of learning remains hidden from view, yet its existence can be taken for granted and must be taken into account.[143]

There are several ways in which the poets in the modern world differ from those in the Middle Ages. One of them may be approached in terms of 'creativity' or 'originality'. While dimensions of these are not totally absent from the works of the medieval poets, they are apparently not of the importance which is attached to them in our times. It is advisable to recall the concept of craftsmanship associated with the men of learning. There are several indications that more important than creativity or originality was the task of working in generally accepted forms and genres which had specific functions in their societies. Creativity was permitted within fairly narrow limits; originality of form was not desired.

It is true that there were different genres in the poetry of medieval Ireland and Wales, but these were not the creations of individuals against existing conventions. New forms, however they originated, might become conventions generally followed. This may be shown in the scholarly terminology concerning medieval Welsh poetry which is divided into work of the *cynfeirdd*, 'early poets'[144] and *gogynfeirdd*, 'fairly early poets', with the dividing line around 1100.[145] In Ireland a similar substantial change can be dated to around 1200 which signals the rise of what is known technically as bardic poetry, written in Classical Irish.[146]

What characterizes the professional poetry in early medieval Ireland and Wales is the observance of general forms within the boundaries of which the

---

the legal decision which they delivered was not clear to the kings and to the (other) *filid*.'
'Scel na Fir Flatha', Stokes, W., ed., 204.
143 See notes 180ff on the numbers involved.
144 This term is believed to have been coined by Robert Vaughan (? 1592-1667): see Huws, D., 'Canu Aneirin: the other manuscripts', in *Early Welsh poetry*, Roberts, B.F., ed., Aberystwyth 1988, 43-56, at 47.
145 For a brief but useful survey see Parry, J.J., 'The court poets of the Welsh princes', *PMLA* 67, 1952, 511-20.
146 Bergin, O., *Irish bardic poetry*.

craftsmen could demonstrate their accomplishment, could express elevated thought and use language to stir the imagination and emotions.

Indeed, the greatest difference between the work of the medieval poet and that of his modern namesake is the public nature of the former's work. The medieval poet held a position at the centre of society, and it was his task to keep alive the social values of the society as they were believed to have existed in the past. They had shown their value and for that reason were to be upheld.[147] It is in this respect that the work of the medieval poets can be justifiably termed traditional or conservative and for the same reason originality and creativity were not wanted.

This is also the area in which the work of the poets somewhat diverges from that of the legal experts: law could be imagined to have an existence separate from individuals; it was a set of rules believed to be of general usefulness which had to be observed by everybody. The legal experts were guardians of tradition *par excellence*, and it is not surprising that they are very rarely mentioned individually in the sources. The poets were also guardians of tradition, as we have heard, but besides that they also composed poetry for their patrons which offered them the chance to make a personal impact.

Through their work, the poets showed that people who wielded power in society were entitled to do so because they belonged to the right families and also because they acted in socially acceptable ways. In this manner, the poets were mediators in more than one way: between the past and the present, and between the top and bottom of their society. They held a cardinal position, they were the hinges on which society turned. The interaction between poets and political leaders is best attested, although the way in which the base of society was affected by their activity has left some traces in the records which will be considered later.

Y TRI CHOF

There has survived from Wales, dating from the seventeenth century, a brief account of unknown date in English translation concerning the tasks of the poets in Welsh society, tasks which have parallels in Ireland: 'Tri chof ynys Brydain', 'the three records or memorials of the island of Britain'.[148] The threefold task of the poets is outlined as follows:

147 For this reason the works of the poets in the Middle Ages are potentially most important sources for the historian. While they may not contribute to writing 'dispassionate history' (so Quiggin, E.G., 'Prolegomena to the study of the later Irish bards, 1200-1500', *PBA* 5, 1911/12, 89-143, at 120), they give valuable access to 'mentalities' which is only beginning to be investigated, see, for Ireland, Simms, K., *From kings to warlords*, Woodbridge 1987; for Wales, Williams, G., *Recovery, reorientation and reformation. Wales c.1415-1642* (= History of Wales vol. III), Oxford 1987, esp. 98-102, 108, 115f., 182, 197, 383, 465.
148 See Lloyd, E.M., ed., *A Book of Wales*, London 1953, 104-8; my attention was drawn to this document by Bloomfield and Dunn, *Role of the poet*, 85.

> The one of the sayd three 'Cof' is the History of the notable Acts of the kings and princes of this land of Bruttaen and Cambria; and the second of the sayd three cof is the languaige of the Bruttons for which thee bards ought to give accompt for every word and sillable there in whey they are demaunded thereof ... and the Thyrd cof was, to keepe the genealogies or Descents of the Nobilitie, there Division of lands and there Aarmes. ...[149]

We note that the cultivation of the language was regarded as one of the essential tasks of the poets; it was in fact equal in importance to the recording of the deeds of the kings and the nobility. They stored what was worth preserving and guaranteed its transmission in the appropriate form.

These tasks are also mentioned in the twelfth century by Giraldus Cambrensis in his *Descriptio Kambriae*: bards guard the genealogies of the noble families even though these are reported to be available by then in Welsh in written form:

> Hoc etiam mihi notandum videtur, quod bardi Kambrenses, et cantores, seu recitatores, genealogiam habent praedictorum principum in libris eorum antiquis et authenticis, sed tamen Kambrice scriptam.[150]

Giraldus also comments positively on the care which the bards take with the language in which they express their works:

> In cantilenis rhythmicis, et dictamine, tam subtiles inveniuntur, ut mirae et exquisitae inventionis lingua propria tam verborum quam sententiarum proferant exornationes. Unde et poetas, quos bardos vocant, ad hoc deputatos in hac natione multos invenies.[151]

This eminently public function of the poets is evident particularly where they appear in close association with people in high position, in authority. It is worth pointing out that the poets were functionally linked with public authority.

These references occur in what one might classify as traditional 'historical' sources; these confirm what can be taken from 'literary' material that was the product of the men of learning and therefore without the necessary distance from the issue. However, the references in the non-literary sources encourage

---

149 Lloyd, 105. Roberts, B.F., 'Oral tradition and Welsh literature. A description and survey', *Oral Tradition* 3, 1988, 61-87, quotes p. 62: 'a bardic triad notes the three features which give a poet amplitude: knowledge of history, poetry and heroic verse'.
150 *Descriptio Kambr*. I, iii, RS 21.6, 167f. Cf. also I, xvii: 'Genealogiam quoque generis sui etiam de populis quilibet observat ... memoriter et prompte genus enarrat ...' 200.
151 *Descr. Kambr*. I, xii, p. 187.

the acceptance of the information contained in the literary material as being plausible.

In the course of the early Middle Ages the position of the kings gained strength in Ireland and Wales, as indeed on the continent.[152] The rise of the king in society would have repercussions also on the men of learning associated with them. The early Irish law-tracts placed the men of learning on a par with the king; later the poet appears rather as one of the king's officials, in a position of subordination rather than equality. This is, however, only a hypothesis; beyond question is the close link between king and poet, a relationship which would have had implications for both parties.

RECIPROCITY

This comes out clearly in an analysis of the terminology for the work of the men of learning. Their most important task was to express appropriately the authority and achievements of their patrons, which was done in verse form.

The most general term for 'poem' in Old Irish is *dúan* (late medieval books of poetry associated with aristocratic families are called *dúanaire*). This term is cognate with Latin *donum*, 'gift'. As in many traditional societies, the *dúan/donum* required, indeed demanded, an adequate counter-gift, namely appropriate remuneration.[153] The position of the poets among the leading circles of society sheds from this angle a new light on the importance attached to their work in early Ireland and Wales. They performed an essential task, and for their work they were entitled to appropriate payment. Thus one finds written: 'eochair dúaisi dúana', 'the key of recompense is poems'.[154]

Here one encounters the poet as fully integrated in society where he held a central place.[155] It goes without saying that the work he was expected to deliver met the expectations of those for whom he was active. One thinks especially of the praise poetry. This celebrated the worthy deeds of people of

---

152 For the continent see chapter 1. The Welsh evidence has most recently been reviewed by Davies, W., *Patterns of power in early Wales*, Oxford 1990. For Ireland see Ó Corráin, D., 'Nationality and kingship in pre-Norman Ireland', in *Nationality and the pursuit of national independence* (= Historical Studies XI), Moody, T.W., ed., Belfast 1978, 1-35, esp. 16ff. More discussion of this issue can be expected in the O'Donnell lectures of Dr David Dumville, which have remained unpublished for more than ten years.
153 See esp. Watkins, C., 'The etymology of Irish dúan', *Celtica* 11, 1976, 270-76; also id., 'New parameters', esp. 788. The classic work on gift-exchange in traditional societies, Mauss, M., *Le don*, Paris 1925, raised issues which have since then been highlighted in many societies; for the Middle Ages: see especially Gurevich, A.J., *Categories of medieval culture*, London 1985, ch. 5 (Russian original Moscow 1972). For the linguistic evidence see Benveniste, E., *Le vocabulaire des institutions indo-européennes*, vol. I, Paris 1969, 81-86.
154 ZCP 6, 1908, 270.
155 For surveys see Williams, J.E.C., 'The court poet in medieval Ireland', *PBA* 57, 1971, 1-51; Lloyd-Jones, J., 'The court poets of the Welsh princes', *PBA* 34, 1948, 167-97.

influence, confirmed their living up to the expectations brought to them within their society, in this way upholding the value system of the society. It is not surprising that this praise poetry places little emphasis on individual features; instead, it aimed at fitting a given person into a pre-existing framework of reference. This, however, could be done through highly artistic use of language. In praising generosity, for example, the poets would raise the issue of their own rewards in more or less subtle manner.

The poet appears thus as a person of great influence in society. His contribution lay in making acceptable the existing order as the best possible one. Such a system functioned as long as the products of the men of learning were accepted by society. As long as they abided by the norms, this seems to have been the case. In this light the social system appears as a closed one, with congruence characterizing the relationship between expectation and realization.[156] This gave the poets a position of power, matched, however, by a great responsibility since they had to work within traditional norms. The power worked as long as the general trends in society were taken into account.

The poet was recognizable publicly by his dress.[157] One of the names for the special garment of the poet, Ir. *tuigen*, or *tugan, tuignech*' is etymologized by the tenth-century scholar Cormac as *tuge én*, 'thatch of birds'[158] from whence arises the idea that the poet was adorned with bird feathers.[159]

What has been presented so far may appear as an idealized outline; it is difficult to penetrate the smokescreen of the ideal which is erected by the stereotyped work of the men practising wordcraft. That there must have existed more than is clearly visible is suggested by the historical sources, which are full of particular cases where political disharmony, within groups and between groups, was the order of the day, a situation which had to be mastered by those who were called to mediate. The sources do hint, however, that the men of learning were not always viewed without criticism or resentment. Proinsias Mac Cana, who has contributed much to the elucidation of native Irish learning, refers in passing to the greed of the *filid*. He characterizes their activity as 'a blend of idealism and gross materialism';[160] both these terms are modern concepts with moral implications. I am not sure whether 'idealism' would describe their activity more properly than masterly craftsmanship. On

---

156 On congruence see Vansina, *Oral tradition*, 114. T.M. Charles-Edwards, *The Welsh laws*, 8, writes in a similar context about a 'happy harmony'.
157 Breatnach, P.A., 'The chief's poet' *PRIA*, 83, 1983, 37-79, at 68; Vendryes, J., 'La poésie de cour en Irlande et en Galles', in *Choix d'etudes linguistiques et Celtiques*, Paris 1952, 209-24, at 215f.
158 See *CMCS* 19, 1990, p. 31, n. 26.
159 This is mentioned in passing by Chadwick, N.K., *Poetry and prophecy*, Cambridge 1942, 58.
160 Mac Cana, 'Regnum and sacerdotium. Notes on Irish tradition', *PBA* 65, 1979, 443-79, at 458, 461.

the other hand, one certainly needs to be aware of the burden which the demands of the men of learning made on society. Even 'gross materialism' seems to me to impose modern concepts on those societies where mind and money were not closely intertwined. Mac Cana even suggests that there was 'a permanent, generally latent tension between the *filid* and the secular ruling class'.[161] I do not know on what evidence this suggestion is based; but if it points in the right direction, then this would imply that the men of learning were even more essential to society in Ireland and Wales than is normally conceded, for if they were indeed excessively greedy, their demands were nonetheless met, they were tolerated in their behaviour, albeit perhaps with gritted teeth.

MODES OF TRANSMISSION/EXPRESSION

The way in which the work of the poets was actually presented is nowhere explicitly described; it has to be gleaned from incidental references, which, nevertheless, are in broad agreement with each other.

We find written in the Welsh laws relating to the pencerdd: 'Cum regi placuerit carmina audire, unum de Deo, alterum de regibus debet cantare in anteriori parte aule'.[162] Thus the works of the 'chief of song' were sung in the royal hall; a song in honour of God had precedence over the traditional topic, the deeds of the ancestors. While it is not stated whether the *pencerdd* sang to musical accompaniment, it is written about the *bard teylu* that, when he was conferred his position, he was given a harp which he was to have always with him:

> Quando bart teulu datur officium suum, rex dabit ei citharam, et regina anulum. Numquam a se cytharam dimittet.[163]

Also from Wales one hears as early as the twelfth century of secular rulers who composed poetry. This was then no longer as strictly the reserve of professionals as appears to have been the case before.

However, in Wales as in Ireland the work of the poets was performed to music; hence the frequent use of terms like *carmen* or *cantare*. After the quotation from the Welsh laws, we may once again refer to a stereotyped way of expressing this activity, from the *Life of Ciaran of Saighir* reporting of Oengus, king of Munster:

> Ipse rex Mumenie Aengus cytharistas optimos habuit, qui dulciter coram eo acta heroum in carmine cytharizantes cantabant.[164]

161 Mac Cana, 'Regnum', 468.
162 Emanuel, *Latin texts*, Red. E, 447.
163 Emanuel, *Latin texts*, Red. D, 329.
164 *Vitae Sanctorum Hiberniae*, ed. Plummer, 222; note the 'figura etymologica' which was a

This reference is apparently unique in the Latin sources from early medieval Ireland[165] where otherwise the native terminology occurred.

A 'chief harpist' is mentioned incidentally in Wales in the twelfth-century *Hanes Gruffydd ap Cynan*;[166] he had accompanied King Gruffudd in battle, where he fell in 1094.

As was mentioned earlier, the Irish legal material was stated to have been preserved by chanting, Old Irish *for-cain*; this verb is cognate with Latin *canere* with a wide range of connotations, including that of reciting and enchanting, and including *vaticinium*.[167] Clearly, the material conveyed by the men of learning was not pronounced in ordinary speech but instead in an elevated register. Also, it was cast in a language that offered the opportunity of displaying artistry. In later medieval Ireland, this language was referred to as *berla na filed*, 'speech/language of the poets'. The close relationship between reciting and singing is well expressed in early Welsh. *Cerdd dafod*, 'craft of the tongue' (= poetry) is put alongside *cerdd dant*, 'craft of the string'.[168]

We have heard that music was part of the oral tradition in action. It is not clear whether the person playing an instrument was distinct from the person who chanted the tradition. It is not even possible to be precise about the nature of the instrument called *cithara* or *rotta* in Latin, *crott* in Irish.[169] While I have no difficulty in regarding *rotta* and *crott* as cognate terms,[170] I suggest that the instrument in question was a lyre rather than a harp. In any case, it was a stringed instrument intended to be plucked.[171]

NUMBERS INVOLVED

In early and medieval Ireland poetry or at least verse was woven into the whole fabric of society and that society could not exist without it.[172]

favourite form among the Irish; but see also Rev. 14:2 'citharoedorum citharizantium in citharis suis'. For *optimus* see above pp. 204f and *sui cruithirechta*, as in AU 1100.

165 This statement is based on the results of a word search at the Royal Irish Academy in Dublin.
166 Jones, A., ed., *The History of Gruffydd ap Cynan*, Manchester 1910, 139. In 1110, AU mention a 'master harpist' *sui cruitirecha*, who is also styled *fer léiginn*.
167 See Watkins, C., 'Indoeuropean metrics and archaic Irish verse', *Celtica* 6, 1963, 194-249, at 214. For the range of meanings of cantare see Allen, W., 'Ovid's cantare and Cicero's Cantores Euphorionis', *Transactions and Proceedings of the American Philological Association* 103 , 1972, 1-14.
168 Cf. Ford, P., *The poetry of Llywarch Hen*, Berkeley, Los Angeles and London 1974, 40.
169 For an Old-Irish gloss in this matter see Ml f. 51c (*Thesaurus Palaeohibernicus* I, 160).
170 See the discussion in Steger, H., 'Die Rotte. Studien über ein germanisches Musikinstrument im Mittelalter', *Deutsche Vierteljahrsschrift für Literaturwissenschaft und Geistesgeschichte* 35, 1961, 96-147.
171 Cf. Bruford, A., 'Song and recitation in early Ireland', *Celtica* 21, 1990, 61-74.
172 Carney, J., 'Society and the bardic poet', *Studies* 62, 1973, 233-50, at 239.

Here I intend to investigate the numbers involved as regards the men of learning in medieval Ireland and Wales. In view of the fact that we are dealing with a period where reliable demographic figures are not available, expectations will have to be realistic at the outset. The Irish annals between c.660 and 1100 contain the obits of some 400 named scholars (which is unique in Europe at that time);[173] there is every reason to believe that these sources reveal only the proverbial tip of the iceberg. However, only a small proportion of these scholars appears to have been men of learning of the Irish tradition, the majority were Christian scholars.

Even rough figures are not available before c.1000. When figures do occur, they have to be 'decoded'. Ultimately, one has to be satisfied with statements of the kind that numbers were 'small', 'medium' or 'large'.

The following discussion is helped, however, by the awareness that the men of learning were an integral part of the existing society. Ireland and Wales in the early medieval centuries were politically fragmented;[174] there existed a great number of kingdoms.[175] According to the law tracts, a proper king required men of learning in his entourage. Scores of kings imply more scores of men of learning.

We have seen earlier that both kings and nobles required the skills of the men of learning; kings had them as their constant companions and close advisors. To what extent this was also the case among the nobility is impossible to say. We have further seen that in Ireland the men of learning were hierarchically structured; in Wales there are only hints of such a situation. It is not surprising that in the entourage of kings were men representing the highest grades of learning; perhaps lower grades were also represented there.[176]

As to the learned profession itself, one would imagine that not every man of learning made it to the top and became an *ollam*; in other words, it is to be assumed that for every *ollam* recorded there existed several men representing the lower grades of learning. Great numbers would favour competition, and this in turn would benefit the quality of the work.

In his *Descriptio Kambriae*, written in the late twelfth century, Giraldus Cambrensis states: 'Unde et poetas, quos bardos vocant, . . . in hac natione multos invenies' (I, xii). Giraldus was sufficiently familiar with Welsh society

173 Cf. McCone, *Pagan past*, 21ff. For more see Richter, 'The scholars of early Christian Ireland'.
174 McCone, *Pagan past*, 'early Ireland had a reasonably typical medieval Western European social structure', p. 25, is vague and unhelpful.
175 For Ireland one has to reckon with scores of them, not all of the same standing. Numbers are disputed; they are put rather low by Ó Corráin, D., 'Nationality and kingship', 1978. However, the guarantor list of *Cáin Adomnáin* of c.697 includes names of 50 kings; the *Tripartite Life of Patrick*, Stokes, W., ed., RS 89.1, 1887, from the ninth century, contains a great number of them. It is impossible to give absolute figures.
176 See above at notes 103f.

for his statement to be considered as well informed. He was also familiar with other societies, particularly in England and France, to appreciate differences between the various societies. His statement must be interpreted that in his experience it was characteristic of Welsh society to have high numbers of people of native learning.

An Irish poem from the late tenth century mentions in passing the killing of 150 men of learning ('tri choicait eecess') in the course of a dispute between two secular lords.[177] One should note the traditional Irish 'three fifties'[178] which, however, ought not to be taken literally. Nevertheless 'a high number' is clearly implied. We have here also the allusion to the close association between men of learning and secular power.

We shall now consider in some detail an account of the position of the men of learning in Irish society, a report contained in the prose preface to the *Amra Coluim Chille* (ACC).[179] The ACC is regarded as one of the earliest poems in the Irish language to have survived; it is believed to have been composed not long after the death of Colum Cille in 597.[180] The prose preface is of a later date, of the early eleventh century according to the most recent discussion of this text.[181]

This prose text has as its subject a public gathering held at Druim Cett, traditionally dated to AD 575, at which, among other business, it was discussed whether the poets should be expelled from Ireland. The reason for this intended expulsion is not given. It has been suggested that there had been tension between the secular leaders and the poets;[182] a more plausible reason would appear to be that there had been serious objections to the influence of the guardians of native traditional learning from committed Christians. Be that as it may, according to this account, Colum Cille, abbot of Iona since 563, who was present at Druim Cett, spoke out in favour of the poets, whose expulsion was thereupon not carried out.

The preface is as difficult a document as is the elegy which follows it, albeit for different reasons. Here we are only concerned with the matter relating to the poets, where it states:

> Now the men of Ireland rejected the poets thrice, but the Ulaid, from

177 Mac Cana, P., 'Two notes', *Celtica* 11, 1976, 130.
178 See Richter, *Medieval Ireland*, 15.
179 Stokes, W., 'The Bodleian *Amra Choluimb Chille*', RC 20, 1899, 30-55, 132-83, 248-89, 400-37.
180 On Colum Cille see Smyth, A.P., *Warlords and holy men. Scotland AD 80-1000*, London 1984, ch. 3, pp. 84-115, and more recently Herbert, M., *Iona, Kells and Derry. The history and hagiography of the monastic familia of Columba*, Oxford 1988; also Richter, *Medieval Ireland*, 54f.
181 Herbert, M., 'The preface to *Amra Coluim Cille*', in *Sages, saints and storytellers* (= FS James Carney), O Corráin D. et al., ed., Maynooth 1989, 67-75.
182 Thus Herbert, 'Preface', 71.

their generosity, retained them. Twelve hundred was their number at the first proscription, when Conchobar and the nobles of the Ulaid kept them for seven years. The second proscription was when Eochaid the king-poet (*ríceges*) with seven hundred was refused; but Fiachna, son of Baetán, retained them. Now the third time was the great proscription of the twelve hundred poets, including Eochaid the king-poet.[183]

The poets survived this threat to their existence in Irish society, even though with somewhat reduced influence: 'Thereafter the poets were billeted throughout Ireland; but their retinue was diminished, namely, twenty-four in the *ollam*'s retinue and twelve in the *anrud*'s.[184]

Profound scepticism has been expressed concerning the historicity of this part of the meeting at Druim Cett.[185] Indeed it would be unwise to infer anything concerning the position of poets in Irish society in the sixth century from this document.[186] However, the elegy which follows the prose preface is generally believed to have been composed, shortly after Colum Cille's death, by a celebrated Irish poet, Dallán Forgaill. It is impossible to classify that elegy as either purely Christian or purely traditional, heroic; it combines elements of the two traditions. The very existence of the poem highlights the respect voiced by an outstanding Irish poet for an outstanding representative of Irish society who also held an important office in the Church. In this respect, as well as in being preserved in written form, the ACC epitomizes the coexistence of pre-Christian tradition and Christian life in Ireland around AD 600.

While the preface to the ACC cannot be taken as a document conveying reliable information about events in the late sixth century, it is of value to the historian in shedding light on the position of men of learning at the time when the preface was written, thus for the situation around AD 1000.[187] The preface can be considered as an aetiological tale. As such, the text would thus give insight into what its author believed could have been the situation in the past; the past would have been viewed as having given rise to the situation at the time the preface was written.

The preface to the ACC refers to poets; by the time this was written, *filid*. were no longer in charge of legal learning; it is not certain whether they still had to master the 'compositions' as stated in *Uraicecht na ríar* relating to the eighth century. It is thus most likely that in the preface to ACC we are dealing with 'poets' in the more traditional sense as discussed earlier.

183 Stokes, 43.
184 Stokes, 45.
185 See Bannermann, J., 'The convention of Druim Cett', in id., ed., *Studies in the history of Dal Riada*, Edinburgh 1974, 157-70.
186 Mac Cana, '*Regnum*', 462-70, 476f.
187 For the dating see Herbert, 'Preface', 68.

The preface to ACC mentions the figure of 1200 poets and a multiple, roughly of five to ten, of retinue associated with them. In the light of the reputation of the Celts for boasting[188] one might be inclined to be sceptical about these figures. However, one should take into account that this text was written, neither for posterity nor for the outside world, but for the society of the author. One may thus conclude that, even if this text may not be 'historical', the figures mentioned in it must have appreared as not unreasonable around 1000. Furthermore, they dovetail with what has been proposed earlier.

It is thus suggested more concretely now that around 1000 native learning was very broadly based in Ireland; the poets to whom the prose preface refers were only one segment of the men of learning; the *oes dána*, as a whole, appear to have been very numerous indeed. Since they were also very demanding, the institution of organized native learning in Ireland was extremely costly, but apparently considered, on balance, as worth having. It can be argued further that in the course of the half-millennium since the establishment of Christianity, the conditions for the cultivation of traditional learning had not developed favourably, had at best stayed as before, but perhaps even deteriorated (as hinted at in the prose preface). The men of learning were, however, around 1000, by any standards, a most impressive segment of society; it seems likely that this had also been the situation, perhaps even more impressively so, before the establishment of Christianity.

The men of learning expected adequate remuneration for their skills; they kept a retinue that displayed their standing in society, a retinue which also had to be maintained. In the light of these considerations resentment against the men of learning is not surprising, but their maintenace in spite of the cost involved is a fact. It was unthinkable to dispense with them, even though traditional learning was a heavy material burden.

The available documentation makes the general expense for native learning an unlikely subject of discussion; it was accepted as a fact of life, even when resented. Instead, one is treated occasionally to more superficial aspects of it, like the splendour or spectacle which were part of this institution. Thus the Welsh Chronicle, *Brut y Tywysogyon*, contains an account of a public competition sponsored by the lord of Deheubarth in 1176:

> And then the Lord Rhys held a special feast at Cardigan, and he set two kinds of contest: one between the bards and the poets, and another between the crowders and the pipers and the various classes of string music. And he set two chairs for the victors in the contests. And those he enriched with great gifts. And then a young man from his own court

---

188 For some references see Richter, M., 'Die Kelten im Mittelalter', *HZ* 246, 1988, 265-95, at 271.

won the victory for string music. And the men from Gwynedd won the victory for poetry. And all the other minstrels received from the Lord Rhys as much as they asked, so that no one was refused. And the feast was proclaimed a year before it was held in Wales and England and Scotland and Ireland and many other lands.[189]

It is not clear how exceptional this event was to find its way into the Chronicle. It is noteworthy that this was an international competition, though it was the Welsh who won the two competitions. However, we get also in this text reference to the men of learning at court as a matter of fact, mentioned in connection with the winner of the chair of string music. In addition, appropriate remuneration of all participants is also mentioned. The competitive nature of this traditional culture was bound to produce high standards even without feasts. Such culture required patronage and adequate recognition, of a material as well as an non-material nature.

Continental Christian rulers also held court regularly, especially on the occasion of the great feasts of the Christian calendar. These were some of the occasions for appropriate entertainment which included the appearance of the guardians of the oral tradition.[190] The situation appears to have been similar to that of the Irish and Welsh rulers although there is less evidence as to the number of people involved in the practice of the oral tradition there. They had to exercise generosity and hospitality in order to continue to attract followers. This was so much part of the norm that chroniclers did not mention such occasions if they passed off without a hitch.[191] On these ocasions wealth was lavishly distributed, generosity displayed, loyalty purchased, and the host was praised appropriately.

COEXISTENCE OR SYMBIOSIS?

We have recovered—with the help of written sources—a number of facets of the organization of oral learning in early medieval Ireland and some facets of it in Wales. But how is one to imagine the two types of learning in these societies? An answer based on some information can be attempted only for Ireland but it may be of a paradigmatic nature.

We may begin at the very end of the period being investigated here. There is a ruling from the first synod of Cashel of 1101 which states: 'Gan chion in chléirig nó in filed do tabairt do'n tuata' which A. Gwynn translates as follows: 'That the share of clerics or poets should not be given to a layman.'[192] Here

---

189 *Brut y Tywysogyon* (The Chronicle of the Princes), Red Book of Hergest Version, Jones, T., ed., (Board of Celtic Studies, History and Law Series XVI), Cardiff 1955, 167.
190 Cf. chapter 6.
191 There are references to exceptions in chapter 6 above.
192 Gwynn, A., 'The first synod of Cashel', *Irish Ecclesiastical Record* 67, 1946, 109-22, at 109.

we find that the reformers within the Irish Church took for granted the privileged position in society of clergy and *filid*. The latter should be taken as representing the *oes dána* more generally, whose activity in Irish society is amply attested throughout the Middle Ages. Thus Irish churchmen, indeed reformers, approved of them. Furthermore, it is implied that the *oes dána* were recognizably different from clerics. Thus we have a normative, authoritative statement from the early twelfth century of the existence in Irish society of two kinds of learning.

There are enough pointers to the existence of oral learning in Irish society before the coming of Christianity.[193] We can now say confidently that traditional learning continued to be practised in what is called 'Christian Ireland' for many centuries. Book learning associated with the Christian religion did not oust traditional oral learning. The two types of learning existed side by side; however, there is no easy answer to the question as to what extent they influenced each other.

There is an intriguing reference in an eighth-century manuscript now at Würzburg which conveys the idea that even learning associated with Christianity, learning in a subject as technical as the *computus*, was retained by Irish ecclesiastics by memory (orally) before it was written down:

> Mosinu maccumin scriba et abbas benncuir primus hebernensium compotem a graeco quodam sapiente memoraliter dedicit. Deinde mocuoroc maccumin semon quem romani doctorem totius mundi nominabant alumnusque praefati scribae in insola quae dicitur Crannach Duinlethglaisse hanc scientiam literis fixit ne memoria laberetur.
>
> (Mo-Sinu maccu Min, scholar and abbot of Bangor, was the first of the Irish who learned the computus by heart from a certain learned Greek. Afterwards, Mo-Chuoróc maccu Neth Sémon, whom the Romani styled doctor of the whole world, and a pupil of the aforesaid scholar, in the island called Crannach of Downpatrick, committed this knowledge to writing, lest it should fade from memory.)[194]

We note that the abbot in question is twice styled *scriba*, that the man from whom he learned the *computus* is styled *sapiens*. We thus encounter the

---

193 'It is not the beginnings of a literature which we see then (sixth century), but the full flowering of a long tradition, pre-Christian, pre-literate, and uninfluenced by the Graeco-Roman world', Watkins, C., 'Indo-European metrics', 217.

194 This is written on a leaf now in Würzburg, Universitätsbibliothek MS M.p.th.f. 61. See further Ó Cróinín, D., 'Mo-Sinnu moccu min and the computus of Bangor', *Peritia* 1, 1982, 281–95, at 283 ('edited' text), 284 (reproduction), 286 (translation). See also p. 50 above at n. 26.

terminology which we have elaborated earlier for Christian scholars at that time in the annals. However, the abbot is said to have retained the knowledge about the *computus* orally, in the traditional Irish manner of learning. It cannot be taken for granted that the great scholar Mo-chuoróc maccu Neth Sémon did the writing of this material himself or organized that it be written.[195]

In the light of this information, and on the basis of what has been stated elsewhere about the technology of writing, one must approach the issue of new, Christian learning as a kind of learning connected intricately with writing, in a differentiating manner. One has to distinguish the physical act of writing from the occupation with material that was fixed in writing even though it was studied orally. It is necessary to keep in mind the technical expertise necessary for writing the medieval manuscripts. This expertise was certainly cultivated in the Christian milieu, and the monasteries provided the most suitable environment for it. Irish secular society was not yet built upon the written word; it did not yet provide the infrastructure for teaching the skill of writing.

In the light of the existence of monasteries throughout Ireland, as well as the existence in Ireland of traditional men of learning in great numbers and taking into account the overall population of Ireland in the early medieval centuries, it is hard to avoid the conclusion that Christian learning and traditional learning lived in close proximity to each other. It is all the more important to find that they were still considered as separate by church reformers in the early twelfth century.

We have seen already that the pre-Christian past was considered as respectable in Irish Christian society; it appears that on the whole traditional men of learning continued to be respected, by churchmen and lay people alike. This is confirmed by a casual reference in Adomnán's *Vita Columbae* of a poet visiting the monastic community of Iona; the monks were merely astonished that their abbot did not request a poem in 'payment' for hospitality received: 'Quidam ad eos scoticus poeta devenit. Qui cum post aliquam recessisset sermocinationem, fratres ad sanctum: "Cur", aiunt, "a nobís regrediente Cronano poeta aliquod ex more suae artis canticum non postulasti modolabiliter decantari?" '[196] In like manner, the Life of St Molua (eighth century) refers to a poet in the company of the saint as a man not used to manual labour.[197] These are only stray references showing how the two kinds of learning co-existed.

In later Irish tradition the story of Cenn Faelad mac Ailella and his famous

195 For a comparable case see chapter 6, n. 46
196 Adomnan, *Vita Columbae* 43a/b.
197 Heist, W.W., ed., *Vitae Sanctorum Hiberniae*, Bruxelles 1965, 139: 'Fuit quoque apud Lugidum quidam poeta, Conanus nomine, qui laborare suis manibus peritus non erat.' Note the Hibernicism *apud*.

inchinn dermait, 'brain of forgetting' is associated with the practice of writing native and Christian learning.[198] There is a 'Cenn Faelad sapiens' listed in the annals as having died in 679. However, it is not necessary to regard the story of Cenn Faelad the scholar in three disciplines as historically accurate; more likely, the account should be considered as an aetiological tale about the practice of writing material that had traditionally been transmitted orally.

It has been pointed out that there are few references from early Ireland about Irish men of learning becoming leading Christians like Colmán mac Léneni, first a poet, then the founder of the monastery of Cloyne who died in 604.[199] However, it must be recalled that the Irish annals mention men of learning only rarely compared to Christian scholars, and the early period is particularly poorly covered for either group.

The Irish annals rarely mention Christian dignitaries who were also experts in Irish traditional learning. One may refer to 'Ailill m. Cormaicc, abbas Slane, sapiens 7 iudex optimus'[200] as an example. The abbot Ailill was commemorated as a leading legal expert. This shows that traditional learning was practised by ecclesiastics without being subsumed into Christian learning. One can easily imagine that many of the leading Christian scholars mentioned in the annals were nevertheless interested in native learning without being famous for their knowledge of it. These, and scholars of a lesser calibre (of whom there must have been a great many), as well as men like Ailill, can be imagined as patronizing tradition learning, alongside Christian scholarship. It is easiest to visualize here the milieu in which the material containing traditional learning found its way into writing. An alternative would be that men of learning borrowed the expertise of professional scribes (who would have been trained in monasteries) to write what they wished to preserve in this manner. However, I am very sceptical that this was actually done. The modern connotation of 'schools' may be very misleading.[201]

Here it is necessary to stress once again that texts of traditional material are not 'oral tradition in written form'. We have seen earlier that oral tradition

---

198 The story occurs in *Bretha Etigid* as well as in *Auraicept na nÉces*, Calder, G., ed., Edinburgh 1917, lines 63ff and 2616ff. Mac Cana, P., 'The three languages and the three laws', *Stud. Celt.* 5, 1970, 62-78; see also Slotkin, E.M., 'Medieval Irish scribes and fixed texts', *Éigse* 17, 1977-79, 437-50; Tristram, H.L.C., 'Warum Cenn Faelad sein "Gehirn des Vergessens" verlor. Wort und Schrift in der älteren irischen Literatur', in *Deutsche, Kelten und Iren. 150 Jahre deutsche Keltologie* (FS Gearóid Mac Eoin), Hamburg 1990, 207-48.
199 Búrca, S. de, 'Aspects of transmission', *Éigse* 15, 1973-74, 51-65, esp. 54. See also Thurneysen, R., 'Colmán Mac Léneni und Senchán Torpéist', *ZCP* 19, 1933, 193-209.
200 AU 802, AFM 797.
201 See Binchy, D.A., 'Ancient Irish law', *Irish Jurist* 1, 1966, 88: 'By the seventh (or perhaps even the sixth) century writing in the Latin alphabet had seeped from the monastic into the native schools, and "the ancient lore of the Irish" was committed to parchment.' A similar statement is found in his contribution 'Celtic suretyship, a fossilized Indo-European institution?', *Irish Jurist* 7, 1972, 360-72, at 365.

involves much more than 'texts', even texts read out aloud.[202] This is also the reason why we did not have to deal with Irish literature as such even though this literature is surely more than just a window on the oral tradition. This literature informs us about social values as well as political life and strife, about expectations brought to individuals and groups. The texts can give us much more than just an idea of the subject of the oral tradition even where one may detect possible signs of censorship.[203] The enormous corpus of medieval literature written in Irish conveys an impressively wide range of material cultivated in the oral tradition. There are good reasons to believe that many Irishmen, like their continental equivalents, continued to be attracted by the traditional culture even after donning the clerical garb. There is, thus, a great amount of indirect evidence that people who were professed Christians did enjoy ways of life, including entertainment and remembering the Irish heroic past, which would not be approved of by zealous Christians. There is a general tendency for such lenient Christian behaviour to be less fully represented in the sources than more rigorous attitudes.[204] While this is hardly surprising, it must be taken into account in a general assessment. Clearly, the Middle Ages were also in Ireland not as 'Christian' as some Christian sources seem to suggest. Christianity had not been able to replace many traditional values. On the contrary, as has been well written about the Irish Church: 'Her strength and weakness lay in her full adjustment to her environment.'[205]

In one manuscript version of the Irish national epic, the *Táin Bó Cúalnge* (The cattle-raid of Cooley) there are at the end two colophons. The one in Irish reads: 'Bendacht ar cech óen mebraigfes go hindraic Táin amlaid seo 7 ná tuillfe cruth aile furri'. (A blessing on every one who shall faithfully memorise the Táin as it is written here and shall not add any other form to it.) This is followed by one in Latin: 'Sed ego qui scripsi hanc historiam aut verius fabulam quibusdam fidem in hac historia aut fabula non accommodo. Quaedam enim ibi sunt praestrigia demonum, quaedam autem figmenta poetica, quaedam similia vero, quaedam non, quaedam ad delectationem stultorum'. (But I who have written this history, or rather this fable, give no credence to the various incidents related in it. For some things in it are the deceptions of demons, others poetic figments; some are probable, others improbable; while still others are intended for the delectation of foolish men.)[206] Here we have a case where a copyist disagrees with the matter he is asked to copy. The text is measured by Christian values and is found wanting. Even

202 See chapter 4.
203 Mac Cana, P., 'Conservation and innovation in early Celtic literature', *Études Celtiques* 13, 1972, 61-119, esp. 99ff.
204 See above, *Kanonensammlung* Book X (Carthage).
205 Hughes, *The Church in early Irish society*, 156.
206 *Táin Bó Cúalnge from the Book of Leinster*, O'Rahilly, C., ed., Dublin 1970, 136 texts, 272 translation. The editor translates *historia* here as 'story' which makes the text less poignant.

enjoyment of the material is considered in a negative way. The person who composed the Irish colophon, by contrast, believed in the lasting worth of this epic and envisaged it to be orally transmitted. This is a classic example of coexistence of two forms and kinds of culture.

How, then, is one to imagine the two kinds of learning in early medieval Ireland? I think that one has to qualify the suggestive statement by Kathleen Hughes that 'the Christian church had embraced all that was congenial in heroic society, its honour and generosity, its splendour and display, its enthusiasm, its respect for learning.'[207] Nor can I subscribe to Proinsias Mac Cana's statement that 'the pagan heritage was . . . a large ingredient in the making of the Irish Church'.[208] I suggest instead that the two types of learning existed, by and large, side by side each other, each pursuing their own forms of learning. This co-existence can be imagined as very close, which allowed for some overlapping without the two merging. The two types of learning had different aims and a different place in society while the society was affected by them both. This is one of the reasons why Irish society in the early Middle Ages shows signs of an exceptional vitality.[209] Nowhere else is the information on traditional culture as well attested, on the whole without a pejorative slant, in its own terms and in such strength. It is possible that the oral tradition was indeed stronger in Ireland than anywhere else in the early Middle Ages; this could well be due to the fact that Ireland had never been exposed to Romanization or any other foreign occupation at a time when many other parts of Europe, including Britain, suffered such disruptions.

How accommodation between the two types of learning had been achieved, how, to put it differently, Christianity had embedded itself in Irish society, is impossible to say. The decisive fifth and sixth centuries have left few contemporary sources. It would be hard to imagine a St Patrick or a St Columbanus being very tolerant of traditional culture; on the other hand, Adomnán apparently had come to accept it as given, and he had surely many contemporary colleagues who would have been less zealous than he was. It may have taken quite a while for mutual tolerance to have been achieved, but in the centuries of contemporary written sources such tolerance can be seen as existing, and it was to continue for many centuries until the destruction of the Irish traditional social order at the end of the Middle Ages.

207 Hughes, K., *Church*, 156.
208 Mac Cana, P., 'Regnum and sacerdotium', 478.
209 Its attractiveness to foreigners was emphasized by Aldhelm, see Eph 5: 'Cur, inquam, Hibernia, quo catervatim istinc lectitantes classibus advecti confluunt . . . ? Quamvis enim praedictum Hiberniae rus discentium opulans vernansque, ut ita dixerim, pascuosa numerositate lectorum, quemadmodum poli cardines astriferis micantium vibraminibus siderum, ornetur?', MGH AA 15, 492.

10

ORAL CULTURE AND EARLY VERNACULAR LITERATURE

As we have seen, oral culture was a virtually universal phenomenon among the barbarians, presumably familiar to all echelons of society, even though it is attested very inadequately as well as unevenly in the available sources, and mainly for the higher strata. There have been various suggestions as to why this was the case.

Accessible on the whole through the Latin language, a language not suitable for this purpose, oral culture was cultivated predominantly in verse, as has been shown. In performance, in its actualization, it was sung or recited, in such a form as to give pleasure to those exposed to it. In the terms of Regino of Prüm,[1] music or song pervaded lives almost everywhere, whether the individual was participating in it as performer or as audience. The oral culture was broadly based, and thus it gives access to the ontology of the barbarians.

The implications of all this are that barbarians were familiar with language used skilfully and in memorable form, a fact which has far-reaching consequences. There was a relationship of reciprocity and mutual esteem among those who took part in the performance of their culture. This was the channel through which social values were maintained, continuously enhanced as well as deepened through repetition.[2] Everything points to wordcraft as a crucial element in barbarian societies.

One main topic remains to be considered, at least in general outline, namely the relationship between the oral culture and early vernacular literature. It is a topic that has been dealt with often in the past; however, since the oral culture as a whole has not, so far, received satisfactory treatment, the earlier accounts are, on balance, defective in important respects. A reassessment of the kind offered here naturally cannot claim to answer all the questions that

---

1 See chapter 5 at n. 29.
2 These and similar ideas have been advanced especially by Havelock, E.A., *Preface to Plato*, Harvard 1963, and are of value beyond pre-historic Greece. This does not mean that I share all the ideas put forward concerning the genesis of the Homeric epics in Havelock's various publications.

arise. It will have served its purpose if it points in a general direction where work is necessary and stimulates a discussion of this problem on a new basis.

In the course of the early medieval centuries, the vernacular languages came to be written with ease in the West.[3] The process began in Ireland, Wales and England around 600, in Germany in the eighth, in France in the ninth century. In each case there were particular preconditions which contributed to the characteristics of this early vernacular literature.[4] The rise of written vernacular culture was gradual, and occurred in each case within an existing oral culture. It was shaped prominently by the Latin tradition that came from Roman antiquity and through the Church. However, there can be no doubt that the oral culture played a part as well. The question is, how this contribution can be pinpointed.

This topic has been treated in various different ways, but in every instance so far the lack of adequate attention to the oral culture has had negative implications for the treatment. As has been stated at the beginning of this work, the concepts with which one approaches any issue and the terminology one uses are crucial. Generally, and in a way quite rightly, the early phases of vernacular literature form part of the work of those scholars who deal predominantly with the history of literature. Thus the concepts normally used for literature are applied to its earliest manifestations as well, which is perfectly legitimate; but they also are used for the pre-literate background without questioning whether they apply universally to cultural material.[5]

In these accounts, a point that is normally passed over quickly is the quantity of early vernacular literature. It has been mentioned earlier that, generally speaking, the technology of writing came to the barbarians with Christianity, and that the means of writing—including the vernacular—were available wherever the Christian religion had gained a foothold. However, only exceptionally, as for example in Ireland, was the vernacular written extensively at an early stage. Of course, for all areas, including Ireland, one has to reckon that material was lost, on a scale impossible to calculate.[6] However, this is not a sufficient explanation of the relatively meagre corpus of vernacular literature in the continental West before c.1100. We have seen that the oral tradition remained as an important and viable method of storing culture; this is therefore the better explanation for the small corpus of vernacular literature. Oral

---

3 The discussion of the technical difficulties of writing the Frankish language by means of the Latin alphabet by Otfrid (pp. 173f above), is certainly interesting but should not be over-rated.
4 McKitterick, *Uses of literacy*; Banniard, M., ed., 'La voie et l'écriture', *Médiévales* 25, 1993.
5 For a classic manifestation of this see Bezzola, R.R., *Les origines et la formation de la littérature courtoise en occident (500–1200)*, vol. I, Paris 1958.
6 Eis, G., 'Von der verlorenen altdeutschen Dichtung. Erwägungen und Schätzungen', *Germanisch-Romanische Monatsschrift* Neue Folge 6 (37), 1956, 175-89.

transmission of barbarian culture remained the preferred medium for centuries; it had had a respectable past and was familiar and adequate. Thus a discussion of the relationship of the existing vernacular literature to that oral tradition is imperative.

ORAL LITERATURE

There have been influential studies, and these must be examined. They claim to provide a relatively simple solution of the problem. One model is the concept of oral literature; another, related but to be dealt with separately, is the concept that, under certain conditions, early vernacular poetry is in fact oral tradition.

The concept of oral literature goes back to the nineteenth century.[7] It is used, at times defiantly, to the present time.[8] More often, however, it seems to be taken for granted without being considered as questionable. Apparently our familiar concepts make it exceedingly difficult to do justice to the oral culture of the past. Thus the Chadwicks, whose contribution to the subject generally remains fundamental despite all the quibbles that can be raised on individual points, used inverted commas when employing the term 'literature' for the early material. But terminology in inverted commas is a curse because these diacritical marks carry no sound[9] while indicating at the same time that the term in question is not used in the ordinary sense, although the difference is not spelled out. This is clearly no solution and must therefore be avoided. In one place, the Chadwicks referred to the oral tradition as 'records of intellectual activity preserved in speech'.[10] In this phrase, 'intellectual' seems to be just as misleading as 'literature'.

There is one apparent justification for regarding the products of oral culture, at least loosely, as literature: the terminology by which it is referred to in the sources—not invariably, but often enough. Yet this situation can also be seen as a vicious circle. One is confronted with the plight of the medieval authors writing Latin at second hand with their wretched box of a very limited

7 Zumthor, P., *Introduction à la poésie orale*, Paris 1983, p. 45, ascribes its formulation to P. Sébillot in 1881.
8 See especially Finnegan, R., *Oral poetry. Its nature, significance and social context*, Cambridge 1977. This position is upheld, even though occasionally with modifications or the use of inverted commas, in her later publications, see Finnegan, R., *Literacy and Orality. Studies in the technology of communication*, Oxford 1988; Finnegan, R., 'Tradition. But what tradition and for whom?', *Oral Tradition* 6, 1991, 104-24. It has to be stressed that Ruth Finnegan is an anthropologist, not a literary historian. Nevertheless, it happens frequently that identical terminology is used with different connotations in different disciplines, which makes a dialogue across the frontiers of disciplines difficult.
9 To use gestures for them as tends to be done in the English-speaking scholarly world in oral delivery is no help.
10 Chadwick, H.M., and Chadwick, N.K., *The Growth of Literature: vol. I: the ancient literatures of Europe*, Cambridge 1932, xi.

number of vocal beads. Terms like *carmen* or *cantilena*, while strictly speaking denoting, not sign but sound, had from antiquity acquired connotations of written material. It is significant that when describing the oral material they are often used in conjunction with qualifying adjectives, such as *saecularis* or *vulgaris*, and these adjectives not infrequently carry connotations which are normally considered negative. Much the same applies to the term *poeta vulgaris*.[11]

This terminology for elements of oral culture apparently gives rise to misconceptions. It is more appropriate, and it also has been shown, that important aspects of oral culture had their own terminology in Latin, through the formation of new terms or by way of semantic changes of traditional terms.[12] There are furthermore indications that there existed a vernacular terminology of perhaps great variety for the vernacular products.[13]

On the other hand, there have been scholars who objected on principle to the concept of oral literature. There is, of course, the essential fact that the term 'literature' is derived from *littera* and thus entails the use of writing for its existence. It is true that any term can be used on a wide scale of meanings, but this becomes dangerous, as in the present case, when the essence of a term is contradicted. Walter Ong, for example, called 'oral literature' a monstrous concept, a preposterous term,[14] and he explained why this should be avoided: 'In view of this pre-emptiveness of literacy, it appears quite impossible to use the term "literature" to include oral tradition and performance without subtly but irremediably reducing these somehow to variants of writing', for '"preliterate" presents orality . . . as an anachronistic deviant from the "secondary modeling system" that follows it.'[15]

In this respect there appears to be at least an inner consistency for Ruth Finnegan to use the term since, in her opinion, 'there is no clear-cut line between "oral" and "written" literature'.[16] Unless there is, indeed, the term could be acceptable. Its rejection has to be more than a gut-reaction. Ruth Finnegan claims that 'oral' and 'written' literature have in common that 'they possess a verbal text. But in one respect it is different: a piece of oral literature, to reach its full actualization, must be performed.'[17] If this is the case—and

11 See above Bede in chapter 7. The vernacular terminology occurs naturally in vernacular literature, generally with positive connotations, see See, K. v., 'Skop und Skald. Zur Auffassung des Dichters bei den Germanen', *Germanisch-Romanische Monatsschrift* 45, 1964, 1-14.
12 See above, chapter 5.
13 See notes 36ff below.
14 Ong, W.J., *Orality and literacy*, 11.
15 Ong, *Orality and literacy*, 12f.
16 Finnegan, R., *Oral poetry. Its nature, significance and social context*, Cambridge 1977, 2, 16, 24.
17 *Oral poetry*, 28.

we have seen that this applies to the early medieval material—then all its implications have to be considered. 'Verbal text', though not particularly attractive, is a term at least not loaded from the beginning like 'literature'.

We have said earlier that written material was generally communicated, in the period here investigated, by reading aloud. This could be done in a variety of manners, by varying the tone of the voice, by accompanying gestures, as well as by silences. In this respect reading a text aloud could have the essential characteristics of a performance.[18] All this seems to speak in favour of Finnegan's assertion. We have it on record from people who have experienced oral culture that it cannot be reduced to verbal texts, and that it is impossible to endeavour to record the performance of oral culture.[19]

Now, it is certainly possible to transcribe the verbal text of a performance, and indeed this has been done by many anthropologists. On the other hand, by defining the oral tradition as significant oral messages based on previous oral messages of a certain age,[20] one accepts, indeed has to accept, that there are potentially countless performances of a particular oral tradition, similar to each other in the verbal text, but never identical. From many verbal texts of oral performances that have been transcribed more than once, it has emerged as a characteristic feature that the verbal text was not identical in the different recordings. Indeed, the essence of performances of traditional culture is the interaction of performer and audience, a constellation in which all build on a close familiarity with the material, and where the quality of a particular performance depends on the excellence of the performer as well as the appreciation of the audience. Thus, while indeed literature and oral tradition share the phenomenon of 'verbal text', in literature this text is fixed, written and finite, whereas in oral culture there is not, as a rule, a fixed verbal text but instead, and characteristically, potentially infinite variety within the subject area. That the finite nature of the written text affects its contents as regards inner consistency, cross-references and the like, can be stated here but need not be developed further. It is sufficient to have clarified that Finnegan's claim about there being no clear-cut line between 'oral' and 'written' literature cannot be accepted.

As a matter of fact, the alleged oral quality of early medieval vernacular literature has received attention in the scholarly world in the last generation, as a reaction to the second phenomenon indicated earlier, the—quite recent— claim that early vernacular poetry in written form was, basically, oral. This position requires elaboration.

A vital oral tradition in the first half of this century in Yugoslavia has been brought to the attention of an unusually wide public, including the world

18   See above, chapter 3.
19   See above, chapter 4.
20   See chapter 4, notes 8-11.

of scholarship, by Albert Lord's *The Singer of Tales*, published in 1960. In this book he summarized field work and subsequent analysis carried out by himself and his teacher Milman Parry over a period of about thirty years. The field work of Parry was undertaken initially in order to reach a better understanding of the Homeric epics, stemming as they do from a non-literate society.

The singer of tales is the Yugoslav *guslar* who performs narrative poetry sung to a one-stringed instrument, the *gusle*. The tales can be of considerable length, consisting sometimes of several thousand lines. They were performed typically in coffee-houses before a public that was familiar with the genre and thus appreciative of a good performance, critical of a poor one. Among Muslims, entertainment by *guslars* tended to take place especially during the nights of the month Rhamadan, and for this reason experienced *guslars* often had about thirty tales in their repertoire. The *guslar* was a specialist (though no professional, in the sense that his skill in this field would be his only or even major source of income), but obviously narrative poetry of considerable length was involved, and the mastery of the art required apprenticeship leading to mastery within the tradition.

Lord's *Singer of Tales* investigates principally the process of composition of oral narrative poetry. This was done by detailed analysis of a considerable corpus of material collected with the help of recording machines and later transcribed. Among the important results was the discovery that the narrative poetry of the *guslar* was not a reproduction of a fixed text which had been memorized. Instead, the narrative was composed in the course of the performance; this implies that literary concepts or categories like 'original' or 'authorship' are meaningless as regards this material (101).

Most of the *guslars* whom Parry and Lord studied were illiterate; with their skills they stood in a long tradition, and their task was to do justice to the tradition as well as possible. Competent *guslars* claimed to be able to acquire a tale after hearing it only once, and to be able to reproduce it completely. The analysis of the same tale sung by various singers in different places has shown that in fact these versions varied one from another. The claim of the *guslar* to produce a tale as heard from another guslar must be taken within a culture without literacy where literary concepts do not exist and are thus inapplicable. 'Fixed text' has no place in non-literate cultures.

The ability to deliver oral narrative poetry several thousand lines in length obviously requires talent as well as training. Lord observed and learned from *guslars* that the skill was acquired through observation, imitation and creation of other experts. Favourite themes were treated by the various guslars in similar manners; the poetic narrative included a considerable amount of formulae. These are, in the words of Lord, 'a group of words which is regularly employed under the same metrical conditions to express a given essential idea' (30). The good formulae have become set in the poet's mind; if successful, they are used frequently. Thus oral narrative poetry as studied here is, within the bounds of tradition, rather fluid. With the aid of the formulae, the skilled singer of tales is capable of rapid composition in performance. However, the musical accompaniment is an integral and essential part of the performance (99). The singer performs before various audiences and is able and free to vary a tale, in length as well as in content, depending on the preferences of the audience.

Part of the work of Parry and Lord consisted also in taking down tales from dictation. It is important to learn that 'a dictated text is never a sung text' (127). Two explanations seem plausible: dictation slows down the flow of the narrative or even interrupts it; and there is no audience in the traditional sense, audience not as passive recipient but stimulating and inciting the singer to provide the best possible quality. This also suggests that there is no smooth transition from oral narrative poetry to poetry composed in the medium of writing. Lord is emphatic that 'transitional texts', half way between sung texts and written texts, are inconceivable, because the two manners are mutually exclusive, the techniques contradictory (128-32).

Besides the use of formula, the paratactic ("adding", Parry) style appears as characteristic. Of course, the illiterate *guslar* lacks the concept of metre and even of line while nevertheless observing them. Lord maintained that 'we can with a high degree of certainty determine whether any text before us was formed by a traditional bard in the crucible of oral composition' (45). Although this is not explicitly stated, I take it that Lord's claim extends here only to material from southern Yugoslavia. Finally, there is the useful reminder that a written style is not *eo ipso* superior to an oral one.

In a paper published twenty-six years later,[21] Albert Lord takes up some of the points in his earlier book and adds some others. It seems important to emphasize that *guslars* were apparently very numerous. Lord further draws a sharp line between the language of the *guslars* and the highly artistic literary language, *Slaveno-srpski*, and later on refers to folk speech and folk literature on which the singers had drawn.[22] He states that 'it is an intriguing question whether the world of literacy has as great a difficulty in comprehending the world of orality as we have found that the world of orality has in understanding the world of literacy. The gap is felt on both sides.'[23] This statement contrasts with the title of the contribution: 'the merging of two worlds'. It should be added that Lord uses the term 'oral literature' freely, in his early work as well as in the later contribution.

21 Lord, A.B., 'The merging of two worlds: oral and written poetry as carriers of ancient values', in Foley, J.M. ed., *Oral tradition in literature. Interpretation in context*, Columbia 1986, 19-64, at 31.
22 Ibid., 44f.
23 Ibid., 50.

The most important aspect of the work of Parry and Lord is its demonstration that illiterate singers could present sizeable verse accounts of widely known material which they composed as they performed them. Since this was possible among Yugoslav illiterate professionals, it was reasonable to argue that something comparable was feasible in archaic Greece, and that, on these terms, the Homeric epics could be taken as products that originated in a non-literate society. Of course, what Parry and Lord came to call 'the formula' had been noticed in the Homeric epics long before them and can be shown to have been regarded as important by Parry at an early stage of his work.[24] What was new in the work of Parry and Lord was their transcultural contribution, their field work for the sake of coming to a better understanding of a remarkable cultural phenomenon perhaps three thousand years older and originating in a different society. It is this last element which has proved highly attractive to scholars of early medieval European literature. Over the last generation virtually every discussion of oral culture and early literature did so with reference to Parry and Lord. The results of their work have been subsequently applied to other areas, other periods and other cultures, with very different consequences, which shows that they can be read in different ways. The extent to which this is meaningful is being debated.

A number of scholars, particularly in the English-speaking world, applied the characteristics of 'the formula' to early vernacular poetry, discovered 'formulaic language' in very many places and thus asserted that these works were 'oral poetry'. One of its prominent exponents, John Miles Foley, proudly claimed that the oral formulaic theory was 'carried by them [Parry and Lord] and other scholars into more than one hundred separate language areas.'[25] This approach is epitomized by the launching in 1986 of a new scholarly journal with the title *Oral tradition* which shows a steadily widening application of the ideas of Parry and Lord.[26] I know of no vigorous objection to this expansion on the part of Albert Lord (who died in 1991).

It must be stated, however, that warnings against too generous an application of the Parry-Lord theory were raised at an early stage and continue to be raised. It has been pointed out that formulaic language of sorts is a characteristic of poetic language *tout court*, and that its manifestation by itself was no sign of the oral nature of such works.[27]

24 This has been discussed by Foley, J. M., *The theory of oral composition. History and methodology*, Bloomington 1988, esp. ch. 1.
25 Foley, *Theory*, Preface, xiii.
26 Cf. also Foley, J.M., ed., *Oral-formulaic theory and research*, New York 1985.
27 For a concise and wide-ranging criticism see Curschmann, M. 'Oral poetry in medieval English, French and German literature: Some notes on recent research', *Speculum* 42, 1967, 36-52. See also Curschmann's two reviews of books dealing with aspects of 'oral literature' by various authors—Foley, J.M., ed., *Oral traditional literature. A Festschrift for Albert Bates Lord*, Columbus, Ohio 1981, in *Speculum* 58, 1983, 460-3 and *Oral poetry. Das Problem der*

Nevertheless, it is heartening to see how the ideas developed by Parry and Lord have had tremendous repercussions far beyond the area within which they were originally developed. Even disagreement with the Parry-Lord theory as applied to early medieval vernacular literature has resulted in deepened interest in that literature and attempts to arrive at alternative ways of coming to terms with them.

It may well be that the sum total of the findings of Parry and Lord applies only to the Yugoslav situation. The sum total is made up of various components, each of which is essential while only contributory to the sum total. This seems to account for the application of the Parry-Lord findings to other material.

It is remarkable, in any case, to note that attempts to apply the Parry-Lord theory to other works of poetry were mainly made by concentrating on the formula. However, the purpose which the formula served, that is, the poetic production in performance, every time it happened in a unique situation, was no longer taken into account. It is evident, however, in the work of Parry and Lord, that the formula was a means to an end, and that the whole context in which it made its appearance has to be taken into account. Here again it is imperative to heed the warning that oral tradition is much else besides the verbal text, that it seems to require music in an essential manner.[28] Furthermore, generally speaking, oral tradition does not encompass the phenomenon of a fixed verbal text but instead varies infinitely with each performance. In the light of these considerations, it is out of the question to take early vernacular poetry, including epic poetry, as oral literature in written form. There can be no such thing.[29]

I should like to conclude this section by reference to the work of Paul Zumthor in this area. When using inverted commas in his work on medieval literature,[30] he does so for different reasons than those of the Chadwicks. For in this work he focuses on the literature of the Middle Ages in general, not only its early manifestations, and he thus works on the literature as the product of a milieu that had come to use writing as a matter of course. However, he concentrates on the ways and means by which this literature was received. In emphasizing the oral element ('vocalité', p. 21) he is not original,[31] but his is the most extensive treatment of this aspect to date. His work, not unlike the

Mündlichkeit mittelalterlicher epischer Dichtung, Voorwinden, N., and Haan, M. de, ed., Darmstadt 1979, in *Mittellateinisches Jahrbuch* 16, 1981, 379-82.

28 See Lord, *Singer*, 99.
29 Curschmann, 'Oral poetry', briefly toyed with the concept of 'transitional texts', 45-9; however, he quickly admitted that this was unsuitable.
30 Zumthor, *La lettre et la voix*, which should be considered in conjunction with id., *Introduction à la poésie orale*, Paris 1983.
31 See chapter 3 above. Reference is often made in this subject to the article of Crosby, R., 'Oral delivery in the Middle Ages' which is by now completely dated.

present one, in tackling apparently familiar issues, gives rise to all sorts of problems which demand extensive further research. Zumthor maintains that the leading modern scholars of medieval literature tend to approach this material with modern connotations which cannot do justice to that material. He explains, rightly, that this is so because the 'performance' dimension of this material, central to it, is not normally taken into account. He aims at 'percevant— et analysant—l'oeuvre orale dans son existence discursive'.[32] Thus his oral dimension of medieval literature is a different one from that of Ruth Finnegan. For her the oral element was part of creation; for Zumthor it is the production that counts.

These are some of the ways in which the issue of oral tradition and literature have been tackled recently. It is remarkable to see how apparently straightforward terms such as literature and orality can give rise to a great variety of interpretations. There is no need to add yet another variant, for the present study has a different focus.

Where does all this leave us in the light of the evidence of the barbarian culture in the early medieval West? It is easily stated that the situation is complex, but surely this is not enough. My dissatisfaction with the concept of oral literature is plain, and the concept of transitional or intermediary texts also seems to indicate a refusal to take a definite stand.

On the other hand, to assign the early vernacular literature simply to *litterati* cannot be compelling in the light of what has been elaborated earlier about the mechanical aspects of writing. While there is still a great deal of uncertainty about who wrote in the early medieval West, evidence of this skill outside clerical circles is slight.[33] Thus vernacular literature, including verse, could have been initiated by anybody who had access to scribes.

But one has to go further. We have seen that oral culture held a prominent place in the early medieval West. Its continued functioning required a broad base, which can thus be taken as fact. The verbal texts, in the hands of professionals, would have been of high artistic standard;[34] the competition between those who were in charge of the culture would guarantee this. We have had ample evidence that the barbarian culture was appreciated even in clerical circles—evidence of its strong attraction. Thus those who are normally associated with literacy were still exposed to the oral culture of the society within which they lived. If these factors are kept in mind, as I think they have to be, then one can posit a profound influence of the oral culture on early vernacular literature.

32 Zumthor, *Lettre*, 126.
33 See chapter 3 above.
34 Complaints about the inferiority of the vernacular languages *vis-à-vis* Latin, coming as they do from clerical authors writing in Latin, smack of topoi and should not be taken at face value. See Haubrichs, *Anfänge*, esp. 38-43, who does not make this qualification, but who has useful comments on the lack of a uniform Old German language.

We have seen that the term 'literature' is very unsuitable for the products of barbarian oral culture. This is so because when used in the ordinary sense it carries connotations which just do not apply to oral culture. Nevertheless, it has to be admitted that a viable alternative term is not available at present.

It is now necessary to turn to the terms used by contemporaries for the products of oral culture as well as for the people involved in its performance. In the previous chapters we have met products and performers in the Latin terminology of the sources. Thus we have encountered the *ioculator, mimus, scurra, histrio*, apparently terms used synonymously. From the semantic range of each of these terms and from the contexts in which they were used, it has sometimes been possible to associate people so named as involved in performance. From this it has been possible to deduce that this was also the case where the context did not allow such conclusions as long as it did not explicitly exclude the possibility.

We have also encountered terminology traditionally associated with products of literature, such as *carmen*, used with qualifying adjectives (*rusticus, vulgaris* and the like). This conveys the idea that one is not dealing with the product as normally understood. However, it is impossible to generalize.[35] Something comparable is found as regards *poeta. Poeta vulgaris* or *poeta secularis* (which I take to be synonymous), as attested from England in the mid-eighth century,[36] must surely be understood as being of a different kind than *poetae tout court*. In seventh-century Ireland we have encountered the *poeta optimus*, a term which, as material from the ninth century makes evident, attempts to convey in Latin a technical term in Irish, in this case *rígfile* or *ollam filed*.[37] It could further be shown that the term *file* at that time had a much wider semantic range than later when *poeta* would indeed become a suitable equivalent in Latin and 'poet' in English.

In other words, it is necessary to say something about the vernacular terminology concerning the personalities and the products of the oral culture. However, this is easier said than done—for the following reason: unless vernacular terms are Latinized to such an extent that the vernacular term can still be recognized, as happens occasionally, one encounters them only in vernacular literature, thus generally rather late, and the extent to which this literature reflects daily life and its oral culture cannot be fathomed.

There is a further possibility, namely the appearance of vernacular terms in early glossaries, which is of course invaluable evidence. However, terms appear in glossaries normally without a context, which is a very serious obstacle

---

35 See below on the *plebei psalmi*. Thus Rabanus Maurus, *De clericorum institutione* II, xlix writes: 'Carmina autem quaecunque in laudem Dei dicuntur, hymni vocantur'. PL 107, 362. (= Isidore of Seville, *De ecclesiasticis officiis* I, 6).
36 See above, pp. 147-9.
37 See chapter 9 at n. 108.

to a recovery of their semantic range.[38] A case in point are the *ioca turpia et obscena*. Each of these terms, taken out of time when it is attested, makes perfectly good sense, and the same can be said about them in combination. However, in this combination these terms are not attested in classical Latin nor in the Vulgate. As we have seen, the combination became a standard expression in the Latin vocabulary of the authors in the early Middle Ages.[39]

Generally, the situation is much less manageable. Take the case of the Old High German term *spilman*. It has the appearance of a calque on Latin *ioculator* in its medieval meaning. In Old High German, it is attested only once, and then not as a gloss on *ioculator* but on *istrio*.[40] This, incidentally, is a further confirmation that *ioculator* and *histrio* were used synonymously in the early Middle Ages. But we have no clue as to when *spilman* began to be used, which may well have been before *ioculator* had evolved its medieval meaning. One can assume that *spilman* was a standard term to denote the person named in the Latin sources by the Latin terminology for the people involved in performance. *Spilman* must have been widely used orally in the early medieval centuries. It is not attested otherwise because there was Latin terminology available for the authors writing in Latin, and there was no literature before the eleventh century when the German term became quite frequent in its Middle High German form *spileman*. With these considerations we have not yet touched upon the exact function of the *spilman* before the eleventh century. But we have elucidated further that the culture of the barbarians had its authentic vocabulary.

The singular attestation of OHG *spilman* has had the effect that this term is not normally discussed when the OHG terminology for 'poet' is investigated. On the other hand, the term *scof*, attested more often in OGH and Old English, is normally discussed with reference to these two languages.[41] However, it has to be taken into account that in Old English there are two other vernacular terms for 'poet' with no equivalent in OHG, and there is no obvious equivalent in Old English for *spilman*. So the differences have to be taken into account along with the parallels.

In OHG *scof* is attested, from the ninth century on, only in glosses, thus without context. It glosses Lat. *poeta*[42] and occurs as a compound in

38 Watkins, C., 'New parameters', 788.
39 See above, chapter 5.
40 Steinmeyer, Sievers, *Althochdeutsche Glossen* (= SS) III, 319, n. 1.
41 Wissmann, W., 'Skop', *Sitzungsberichte der deutschen Akademie der Wissenschaften zu Berlin, Klasse für Sprachen, Literatur und Kunst* 1954, Nr. 2; See, K. v., 'Skop und Skald. Zur Auffassung des Dichters bei den Germanen'; Werlich, E., 'Der westgermanische Scop', *Zeitschrift für deutsche Philologie* 86, 1967, 352-75; Hollowell, I., Scop and wodbora in Old English poetry', *Journal of English and Germanic Philology* 77, 1978, 317-29.
42 SS IV, 244.17, [Wissmann has 247.17] and cf. IV, 23.11 (*uates*).

terminology associated with Christianity: *salmscoph*;[43] but it occurs also in the context of verse, the nature of which is far from clear: 'plebeios psalmos, cantica rustica et inepta = ódo uuinileod, ódo scofleod'.[44] The unspecific semantic field of OHG *skop* is worth noting. To consider this term, as is normally done, in analogy to the Old English term, is thus possibly misleading. The compound *salmscoph* suggests that *skop* primarily denoted a versifyer of secular material. Since it is known from Tacitus that 'the Germans' had *carmina*, it is very likely that they also had specialists in charge of that material, known by specific terms (what these were is unfortunately not known).

On the basis of our previous considerations it is possibly misleading to refer to the *skop* as 'poet', a term with connotations not appropriate to the time here considered. It appears more appropriate to regard him as an expert in charge of oral tradition, which, as we have seen, was largely executed in verse. There is nothing in the vernacular German sources to justify the term 'court poet' in analogy to the English material. Indeed we have seen indications, not more, in the Latin sources from the ninth century, that performers of the oral culture may have held a permanent position in the entourage of the ruler.[45] Are *scof* and *spilman* then synonyms or terms for separate institutions? On the basis of the German material this cannot be decided; the contemporary Latin terminology would suggest synonyms; the vernacular terminology from England as well (as the Celtic countries) points in the direction of different professions.

In Old English poetry the *scop* figures mainly among the *comitatus* in the entourage of the king.[46] The term occurs also, in translations of Latin works, in association with men of literature from antiquity.[47] Thus the *scop* figures here both as 'singer' and as 'poet'. The Old English language has, in addition, the term *gléoman*, 'man of joy' for the poet.[48] If this is taken as meaning something comparable to the jongleur, we recall from our Latin material that an essential task of the performers was the stimulation of pleasure;[49] there is no justification to consider the *gléoman* as 'a lower-class scop'.[50] There is further in Old English the term *wodbora*, which has a semantic field similar

43 SS II, 346.53.
44 SS II, 83.10; 85.32; 86.42; 95.73; 100.59; 113.28; 140.42; IV, 323.2. and see below (*at liod*).
45 See chapter 6.
46 Wissmann, 3-9. See also Opland, J., 'Beowulf on the poet', *Mediaeval Studies* 38, 1976, 442-67.
47 Wissmann, 11.
48 Cf. also the Old English poetical term *gleóbeám* lit. 'beam of joy' for harp.
49 See chapters 1 and 2.
50 So Wissmann, 9. On the subject of joy in this context see also Ostheeren, K., *Studien zum Begriff der "Freude" in altenglischen Texten*, Heidelberg 1964, an exceptionally informative study. Cf. also Lindheim, B. v., 'OE "dream" and its subsequent development', *Review of English Studies* 25, 1949, 193-209.

to the other two without being a synonym.[51] The element *wod-* should be taken as related to IE **vat-* with the connotations of 'inspired'. This suggests that the *wodbora* is comparable to Latin *vates* and the Old Irish *fáith*.[52] It is furthermore worth noting that the *wodbora* was not among the *comitatus* but is found as travelling the world.[53] 'The *wodbora* is dealing with the core of existence, serving as mediator between what to his contemporaries would be the mysterious and powerful forces of nature on the one hand, and the mind of man on the other. He has knowledge not even hinted at for the *scop*.'[54] There are furthermore compounds involving the element *wod-*, such as *wothgifu*, 'gift of voice, poetry', *wodcraeft*, 'poetry'.[55]

There is no reason to assume that the social function of verse was less complex among the Germans than among the English even though this is not evident from the available terminology concerning the men of versecraft. The Old High German *liod*, attested in the Latinized form twice as early as the sixth century yet unattested for two centuries thereafter, certainly going back much further, carried the connotation of 'praise-song' in an original manner and retained this connotation.[56] It is itself a sub-category of OHG *sang*, 'song'.[57] Several sub-categories of *liod* are known also in Latinized guise.[58] In this technical meaning as 'praise-song' it remained current into the eleventh century, apparently predominantly, if not exclusively, used for secular song.[59] A great variety of genre names in vernacular literature is known from early medieval Ireland. We have seen that there is good reason to believe that part

51 On this see Hollowell, 323.
52 See chapter 9, pp. 200f.
53 See Hollowell, 325 and the reference to the poem "The order of the world" quoted there, esp. line 9.
54 Hollowell, 323.
55 These terms occur in an ecclesiastical context, see See, 3.
56 See Schwarz, H., 'Ahd. liod und sein sprachliches Feld', *Beiträge zur Geschichte der deutschen Sprache und Literatur* 75, 1953, 321-65, esp. 336, 348, 354.
57 Ibid., 333, 342.
58 See the *winileodos* in the capitulary 23.19 of 789, MGH Capit. I, 63. The precise meaning of this term is not clear, see the summary by Smet, G. de, 'Die winileod in Karls Edikt von 789', in: *Studien zur deutschen Literatur und Sprache des Mittelalters* (FS Hugo Moser), Berlin 1974, 1-7. Cf. also 'skifliod', 'skofliod', 'todliod', 'gartliod', 'huorliod' attested in the glosses, Schwarz, passim. *uuinileod*, explaining *plebeii psalmi* in this manner would refer to song in church apart from authorized psalms or hymns, but nevertheless of a Christian kind. It is found in the canons of the Council of Laodicea (s. IV/2) c. LIX, to be taken in conjunction with c. XV, Mansi 2, 578, 582. For a ninth-century attestation see Agobard of Lyon, *Liber de divina psalmodia*, PL 104, 327. For a lucid discussion see Kelle, J., 'Die Bestimmungen im Kanon 19 des Legationsedictum von 789', SBB Wien, Phil.-hist. Kl. 161, 1908, 9. Abh., esp. 6-9; id., 'Chori secularium—cantica puellarum', SBB Wien, Phil.-hist. Kl. 161, 1908, 2. Abh.
59 Schwarz, 331, points out that Notker Labeo in his translations from Latin does not once translate *carmen* as *liod*.

at least of the oral culture was the product of high professionalism, a phenomenon which in turn would have encouraged the use of specialised terminology. This is a dimension of the demand for barbarian culture to be taken on its own terms.[60]

We shall now examine two instances in which the existing vernacular early medieval literature can be shown to illuminate the existing oral tradition, different in kind and thus shedding different light on the situation; they were chosen also because they allow statements beyond mere guesswork about the influence of oral culture on vernacular literature.

BIBLE EPIC: THE *HELIAND*

The first case is that of the versification in the vernacular of parts of the bible, attested in Germany as well as in England for the early ninth century. The case is best documented for the Old Saxon Bible versification *Heliand* ('the Saviour'). There is a Latin prose preface to this work, anonymous and of unknown date, which, however, fits quite well the subject of the ensuing work.

According to the preface, it was the emperor Louis who initiated this versification in order to grant access to the Word of God to those people who knew no Latin: 'ut cunctus populus suae ditioni subditus, Theudisca loquens lingua, eiusdem divinae lectionis nihilominus notionem acceperit'.[61] It is not certain which Louis is meant here: the population of the empire of Louis the Pious was more than just German-speaking while the East Frankish son of Louis the Pious, Louis 'the German', did have a German-speaking subject population but was never emperor.

We have discussed earlier that Louis chose for this task a Saxon whose expertise in the field of vernacular poetry was well known and appreciated.[62] This is a reference to a Saxon skilled in wordcraft who, by implication, would have acquired his reputation as a professional in secular poetry. The choice of such a man by or on behalf of the ruler is further evidence that this kind of activity was familiar in his circles and was appreciated. We have had other, similar evidence independently pointing in the same direction.

The *Heliand* is the oldest known biblical verse epic in the Germanic vernacular, in this case in Old Saxon. Its poetic qualities are surely a reflection of the high standard of verse commonly in use among the continental Saxons.[63]

---

60   See chapter 4.
61   *Heliand und Genesis*, Behaghel, O, ed., 9th ed. rev. by Taeger, B., Tübingen 1984, 1.
62   See p. 143.
63   Cf. Hofmann, D., 'Die altsächsische Bibelepik zwischen Gedächtniskultur und Schriftkultur', *Settimane di Studio . . . Spoleto* 32, 1986, 453-83, at 466. The concept of 'Gedächtniskultur' which he took from Gaechter, P., 'Die Gedächtniskultur in Irland', *Innsbrucker Beiträge zur Sprachwissenschaft*, II, Innsbruck 1970, is highly misleading.

The *Heliand* is a suitable example how language and ethics are closely intertwined. We have stressed repeatedly that Christian ethics and barbarian culture were in many respects incompatible. Transferring the Christian message into the language which the lay audience would understand was a great challenge. The author of the Latin preface implies that the task had been fulfilled adequately.

Many scholars have pointed out that the poet was familiar with the theological legacy of the Carolingian age which he applied in his work. He 'aims to present Christ's life with sensitivity to their doctrinal significance ... (yet) the poet draws on the technique, imagery and values of Germanic poetry.'[64] Thus Christ and his disciples are described in terms of the lord and his warband. More significant even is the loving detail with which feasts are described, occasions, of course, which demonstrate the close relationship betwen the lord and the *comitatus*. There was nothing in the Bible to justify the positive description of inebriation on these occasions. Thus in the Latin Bible commentary of Rabanus Maurus, for example, a contemporary of the *Heliand* poet, Herod's feast, leading to the beheading of John the Baptist, is, appropriately, presented as a manifestation of *luxuria*,[65] a term with decidedly negative connotations in Christian teaching. By contrast, in the *Heliand*, Herod himself is depicted as 'ring-giving, generous to his retainers, wishing to please the people'.[66]

Thus barbarian ethics are articulated in familiar terms, and they are not castigated where it would have been justifiable due to the material which the poet wished to make known. In this respect the *Heliand* is a good example of a 'localizing' of the Christian message.[67] Since the ethos of the Bible is not followed in some significant respects, this can be taken as an indication of the strength of the barbarian ethos which the poet elaborated.[68] This conclusion seems to be unavoidable even when it is not liked by some scholars.[69]

---

64 Magennis, H., 'The treatment of feasting in the *Heliand*', *Neophilologus* 69, 1985, 126-33, at 126.
65 *Commentarium in Mattaeum* V, PL 107, 960: 'luxuriando celebrare, in luxuria conviviorum' (? mistake for 'convivorum').
66 Magennis 130, referring to *Heliand* 2731-44. For some other aspects of barbarian ethics in the *Heliand* see Schücking, L. L., 'Heldenstolz und Würde im Angelsächsischen', *Sächsische Akademie der Wissenschaften, Phil.-Hist. Klasse* 42, 5, 1933, esp. 3 and 25.
67 For this concept see chapter 2, n. 12.
68 For the opposite attitude in Anglo-Saxon poetry see Hume, K., 'The concept of the hall in Old English poetry', *Anglo-Saxon England* 3, 1974, 63-74.
69 Haubrichs, *Anfänge*, 26: 'Darin drückt sich kaum eine "Germanisierung" der Frömmigkeit aus, wie man lange meinte, es handelt sich vielmehr um das Ergreifen der biblischen Vorzeitwelt in den Denkformen einer archaischen Gesellschaft.'

SECULAR EPIC AND ORAL TRADITION: THE *NIBELUNGENLIED*

The Middle High German *Nibelungenlied* (NL) is one of the famous vernacular verse narratives from the central Middle Ages. Some of its main scenes have become known worldwide in Richard Wagner's opera cycle 'Der Ring der Nibelungen'. The NL, as a piece of literature, has to be placed into the context of other medieval vernacular literature from the eleventh, twelfth and thirteenth centuries, which is not the task of the present study. Rather, it receives consideration here because it shows, more clearly than many other works of literature from that time, a dependence on oral tradition. It has been rightly called 'a poem with an exclusively oral past'.[70] It is this oral past which is our concern.

The NL clearly is a piece of literature in the traditional sense of this term, even though it has features that are special and can be linked to its oral past. A work of a very high standard, of which no author is known, it is available in three different, though related versions. This raises the question of whether it had one author or more than one. Some scholars believe that it was patronized by Wolfger of Erla, bishop of Passau; in any case, an origin in the Bavarian-Austrian border area is virtually unanimously assumed today, as well as a date around 1200 for its composition.

The NL is known, in its entirety, by the Middle High German term *liet*.[71] It is composed in stanzas of four lines each. Altogether, it consists of 39 episodes called 'aventiures'. The tale can be roughly divided into two parts. Aventiures 1-19, the first part, take place in the kingdom of the Burgundians centred on Worms on the Rhine. It relates the stories of some principal figures, primarily king Gunter (less so his brothers Gernot and Giselhere) and their sister Kriemhild. These are joined later by Brunhild and Siegfried, who in the course of time marry Gunter and Kriemhild. The first part culminates in the murder of Siegfried with the connivance of Gunter. The second part, aventiures 20-39, sees Kriemhild married to Etzel, king of the Huns. On her invitation her Burgundian relatives come on a visit. Kriemhild revenges the slaying of Siegfried by bringing about the death of her Burgundian relatives and their entourage. The tale ends with the slaying of Kriemhild by Dietrich.

Some of the main characters in the NL are based on historically attested personalities. Thus Gunter can be associated with the Burgundian king

---

70 Curschmann, M., 'The concept of the oral formula as an impediment to our understanding of medieval oral poetry', *Medievalia et Humanistica* NS 8, 1977, 63-76, at 66. This and other publications by Michael Curschmann have helped me greatly to come to a better appreciation of the highly complex co-existence of oral and written culture in the high Middle Ages in general and the NL in particular.

71 This is attested only at the end of version C, see Curschmann, M., ' "Dichter alter maere". Zur Prologstrophe des Nibelungenliedes im Spannungsfeld von mündlicher Erzähltradition und laikaler Schriftkultur', in Hahn, G., Ragotzky, H., ed., *Grundlagen des Verstehens mittelalterlicher Literatur*, Stuttgart 1992, 55-71, at 63.

Gundahar who was killed in the course of the destruction of the 'first Burgundian kingdom' in 436, where the main enemies of the Burgundians were the Romans under Aetius aided by the Huns. Likewise, Etzel of the NL is easily associated with the Hunnish king Attila, a towering figure on the Western European scene before his death in 453. Dietrich, in the NL an exile at the court of Attila, is associated with the Ostrogothic king Theodoric.[72]

There is, thus, a vaguely historical dimension to the NL even though not all main characters can be as easily associated with identifiable personalities. However, Theodoric was not a contemporary of either Gunter or Attila, but then the NL does not claim to be 'historical'. Its unhistoricity points to a different function of this account.

It is not our task to analyze the NL as a piece of literature the oral past of which has been very widely discussed. We have a different aim: to show, in a limited way, that the NL, in the historical information it contains, presupposes a functioning oral tradition over several centuries. Furthermore, there are occasionally signs in the Latin sources before 1200 which vaguely suggest familiarity with the Nibelungen material for which there are no other historical sources.

We have seen in a previous chapter that the history of the Burgundians in the fifth century is very poorly attested. On the basis of contemporary sources now available, it is not possible to locate the 'first' Burgundian kingdom in the Worms area. Archaeological finds on the other hand would not exclude such a placement.

It is most remarkable, furthermore, that the epic contains information for which no written sources are now known but which can be shown to have a historical foundation. One can point here to the basically amicable relations between the Burgundians and the Huns that are, in the NL, a precondition for the marriage of Kriemhild and Etzel. A historical basis of such a relationship has been highlighted by archaeology. The Huns had the fashion of deforming the skulls of their infants artificially ("Turmschädel"); this fashion is attested among several Western European peoples in the fifth century, particularly the Burgundians. This is evidence of a substantial cultural impact by the Huns on the Burgundians.[73]

The Burgundian law code of c.500, *Lex Gundobada*, lists four of Gundobad's predecessors as Burgundian kings: 'Gibicam', 'Gundomarem', 'Gislahar-

---

[72] Of course the literature on the NL is vast. Quite a good summary of the historical background is provided by Nagel, B., *Das Nibelungenlied. Stoff—Form—Ethos*, 2nd ed., Frankfurt 1970, esp. 14-33: however, we have shown that the accounts of the fifth and sixth centuries respectively can be evaluated somewhat differently.

[73] J. Werner, 'Beiträge', 1956; Stroheker, K. F., 'Studien zu den historisch-geographischen Grundlagen der Nibelungendichtung', *Deutsche Vierteljahrsschrift für Literaturwissenschaft und Geistesgeschichte* 32, 1958, 216-40.

ium', 'Gundaharium'.[74] Thus Giselhere and Gunter were indeed Burgundian kings in the fifth century, although this source does not indicate (but does not exclude either) that they were brothers.

The earliest traces of what appears to be an oral tradition concerning the Burgundians and the Huns can be made out in the eighth century, thus a good three centuries after the events and in this indicating a functioning tradition.

In his *Historia Romana* Paul the Deacon, working in the last quarter of the eighth century, mentions in passing that Attila killed king Gunter: 'Attila ... Gundicarium Burgundionum regem sibi occurrentem protrivit.'[75] We have already referred to the profound interest of Charlemagne in Theodoric, whom he must have considered as an exemplary king.[76] Likewise, his interest in the *barbara et antiquissima carmina* is recorded by Einhart. The *Hildebrandslied*, first written *c*.800, similarly attests familiarity with material from the circle around Theodoric. There, the Ostrogothic king was portrayed as an exile from his kingdom for many years, as he also appears in the NL. It is unlikely that this aspect of Theodoric would have impressed Charlemagne to the extent he apparently did. One must surely assume that other traditions about Theodoric were current in the Frankish kingdom at that time.

The other bulk of evidence indicating an oral tradition about the Burgundians in the eighth century is seen in the popularity of the names attested then which also occurred in the NL. There is especially the name Nibelung itself. In the NL, it makes a sudden appearance towards the end of the first part as an alternative name of 'Burgundians', perhaps in the function of an ethnic, more likely however as a dynastic name. A prominent attestation as a personal name can be taken from the mid-eighth century: a cousin of Pippin, usurper-king of the Franks, was called Nibelung; his father's name was Childebrand, and both were behind the writing of a very important historical work in favour of the Arnulfings:

> Usque nunc inluster vir Childebrandus comes, avunculus praedicto rege Pippino, hanc historiam vel gesta Francorum diligentissime scribere procuravit. Abhinc ab illustre viro Nibelungo, filium ipsius Childebrando, itemque comite, succedat auctoritas.[77]

In the ninth century, Nibelung was the name of six successive counts of Burgundy.[78] More names associated with the Nibelung tradition have been

74 MGH LL I, II, 1, 43.
75 MGH SS in us. schol. 49, 112.
76 See chapter 6, p. 135.
77 *Chronicarum quae dicuntur Fredegarii scholastici continuationes* c. 34, MGH SS rer. Merov. II, 182.
78 Cf. Rosenfeld, H., 'Die Namen Nibelung, Nibelungen und die Burgunder', *Blätter für oberdeutsche Namenforschung* 9, 1968, 16-21.

traced in charters particularly from Bavaria in the eighth and ninth centuries. While this can indeed be interpreted as reflecting the popularity of a Nibelung tradition at certain times and in certain regions, it can hardly be considered, as is normally done, as a specifically aristocratic interest in this tradition,[79] for it has to be kept in mind that other social groups that might have carried such names are under-represented in this type of material.[80]

It must be stressed that this kind of evidence can be adduced only in the knowledge that there existed an oral tradition relating to the leading figures from the time of the transformation of the Roman world. Oral tradition has to be continuous, and one is here merely confronted with a temporary surfacing of traces of such a tradition in the sources. Thus the alleged importance of the Carolingians for the Nibelungen tradition is merely an optical illusion.

The next remarkable reference to such a tradition comes from the mid-eleventh century. A canon of the cathedral of Bamberg, Meinhard, in a letter to an unnamed colleague, complained about the cultural preferences of his bishop Gunter: 'Numquam ille Augustinum, numquam ille Gregorium recolit, semper ille Attalam, semper amalungum et cetera genus portare tractat.'[81] We have here yet another example of the secular tradition being considered with favour in high clerical circles. Surely the bishop would have shared his taste with his *familia* and friends. But there is more to this sentence. The writer of these lines, a cleric himself, mentions the subject in such a way that one must conclude that he and his addressee were likewise familiar with the material. Meinrad's 'et cetera genus' is very telling even though one would wish that he had been more specific. Gunter (bishop of Bamberg 1057-65) is known otherwise also as a patron of learning and vernacular Christian poetry.[82]

A further important attestation comes from the first half of the twelfth century, also from Bamberg, as it happens. The chronicler Frutolf of Michelsberg, in his world chronicle, when writing about the events in the fourth, fifth and sixth centuries, drew explicitly on the Gothic history of

79 So Störmer, W., 'Nibelungentradition als Hausüberlieferung in frühmittelalterlichen Adelsfamilien? Beobachtungen zu Nibelungennamen vornehmlich in Bayern', in Knapp, F. P., ed., *Nibelungenlied und Klage. Sage und Geschichte, Struktur und Gattung* (= Passauer Nibelungengespräche 1985), Heidelberg 1987, 1-19.
80 Cf. Richter, *Oral tradition*, ch. 5. See also Wenskus, R., 'Wie die Nibelungenüberlieferung nach Bayern kam', *Zeitschrift für Bayerische Landesgeschichte* 36, 1973, 393-449.
81 MGH, *Briefsammlungen der Zeit Heinrichs* IV, no. 73, p. 121.
82 *Vita Altmanni episcopi Pataviensis*, MGH SS 12, 230: 'Guntherus Babinbergensis episcopus, vir tam corporis elegantia quam animi sapientia conspicuus; in cuius comitatu multi nominati viri et clerici et laici, tam de Orientali Francia quam de Bawaria fuerunt. Inter quos praecipui duo canonici extiterunt; videlicet Ezzo scolasticus, vir omni sapientia et eloquentia praeditus, qui in eodem itinere cantilenam de miraculis Christi patria lingua nobiliter composuit; et Counradus, omni scientia et facundia ornatus.' See also Ploss, E., 'Bamberg und die deutsche Literatur des 11. und 12. Jahrhunderts', *Jahrbuch für fränkische Landesforschung* 19, 1959, 275-302.

Jordanes. In this context, he referred to contemporary oral accounts concerning that part of the past: 'quod non solum vulgari fabulatione et cantilenarum modulatione usitatur, verum etiam in quibusdam cronicis adnotatur'.[83] One notes here a distinction between oral tradition in prose and verse. Further on the author suggested that the Gothic kings Ermanaric and Theodoric were not contemporaries of Attila; thus either the oral tradition was mistaken ('aut vulgaris opinio fallitur et fallit') or there must have been other (unknown) kings with those names contemporary with Attila. It is important to note that Frutolf attests in this passage the co-existence of oral and written kinds of history. It should not be read, as is customarily done, to indicate that he regarded written history as superior. If one regards his genre terms 'vulgaris fabulatio et cantilenarum modulatio' as technical terms for vernacular prose and verse without a pejorative association, the passage then indicates that at that time oral tradition as history was taken seriously, even by professional historians writing in Latin.[84]

Another aspect of the Nibelungen material can be found in an account of the Danish historian Saxo Grammmaticus concerning the fate of Cnut, duke of Schleswig (d. 1131) who was the object of the Danish King Magnus's intrigues. A Saxon jongleur ('genere Saxonem, arte cantorem')[85] who held a delicate position of intermediary between the two, is said to have performed a very beautiful song concerning the most infamous treachery of Kriemhild towards her brothers: 'speciosissimi carminis contextu notissimam Grimildae erga fratres perfidiam de industria memorare adorsus'.[86] This performance was supposed to act as an indirect warning to the duke, which in turn would only have made sense if the audience was familiar with the gist of the story which, on this occasion, was simply recalled.

There is, finally, a further attestation of existing oral traditions of this material in the late twelfth century. It is found, without a context, in the chronicle of Deutz. Reference here is made likewise to the Gothic kings Ermanaric and Theodoric and the Hun Attila 'whose deeds and praises are recited in accounts of the forefathers throughout the world': 'quorum actus

---

83 MGH SS 6, 130.
84 This view is not held by Erdmann, K., 'Fabulae curiales. Neues zum Spielmannsgesang und zum Ezzo-Liede', *Zeitschrift für deutsches Altertum und deutsche Literatur* 73, 1936, 87-98.
85 As far as I am aware, Saxo's use of *cantor* for jongleurs is exceptional; see above, p. 171. This term otherwise generally applies certainly by this time to men active in the divine service. See Reimer, E., 'Musicus und Cantor. Zur Sozialgeschichte eines musikalischen Lehrstücks', *Archiv für Musikwissenschaft* 35, 1978, 1-32.
86 *Saxonis Gesta Danorum*, Olrik, J., Raeder, H., ed., 1931, XIV, VI, 7, p. 355. Another *Cantor Germanicus* who entertained Danish court after a banquet, is attested: ibid. XIV, XVIII, p. 404.

vel preconia veterum narrationibus tragicorumque decantationibus toto orbe declamantur'.[87]

'Toto orbe' is a telling expression. It articulates a phenomenon that had already earlier become apparent: the traditions associated with the Nibelungen material, with the fall of the Burgundians, was not or no longer the property of a particular ethnic group (in this case the Burgundians being the most likely candidates), but had been taken over more widely. The available evidence does not allow to trace how or when this diffusion happened, let alone why; one can only state the fact. It can furthermore be added that in one kind of tradition the person of Theodoric as an exile at the Hunnish court, as he figures in the NL, appears in this manner already four hundred years earlier.

With reference to early Germanic epic it has been observed that much of it is of a kind that presupposes knowledge not given in the poetry.[88] This means, in other words, that the stories of the heroic poetry were embedded in a larger body of information which the composer of the poetry could take for granted among the audience. Much the same can be said about the material from the Celtic countries. In this respect the scholar who has a grasp of the whole corpus of literature based on oral tradition has to keep in mind that this cannot be assumed for the medieval audience. Thus in one respect he has an advantage over the medieval public where in other respects his position is less favourable.

There have been extended debates as to the form in which the material was transmitted orally before it found its way into writing. Answers must be of necessity approximations at best. As to the NL, however, it is most important that the stanza form with end rhyme in which it is cast did not develop before the mid-twelfth century, a change in poetic customs which has rightly been called momentous.[89] This is the clearest sign that can be imagined that the oral transmission did not continuously take the same form. We have seen that the terms which are used in the Latin sources for the oral culture point to transmission in verse as well as to performance in song. This is the most frequent kind of information conveyed. It has been rightly stressed over the past generation that in this field the Parry-Lord research has been of very great importance. It is no longer necessary, when meeting terms like *carmen*

---

87 *Archiv für die Geschichte des Niederrheins* 5, Düsseldorf 1866, 322. I owe this reference to Curschmann, M., 'Zur Wechselwirkung von Literatur und Sage. Das "Buch von Kriemhild" und Dietrich von Bern', *Beiträge zur Geschichte der deutschen Sprache und Literatur* 111, 1989, 380-410, 384, n. 11.

88 See Kuhn, Hans, 'Heldensage vor und außerhalb der Dichtung', in Schneider, H., ed., *Edda, Skalden, Saga* (FS Felix Genzmer), Heidelberg 1952, 262-78, at 268. This has been taken up in turn by Haymes, E.R., 'Oral poetry and the Germanic Heldenlied', *Rice University Studies* 62, 1976, 47-54.

89 Curschmann, M., ' "Dichter alter maere", 61: 'dramatische Veränderungen der dichterischen Diktion'.

or *cantilena* being performed, to think of compositions with fixed texts which were transmitted through memorisation (German: *Liedtheorie*). When one opens oneself to the potentials of oral culture, then the model Parry-Lord is perfectly acceptable.[90] However, it is important in this respect to stress the term 'model': it is not claimed that the situation in the early medieval West is comparable to that of Yugoslavia in the first half of the twentieth century. However, this does not exclude the possibility to learn from the one about potentials for the other.

Besides transmission in verse one should not exclude the possibility of oral tradition also being handed on in prose although verse was a better medium for memorable formulation. It may be an accident of the medieval material, but I have found the term *fabulae* being used increasingly in the eleventh and twelfth centuries, mainly with negative connotations. These may well refer to prose accounts or tales which the historians who mentioned them disapproved of. At least this should be kept in mind as a possibility.

In this way the epic literature can be taken as an additional indication of oral culture that preceded this literature. The opening stanza of the Nibelungenlied makes just this point:

> Uns ist in alten maeren wunders vil geseit
> von helden lobebaeren von grôzer arebeit
> von frôuden, hôchgezîten von weinen und von klagen
> von kuener recken strîten muget ir nu wunder hoeren sagen.

We have seen that this statement expressed the situation most poignantly.[91]

It should be apparent now, however, why I have chosen the vernacular literature only at the end and only as an illustration. For far too long scholars of medieval vernacular literature have taken the oral past for granted and largely left it at that. This made the present study a desideratum. One of its conclusions is that the oral tradition has dimensions well beyond the verbal plane.

There is lastly the question whether one should distinguish an aristocratic oral culture from one among the lower echelons of society. The sources present prominently the higher echelons throughout so that there is the widespread view that one is confronted with a culture of a specific class rather than a general one. Against this it may be stated that a 'culture of the lower classes' is hardly ever referred to. We have seen also that the terms *rusticus* and *vulgaris*, which might equally be taken as referring to the common people, are often used in the sense of 'vernacular' rather than 'vulgar' or 'boorish', as indeed

90 See Bäuml, F.H., Ward, D.J., 'Zur mündlichen Überlieferung des Nibelungenliedes', *Deutsche Vierteljahrsschrift für Literaturwissenschaft und Geistesgeschichte* 41, 1967, 351-90.
91 See the brilliant interpretation by Curschmann, ' "Dichter alter maere" '.

the term *barbarus*. Thus what the Latin sources imply is rather a distinction along the lines Latin-Christian and vernacular-not-Christian rather than aristocratic versus popular. Even here we have had many instances to show that such a distinction was wishful thinking on the past of zealous clerics rather than a reflection of how things were in life. Oral culture, as a primal mode of cultural expression and transmission, the origins of which lie far beyond the appearance of Christianity, had strong roots and bore, in the period here discussed, correspondingly strong fruit.

We have seen that in the early medieval centuries a strong oral culture was widespread in societies where alphabetic writing was available. For centuries virtually nothing of this oral culture found its way into writing on the continent as far as the evidence goes. This must not be taken as a sign of inferiority of this culture as it is often portrayed in the clerical accounts but rather as a sign of its vitality. Oral culture also survived the establishment of vernacular literature, including that literature with a strong oral past. To study this, and especially the complex and delicate symbiosis of oral and written culture, must remain in the first place the task of the scholars of medieval literature.[92]

---

92   For an exemplary study see Curschmann, 'Wechselwirkung'.

11

RESULTS

Our studies of the barbarian culture in the early Middle Ages have shown that there existed a kind of culture that was characterized by oral transmission. Since the oral element is essentially transitory, access to this culture is by definition indirect. We have at our disposal a relatively small corpus of information which, when properly decoded, yields a picture of oral culture in the early medieval West which is truly remarkable. This is the place to present some results and to suggest some desiderata.

Access to the oral culture is possible only through written sources; this implies that oral culture existed in those societies where written culture was present. One should go further and observe that oral culture persisted alongside written culture. It follows that written culture was not considered as superior by those societies, that oral culture instead continued as a viable means of cultural transmission. This is a message which greatly reduces the social significance of literate culture; we have seen other indications pointing in the same direction.

In modern society written culture is almost invariably considered as superior to oral culture, and it does indeed have inherent qualities that are, objectively speaking, superior to those of oral culture. The fact of the continued existence of oral culture in the early medieval West thus assumes a new dimension. If one takes into account how complex and costly it was to maintain, it must have been regarded as highly important.

We have seen, albeit from oblique and distorting perspectives, that oral culture was at all times cherished in the highest social circles—another indication of its entrenched position. However, it would be wrong to label it an aristocratic culture. In view of the fact that the upper echelons of society are over-represented in the available sources, the indications which we have noted that this culture extended beyond the highest circles of society must be taken as showing that this culture enjoyed wide popularity. Nevertheless, to call it 'popular' would be equally misleading. While in its value-orientation everything but 'Christian', the term 'lay culture' could also be misleading when taken to mean that clerics did not partake in it. We have seen, in many instances, that clerics of all ranks enjoyed this culture; apparently its critics were in a minority even though they are rather prominent in the sources. It is tempting to suggest that the oral culture was the dominant form of culture in the early medieval West, the primary factor in its formation—in which case it goes without saying that further research is urgently called for.

In order to function, oral culture requires continuity and allows no interruption. This makes it essentially different from any culture associated with writing. This factor offers distinct advantages to the researcher. For, once the features of oral culture are clear to us there is no need for a continuous attestation of its existence. An oral tradition attested at one particular time implies its previous existence and cultivation. Thus it is possible to posit an oral culture for seven centuries between the transformation of the Roman world and the composition of the *Nibelungenlied* (around 1200). Attestation of this particular oral tradition surfaced quite late, around the eighth century, but this is best explained by the limited use of writing in societies that cherished the oral culture.

A price has to be paid, literally and metaphorically, if oral culture is to survive. While one should not assume that it involved everyone to the same extent, it did need a broad base. As I see it, oral culture was an institution of cultural importance; it was not something on the margin of society. It is in this field that traditional views need to be drastically revised.

A socially respected, broadly-based oral culture would elicit competition between the various performers; this in turn would make for excellence and refinement of the forms in which the culture was cast. Continuous cultivation of oral tradition meant that much of the culture had a solid base among the recipients. Passive acquaintance was a precondition for appreciation. The repertoire of such passive acquaintance would increase over the years for every individual.[1]

There are enough indications from the barbarians in the early medieval West to maintain that 'poetry or at least verse was woven into the whole fabric of society, and that society could not exist without it, unless by changing its whole character.' This statement was made with regard to medieval Ireland;[2] it was further maintained that this was a feature which 'differentiated Irish from European society'.[3] On the basis of our investigation there is sufficient reason to suggest that this evaluation has to be qualified.[4]

---

1 The nearest analogy that comes to my mind is the passive repertoire of music, classical or popular, in modern Western society, where familiarity produces refinement in appreciation.
2 Carney, J., 'Society and the bardic poet', 239.
3 Ibid., 241: 'the bardic tradition was the most characteristically Irish phenomenon'.
4 Thus Havelock, E.A., *Preface to Plato*, stated about early Greek society: 'The whole memory of a people was poetised, and this exercised a constant control over the ways in which they expressed themselves', 134.

The assessment quoted here did not rest on a thorough discussion of the issue of oral culture and vernacular literature. It derived, however, from a deep familiarity with early Irish literature, much of which is in verse. To what extent can the situation in the Celtic countries be compared with that in the other societies? Is one faced with a difference in quantity of evidence or in the quality of the institutions that carried the culture? Would it not be appropriate to refer to the phenomenon of oral culture as 'barbarian' rather than either 'Celtic' or 'Germanic'? This is an extremely attractive result of our investigations.

We may extend the statement concerning the omnipresence of verse by maintaining that sung verse was woven into the whole fabric of society, and that this sung verse was a very prominent feature of the various societies in the early medieval West. A vital oral culture was the characteristic feature of all barbarian societies in the early medieval West. Its existence implies organization, social acceptance and thus relevance to each society concerned.

What makes Irish society in this respect special and exceptional is the extent to which the oral culture percolated at an early stage into writing. Indeed, Ireland offers the richest vernacular literature in the early medieval West. However, it is necessary to be clear as to how this relates to oral culture. This literature cannot be considered, as is frequently implied, as a direct manifestation of oral culture in Irish society; it is at best the secondary product of a primal oral culture. This means that also in Ireland the oral culture persisted side by side with the imported written culture which was initially completely geared to Christian material written in Latin. This is a good indication that writing was not considered as necessarily superior to orality as a form of transmission. There are parallels to this situation in ancient Greece as well as in Rome. But here also, one can and indeed must go further in one's search.

Thus the continental barbarian societies of the early medieval West can be viewed in analogy to Ireland, even though the attestation is much poorer. But even this poorer continental attestation must be accounted for. It can be taken as indicative that the oral culture was strong and well entrenched there. It can further be suggested that the rather modest corpus of vernacular works from Wales as compared to Ireland before 1100 may be indicative that the continuous oral culture there was sufficient to maintain cultural identity. Indeed, the whole issue of the relationship of vernacular literature and oral culture requires new investigation.

What makes a great difference between Ireland (and to a lesser extent Wales) and the other societies in the early medieval West is the fact that owing to the available early Irish literature one can approach aspects of the Irish oral culture on its own terms and in various ramifications; when the oral culture is expressed in Latin, which also happens, though rarely, the insufficiency of this language becomes evident and very notable. In this respect one can suggest that the case of Irish early medieval society provides a model on to which the continental barbarians can be fitted.[5]

Indirect access to oral culture by way of written information can be hazardous for various reasons. The Latin language of the majority of our continental sources is help and hindrance: it provides access to this culture even though it is impossible to do full justice to non-Latin phenomena in and through Latin. Also, the Latin terminology suggests a uniformity which may have had no equivalent in reality.

In our source material relating to the early medieval West, we were able to trace information about oral culture once we established that key terms had changed their meaning over time. While it is common knowledge that the early Latin writers relied generally on the authority of the late Church Fathers, it is one thing for them to have done so in matters of doctrine—and quite another to have done so in questions relating to the broader cultural context, since that context was a very different one in medieval times. It is startling to see with what apparent ease these medieval authors at times took over the pronouncements of church councils and church Fathers.[6] They must have considered these as relevant to their own times. This is one reason why Latin appears here as a great leveller. Nowhere is this as obvious and frustrating as in the field of music. The issue is epitomized by the very varying use of *cantare* as well as by the shunning of this term.

It is only apparently a contradiction to suggest that there were basic similarities in the oral culture of the various barbarian peoples. For each of these had its own language with its own terminology relating to the specific manifestation of oral culture. Thus Bede's *poeta vulgaris* surely obliterates a native technical term; indeed, *poeta* is used frequently as the term to denote the person involved in oral culture, including his function as performer, which is a far cry from the classical and indeed in the modern meaning of this term. This is therefore a prime illustration of the assertion that Latin must be considered a most ominous obstacle to access to barbarian culture. Comparable reservations must be made concerning the *carmina* or the *ioca turpia*. *Carmina* conveys fixed forms which may well not apply to all of the barbarian material. It is advisable therefore to think in more neutral terms such as verse or indeed song. For it has hitherto been overlooked that the *ioca* were in fact performed, and that the *carmina* like the *cantilenae* were sung or recited, uttered in a form

---

5 Richter, M., 'Die Symbiose von Christentum und archaischer Gesellschaft in Irland, 400-800', in Tristram, H.L.C., ed., *Studien zur Táin Bó Cuailgne*, Tübingen 1993, 158-72, esp. 170f, in response to McCone, *Pagan past*.
6 See e.g. Agobard of Lyon, *Lib. de corr. Antiphon.*, PL 104, esp. chs. XI-XV, 334-6, particularly XII where he follows Jerome (= PL 26, 561-62) on the question of singing which in the ninth century had found a firm place in divine service.

of speech recognizably different from that of everyday parlance. Thus the oral culture had three dimensions, as it were, words, sound and movement, and all of these can be posited even where only one or two of them are found in the sources. Indeed, this is one of the keys to our material. Once it is clear what an oral culture entails, even the most fleeting reference to it in the sources allows far-reaching conclusions. Due to the nature of the available sources, it is unreasonable to expect a full positive presentation of this culture in them, but this is not essential.

Thus there is good reason to argue that everywhere in the early medieval West the barbarian culture was vital and viable. Even as narrowly Christian a person as Bede deigned to concede to the products of oral culture the term *ars*. That so little about it is known from the available sources—though considerably more than has hitherto been assumed—is due to the fact that the sources on the continent are virtually exclusively in Latin. The paucity of these sources outside the Romania can in a way be considered as confirming that very position: there was little need for written culture, and even less so in a foreign language. A further barrier against a full appreciation of the early medieval oral culture was the treatment of the manifestations of this culture in terms of literature. In the modern understanding of literature, two of the three dimensions of oral culture are either totally absent or play only insignificant parts.

There were specific terms in the vernacular languages for the products of the oral culture as well as for the people professionally involved in them. One cannot be sure that all terms which were available are actually attested in the sources. The different appearance of the OHG *scof* and the Anglo-Saxon *scop* is a case in point. One gets the impression that the vernacular languages are very inadequately represented in the sources where Latin is the predominant medium of written culture. The singular attestation in OHG material of the term *spîlman*[7] is another example. It gives rise to important questions which cannot be answered satisfactorily, particularly the time when it originated. Yet the one attestation permits the conclusion that this calque on *ioculator* was then current; in a similar manner, the singular attestation of *wordcraeft* in Old English is direct evidence of the great respect brought to the native oral culture. Furthermore, such fleeting attestation of terms is not a characteristic of the vernacular languages alone. The lack of attestation for three centuries of the term *musica artificialis* is a reminder that Latin occasionally does not fare much better. Our available written sources thus have to be used more dynamically than is normally done.

We have been able to clarify several instances of semantic changes in individual terminology, a very difficult task on the basis of the material that

7   See the section on *jongleur* in chapter 5.

is available; these changes in language are in turn manifestations of changes in the relationship between society and the language referring to it.

The recognition of oral culture as a feature of central importance in the barbarian societies in the early medieval West has profound repercussions for the appreciation of the period generally. It helps to explain the rather hesitant expansion of writing into the areas of the non-Latin languages. These were cultivated orally, intensely so as one now can state, and there was little motivation as yet to transpose them into the milieu of writing. In this respect Ireland is an exceptional case in that the native language of learning was early and widely used in writing. We have seen that the rich corpus of vernacular writing in Ireland is at most a reflex of a vibrant oral culture there, certainly not a direct manifestation of it.

The other effect of the central importance of oral culture is a re-evaluation of the written sources in the early medieval West. The more the oral culture is seen as socially highly relevant, the more will the written sources emerge as in no respect representative of the early medieval societies.[8] To assign the written sources of these centuries their appropriate place in their respective societies is a task that now lies ahead. The reduction of output of written material after the end of the Roman Empire in the West must be seen as evidence that the oral transmission of culture was of a quality which allowed the barbarian societies to forego writing almost completely even when it was available in their midst attached to the institutions of Christianity.

The written sources provide information which will lead to different results than those hitherto obtained. In this respect, it will be easier to evaluate the Latin of the sources in the barbarian societies. To many people in the early Middle Ages the Latin language of these sources presented a linguistic barrier which the modern historian has to take into account. In the course of our investigation we have noticed that much remains to be discovered in these Latin sources—that many apparently simple and unproblematical terms are more complex than hitherto perceived.[9]

There is the further issue of the performance of oral culture and the vocalization of the written material. We have seen indications that both kinds of verbal performance took comparable forms. Writing as a method of cultural storage is of rather recent date; oral transmission by contrast goes back into the untraceable past, but it must have been organized and sophisticated by the

---

8   See especially chapter 6. A good example is the case of Alcuin. He has left 310 letters, roughly a quarter of all the letters from the period. Yet his determined efforts to suppress oral culture had only little effect.
9   *Memoriae mandare/ commendare* in the sense of 'writing' rather than memorizing, attested in Einhart and Otfrid, suggests this to have been an agreed language use then; it is of course a common expression in classical Latin.

time that writing came. One can suggest now that the vocalization of the written material took place in forms and with features characteristic of oral performance, in special language registers which had been developed for oral performances. The extent to which music, singing or chanting, was involved in either of these kinds of vocalization remains ultimately unclear.

It has also emerged that music held a very important place in barbarian societies from pre-historic times onwards. The field of music in the secular sphere in the early medieval West is as yet unexplored. However, instrumental music in association with oral culture, with the performance of verse, is attested in the Latin sources from the earliest times onwards. Modern musicologists have so far failed to come up with an exact description of how song and instrumental music combined. The musical dimension of a performance often appears as more than just the strumming of the occasional chord. It is true that we have no notation for this material, nor have we the texts to which that music sounded—but then all the evidence of oral culture, not just its musical dimension, is accessible at second hand only and is nevertheless a viable subject of study. It is desirable to have experts in music look at this secondary information. What is clear even at this stage is that the close interrelation between verse and singing in the oral culture placed this form of communication on a higher level than everyday communication, even where basically the same language was used for both forms of communication.

There are firm indications that music in the early medieval centuries had also an oral dimension as it were; this is suggested by the fact that writing music developed fairly late and then initially not in a comprehensive way but apparently as a prop to memory. An enduring and deep-rooted tradition of music as well as singing had long provided ways of transmission and cultivation outside the written sphere.

The musical dimension confirms the tremendous strength of the oral culture of the barbarians. Nothing shows this more clearly than the fact that in the course of the early Middle Ages music, in the form of singing (and gradually even in the form of instrumental music) found acceptance in the Church; this should not have been the case, or only within exceedingly narrow limits, according to the teaching of the Church Fathers. Music was associated with physical pleasure[10] and as such was suspect to rigorous Christians. It is important to learn that thus music was appreciated for its own sake, not just in the service of conveying verbal information in memorable form. Rigorous Christians found themselves out of tune with the demands, expectations and value systems supported by the overwhelming majority of people, including ecclesiastical officials in utterly respectable positions. As regards song and

---

10   This was established also for the Homeric material: see Havelock, *Preface to Plato*, esp. 152, 157f.

music, Christianity in the early medieval West was more 'localized'[11] than has hitherto been granted or even perceived. This would mean that very important aspects of the barbarian culture remained formative in the centuries of the transformation of the Roman world.

Generally speaking, the availability of writing did not destroy or even marginalize oral culture. Writing was throughout the early medieval centuries the domain of a small circle of specialists for rather narrowly circumscribed purposes, and this situation was in fact facilitated by the existence of an entrenched oral culture which catered adequately for important social needs.

When dealing with the sources which inform us about oral culture, one gets indications, in more ways than one, that this was a highly ritualized form of socialization. Familiarity with it through frequent performance resulted in social cohesion and confidence in values. Thus oral culture formed part of a more wide-reaching ritualization of society. This is extremely difficult to recover from narrative or normative historical sources. We have encountered some aspects of the further reaching socialization in the form of feasts and in communal inebriation. In this domain, the material culture can contribute substantially to our perception[12] which, on the basis of the written sources, remains rather weak. Medieval literature can shed further light on the matter.[13] even though the relationship of literature to life is an extremely complex and delicate field. However, what becomes increasingly clear is that the historian who disregards literary material will voluntarily forego important avenues of information, while the scholar specialized in medieval literature will likewise miss a great deal when disregarding the social context of literature. More interdisciplinary work is called for.

Our investigation was confined to the first half of the Middle Ages. The oral culture was investigated with tools which historians normally employ. The available sources, all of them in print, most of them for a century or more, were investigated concerning a specific issue. That this topic, oral culture, appears in the sources frequently in a negative light, does not imply that it was considered in this way by most contemporaries. However, an essential task preceding this investigation was the fathoming of problems and possibilities of oral culture. This was done with the help of modern anthropological research. Once it was clear what oral culture can imply, then manifestations of it could be explored in the traditional sources. Although there are more references in the sources to oral culture than has been generally maintained, it has to be granted that the overall corpus of material discussed here remains

11 For this term see chapter 3 at n. 12.
12 Vierck, 'Hallenfreude'.
13 Enright, 'Lady with the mead cup'.

rather small. The inferences derived from this may strike the reader as disproportionate, and this they may well be, but then this first book on the topic may be forgiven a lack of refinement in the exploration of largely uncharted territory. For the exposure of the oral culture in the early medieval West has made this period more interesting than before in granting it autonomous qualities hitherto unnoticed.

This work does not claim that there was no oral culture in the second half of the Middle Ages and even later. That later period also merits research into its oral culture. However, because of the profusion of the source material, the researcher will have to develop special approaches to deal with that new cultural context.

The upsurge of writing in the vernacular, and an undeniable increase of written culture, should not tempt one to assume that oral culture declined or was marginalized. The enormous increase in written sources generally and in sources written in languages other than Latin poses the question of how this material was voiced and what its relationship was to oral culture. The 'Irish question' from the early medieval centuries merges into a European issue in the twelfth century at the latest. In this respect it is hoped that this book will encourage further research in this potentially rich even if thorny field.

BIBLIOGRAPHY

SOURCES

Individual works from the MGH are included only exceptionally; works widely available in more than one edition are normally given in only one edition.

Adamnan, *De Locis Sanctis*, Meehan, D., ed., (Scriptores Latini Hiberniae 3), Dublin 1958.
Adomnan's Life of Columba, Anderson, A.O., Anderson M.O., ed., Edinburgh 1961.
Agobard of Lyon, *Epistolae*, MGH Epp. V.
Agobard of Lyon, *Liber de correctione antiphonarii*, PL 104.
Alcuin, *Epistolae*, MGH Epp. IV.
Alcuin, *Liber de virtutibus et vitiis*, PL 101.
Alcuin, *Vita Willibrordi*, MGH SS rer. Merov. 7.
Aldhelm, *Epistolae*, MGH AA 15.
Ambrose, *Epistolae*, PL 16.
Ambrose, *Liber de Elia et jejunio*, PL 14.
Ammiani Marcellini rerum gestarum libri qui supersunt (Teubner), Stuttgart 1967.
Annales Hildesheimenses, MGH SS 3.
Annales Quedlinburgenses, MGH SS 3.
Anonymi Valesiani pars posterior, MGH AA 9.
Anselmi gesta episcoporum Leod., MGH SS 7.
Asser, *De rebus gestis Aelfridi*, Stevenson, H. W., ed., Oxford 1904, repr. 1959.
Augustine, *Confessiones*, CCSL XXVII.
Augustine, *De doctrina christiana*, PL 34.
Augustine, *De catechizandis rudibus*, CCSL XLVI.
Augustine, *De Civitate Dei*, CCSL XLVII-XLVIII..
Augustine, *De catechizandis rudibis*, CCSL XLVI, 1969.
Augustine, *Enarrationes in psalmos*, PL 36.
Augustine, *Epistolae*, PL 33.
Augustine, *Sermons: Sancti Augustini sermones post Maurinos reperti*, in *Miscellanea Agostiniana*, Morin, G., ed., vol. 1, Rome 1930.
Augustine, *Tractatus in Iohannem*, CCSL XXXVI.
Auraicept na nÉces, Calder, G., ed., Edinburgh 1917.
Bede, *De arte metrica*, see *Grammatici Latini*.
Bede's *Ecclesiastical History of the English people*, ed. Colgrave, B., and Mynors, R.A.B.,

Oxford 1969.
Bede, *Epistola Bede ad Ecgbertum episcopum,* in *Historia Ecclesiastica,* Plummer, C., ed., Oxford 1896.
Bede, *Historia Abbatum,* in *Historia Ecclesiastica.*
Bede, *Historia Ecclesiastica gentis Anglorum,* ed. Plummer, C., Oxford 1896
Bede, *Letter to Bishop Acca,* PL 92.
Bethu Phátraic, Mulchrone, K., ed., Dublin 1939.
Boethius, *De institutione musica,* in B., *De institutione arithmetica,* Friedlein, G., ed., Leipzig 1867.
Boniface, S. *Bonifatii et Lulli epistolae,* MGH Epp. sel. 1
Briefsammlungen der Zeit Heinrichs IV., MGH, Die Briefe der deutschen Kaiserzeit 5.
Brut y Tywysogyon (The Chronicle of the Princes), Red Book of Hergest Version, (Board of Celtic Studies, History and Law Series XVI), Thomas, J., ed., Cardiff 1955.
Caesarius of Arles, *Sermones,* Morin, D.G., ed., CCSL CIII.
Caesarius of Arles, *Sancti Caesarii episcopi Arelatensis Opera omnia,* Morin, D.G., ed., Maretioli 1942.
Cáin Adamnáin, Meyer, K., ed. (= *Anecdota Oxoniensia,* Texts, documents and extracts), Oxford 1905.
Cassiodorus, *Variae,* CCSL XCVI (or MGH AA 12).
Casus Sancti Galli, cf. Ekkehardi IV.
Chronica Gallica, MGH AA 9.
Chronicon Novaliciense, MGH SS 7.
Chronik des Klosters Petershausen, Feger, O., ed. (= Schwäbische Chroniken der Stauferzeit 3), Lindau/Konstanz 1956.
Codex Theodosianus: *Theodosiani Libri XVI* ed. Mommsen, T., Berlin 1904.
Claudian, *Laudes Stilichonis,* MGH AA 10.
Clavis Gerberti, see Regino.
Collectio Canonum Hibernensis, see *Die irische Kanonensammlung.*
Concilia Galliae A. 314 - A. 506, CCSL CXLVIII (= Mansi VIII).
Conciliorum Oecumenicorum Decreta, Alberigo et al., ed., Basel 1962.
Corpus Consuetudinum Monasticarum, Hallinger, K., ed., Siegburg 1963.
Corpus Iuris Hibernici, Binchy, D.A., ed., 6 vols., Dublin 1978.
Councils and Ecclesiastical Documents, Haddan, A.W. and Stubbs, W., ed., Oxford 1871.
Críth Gablach, Binchy, D.A., ed. (= Mediaeval and Modern Irish Series XI), Dublin 1941.
Cronicon Suevicum Universale, MGH SS 13.
De duodecim abusivis saeculi, Hellmann, S., ed., *Pseudo-Cypriani De XII abusivis saeculi,* Leipzig 1909 (or PL 4).
Die irische Kanonensammlung, Wasserschleben, H., ed., second ed., Leipzig 1885, reprint Aalen 1966.
Domesday survey of Gloucestershire, Morris, S., ed., London 1982.
Einhardi Vita Karoli Magni, ed. MGH SS us. schol. 25, 1911.
Ekkehard of Aura, *Ekkehardi chronicon,* MGH SS 6.
Ekkehardi IV Casus sancti Galli, Haefele, H.F., ed., Darmstadt 1980.

Bibliography

Excerpta Valesiana, Leipzig 1967.
Ex chronico universali anonymi Laudunensis, MGH SS 26.
Ex miraculus sancti Benedicti, Recueil des historiens de Gaule et de la France, Delisle, L., ed., XI, Paris 1826.
Fredegar, MGH SS rer. Merov. 2.
Frutolf of Michelsberg, *Ekkehardi Chronicon universale*, MGH SS 6.
Gaudentius of Brescia, *Sermones*, PL 20.
Gelderse Kronik, Mocy, A. J. de, ed., Amsterdam 1950.
Gerhoch von Reichersberg, *Commentarius in psalmos*, MGH Libelli de lite III.
Gildas, *De Excidio Britanniae*, MGH AA 13.
Gildas, *The ruin of Britain and other works* (= Arthurian period sources 7), Winterbottom, M., London and Chichester 1978.
Giraldus Cambrensis, *Descriptio Kambriae*, Brewer, J.S. ed., RS 21.6, 1868.
Gislebert de Mons, *La chronique de Gislebert de Mons*, Vanderkindere, L., ed., Bruxelles 1904.
Grammatici Latini, ed. Keil, H., Leipzig 1857-1870.
Gregory of Tours, *Liber in Gloria Martyrum*, MGH SS rer. Merov. 1, 2.
Gregory of Tours, *Libri Decem Historiarum*, MGH SS rer. Merov. 1.
Gregory of Tours, *De virtutibus S. Martini*, MGH SS rer. Merov. 1, 2.
Gregory the Great, *Dialogi*, PL 77.
Gregory the Great, *Enarrationes in Psalmos*, PL 36.
Gregory the Great, *XL Homiliarum Evangelia in Lib. I*, PL 76.
Gregory the Great, *Moralia in Iob*, PL 75, 76.
Gregory the Great, *Registrum epistolarum*, CCSL.CXL, CXLA.
Gregory the Great, *Regula Pastoralis*, PL 79.
Gregory the Great, In Hiezech.II, Homilia CCSL 42.
Guy of Amiens, *Carmen de Hastingae Proelio*, Morton, C. and Muntz, H., ed., Oxford 1972.
Hanes Gruffydd ap Cynan—The History of Gruffydd ap Cynan, Jones, A., ed., Manchester 1910.
Hariulf, *Chronique de l'abbaye de Saint Riquier*, Lot, F., ed., Paris 1894.
Heliand und Genesis, Behaghel, O., ed., Tübingen 1984.
Henry of Huntingdon, *Henrici archidiaconi Huntendunensis Historia Anglorum*, Arnold, T., ed., RS 74, 1879.
Herbordi Vita Ottonis episcopi Babenb., MGH SS 20.
Hermannus Contractus, *Herimanni Augiensis chronicon*, MGH SS 5.
Honorius Augustodunensis, *Elucidarium*, PL 172.
Hugh of St Victor, *De bestiis et aliis rebus*, PL 177.
Iordanis de origine actibusque Getarum, MGH AA 5, 1.
Irische Texte III, Stokes, W. and Windisch, E., ed., Leipzig 1891.
Isidore of Seville, *De ecclesiasticis officiis*, CCSL CXIII.
Isidore of Seville, *Differentiae*, PL 83.
Isidore of Sevilla, *(Origines) Etymologiarum sive originum libri XX*, Lindsay, W.M., ed., Oxford 1911.
Jerome, *Commentarium in Epist. ad Ephes.*, PL 26.
Jerome, *Commentarium in Michaeam*, PL 25.

Jerome, *Epistolae*, CSEL 56, 1918.
John of Salisbury, *Ioannis Saresberiensis episcopi Policratici sive de nugiis curialium et vestigiis philosophorum libri VIII*, Webb, C.C.I., ed., London 1909.
Jonas of Orleans, *De Institutione Laicali*, PL 106.
Jonas of Orleans, *De Institutione Regia*, Reviron, J., ed., Paris 1930.
Julian the Apostate, Works of, London 1913 (Loeb)
Lamberti Ardensis historia comitum Ghisnensium, MGH SS 24.
Lebor Gabala Erenn. (The Book of the Taking of Ireland), Macalister, R.A.S., ed., Irish Texts Society vol. 41, Dublin 1941.
Lex Romana Curiensis (Die Rechtsquellen des Kantons Graubünden), Meyer-Marthaler, E., ed., Aarau 1959.
Lucian, *Heracles.*, translated by Harmon, A.M., London and Cambridge Mass. 1960.
Manegold von Lautenbach, *Liber contra Wolfelmum*, c. IX, ed. Hartmann, W., MGH Quellen zur Geistesgeschichte des Mittelalters 8, Weimar 1972.
Mansi, *Conciliorum sacrorum nova et amplissima collectio.*
Memorials of St. Dunstan, Stubbs, W., ed., RS 63, 1874.
'Mittelirische Verslehren', *Irische Texte*, Thurneysen, R., Stokes, W., and Windisch, E., ed., Dritte Serie, 1. Heft, Leipzig 1891, Part II.
Notker Balbulus, *Gesta Karoli*, MGH SS 2.
Origen, *Contra Celsum*, translated by Chadwick, H., Cambridge 1965.
Orosius, *Historia adversus paganos*, CSEL 5, 1882.
Otto of Freising, *Ottonis episcopi Frisingensis Chronica sive historia de duabus civitatibus*, Hofmeister, A., ed., MGH us. schol. 45.
Pascasius Radbertus, *Epistolae*, MGH Epp. 6.
Patrick, 'Libri Epistolarum sancti Patricii episcopi', Bieler, L., ed., *Classica et Mediaevalia* 11, 1950.
Paulinus of Aquileia, *Liber exhortationis ad Henricum Forojulianum*, PL 99.
Paulus Diaconus, *Pauli Historia Langobardorum*, MGH, SS us. schol. 48.
Paulus Diaconus, *Historia Romana*, MGH SS us. schol. 49.
Peter Abelard, *Petri Abelardi Opera Theologica*, CCCM XII, 1969.
Peter of Blois, *De confessione*, PL 207.
Peter the Chanter, Pierre le Chantre, *Summa de sacramentis et animae consiliis*, ed. Dugauquier, J., Louvain 1963 (= Analecta Mediaevalia Namurcensia 16).
Peter the Chanter, *Verbum Abbreviatum*, PL 205.
Piper, P., ed., *Die Schriften Notkers und seiner Schule*, Freiburg/Tübingen 1882.
Poeta Saxo, MGH Poetae Latini 4.
Priscus, *Fragmenta Historicorum Graecorum*, Müller, Karl, ed., IV, Paris 1851.
Prosper of Aquitaine, *De vocatione gentium*, PL 51.
Prosper Tiro, MGH AA 9.
Prudentius, *Contra Symmachum*, CSEL 61, 1926.
Quintilian, *Institutio Oratoria.*
Rabanus Maurus, *Carmina XIII*, MGH Poet. Lat. 2.
Rabanus Maurus, *Commentarium in Matthaeum*, PL 107.
Rabanus Maurus, *De clericorum institutione*, PL 107.
Rahewini gesta Friderici imperatoris, Waitz, G., ed., MGH us schol. 46, 1912.
Ratperti Casus sancti Galli, Meyer von Knonau, G., ed., St Gallen 1872.

Reeves, W., ed., *The Life of Columba*, Dublin 1857.
Regino of Prüm, *Chronicon*, MGH SS 1.
Regino of Prüm, De Harmonica institutione monitum, in *Scriptores ecclesiastici de musica sacra potissimum*, Gerbert, M., ed., vol. I, 1784; Bernhard, M., ed., *Clavis Gerberti*, München 1989.
Roger of Howden, *Gesta Regis Henrici Secundi Benedicti abbatis*, Stubbs, W., ed., RS 49, 1867.
Salvian of Marseilles, *De Gubernatione Dei*, MGH AA 1.
Saxo Grammaticus, Saxonis Gesta Danorum, Olrik, J., and Raeder, H., ed., Hauniae 1931.
Scel na Fir Flatha, in: *Irische Texte* III, Stokes, W., ed. and transl., 1891, 185-229.
Steinmeyer, E., Sievers, E., ed., *Die althochdeutschen Glossen*, 5 vols., 1879-98, rep. Dublin/Zürich 1969.
'Synodus Nivhingana sub Tassilone Bojariae duce anno DCCLXXIIII celebrata', Scholinger, H., in *Beiträge zur Vaterländischen Historie, Geographie und Statistik*, Westenrieder, L.v., ed., München 1785, vol. I, 1-30.
Táin Bó Cúalnge from the Book of Leinster, O'Rahilly, C., ed., Dublin 1970.
Thegani vita Hludowici, MGH SS 2.
The Latin texts of the Welsh Laws (Board of Celtic Studies, History and Law Series Nr. 22), Emanuel, H. D., ed., Cardiff 1967.
The Patrician Texts in the Book of Armagh, Bieler, L., ed., Dublin 1979 (= Scriptores Latini Hiberniae 10).
The Tripartite Life of Patrick, ed. Stokes, W., RS 89, 1887.
Thesaurus Palaeohibernicus, Stokes, W. and Strachan, J.J., 2 vols., Oxford 1902, repr. Dublin 1975.
Thomae de Chobham Summa Confessorum, ed. Broomfield, F., Louvain 1968 (= Analecta Mediaevalia Namurcensia 25).
Three Fragments = *Annals of Ireland. Three Fragments*, O'Donovan, ed., 1860.
Translatio Sancti Alexandri, MGH SS 2.
Uraicecht na ríar, Breatnach, L., ed., (Early Irish Law Series vol. II), Dublin 1987.
Varro, *De lingua latina*.
Venantius Fortunatus, *Opera pedestria*, MGH AA 4, 2.
Vitae Sanctorum Hiberniae, ed. Plummer, C., 2 vols., Oxford 1910.
Vitae Sanctorum Hiberniae, Heist, W.W., ed., Bruxelles 1965.
Vita Sancti Liudgeri, Diekamp, W., ed., (Die Geschichtsquellen des Bistums Münster, vol. 4), Münster 1881.
Wace, *Le Roman de Rou de Wace*, Holden, A. J., ed., Paris 1971.
Walahfrid, *De imagine Tetrici*, MGH poet. Latini 2.
Widukind of Corvey, *Rerum Gestarum Saxonicarum libri tres*, Hirsch, P., ed., MGH SS us. schol. 60.
Willelmi Malmesbiriensis monachi de gestis pontificum Anglorum libri quinque, ed. Hamilton, N.S.E.A., RS 52, 1870.
Willelmi Malmesbiriensis monachi de gestis regum Anglorum libri quinque, ed. Stubbs, W., 2 vols., RS 90, 1887-89.

SECONDARY WORKS

Acker, L.v., 'Barbarus und seine Ableitungen im Mittellatein', *Archiv für Kulturgeschichte* 47, 1965, 125-40.
Aitmatov, C., 'Snow on Manas mountain', in *The time to speak out*, Moscow 1988, 30-47.
Akinnaso, F.N., 'Schooling, language and knowledge in literate and nonliterate societies', *CSSH* 34, 1992, 68-109.
Allen, W., 'Ovid's cantare and Cicero's cantores Euphorionis', *Transactions and Proceedings of the American Philological Association* 103, 1972, 1-14.
Altenburg, D. et al., ed., *Feste und Feiern im Mittelalter*, Sigmaringen 1991.
Altheim, F., *Geschichte der Hunnen*, 5 vols., Berlin 1959-1962.
Althoff, G., *Verwandte, Freunde und Getreue*, Darmstadt 1990.
Althoff, G., 'Fest und Bündnis', in *Feste und Feiern im Mittelalter*, Altenburg, D., ed. et al., Sigmaringen 1991, pp. 29-38.
Amory, P., 'The meaning and purpose of ethnic terminology in the Burgundian laws', *Early Medieval Europe* 2, 1993, 1-28.
Angenendt, A., *Das Frühmittelalter. Die abendländische Christenheit von 400 bis 900*, Stuttgart 1990.
Baldwin, L.W., *Masters, princes and merchants. The social view of Peter the Chanter and his circle*, 2 vols., Princeton 1970.
Balogh, J., 'Voces paginarum', *Philologus* 82, 1927, 84-109, 202-40.
Bammesberger, A., Wollmann, A., ed., *Britain 400-600: language and history*, Heidelberg 1990.
Bannermann, J., 'The convention of Druim Cett', in id., *Studies in the history of Dal Riada*, Edinburgh 1974. 157-70.
Banniard, M., 'Le lecteur en Espagne wisigothique d'après Isidore de Séville: de ses fonctions à l'état de la langue', *Revue des Études Augustiniennes* 21, 1975, 112-44.
Banniard, M., *Genèse culturelle de l'Europe*, Paris 1989.
Banniard, M., *Viva voce. Communication écrite et communication orale du IVe au IXe siècle en Occident latin* (Collection des Études Augustiniennes), Paris 1992.
Banton, M., ed., *Anthropological approaches to the study of religion*, London 1966.
Bartlett, R., *Gerald of Wales, 1146-1223*, Oxford 1982.
Bäuml, F.H., Ward, D.J., 'Zur mündlichen Überlieferung des Nibelungenliedes', *Deutsche Vierteljahrsschrift für Literaturwissenschaft und Geistesgeschichte* 41, 1967, 351-90.
Bäuml, F.H., 'Varieties and consequences of medieval literacy and illiteracy, *Speculum* 55, 1980, 237-65.
Beckmann, G.A., 'Aus den letzten Jahrzehnten des Vulgärlateins in Frankreich. Ein parodistischer Zusatz zur Lex Salica und eine Schreiberklage', *Zeitschrift für Romanische Philologie* 79, 1963, 305-34.
Benveniste, É., *Le vocabulaire des institutions indo-europenéennes*, 2 vols., Paris 1969.
Benveniste, É., *Indo-European language and society*, Coral Gables, Florida 1973.
Berg, H., 'Zur Organisation der bayerischen Kirche und zu den bayerischen Synoden des 8. Jahrhunderts', in *Typen der Ethnogenese unter besonderer Berücksichtigung der Bayern*, Wolfram, H., Pohl, W., ed., Wien 1990, 181-97.
Bergin, O., *Irish bardic poetry*, Greene, D., and Kelly, F., ed., Dublin 1970.

Bibliography

Bergmann, R.. ed., *Althochdeutsch*, Heidelberg 1987.
Bernardi, A., 'The economic problems of the Roman Empire at the time of its decline', in *Economic decline of empires*, Cippola, C., ed., London 1970, 16-83.
Berndt, C.H.; Berndt, R.M., *The barbarians*, Harmondsworth 1973.
Bernhard, M., *Studien zur Epistola de armonica institutione des Regino von Prüm*, München 1979 (= Bayerische Akademie der Wissenschaften, Veröffentlichungen der Musikhistorischen Kommission 5), esp. part 2.
Beumann, H., *Widukind von Korvey*, Weimar 1950.
Bezzola, R., *Les origines et la formation de la littérature courtoise en occident (500-1200)*, I, Paris 1958.
Bickel, E., 'vates bei Varro und Vergil', *Rheinisches Museum für Philologie* NF 94, 1951, 257-314.
Bieler, L., 'The island of scholars', *Revue du Moyen-Age Latin* 8, 1952, 213-34.
Binchy, D.A., 'The linguistic and historical value of the Irish law tracts', *PBA* 29, 1943, 195-227.
Binchy, D.A., 'Bretha Nemed', *Ériu* 17, 1955, 4-6.
Binchy, D.A., 'The Date and Provenance of Uraicecht Becc', *Ériu* 18, 1958, 44-54; 113-38.
Binchy, D.A., 'Linguistic and legal archaisms in the Celtic law books', *Transactions of the Philological Society*, 1959, 14-24.
Binchy, D.A., 'Bretha Déin Chécht, *Ériu* 20, 1966, 1-66.
Binchy, D.A., 'Ancient Irish law', *Irish Jurist* 1, 1966, 88.
Binchy, D.A., 'Celtic suretyship, a fossilized Indo-European institution?', *Irish Jurist* 7, 1972, 360-72.
Binchy, D.A., 'The pseudo-historical prologue to the Senchas Mar', *Stud. Celt.* 10-11, 1975/1976, 15-28.
Binchy, D.A., 'A pre-Christian survival in mediaeval Irish hagiography', *Ireland in early mediaeval Europe* (= Studies in memory of Kathleen Hughes), Whitelock, D., et al., ed., Cambridge 1982, 165-78.
Binchy, D.A., 'Corpus Iuris Hibernici: Incipit or finit amen?', *Celtic Studies Congress Galway 1979*, Dublin 1983, 149-64.
Bischoff, B., Hofmann, J., *Libri Sancti Kyliani: die Würzburger Schreibschule und die Dombibliothek im 8. und 9. Jahrhundert*, Würzburg 1952.
Bischoff, B., 'Elementarunterricht und Probationes pennae', (extended version of the 1938 original in ed.), *Mittelalterliche Studien* I, Stuttgart 1966, 74-87.
Bischoff, B., 'Caritas-Lieder', *Mittelalterliche Studien* II, Stuttgart 1967.
Bischoff, B., *Die südostdeutschen Schreibschulen und Bibliotheken in der Karolingerzeit*, vol. I, 3rd ed., Wiesbaden 1974.
Bischoff, B., *Latin palaeography. Antiquity and the Middle Ages*, Cambridge 1990.
Bleicken, J., *Constantin der Große und die Christen* (Historische Zeitschrift, Beihefte, NF 15), 1992.
Bloch, H., 'A new document of the last pagan revival in the West, 393-394', *Harvard Theological Review* 38, 1945, 199-244.
Bloomfield, M.W. and Dunn, C.W., *The role of the poet in early societies*, Cambridge 1989.
Böhner, K., 'Childerich', *Reallexikon der germanischen Altertumskunde*, 4, 1981, 440-60.

Bonner, S.F., *Education in ancient Rome*, London 1977.
Breatnach, L., 'The caldron of poesy', *Ériu* 32, 1981, 45-93.
Breatnach, L., 'Lawyers in early Ireland' in *Brehons, serjeants and attorneys. Studies in the history of the Irish legal profession*, Hogan, D. and Osborough, W.N., ed., Dublin 1991, 1-13.
Breatnach, P.A., 'The chief's poet', *PRIA* 83, 1983, 37-79.
Brommer, P., 'Die bischöfliche Gesetzgebung Theodulfs von Orleans', *ZRG kan.* 91, 1974, 1-120.
Brown, P., *The world of late antiquity*, London 1971.
Brown, P., 'The saint as exemplar in late antiquity', *Representations* 1, 2, 1983, 1-25.
Bruford, A., *Gaelic folk-tales and romances*, Dublin 1969.
Bruford, A., 'Recitation or re-creation? Examples from South Uist storytelling', *Scottish Studies* 22, 1978, 27-44.
Bruford, A., 'Song and recitation in early Ireland', *Celtica* 21, 1990, 61-74.
Brunhölzl, F., 'Fuldensia', in *Historische Forschungen für W. Schlesinger*, Beumann, H., ed., Köln/Wien 1974, 536-47.
Bruyne, E. de, *Études d'esthétique médiévale*, Bruges 1946, 3 vols.
Búrca, S. de, 'Aspects of transmission', *Eigse* 15, 1973-74, 51-65.
Burridge, K., *Encountering aborigines. A case study: anthropology and the Australian aboriginal*, New York 1973.
Byrne, F.J., 'Senchas: the nature of Gaelic historical tradition', *Historical Studies* IX, 1974, 137-159.
Campanile, E., 'L'étymologie du celtique *bard(h)os', *Ogam—Tradition Celtique* 22-25, 1970-73, 235 f.
Campbell, J., ed., *The Anglo-Saxons*, Oxford 1982.
Campbell, J., *Essays in Anglo-Saxon history*, London 1986.
Carey, J., 'The two laws in Dubthach's judgement', *CMCS* 19, 1990, 1-18.
Carney, J., 'Society and the bardic poet', *Studies* 62, 1973, 233-50.
Casgrande, C., Vecchio, S., 'Clercs et jongleurs dans la société médiévale, XIIe et XIIIe siècles', *Annales, E.S.C.* 34, 1979, 913-28.
Cassirer, E., *An essay on man. Introduction to a philosophy of human culture*, New Haven and London 1944.
Chadwick, H., 'Augustine on pagans and Christians: reflections on religious and social change', in *History, Society and the Church* (FS Owen Chadwick), Cambridge 1985, 9-27.
Chadwick, H.M., Chadwick, N.K., *The growth of literature: vol I: the ancient literatures of Europe*, Cambridge 1932.
Chadwick, N.K., *Poetry and prophecy*, Cambridge 1942.
Charles-Edwards, T.M., 'Review article. The Corpus Iuris Hibernici', *Studia Hibernica* 20, 1980, 141-62.
Charles-Edwards, T.M., *The Welsh laws*, Cardiff 1989.
Charles-Edwards, T.M., 'Early Irish Law', *School of Celtic studies. Fiftieth anniversary report, 1940-1990, Dublin 1990*.
Charles-Edwards, T.M., *Early Irish and Welsh kinship*, Oxford 1993.
Christ, K., 'Römer und Barbaren in der hohen Kaiserzeit', *Saeculum* 10, 1959, 273-88.
Chrysos, E.K., ' Die Amaler-Herrschaft in Italien und das Imperium Romanum. Der

Vertragsentwurf des Jahres 535', *Byzantion* 51, 1981, 430-71.
Chrysos, E.K., 'Legal concepts and patterns for the barbarian settlement on Roman soil', in *Das Reich und die Barbaren*, Chrysos, E.K., Schwarcz, A., ed., Wien/Köln 1989, 13-23.
Chrysos, E.K., Schwarcz, A., ed., *Das Reich und die Barbaren*, Wien/Köln 1989.
Cippola, C., ed., Economic decline of empires, London 1970.
Clanchy, M.T., 'Remembering the past and the good old law', *History* 55, 1970, 165-76
Clanchy, M.T., *From memory to written record. England 1066-1307*, London 1979.
Clanchy, M.T., Review of Rosamond McKitterick, *Uses of literacy*, EHR 107, 1992, 678-80.
Claude, D., 'Zur Königserhebung Theoderichs des Großen', in *Geschichtsschreibung und geistiges Leben im Mittelalter* (FS Heinz Löwe), Hauck, K., Mordeck, H., ed., Köln/Wien, 1978, 1-13.
Claude, D., 'Universale und partikulare Züge in der Politik Theoderichs', *Francia* 6, 1978, 19-58.
Cleary, E., *The ending of Roman Britain*, London 1989.
Cristianizzazione ed organizzazione ecclesiastica delle campagne nell'alto medioevo: espansione e resistenze, Settimane di studio... Spoleto 1982, 1205-221.
Curschmann, M., 'Oral poetry in medieval English, French and German literature: Some notes on recent research', *Speculum* 42, 1967, 36-52.
Curschmann, M., *Spielmannsepik. Wege und Ergebnisse der Forschung von 1907-1965*, Stuttgart 1968.
Curschmann, M., 'The concept of the oral formula as an impediment to our understanding of medieval oral poetry', *Medievalia et Humanistica* NS 8, 1977, 63-76.
Curschmann, M., Review of *Oral poetry. Das Problem der Mündlichkeit mittelalterlicher epischer Dichtung*, Voorwinden, N., and Haan, M. de, ed., Darmstadt 1979, in *Mittellateinisches Jahrbuch* 16, 1981, 379-82.
Curschmann, M., Review of *Oral tradition literature. A Festschrift for Albert Bates Lord*, Foley, J.M., ed., Columbus, Ohio 1981, in *Speculum* 58, 1983, 460-63.
Curschmann, M., 'Zur Wechselwirkung von Literatur und Sage. Das "Buch von Kriemhild" und Dietrich von Bern', *Beiträge zur Geschichte der deutschen Sprache und Literatur* 111, 1989, 380-410.
Curschmann, M., ' "Dichter alter maere". Zur Prologstrophe des Nibelungenliedes im Spannungsfeld von mündlicher Erzähltradition und laikaler Schriftkultur', in: Hahn, G., Ragotzky, H., ed., *Grundlagen des Verstehens mittelalterlicher Literatur*, Stuttgart 1992, 55-71.
Crosby, R., 'Oral delivery in the Middle Ages', *Speculum* 11, 1936, 88-110.
Dagron, G., 'Aux origines de la civilisation byzantine: langue de culture et langue d'État', *Revue Historique* 241, 1969, 23-56.
Dahlmann, H., 'Vates', *Philologus* 97, 1948, 337-53.
Davies, R.R., ed. et al., *Welsh society and nationhood* (FS Glanmor Williams), Cardiff 1984.
Davies, W., *Patterns of power in early Wales*, Oxford 1990.
Deferrari, R.J., 'St. Augustine's method of composing and delivering sermons', *American Journal of Philology* 43, 1922, 97-123; 193-219.

Delargy, J.H., 'The Gaelic story-teller', *PBA* 31, 1945, 177-221.
Demougeot, E., 'Une lettre de l'empereur Honorius sur l'hospitium des soldats', *Revue Historique de Droit Français et Étranger*, Quatrième Série 34, 1956, 25-49.
Diamond, S., 'The search for the primitive', in *Man's image in medicine and anthropology*, Galdston, I., ed., New York 1963, 62-115.
Dodds, E.R., *Pagan and Christian in an age of anxiety*, Cambridge 1965.
Dolbeau, F., 'Nouveaux sermons de saint Augustin pour la conversion des païens et des donatistes', *Revue des Études Augustiniennes* 37, 1991, 37-78.
Ebel, U., 'Historizität und Kodifizierung. Überlegungen zu einem zentralen Aspekt des germanischen Heldenliedes', in *Althochdeutsch*, Bergmann, R., ed., Heidelberg 1987, I, 685-714.
Edwards, J.G., 'Studies in the Welsh laws since 1928', *WHR* special number 1963: The Welsh Laws.
Edwards, N., *The archaeology of early medieval Ireland*, London 1990.
Eis, G., 'Von der verlorenen altdeutschen Dichtung. Erwägungen und Schätzungen', *Germanisch—Romanische Monatsschrift Neue Folge* 6 (37), 1956, 175-89.
Eliade, M., *Australian religions. An introduction*, Ithaca and London 1973.
Elliott, T.G., 'Constantine and "the Arian reaction after Nicaea"', *Journal of Ecclesiastical History* 43, 1992, 169-94.
Engen, J. v., 'The Christian Middle Ages as an historiographical problem', *AHR* 91, 1986, 519-52.
Enright, M.J., 'Lady with a mead-cup. Ritual group cohesion and hierarchy in the Germanic warband', *Frühmittelalterliche Studien* 22, 1988, 170-203.
Erdmann, K., Fabulae curiales. Neues zum Spielmannsgesang und zum Ezzo-Liede', *Zeitschrift für deutsches Altertum und deutsche Literatur* 73, 1936, 87-98.
Evans, D.E., 'Insular Celtic and the emergence of the Welsh language', in *Britain 400-600: Language and History*, Bammesberger, A., Wollmann, A., ed., Heidelberg 1990, 149-77.
Evans-Pritchard, E.E., *Anthropology and history*, Manchester 1961.
Faral, E., *Les jongleurs en France au moyen-age*, Paris 1910.
Faussner, H.C., 'Die staatsrechtliche Grundlage des Rex Francorum', *ZRG germ. Abt.* 103, 1986, 42-103.
Ferreiro, A., 'Frequenter legere. The propagation of literacy, education and divine wisdom in Caesarius of Arles', *Journal of Ecclesiastical History* 43, 1992, 5-15.
Finnegan, R., 'Literacy versus non-literacy: the great divide? Some comments on the significance of "literature" in non-literate cultures', in *Modes of thought. Essays on thinking in Western and non-Western societies*, Horton, R., Finnegan, R., ed., London 1973, 112-44.
Finnegan, R., *Oral poetry. Its nature, significance and social context*, Cambridge 1977.
Finnegan, R., *Literacy and Orality. Studies in the technology of communication*, Oxford 1988.
Finnegan, R., 'Tradition. But what tradition and for whom?', *Oral Tradition* 6, 1991, 104-24.
Flint, V.I.J., *The rise of magic in early medieval Europe*, Oxford 1991.
Foley, E., 'The cantor in historical perspective', *Worship* 56, 1982, 194-213.
Foley, J.M., ed., *Oral-formulaic theory and research*, New York, 1985.

Foley, J.M., ed., *Oral tradition in literature. Interpretation in context*, Columbia 1986.
Foley, J.M., *The theory of oral composition. History and methodology*, Bloomington 1988.
Ford, P., *The poetry of Llywarch Hen*, Berkeley and London 1974.
Ford, P., 'The poet as cyfarwydd in early Welsh tradition', *Stud. Celt.* 10-11, 1975-76, 152-62.
Fortes, M., 'Culture contact as a dynamic process. An investigation in the Northern territories of the Gold Coast', *Africa* 9, 1936, 24-55.
Fowden, G., 'Bishops and temples in the eastern Roman empire, A.D. 320-435', *Journal of Theological Studies* NS 29, 1978, 53-78.
Fritze, W., 'Universalis gentium confessio. Formen, Träger und Wege universalmissionarischen Denkens im 7. Jahrhundert', *Frühmittelalterliche Studien* 3, 1969, 78-132.
Fröschl, J.M., 'Imperitia litterarum. Zur Frage der Beachtlichkeit des Analphabetismus im römischen Recht', *ZRG rom, Abt.* 104, 1987, 84-155.
Fuchs, H., *Der Friedensgedanke bei Augustin: Untersuchungen zum 19. Buch der Civitas Dei*, Berlin 1926.
Gaechter, P., 'Die Gedächtniskultur in Irland', *Innsbrucker Beiträge zur Sprachwissenschaft*, II, Innsbruck 1970.
Ganshof, F.L., 'Charlemagne et l'usage de l'écrit en matière administrative', *Le Moyen-Age* 57, 1951, 1-25.
Galdston, I., ed., *Man's image in medicine and anthropology*, New York 1963.
Geary, P.J., 'Ethnic identity as a situational construct in the early Middle Ages', *Mitteilungen der Anthropologischen Gesellschaft in Wien* 113, 1983, 15-26.
Geary, P.J., *Before France and Germany. The creation and transformation of the Merowingian world*, New York, Oxford, 1988.
Geertz, C., 'Religion as a cultural system', in *Anthropological approaches to the study of religion*, Banton, M., ed., London 1966, 1-46.
Geertz, C., *The interpretation of cultures*, New York 1973.
Geertz, C., *Works and Lives. The Anthropologist as author*, Stanford 1988.
Gellner, E., 'Concepts and society', in *Transactions of the fifth world congress of sociology* vol. 1, Louvain 1962, 153-83.
Gill, S.D., *Beyond "the primitive". The religions of nonliterate peoples*, Englewood Cliffs, 1982.
Gillies, W., 'The craftsman in early Celtic literature', *Scottish Archaeological Forum* 11, 1981, 70-85.
Glassie, H., *Passing the time. Folklore and history of an Ulster community*, Dublin 1982.
Godman, P., *Poets and emperors. Frankish politics and Carolingian poetry*, Oxford 1987.
Goffart, W., *Barbarians and Romans. A.D. 418-584. The techniques of accommodation*, Princeton 1980.
Goffart, W., 'Rome, Constantinople and the barbarians', *AHR* 86, 1981, 275-306.
Goody, J.; Watt, I., 'The consequences of literacy', *CSSH* 5, 1962-3, 304-45.
Goody, J., ed., *Literacy in traditional societies*, Cambridge 1968.
Goody, J., *The domestication of the savage mind*, Cambridge 1977.
Goody, J., *The logic of writing and the organisation of society*, Cambridge 1986.
Gordon, A.E., 'On the origins of the Latin alphabet: modern views', *California Studies in Classical Antiquity* 2, 1969, 157-70.

Graus, F., *Lebendige Vergangenheit. Überlieferung im Mittelalter und in den Vorstellungen vom Mittelalter*, Köln 1975.
Grundmann, H., 'Litteratus—illiteratus', *Archiv für Kulturgeschichte* 40, 1958, 1-65.
Günther, H., 'Probleme beim Verschriftlichen der Muttersprache. Otfrid von Weissenberg und die lingua theotisca.' *Zeitschrift für Literaturwissenschaft und Linguistik* 59, 1985.
Gurevich, A.J., *Categories of medieval culture*, London 1985 (Russian original Moscow 1972).
Gurevich, A.J., *Medieval popular culture*, Cambridge 1988 (Russian original Moscow 1981).
Gwynn, A., 'The first synod of Cashel', *Irish Ecclesiastical Record* 67, 1946, 109-22.
Gwynn, E.J., 'An Old-Irish tract on the privileges and responsibilities of poets', *Ériu* 13, 1940, 1-60; 220-36.
Hahn, G., Ragotzky, H., ed., *Grundlagen des Verstehens mittelalterlicher Literatur*, Stuttgart 1992.
Hammerstein, R., *Diabolus in musica. Studien zur Ikonographie der Musik im Mittelalter*, Bern, München 1974.
Hamp, E.P., 'Social gradience in British spoken Latin', *Britannia* 6, 1975, 150-62.
Harl, K.W., 'Sacrifice and pagan belief in fifth- and sixth- century Byzantium', *Past and Present* 128, 1990, 7-27.
Harris, W.V., 'Literacy and epigraphy', *Zeitschrift für Papyrologie und Epigraphik* 52, 1983, 87-111.
Harris, W.V., *Ancient literacy*, Cambridge, Mass. and London 1989.
Hartmann, W., *Die Synoden der Karolingerzeit im Frankenreich und in Italien*, Paderborn 1989.
Hartung, W., *Die Spielleute. Eine Randgruppe in der Gesellschaft des Mittelalters* (VSWG Beiheft 72), Wiesbaden 1982.
Harvey, A., 'Early literacy in Ireland: the evidence from ogam', *CMCS* 14, 1987, 1-15.
Haubrichs, W., *Die Anfänge* (= Geschichte der deutschen Literatur von den Anfängen bis zum Beginn der Neuzeit, Heinzle, J., ed., I, 1,), Frankfurt 1988.
Hauck, K., 'Heldendichtung und Heldensage als Geschichtsbewußtsein', in *Alteuropa und die moderne Gesellschaft* (FS Otto Brunner), Göttingen 1963, 118-169.
Hauck, K., 'Von einer spätantiken Randkultur zum karolingischen Europa', *Frühmittelalterliche Studien* 1, 1967, 3-93.
Havelock, E.A., *Preface to Plato*, Harvard 1963.
Hayes, W.C., ed., *Australian essays in world religions*, Adelaide 1977.
Haymes, E.R., 'Oral poetry and the Germanic Heldenlied', *Rice University Studies* 62, 1976, 47-54.
Henry, P.L., 'The caldron of poesy', *Stud. Celt.* 14-15, 1979-80, 114-28.
Herbert, M., *Iona, Kells and Derry. The history and hagiography of the monastic familia of Columba*, Oxford 1988.
Herbert, M., 'The preface to Amra Coluim Cille', in *Sages, saints and storytellers* (FS James Carney), O Corráin, D., et al., ed., Maynooth 1989, 67-75.
Herren, M., 'Insular Latin C(h)araxare (Craxare) and its derivatives', *Peritia* 1, 1982, 273-77.
Herrin, J., *The formation of Christendom*, Oxford 1987.

Hildebrandt, M.M., *The external school in Carolingian society*, Leiden 1992.
Hillgarth, J.N., ed., *Christianity and paganism. 350–750. The conversion of Western Europe*, Philadelphia 1986.
Hillgarth, J.N., 'Modes of evangelisation of Western Europe in the seventh century', in *Ireland and Christendom—The Bible and the missions*, Chatháin, P. Ní and Richter, M., ed., Stuttgart 1987, 311-31.
Hodges, R., *The Anglo-Saxon achievement. Archaeology and the beginnings of English society*, London 1989.
Höfler, O., 'Theoderich der Große und sein Bild in der Sage', *Österreichische Akademie der Wissenschaften, Phil.- hist. Klasse, Anzeiger* 111, 1974, 349-72.
Hoffmann, H., 'Die Aachener Teoderichstatue', in *Das erste Jahrtausend. Kultur und Kunst im werdenden Abendland an Rhein und Ruhr*, Textband I, Elbern, V.H., ed., Düsseldorf 1962, 318-35.
Hoffmann, H., *Buchkunst und Königtum im ottonischen und frühsalischen Reich* (Schriften der MGH 30.1), Stuttgart 1986.
Hofmann, D., 'Die altsächsische Bibelepik zwischen Gedächtniskultur und Schriftkultur', *Settimane di studio . . . Spoleto* 32, 1986, 453-483.
Hollowell, I., 'Scop and wodbora in Old English poetry', *Journal of English and Germanic Philology* 77, 1978, 317-29.
Holtzmann, R., 'Die Quedlinburger Annalen', *Sachsen und Anhalt* 1, 1925, 64-125.
Hope-Taylor, B., *Yeavering*, London 1977.
Horton, R., 'Destiny and the unconscious in West Africa', *Africa* 31, 1961, 110-16.
Horton, R., 'Ritual man in Africa', *Africa* 34, 1964, 85-104.
Horton, R., 'African traditional thought and Western Science', *Africa* 37, 1967, 50-71.
Horton, R., 'The Romantic illusion: Roger Bastide on Africa and the West', *Odu* N.S. 3, 1970, 87-115.
Horton, R., 'African conversion', *Africa* 41, 1971, 86-108.
Horton, R., Finnegan, R., ed., *Modes of thought. Essays on thinking in Western and non-Western societies*, London 1973.
Hsu, F.L.K., 'Rethinking the concept "primitive"', *Current Anthropology* 5, 1964, 169-78.
Hughes, K., The Church and the world in early Christian Ireland', *Irish Historical Studies* 13, 1962-63, 99-113.
Hughes, K., *The Church in early Irish society*, London 1966.
Hughes, K., 'Sanctity and secularity in the early Irish Church', *Studies in Church History* 10, 1973, 21-37.
Huizinga, J., *Homo ludens*, ch. 2 (German pbk edition, Hamburg 1956).
Hume, K., 'The concept of the hall in Old English poetry', *Anglo-Saxon England* 3, 1974, 63-74.
Hungerford, T.R.G., ed., *Australian signposts*, Melbourne 1956.
Huws, D., 'Canu Aneirin: the other manuscripts', in *Early Welsh Poetry*, Roberts, B.F., ed., Aberystwyth 1988, 43-56.
I Celti, Venice 1991.
Illich, I., Sanders, B., *The alphabetization of the popular mind*, San Francisco 1988.
Illmer, D., *Formen der Erziehung und Wissensvermittlung im frühen Mittelalter*, München 1971.

Jackson, K.H., 'Common Celtic', *PBA* 37, 1951, 71-97.
Jackson, K.H., *Language and History in early Britain. First to twelfth century*, Edinburgh 1953, repr. Dublin 1994.
Jahnkuhn, H., et al., ed., *Das Handwerk in vor- und frühgeschichtlicher Zeit*, Teil II, Göttingen 1983.
James, E., *The Franks*, Oxford 1988.
James, M. R., 'Two Lives of St Ethelbert, king and martyr', *EHR* 32, 1917, 214-44.
Jarman, A.O.H., *The Cynfeirdd. Early Welsh poets and poetry*, Cardiff 1981.
Jeffrey, P., 'The introduction of psalmody into the Roman Mass by Pope Celestine I (422-32): reinterpreting a passage in the Liber Pontificalis', *Archiv für Liturgiewissenschaft* 26, 1984, 147-65.
Jenkins, D., Owen, M.E., 'The Welsh marginalia in the Lichfield Gospels. Part I.', *CMCS* 5, 1983, 37-66.
Jones, A.H.M., 'The decline and fall of the Roman Empire', *History* 40, 1955, 209-26.
Jones, D.M., 'bardd', *BBCS* 11, 1941-44, 138-40.
Jones, W.R., 'The image of the barbarian in medieval Europe', *CSSH* 13, 1971, 376-404.
Jonsson, R., and Treitler, L., 'Medieval music and language: a reconsideration of the relationship', in *Studies in the history of music. I. Music and language*, New York 1983.
Jürgens, H., *Pompa diaboli. Die lateinischen Kirchenväter und das antike Theater*, Stuttgart 1972.
Kaster, R.A., 'Notes on primary and secondary schools in late antiquity', *Transactions of the American Philological Association* 113, 1983, 323-46.
Kazanski, M., Perin, P., 'Le mobilier funéraire de la tombe de Childéric I. état de la question et perspectives', *Revue archéologique de Picardie* 1986, 13-38.
Kelle, J., Die Bestimmungen im Kanon 19 des Legationsedictum von 789', *SBB Wien, Phil.-hist. Kl.* 161, 1908, 9. Abh.
Kelle, J., 'Chori secularium—cantica puellarum', *SBB Wien, Phil.-hist. Kl.* 161, 1908, 2. Abh.
Keller, H., 'Die Entwicklung der europäischen Schriftkultur im Spiegel der mittelalterlichen Überlieferung', in *Geschichte und Geschichtsbewußtsein* (FS K.E. Jeismann), Leidiger, P. and Metzler, D., ed., Münster 1990, 174-204.
Keller, H., ed., *Pragmatische Schriftlichkeit im Mittelalter. Erscheinungsformen und Entwicklungsstufen*, Münster 1992.
Kelly, F., *A guide to early Irish law*, Dublin 1988.
Kelly, J.F.T., 'Christianity and the Latin tradition in early medieval Ireland', *Bulletin of the John Rylands Library* 68, 1985-86, 410-33.
Kenney, J., *Sources for the early history of Ireland*, vol. I, Ecclesiastical, New York 1929.
Knapp, F.P., ed., *Nibelungenlied und Klage. Sage und Geschichte, Struktur und Gattung* (= Passauer Nibelungengespräche 1985), Heidelberg 1987.
Koch, J.T., 'When was Welsh literature first written down?', *Stud. Celt.* 20-21, 1985-86, 43-66.
Koch, J.T., 'Ériu, Alba and Letha: When was a language ancestral to Gaelic first spoken in Ireland?', *Emania* 9, 1991, 17-27.

Kohl, K.H., *Exotik als Beruf*, Wiesbaden 1979.
Kohl, K.H., 'Abwehr und Verlangen. Das Problem des Eurozentrismus und die Geschichte der Ethnologie', in id., *Abwehr und Verlangen*, Frankfurt 1987.
Kozol, J., *Illiterate America*, New York 1985.
Krusch, B., 'Die Übertragung des H. Alexander von Rom nach Wildeshausen durch den Enkel Widukinds 851. Das älteste niedersächsische Geschichtsdenkmal', *Nachrichten der Gesellschaft der Wissenschaften zu Göttingen, Phil.-hist. Klasse* 1933, 405-36.
Kuhn, H., 'Heldensage vor und außerhalb der Dichtung', in Schneider, H., ed., *Edda, Skalden, Saga* (FS Felix Genzmer), Heidelberg 1952, 262-78.
Ladner, G., 'On Roman attitudes towards barbarians in late antiquity', *Viator* 7, 1976, 1-26.
Lambert, P.Y., 'Le vocabulaire du scribe irlandais', in *Ireland and northern France, AD 600-850*, Picard, J.-M., ed., Dublin 1991, 157-67.
Langosch, K. et al., *Geschichte der Textüberlieferung der antiken und mittelalterlichen Literatur*, vol. 2 (the Middle Ages), Zürich 1964.
Lapidge, M., Dumville, D., ed., *Gildas: New approaches*, Woodbridge 1984.
Lapidge, M. and Sharpe, R., *Bibliography of Celtic-Latin Literature 400-1200*, Dublin 1985.
Lebecq, S., 'Entre tradition orale et littérature héroique: le cas du scop frison Bernlef', *Médiévales* 20, 1991, 17-24.
Levy, K., 'On the origins of neumes', *Early Music History* 7, 1987, 59-90.
Levy, K., 'Charlemagne's archetype of Gregorian chant', *Journal of the American Musicological Society* 40, 1987, 1-31.
Lindheim, B.v., 'OE "dream" and its subsequent development', *Review of English Studies* 25, 1949, 193-209.
Lintzel, M., 'Untersuchungen zur Geschichte der alten Sachsen', *Sachsen und Anhalt* 13, 1937, 28-77.
Lloyd, E.M., ed., *A Book of Wales*, London 1953.
Lloyd-Jones, J., 'The court poets of the Welsh princes', *PBA* 34, 1948, 167-97.
Lord, A.B., *The singer of tales*, Harvard 1960.
Lord, A.B., 'The merging of two worlds: oral and written poetry as carriers of ancient values', in Foley, J.M., ed., *Oral tradition in literature. Interpretation in context*, Columbia 1986, 19-64.
Lowe, E.A., ed., *Codices Latini Antiquiores*, Supplement, Oxford 1971.
Luiselli, B., 'L'idea romana dei barbari nell'età delle grandi invasioni germaniche', *Romanobarbarica* 8, 1984-85, 33-61.
Mac Cana, P., 'The three languages and the three laws', *Stud. Celt.* 5, 1970, 62-78.
Mac Cana, P., 'Mongan Mac Fiachna and Immran Brain', *Ériu* 23, 1972, 102-42.
Mac Cana, P., 'Conservation and innovation in early Celtic literature', *Études Celtiques* 13, 1972, 61-119.
Mac Cana, P., 'Two notes', *Celtica* 11, 1976, 125-32.
Mac Cana, P., 'Regnum and Sacerdotium: Notes on Irish tradition', *PBA* 65, 1979, 443-79.
Mac Cana, P., *The learned tales of medieval Ireland*, Dublin 1980.

Mac Cana, P., 'Christianisme et paganisme dans l'Irlande ancienne' in id., ed., *Rencontres de religions*, Paris 1986, 57-74.
McCone, K., 'Dubthach maccu Lugair and a matter of life and death in the pseudo-historical prologue to the Senchas Mar', *Peritia* 5, 1986, 1-35.
McCone, K., *Pagan past and Christian present*, Maynooth 1990.
McCormick, 'Clovis at Tours. Byzantine public relations and the origins of medieval ruler symbolism', in *Das Reich und die Barbaren, Chrysos*, E.K., Schwarcz, A., ed., Wien, Köln 1989, 155-80.
McKinnon, J.W., *The Church fathers and musical instruments*, New York 1965.
McKinnon, J.W., 'Musical instruments in medieval Psalm commentaries and psalters', *Journal of the American Musicological Society* 21, 1968, 3-20.
McKinnon, J.W., 'The fourth-century origin of the gradual', *Early Music History* 7, 1987, 91-106.
McKinnon, J.W., *Music in early Christian literature*, Cambridge 1989 (originally publ. 1987).
McKitterick, R., *The Frankish Church and the Carolingian reforms, 789-895*, London 1977.
McKitterick, R., *The Carolingians and the written word*, Cambridge 1989.
McKitterick, R., ed., *The uses of literacy in the early Middle Ages*, Cambridge 1990.
McKitterick, R., 'Frauen und Schriftlichkeit im Frühmittelalter', in *Weibliche Lebensgestaltung im frühen Mittelalter*, Goetz, H.-W., ed., Köln/Wien 1991, 65-118.
McManus, D., 'A chronology of the Latin loan-words in early Irish', *Ériu* 34, 1983, 21-71.
McManus, D., 'Ogam: archaizing, orthogaphy and the authenticity of the manuscript key to the alphabet', *Ériu* 37, 1986, 1-31.
Mac Mathuna, L., 'The designation, functions and knowledge of the Irish poet', *Veröffentlichungen der keltischen Kommission Wien*, Nr. 2, 1982, 225-238.
MacMullen, R., *Christianizing the Roman Empire, A.D. 100-400*, New Haven and London 1984.
Mac Néill, E., 'A pioneer of nations', *Studies* 11, 1922, 13- 28, 435-46.
Mac Néill, E., 'Ancient Irish law. The law of status or Franchise', *PRIA* 36, 1923, 265-316.
Mac Néill, E., 'Ireland and Wales in the history of jurisprudence', *Studies* 16, 1927, 245-58; 605-15.
Mackey, J.P., 'Christian past and primal present. The Scots-Irish connection', in FS D.W.D. Shaw, forthcoming.
Mackey, J.P., 'Magic and Celtic primal religion', *ZCP* 45, 1992, 66-84.
Magennis, H., 'The treatment of feasting in the Heliand', *Neophilologus* 69, 1985, 126-33.
Marouzeau, J., *Le Latin*, Toulouse/Paris 1923.
Mauss, M., *Le don*, Paris 1925.
Mayer-Mali, T., 'Rusticitas', *Studi in onore di Cesare Sanfilippo* I, Milan 1983, 307-47.
Mbiti, J.S., 'Christianity and traditional religions in Africa', *International Review of Missions* 59, 1970, 430-40.
Meid, W., 'Dichter und Dichtkunst im alten Irland', Innsbruck 1971.
Meillet, A., *Esquisse d'une histoire de la langue Latine*, Paris 1966.

Meissburger, G., 'Zum sogenannten Heldenbuch Karls des Großen', *Germanisch-Romanische Monatsschrift* 44, 1963, 105-19.
Menéndez Pidal, R., *Poesia juglaresca: y origines de las literaturas romanicas. Problemas de historia literaria y cultural*, Madrid 1957.
Meslin, M., *La fête des kalendes de janvier dans l'empire romain*, Bruxelles 1970 (Collection Latomus 115).
Meyer-Marthaler, E., ed., 'Die Gesetze des Bischofs Remedius von Chur', *Zeitschrift für Schweizerische Kirchengeschichte* 44, 1950, 81-110, 161-88.
Moenckeberg, A., *Die Stellung der Spielleute im Mittelalter*, Berlin and Leipzig 1910.
Moisl, H., 'Anglo-Saxon royal genealogies and Germanic oral tradition', *Journal of Medieval History* 7, 1981, 215-48.
Moisl, H., 'A sixth-century reference to the British bardd', *BBCS* 29, 1980-82, 269-73.
Moisl, H., 'Kingship and orally transmitted Stammestradition among the Lombards and Franks', in Wolfram, H., Schwarcz, A., ed., *Die Bayern und ihre Nachbarn*, vol. I, Wien 1985, 111-19.
Momigliano, A., 'Perizonius, Niebuhr and the character of early Roman tradition', *Journal of Roman Studies* 47, 1957, 104-14.
Momigliano, A., 'Christianity and the decline of the Roman Empire', in id. ed., *The conflict between paganism and Christianity in the fourth century*, Oxford 1963, 1-16.
Momigliano, A., ed., *Pagan and Christian in an age of anxiety*, Oxford 1965.
Morgan, R., 'Old French jogleor and kindred terms', *Romance Philology* 7, 1953-54, 279-325.
Myers, F.R., *Pintupi country. Pintupi self. Sentiment, place and politics among Western desert aborigines*, Berkeley 1986.
Nagel, B., *Das Nibelungenlied. Stoff—Form—Ethos*, 2nd ed., Frankfurt 1970, 14-33.
Ní Chatháin, P., Richter, M., ed., *Ireland and Christendom. The bible and the missions*, Stuttgart 1987.
Nippel, W., Griechen, *Barbaren und Wilde. Alte Geschichte und Sozialanthropologie*, Frankfurt 1990.
Ó Corráin, D., 'Nationality and kingship in pre-Norman Ireland', in *Nationality and the pursuit of national independence* (= Historical Studies XI), Moody, T.W., ed., Belfast 1978, 1-35.
Ó Corráin, D., Breatnach, L., Breen, A., 'The law of the Irish', *Peritia* 3, 1984, 382-438.
Ó Cróinín, D., 'Mo Sinnu moccu min and the computus of Bangor', *Peritia* 1, 1982, 281-95.
O'Donnell, J.J., *Cassiodorus*, Berkeley, Los Angeles 1979.
O'Donnell, J.J., 'The demise of paganism', *Traditio* 35, 1979, 45-88.
Oexle, G.O., 'Gilden als soziale Gruppen der Karolingerzeit', in *Das Handwerk in vor- und frühgeschichtlicher Zeit*, I, Jahnkuhn, H., ed. et al., Abhandlungen der Akademie der Wissenschaften zu Göttingen, phil.-hist. Klasse, 3. Folge 122, Göttingen 1981, 284-354.
Ogilvy, J.D.A., 'Mimi, scurrae, histriones: entertainers of the early Middle Ages', *Speculum* 38, 1963, 603-19.
Okpewho, I., *The epic in Africa: toward a poetics of the oral performance*, New York 1979.
Ong, W.J., *Orality and literacy: the technologizing of the word*, London, 1982.

Opland, J., 'Beowulf on the poet', *Medieval Studies* 38, 1976, 442-67.
Ostheeren, K., *Studien zum Begriff der "Freude" in altenglischen Texten*, Heidelberg 1964.
Parry, J.J., 'The court poets of the Welsh princes', *PMLA* 67, 1952, 511-20.
Pelka, W., 'Studien zur Geschichte des Untergangs des alten Thüringischen Königreichs im Jahre 531 n. Chr.', *Zeitschrift des Vereins für Thüringische Geschichte und Altertumskunde* 2 (NF 14), 1904, 165-228.
Pepperdene, M.W., 'Bede's Historia Ecclesiastica. A new perspective', *Celtica* 4, 1958, 253-62.
Peterson, E., *Der Monotheismus als politisches Problem*, Leipzig 1935.
Pietzsch, G., *Die Musik im Erziehungs- und Bildungsideal des ausgehenden Altertums und frühen Mittelalters*, first publ. 1932, repr. Darmstadt 1969.
Ploss, E., 'Bamberg und die deutsche Literatur des 11. und 12. Jahrhunderts', *Jahrbuch für fränkische Landesforschung* 19, 1959, 275-302.
Plummer, C., 'On the fragmentary state of the text of the Brehon Laws', *ZCP* 17, 1928, 157-66.
Poucet, J., 'Réflexions sur l'écrit et l'écriture dans la Rome des premiers siècles', *Latomus* 48, 1989, 289-311.
Pryce, H., 'The prologues to the Welsh lawbooks', *BBCS* 33, 1986, 151-87.
Pryce, H., *Native law and the Church in medieval Wales*, Oxford 1993.
Quasten J., *Musik und Gesang in den Kulturen der heidnischen Antike und christlichen Frühzeit*, first published 1930, repr. Münster 1973.
Quiggin, E.G., 'Prolegomena to the study of the later Irish bards, 1200-1500', *PBA* 5, 1911/12, 89-143, .
Rädle, F., 'Otfrids Brief an Liutbert', in *Kritische Bewahrung* (FS W. Schröder), Berlin 1975.
Reich, H., *Der Mimus: Ein Literar-entwicklungsgeschichtlicher Versuch*, Berlin 1903.
Reimer, E., 'Musicus und Cantor. Zur Sozialgeschichte eines musikalischen Lehrstücks', *Archiv für Musikwissenschaft* 35, 1978, 1-32.
Rémondon, R., 'L'Égypte et la suprème résistance au christianisme (V^e–VIIe siècles)', *Bulletin de l'Institut Français d'Archéologie Orientale du Caire* 51, 1952, 63-78.
Riché, P., *Éducation et culture dans l'occident barbare, VIe–VIIIe siècle*, Paris 1962.
Riché, P., 'Apprendre à lire et à écrire dans le haut Moyen-Age', *Bulletin de la Société nationale des Antiquaires de France* 1978-1979, 193-203.
Riché, P., *Écoles et enseignement dans le haut moyen-age*, Paris 1979.
Richter, M., 'Kommunikationsprobleme im lateinischen Mittelalter', *HZ* 222, 1976, 43-80.
Richter, M., 'Die Sprachenpolitik Karls des Großen', *Sprachwissenschaft* 7, 1982, 412-37.
Richter, M., 'A quelle époque a-t-on cessé de parler Latin? A propos d'une question mal posée', *Annales, E.S.C.* 38, 1983, 439-48.
Richter, M., 'Bede's Angli—Angles or English?', *Peritia* 3, 1984, 99-114.
Richter, M., 'Practical aspects of the conversion of the Anglo-Saxons', in *Ireland and Christendom. The bible and the missions*, Ní Chatháin, P., Richter, M., ed., Stuttgart 1987, 362-76.
Richter, M., 'Die Kelten im Mittelalter', *HZ* 246, 1988, 265-95.

Richter, M., 'Die mündliche Tradition im Mittelalter. Probleme und Perspektiven der Forschung.', Konstanzer Arbeitskreis für mittelalterliche Geschichte, Konstanzer Reihe, Protokoll 303, 11 June 1988.
Richter, M., *Medieval Ireland—the enduring tradition*, Dublin, London, New York 1988.
Richter, M., 'Is Latin a key to the early medieval world?', in *Odysseus—Man in history today*, Moscow 1991, 125-36.
Richter, M., 'Die Symbiose von Christentum und archaischer Gesellschaft in Irland, 400-800', in Tristram, H.L.C., ed., *Studien zur Táin Bó Cuailgne*, Tübingen 1993, 158-72.
Richter, M., 'Les langages en pays celtiques', in *La voix et l'écriture*, ed., Banniard, M., *Médiévales* 25, 1993, 53-60.
Richter, M., *The oral tradition in the early medieval West*, Typologie des Sources du moyen âge Occidental, fasc. 71, Turnhout 1994.
Richter, M., '. . . quisquis scit scribere, nullum potat abere labore. Zur Laienschriftlichkeit im 8. Jahrhundert', in Jarnut, J., et al., ed., *Karl Martell in seiner Zeit*, Sigmaringen 1994, 393-404.
Richter, M., 'The introduction of alphabetic writing to Ireland: implications and Consequences', (FS Brendan O Hehir), Berkeley 1991 (forthcoming).
Richter, M., 'The scholars of early Christian Ireland', *Australian Conference of Celtic Studies* 1992 (forthcoming).
Richter, M., 'Latein—ein Schlüssel zur Welt des Frühmittelalters?', *Mittellateinisches Jahrbuch* (forthcoming).
Richter, M., 'The reality of the Latin Middle Ages', 1986 (forthcoming).
Richter, M., 'Die mündliche Kultur im früheren Mittelalter—ein Problemaufriß' (lecture Prague 1993, forthcoming).
Roberts, B.F., ed., *Early Welsh poetry*, Aberystwyth 1988.
Roberts, B.F., 'Oral tradition and Welsh literature. A description and survey', *Oral Tradition* 3, 1988, 61-87.
Roberts, C.H., Skeat, T.C., *The birth of the codex*, London 1983.
Rosenfeld, H., 'Die Namen Nibelung, Nibelungen und die Burgunder', *Blätter für oberdeutsche Namenforschung* 9, 1968, 16-21.
Ross, A., *Pagan Celtic Britain*, London 1976.
Rousselle, A., 'Histoire ancienne et oubli du christianisme', *Annales E.S.C.* 1992, 355-68.
Rück, P., ed., *Pergament. Geschichte, Struktur, Restaurierung, Herstellung*, Sigmaringen 1991.
Rugullis, S., *Die Barbaren in den spätrömischen Gesetzen. Eine Untersuchung des Terminus barbarus*, Frankfurt 1992.
Runes, M., 'Geschichte des Wortes vates', *Beiträge zur griechischen und lateinischen Sprachforschung* (FS Paul Kretschmer), Wien, Leipzig and New York 1926, 202-16.
Saenger, P., 'Literacy, Western European', *Dictionary of the Middle Ages* vol. 7, 597-602.
Salmen, W., *Der Spielmann im Mittelalter*, Innsbruck 1983.

Sanders, W., 'Die Buchstaben des Königs Chilperich', *Zeitschrift für deutsches Altertum* 101, 1972, 54-85.
Sawyer, P.H., Wood, I.N., ed., *Early medieval kingship*, Leeds 1977.
Sayers, W., 'The jongleur Taillefer at Hastings: antecedents and literary fate', *Viator* 14, 1980.
Scharf, J., 'Studien zu Smaragdus und Jonas', *Deutsches Archiv* 17, 1961, 333-84.
Scheele, P.-W., 'Motive altirischer Spiritualität in der Passio Kiliani', *Würzburger Diözesangeschichtsblätter* 51, 1989, 181-219.
Scheibelreiter, G., 'Vester est populus meus. Byzantinische Reichsideologie und germanisches Selbstverständnis', in *Das Reich und die Barbaren*, Chrysos, E.K. and Schwarcz, A., ed., Wien 1989, 203-20.
Schlosser, H.-D., 'Die Aufzeichnung des Hildebrandsliedes im historischen Kontext', *Germanisch-Romanische Monatsschrift* 28, 1978, 217-224.
Schmidt, K.H., 'Keltisch-lateinische Sprachkontakte im römischen Gallien der Kaiserzeit', in *Aufstieg und Niedergang der römischen Welt*, Temporini, H. and Haase, W., ed., 29/2, Berlin, New York 1983, 988-1018.
Schmidt, K.H., 'Handwerk und Handwerker in altkeltischen Sprachdenkmälern', in *Das Handwerk in vor- und frühgeschichtlicher Zeit*, Teil II, Jahnkuhn, H. et al., ed., Göttingen 1983, 751-63.
Schmidt, K.H., Ködderitzsch, R., ed., *Geschichte und Kultur der Kelten*, Heidelberg 1986.
Schneider, F., 'Über Kalendae Ianuariae und Martiae im Mittelalter', *Archiv für Religionswissenschaft* 20, 1920-21, 82-134, 360-410.
Schneider, H., ed., *Edda, Skalden, Saga* (FS Felix Genzmer), Heidelberg 1952.
Schott, R., 'Die Funktionen des Rechts in primitiven Gesellschaften', *Jahrbuch für Rechtssoziologie und Rechtstheorie* 1, 1970, 107-174.
Schreier-Hornung, A., *Spielleute, Fahrende, Außenseiter: Künstler der mittelalterlichen Welt*, Göppingen 1981.
Schreuder, D., Oddie, G.: 'What is conversion? History, Christianity and religious change in Colonial Africa and South Asia', *Journal of religious history* 15, 1989, 496-518.
Schücking, L.L., 'Heldenstolz und Würde im Angelsächsischen', *Sächsische Akademie der Wissenschaften, Phil.-Hist. Klasse* 42, 5, 1933.
Schwarz, H., 'Ahd. liod und sein sprachliches Feld', *Beiträge zur Geschichte der deutschen Sprache und Literatur* 75, 1953, 321-65.
See, K.v., 'Skop und Skald. Zur Auffassung des Dichters bei den Germanen', *Germanisch-Romanische Monatsschrift* 45, 1964, 1-14.
See, K.v., *Germanische Heldensage: Stoffe, Probleme*, Methoden, Frankfurt 1971.
Slotkin, E.M., Medieval Irish scribes and fixed texts', *Eigse* 17, 1977-79, 437-50.
Sihler, E.G., 'The Collegium poetarum at Rome', *American Journal of Philology* 26, 1905, 1-21.
Simms, K., *From Kings to Warlords*, Woodbridge 1987.
Sims-Williams, P., 'Gildas and vernacular poetry', in *Gildas: New approaches*, Lapidge, M. and Dumville, D., ed., Woodbridge 1984, 169-92.
Smet, G. de, 'Die winileod in Karls Edikt von 789', in *Studien zur deutschen Literatur und Sprache des Mittelalters* (FS Hugo Moser), Berlin 1974, 1-7.

Smyth, A.P., *Warlords and holy men. Scotland AD 80-1000*, London 1984.
Stacey, R.C., 'Law and order in the very old West: England and Ireland in the early Middle Ages', in *Crossed Paths. Methodological approaches to the Celtic aspect of the European Middle Ages*, Hudson, B.T., Ziegler, V., ed., Lanham, New York and London 1991, 39-60.
Stanner, W.E.H., 'The Dreaming', in *Australian signposts*, Hungerford, T.R.G., ed., Melbourne 1956, 51-65.
Stanner, W.E.H., *On Aboriginal religion* (Oceania Monograph 11), Sydney 1966.
Steger, H., 'Die Rotte. Studien über ein germanisches Musikinstrument im Mittelalter', *Deutsche Vierteljahrsschrift für Literaturwissenschaft und Geistesgeschichte* 35, 1961, 96-147.
Stevenson, J., 'The beginnings of literacy in Ireland', *PRIA* 89, 1989, 127-165.
Stock, B., *The implications of literacy. Written language and models of interpretation in the eleventh and twelfth centuries*, Princeton 1983.
Stokes, W., 'The Bodleian Amra Choluimb Chille', *RC* 20, 1899, 30-55, 132-83, 248-89, 400-437.
Störmer, W., 'Nibelungentradition als Hausüberlieferung in frühmittelalterlichen Adelsfamilien? Beobachtungen zu Nibelungennamenvornehmlich in Bayern', in Knapp, F.P., ed., *Nibelungenlied und Klage. Sage und Geschichte, Struktur und Gattung* (= Passauer Nibelungengespräche 1985), Heidelberg 1987, 1-19.
Straub, J., 'Christliche Geschichtsapologetik in der Krisis des römischen Reiches', *Historia* 1, 1950, 52-81.
Strehlow, T.G.H., 'Anthropology and the study of languages' (lecture), Adelaide 1947.
Strehlow, T.G.H., *Songs of central Australia*, Sydney 1971.
Stroheker, K.F., 'Studien zu den historisch-geographischen Grundlagen der Nibelungendichtung', *Deutsche Vierteljahrsschrift für Literaturwissenschaft und Geistesgeschichte* 32, 1958, 216-240.
Szemerényi, O., 'The origins of Roman drama and Greek tragedy', *Hermes* 103, 1975, 300-332.
Szemerényi, O., 'Studies in the kingship terminology of the Indo-European languages', in *Textes et Mémoires*, vol. VII, Varia 1977 (= Acta Iranica).
Thieme, P., 'Die Wurzel vat-', *Asiatica* (FS Friedrich Weller), Leipzig 1954, 656-66.
Thompson, E.A., 'Britain A.D. 406-410', *Britannia* 8, 1977, 303-18.
Thompson, E. A., 'Zosimus 6.10.2 and the letters of Honorius', *Classical Quarterly* 32, 1982, 445-62.
Thrams, P., *Christianisierung des Römerreiches und heidnischer Widerstand*, Heidelberg 1992.
Thürlemann, F., 'Die Bedeutung der Aachener Theoderich-Statue für Karl den Großen (801) und bei Walahfrid Strabo (829). Materialien zu einer Semiotik visueller Objeckte im frühen Mittelalter', *Archiv für Kulturgeschichte* 59, 1977, 25-65.
Thurneysen, R., 'Le terme Iarmbérla', *RC* 13, 1892, 269.
Thurneysen, R., *Grammatik des Altirischen*, Heidelberg 1909.
Thurneysen, R., 'Aus dem irischen Recht IV. Zu den bisherigen Ausgaben der irischen Rechtstexte', *ZCP* 16, 1927, 167-230.
Thurneysen, R., 'Colmán Mac Lénéni und Senchán Torpéist', *ZCP* 19, 1933, 193-209.

Thurneysen, R., *A grammar of Old Irish*, Dublin 1946.
Tierney, J.J., 'The Celtic ethnography of Posidonius', *PRIA* 60, 1960, 189-275.
Timpe, D., 'Mündlichkeit und Schriftlichkeit als Basis der frührömischen Überlieferung', in *Vergangenheit in mündlicher Überlieferung* (Colloquium Rauricum Bd. 1), Ungern-Sternberg, J.v., Reinau, H., ed., Stuttgart 1988, 266-86.
Treitler, L., 'Oral, written and literate process in the transmission of medieval music', *Speculum* 56, 1981, 471-91.
Treitler, L., 'Reading and singing: on the genesis of occidential music writing', *Early Music History* 4, 1984, 135-208.
Tristram, H.L.C., 'Warum Cenn Faelad sein "Gehirn des Vergessens" verlor. Wort und Schrift in der älteren irischen Literatur', in *Deutsche, Kelten und Iren. 150 Jahre deutsche Keltologie* (FS Gearóid Mac Eoin), Hamburg 1990, 207-48.
Turner, C.H., 'Niceta of Remesiana II. Introduction and text of De psalmodiae bono', *Journal of Theological Studies* 24, 1923, 225-52.
Turner, D.H., *Tradition and transformation. A study of aborigines in the Groote Eylandt area, northern Australia* (Australian Aboriginal Studies No. 53), Canberra 1974.
Turner, D.H., *Life before genesis. A conclusion. An understanding of Australian aboriginal culture*, 2nd ed., New York 1987.
Turner, H., 'The primal religions of the world and their study', in *Australian essays in world religions*, Hayes, V.C., ed., Adelaide 1977, 27-37.
Ullmann, W., 'On the use of the term 'Romani' in the sources of the earlier Middle Ages', *Studia Patristica* 2, 1955, 155-63.
Ungern-Sternberg, J.v., Reinau, H., ed., *Vergangenheit in mündlicher Überlieferung* (Colloquium Rauricum Bd. 1), Stuttgart 1988.
Uytfanghe, M. v., 'Le latin des hagiographes mérovingiens et la protohistoire du francais', *Romanica Gandensia* 16, 1976, 5-89.
Vansina, J., *Oral tradition as history*, London 1985.
Vendryes, J., *Lexique Etymologique de l'ancien irlandais*, Paris 1959-87.
Vendryes, J., 'Druidisme et christianisme dans l'Irlande du Moyen-Age', in id., *Choix d'études linguistiques et celtiques*, Paris 1952, 317-32.
Vendryes, J., 'La poésie de cour en Irlande et en Galles', in *Choix d'études linguistiques et celtiques*, Paris 1952, 209-24.
Viarre, S., 'Un portrait d'Angilbert dans la correspondance d'Alcuin?', in *De Tertullien aux Mozarabes* (FS J. Fontaine), ed. Holtz, L., et al., Paris 1992, vol. II, 267-274.
Vierck, H., 'Hallenfreude. Archäologische Spuren frühmittelalterlicher Trinkgelage und mögliche Wege ihrer Deutung', in *Feste und Feiern im Mittelalter*, Altenburg, D., ed. et al., Sigmaringen 1991, 115-21.
Vollrath, H., 'Das Mittelalter in der Typik oraler Gesellschaften', *HZ* 233, 1981, 571-594.
Walls, A.F., 'Primal religious traditions in today's world', in *Religion in today's world*, Whaling, F., ed., Edinburgh 1987, 250-78.
Wareman, P., *Spielmannsdichtung. Versuch einer Begriffsbestimmung*, Amsterdam 1951.
Wartburg, W. v., *Französisches etymologisches Wörterbuch*, vol. 5, Basel 1950.
Watkins, C., 'Indoeuropean metrics and archaic Irish verse', *Celtica* 6, 1963, 194-249.
Watkins, C., 'The etymology of Irish dúan', *Celtica* 11, 1976, 270-76.

Watkins, C., 'New parameters in historical linguistics, philology and culture history', *Language* 65, 1989, 783-800.
Wattenbach, W., *Das Schriftwesen im Mittelalter*, 3rd. ed., Leipzig 1896.
Weismann, W., *Kirche und Schauspiele. Die Schauspiele im Urteil der lateinischen Kirchenväter unter besonderer Berücksichtigung von Augustin*, Würzburg 1972.
Wenskus, R., *Stammesbildung und Verfassung*, Köln 1961.
Wenskus, R., 'Wie die Nibelungenüberlieferung nach Bayern kam', *Zeitschrift für Bayerische Landesgeschichte* 36, 1973, 393-449.
Werlich, E., 'Der westgermanische Scop', *Zeitschrift für deutsche Philologie* 86, 1967, 352-75.
Werner, J., 'Beiträge zur Archaeologie des Attila-Reiches', *Bayerische Akademie der Wissenschaften*, München 1956.
Whaling, F., ed., *Religion in today's world*, Edinburgh 1987.
Williams, G., *Recovery, reorientation and reformation. Wales c.1415-1642* (= History of Wales vol. III), Oxford 1987.
Williams, J.E.C., 'The court poet in medieval Ireland', *PBA* 57, 1971, 1-51.
Williams, J.E.C., 'Posidonius' Celtic parasites', *Stud. Celt.* 14/15, 1979/80, 313-43.
Williams, J.E.C., 'Gildas, Maelgwn and the bards', in *Welsh society and nationhood* (FS Glanmor Williams), Davies, R.R. et al., ed., Cardiff 1984, 19-34.
Williams, J.E.C., Ford, P.K., *The Irish literary tradition*, Cardiff 1992.
Williman, D., 'Schools, grammar', *Dictionary of the Middle Ages* vol. 11, 1988.
Wirth, G., 'Zur Frage der föderierten Staaten der späteren römischen Kaiserzeit', *Historia* 16, 1967, 231-51.
Wiseman, T.P., 'Roman legend and oral tradition—review article', *Journal of Roman Studies* 79, 1989, 129-37.
Wissmann, W., 'Skop', *SBB Berlin, Klasse für Sprachen, Literatur und Kunst* 1954, Nr. 2.
Wolfe, P., 'On being woken up: the Dreamtime in anthropology and in Australian settler culture', *CSSH* 33, 1991, 197-224.
Wolfram, H., 'Gotisches Königtum und römisches Kaisertum von Theodosius dem Großen bis Justinian I.', *Frühmittelalterliche Studien* 13, 1979, 1-28.
Wolfram, H., 'Zur Ansiedlung reichsangehöriger Föderaten', *MIÖG* 91, 1983, 5-35.
Wolfram, H., 'Die Aufnahme germanischer Völker ins Römerreich: Apekte und Konsequenzen', *Settimane di studio . . . Spoleto* 29, 1983, 87-117.
Wolfram, H., Schwarcz, A., ed., *Die Bayern und ihre Nachbarn*, vol. I, Wien 1985.
Wolfram, H., *History of the Goths*, Berkeley, Los Angeles, London 1988 (German original 1979).
Wolfram, H., *Das Reich und die Germanen*, Berlin 1990.
Wolfram, H., Pohl, W., ed., *Typen der Ethnogenese unter besonderer Berücksichtigung der Bayern*, Wien 1990.
Wood, I., 'The end of Roman Britain; continental evidence and parallels' in: *Gildas: New Approaches*, Lapidge, M. and Dumville, D., ed., Woodbridge 1984, 1-25.
Wormald, P., 'Lex scripta and verbum regis: legislation and Germanic kingship from Euric to Cnut', in Sawyer, P.H., Wood, I.N., ed., *Early medieval kingship*, Leeds 1977, 105-38.
Wright, R., *Late Latin and early Romance*, Liverpool 1982.

Youtie, H.C., 'Ipographeus. The social impact of illiteracy in Graeco-Roman Egypt', *Zeitschrift für Papyrologie und Epigraphik* 17, 1975, 201-21.

Zimmer, H. et al., 'Sprache und Literatur der Kelten im allgemeinen', *Die romanischen Literaturen und Sprachen mit Einschluß des Keltischen*, Berlin/Leipzig 1909 (=Die Kultur der Gegenwart, Teil I, Abt XI, 1).

Zöllner, E., *Geschichte der Franken bis zur Mitte des sechsten Jahrhunderts*, Köln 1970.

Zumthor, P., *La lettre et la voix. De la 'littérature' médiévale*, Paris 1987.

Zumthor, P., *Introduction à la poésie orale*, Paris 1983.

INDEX

This list is confined to personal names; it does not include those of modern scholars.

Abelard, see Peter A.
Absalon of Sprinkirsbach 171
Adalbert of Babenberg 178
Adomnán 227
Aerbo 179
Aetius 17, 248
Agatho 67
Agelmund 141
Agnellus of Ravenna 135 n.
Agobard 137, 141, 244 n., 258 n.
Ailill m. Cormaicc 228
Alaric 6
Albuin 136
Alcuin 42, 43 n., 129, 130, 131, 134, 137, 141, 145, 147, 170 n., 260 n.
Aldhelm 136 n., 151, 230 n.
Alexander III 163, 164
Alfred 174
Amalaberga 176
Amalberga 176
Amandus 155
Ambrose 32, 38 n., 52, 115, 118
Ammianus Marcellinus 17, 158
Anastasius 21, 23
Angilbert 129, 130, 180
Aristotle 186
Arnoldus of Ghisne 171
Asser 174
Athalaric 22, 59
Athanasius 115
Athenaeus 188
Attila 135 n., 159, 179, 248, 249, 251

Atto of Vercelli 73 n.
Augustine 28, 32, 33, 34, 35, 37, 38, 52, 65, 66, 110, 115, 116, 117, 119, 130, 137
Ausonius 57
Avitus of Vienne 152

Baldwin of Ghisne 166
Bardo of Mainz 171
Bede 16, 52 n., 71 n., 104, 147, 148, 149, 150, 151, 175, 234 n., 258, 259
Benedict Biscop 150
Benedict of Nursia 25, 66, 69
Benno II of Osnabrück 179
Bernlef 139
Boethius 25, 59, 111, 113, 117, 158
Boniface 51, 103
Boto 179
Brunhild 247

Caedmon 149, 150
Caesar 12, 186, 187
Caesarius of Arles 35, 36, 37, 64, 65, 110
Cassiodorus 21, 22, 24, 47, 58, 60, 156
Cenn Faelad mac Ailella 227, 228
Charlemagne 42, 52, 69, 70, 71, 72, 73, 74, 75, 76, 125, 133, 134, 135, 136, 137, 138, 141, 142, 143, 144, 145, 171 n., 249
Childebert I 152

Childebrand 249
Childeric 19, 20, 21
Chilperic 68 n., 108
Cicero 53, 66, 107 n.
Claudian 8
Clement of Alexandria 118 n., 119 n.
Clothar 176
Clovis 19, 20, 21, 41, 62, 152, 158
Cnut 251
Colmán mac Lénéni 228
Columbanus 43, 230
Colum Cille 222, 223
Conchobar 223
Conrad I 168
Constantine 29
Constantius 14
Constantius of Lyon 15
Cyprian 137

Dallán Forgaill 223
Desiderius 142
Dietrich 248
Dionysius Exiguus 25, 59
Dubhalthach Mac Firbhisigh 195
Dubthach moccu Lugir 203, 211, 212
Dunstan 174, 175

Eadmer 175
Edwin 16
Egbert of York 148
Einhart 52, 76, 77, 102, 115 n., 125, 133, 134, 136, 137, 260 n.
Ekkehard of Aura 167, 179
Ekkehard IV of St Gall 178, 179, 180
Eligius of Noyon 154
Eochaid 223
Ermanaric 179, 251
Erminfrid 176
Ethelbert, king of East Anglia 151
Etzel 247, 248

Festus 202 n.
Fiacc 204
Fiachna 223
Fredegar 20 n.
Frederick I 167, 180

Frutolf of Michelsberg 178, 250, 251

Gaudentius of Brescia 117, 118
Gennadius of Marseille 110
Gerhoch of Reichersberg 170 n.
Germanus of Auxerre 15
Gernot 247
Gildas 206, 208
Giraldus Cambrensis 98, 102, 216, 221
Giselhere 247, 249
Gratian 110, 116 n.
Gregory of Tours 19, 21, 39, 65, 152, 154, 168 n.
Gregory of Utrecht 146
Gregory the Great 25, 37, 42, 53, 64, 65, 67, 81, 82, 113 n., 116 n., 130 n., 137
Gruffudd ap Cynan 220
Gundahar 17, 248
Gundicarius 17, 135 n.
Gundobad 61, 248
Gundowech 18
Gunter, bishop of Bamberg 250
Gunter, Burgundian king 247, 249
Guntram 152 n.
Gutbert 147
Guy of Amiens 169

Hathagat 177
Hatto of Mainz 178
Heito 128
Helmolt of Bosau 102
Hengist 15
Henry I 168
Henry III, emperor 167, 179
Henry IV, emperor 179
Henry V. emperor 167
Henry of Huntingdon 169
Henry of Friaul
Hermanafrid 61
Hermannus Contractus 167
Higbald 130, 131
Hilarius, pope 18, n.
Honorius, emp. 14
Honorius Augustodunensis 166
Horsa 15

Index

Hugh de Nonant 172
Hugh of St Victor 172

Iring 176, 178
Irminfrid 176
Isidore of Seville 37, 51, 66, 81 n., 108, 111, 116, 118, 120, 121, 200, 201

Jerome 14, 17, 32, 33, 62, 115, 137, 160, 163, 258 n.
John of Salisbury 81 n.
John the archchanter 150, 151
Jonas of Orleans 139, 140, 141
Jordanes 156, 178, 179, 251
Judith 173
Julian the Apostate 34 n., 109 n.
Justinian 24, 25, 62, 108, 156

Kilian 42
Kriemhild 248, 251

Liudger 139
Liutbert of Mainz 173
Loiguire 203, 204
Lothar 74
Louis the Pious 70, 71, 72, 74, 131, 133, 134, 136, 138, 141, 143, 144, 145, 245
Lucan 204 n.
Lucian 188
Lull 50 n., 136 n., 146, 147
Lupus 207

Maelgwn 206
Magnus, Danish king 251
Manegold von Lautenbach 166
Matfrid 140
Mathilda princess 167
Meinhard 250
Mo-Chuoróc maccu Neth-Sémon 226, 227
Mo-Sinu maccu Min 226
Muirchú 203, 204, 205, 208

Nibelung 249

Niceta of Remesiana 116 n.
Notker Balbulus 142
Notker Labeo 244 n.

Odoacer 22
Oengus 219
Origen 28, 38 n.
Orosius 17, 38 n., 204 n.
Otfrid von Weissenburg 173, 174, 232 n., 260 n.
Otto of Bamberg 171
Otto of Freising 178

Paschasius Radbertus 140
Patrick 38 n., 39 n., 43, 189, 203, 204, 205, 211, 212, 230
Paulinus of Aquileia 36 n., 65 n., 140
Paulus Diaconus 135 n., 136, 139, 141, 249
Peter Abelard 165, 166
Peter the Chanter 113 n., 160, 161, 162, 163, 164, 167
Peter of Blois 165
Peter Waldes 167
Pippin 249
Plato 165
Pliny 28, 53
Plutarch 56
Poeta Saxo 135 n.
Posidonius of Apameia 98, 102, 186
Priscus 159
Prosper 17, 38
Prudentius 38

Quintilian 49, 52, 117 n., 118 n.

Rabanus Maurus 50, 51, 241 n., 246
Radegundis 155
Rahewin 180
Ratbod, archbishop of Trier 121
Ratbod, Frisian duke 43 n.
Regino of Prüm 112, 113, 113, 120, 121, 122, 170, 231
Remedius of Chur 75
Remigius of Auxerre 113 n.
Rhys 224, 225

Riculf of Soissons 73
Robert Vaughan 214 n.
Roger of Howden 172
Romulus Augustulus 3, 10, 22
Rudolf of Fulda 177
Rudolf of Rheinfelden 179

Salvian of Marseilles 47
Saxo Grammaticus 251
Seneca 161
Servulus 65
Siegfried 247
Sigibert of East Anglia 71 n.
Stabo 186, 187
Svein 171

Tacitus 12, 159, 201 n.
Taillefer 169, 170
Tertullian 130 n.
Thegan 131, 132, 133, 134, 136, 137, 139, 141
Theodoric 21, 22, 23, 24, 58, 60, 61, 62, 135, 137, 158, 176, 179, 248, 251, 252
Theodosius 28, 29
Theodulf of Orleans 73
Thiudimir 22
Thomas of Chomham 164
Trajan 28

Valens 6
Varro 200
Venantius Fortunatus 153, 155, 158, 207

Walahfrid Strabo 137
Wace 170
Waldemar 171
Widukind of Corvey 175-78, 180
William of Malmesbury 151, 169
Witigis 22
Wolfger of Erla 247
Wulfila 47

Zacharias 103, 146